STUDIES IN JEWISH THEOLOGY

Studies in Jewish Theology

Reflections in the Mirror of Tradition

BYRON L. SHERWIN

VALLENTINE MITCHELL
LONDON • PORTLAND, OR

First published in 2007 in Great Britain by
VALLENTINE MITCHELL
Suite 314, Premier House, 112–114 Station Road,
Edgware, Middlesex HA8 7BJ

and in the United States of America by
VALLENTINE MITCHELL
c/o ISBS, 920 NE 58th Avenue, Suite 300
Portland, OR 97213-3786

www.vmbooks.com

British Library Cataloguing in Publication Data

Sherwin, Byron L.
Studies in Jewish theology : reflections in the mirror of tradition
1. Judaism – Doctrines
I. Title
296.3

ISBN 978 0 85303 692 0 (cloth)
ISBN 978 0 85303 694 4 (paper)

Library of Congress Cataloging-in-Publication Data
A catalog record has been applied for

Printed in Great Britain by Biddles Ltd, King's Lynn, Norfolk

In memory of my teachers:
William Barrett
Louis Finkelstein
Sidney Hook
Max Kadushin
Arcadius Kahan
Seymour Siegel
James Walsh
Karl J. Weintraub
Moshe Zucker,
and my mentor,
Abraham Joshua Heschel

Torah is like a mirror.
The mirror stays the same,
but each generation must find
its own reflection therein.
—Abraham Isaac Kook

Contents

Foreword

Byron Sherwin is not as well known in this country as he deserves to be. I ask myself 'why'. It must have something to do with the fact that he defies neat categorization. He is not a leading academic from an institution like Harvard. But nor is he an authority figure from one of the great American Jewish denominational institutions like Hebrew Union College, the Jewish Theological Seminary or Yeshiva University. He is a significant theologian within the mainstream of Jewish theology, but theology itself is a problematic subject these days.

The radical Anglican theologian John Bowden has argued that an effective way of understanding secularization is to trace the 'development' of the university from its origins as a seat of religious learning to the present day institution as the bastion of secular scholarship. He points out that in Germany – the country where the secularizing process began – a point was reached where serious discussions took place about the appropriateness of the study of theology in a modern university at all. The argument is both simple and significant. Theology demands commitment and is therefore incompatible with the detachment demanded of modern scholarship.

Byron Sherwin would be the ultimate case in point. He is a theologian and his passionate commitment is his defining characteristic. His approach does not sit easily with academic detachment. But nor is he comfortable with the ideological constraints of denominational institutions. Thank goodness for Spertus College in Chicago.

He opens this characteristically stimulating collection of essays with advocacy for the Jewish theological enterprise itself. Reworking Jacob Neusner, Sherwin argues that Jewish theology demands four characteristics – coherence, authenticity, contemporaneity and communal acceptance.

Coherence in turn demands clarity, communicability and cohesion. Sherwin is a marvellous example of fidelity to his own criteria.

What he has to say has clarity and conviction; contains passage after passage of compelling, flashing insight; and could not be further divorced from the impenetrable jargon of so many who approach theology out of the tradition of Western philosophy. Sherwin's theology is emphatically not applied Western philosophy. Indeed, he is fiercely critical of those who try to fit Judaism to a procrustean bed. Amongst his targets are Maimonides and Gersonides. It is worth pointing out how little the Western philosophical tradition impacted upon Judaism during the centuries between Philo of Alexandria and Saadia. Many of the rabbinic texts which are Sherwin's source material come from precisely this period.

Sherwin demands authenticity, by which he means that the theology must emerge from the tradition, from the sources to which the theologian must be wholly/holy committed. The theologian cannot be a disconnected observer and Sherwin rams home his point with a quotation from the Midrash: 'If one studies Torah without the intention to observe it, it is better that he had not been born … it would have been better that he had been strangled by the placenta at birth and had never ventured forth into the world' (Leviticus Rabbah 35:7). He is particularly scathing about nineteenth-century Jüdische Wissenschaft and it is hard, even for a Reform rabbi like me, not to sympathise with his withering assault.

Along with commitment goes a profound rooting in the sources. Here Sherwin is reminiscent of his revered older contemporary Rabbi Dr Louis Jacobs. Sherwin's knowledge of the sources is remarkable in its breadth and richness. The scholarship is formidable but so is the passion for the affective dimension of the material.

Sherwin finds particularly helpful resonances in the Jewish mystical tradition, specifically in the Lurianic Kabbalah which he uses, not for the sake of the scholarly or academic, but because of its contemporary relevance.

The third characteristic of Jewish theology as defined by Sherwin is contemporaneity. This, above all else, makes Sherwin so enjoyable and exciting. There is a widespread tendency in Jewish life today to ignore the elephant in the room, to avoid addressing the range of profound questions made inevitable by the cluster of paradigm shifts that constitute modern and post-modern thought. His essay on the Flood story, for instance, is so rich in insights on theodicy and the acute challenges of contemporary life that the book would be worth it simply for that one essay.

Sherwin takes the familiar Lurianic doctrine of ***tsimtsum***, of God contracting into God's self, and opens up rich veins of thinking. If God alone is perfect and God contracts into God's self to make a place for the universe, then creation, the universe is by definition imperfect. That has profound implications for theodicy. It also has implications for Torah and Halakhah – since Torah is only perfect in the realm of the transcendent, when it is with God in God's essence, but when Torah is in this world it is, by definition, imperfect. As Sherwin points out, the blessing recited on being called to the Torah ends in the present tense, ***notein haTorah***, Who ***is giving*** us the Torah.

The Lurianic system opens up remarkable possibilities for the immanent God, gloriously a theologian's rather than philosopher's God. In perhaps the most daring essay of all, God is an artist and an artist who makes mistakes, who is open to accusation and blame. Finally, the Lurianic framework has implications for human beings – here Sherwin taps in to the rich Jewish tradition of partnership between God and His creation.

Following coherence, authenticity, contemporaneity, as Sherwin's fourth characteristic of Jewish theology is communal acceptance. Sherwin acknowledges that some form of communal acceptance is indispensable for theology but he is clear that, for many reasons, not the least of them the strictures of the institutional, the role of the theologian is frequently to be subversive. Sherwin, a graduate of the Jewish Theological Seminary, is truly subversive in a long and magisterial essay on Halakhah in which he attacks the 'monologic' approach and argues passionately for the 'dialogic'. In so doing he not only takes on Hirsch and Soloveitchik but the whole process of codification. Once again, Maimonides feels the lash.

Byron Sherwin acknowledges three heroes – Schechter, Heschel and Jacobs. But he is not Schechter straddling Europe and America. Sherwin is a full-blown American theologian, but one whose primary allegiance is not to the Western philosophic tradition, nor to sociology, but to the texts which constitute Jewish tradition. He was taught by Heschel and there are times when Heschel's passion for language comes shining through. He shares Heschel's deep ethical commitment. But he is also much more liberal. The liberality and generosity is quite remarkable – in his treatment of such diverse subjects as euthanasia and Christianity.

The attraction of Jacobs is clear and understandable – the shared love and breadth of learning that distinguish both of them. But he is less wedded to reason than Jacobs and more radical. If you read Jacobs' introduction to Sherwin's 2000 book, *Jewish Ethics for the Twenty-First Century*, you will experience both the respect and the sense of challenge and anxiety that Sherwin provokes.

Byron Sherwin is a Jewish theologian *par excellence*. In the pages that follow you will find the coherence, authenticity and contemporaneity that make him so compelling. Add to this, liberality and radicality and you will readily understand that his communal acceptance flows from the simple fact that, agree or disagree, this is Jewish theology at its most interesting, exciting and subversive.

Rabbi Dr Tony Bayfield
Head of the Movement for Reform Judaism
and Lecturer in Personal Theology
Leo Baeck College, London
February 2007

Preface

Due to the scarcity of parchment in medieval times, scribes would often write new texts on top of earlier ones. Such writing is called 'palimpsest'. Theological discourse may be considered a form of palimpsest. Theology is always *a posteriori*; it is never *a priori*. Theology is not a *creatio ex nihilo*. Theological discourse always rests upon who and what has gone before, both texts and people. On Exodus 17:6, 'I [God] will be standing there before you', a Midrash explains: 'God said to Moses: Everywhere that you find a human footprint, I have been there before you'. Just as theology may be characterized as thinking God's thoughts after Him, the theologian may be depicted as walking in God's footsteps. The theologian also walks in the footsteps of a specific faith tradition. Consequently, before a theologian can blaze a new path down the well-trodden road of a particular religious faith, he or she must walk in the footsteps of those who came before. Before becoming a pioneer, the theologian must first become an heir.

For more than a century, the claim that Jewish theology does not exist, or that it is irrelevant to contemporary Jewish concerns and communal agendas, has been pervasive. Whereas in medieval times, Jewish theologians felt compelled to demonstrate the existence of God and to defend Jewish theological presuppositions against claims made by advocates of other religions, contemporary Jewish theologians find themselves obliged to demonstrate the very existence of Jewish theology. Under attack from both Jewish secularists and many religiously observant Jews, Jewish theologians find themselves on the defensive against those who depict Jewish theology as 'the search by a blind person in a dark room for a black cat which is not there'.

There are those who claim that there is no Jewish theology because Judaism is a way of living and not also a way of thinking. For some, this means that Judaism is exclusively a religion of law or of ethics. Others claim that there is no Jewish theology because

Judaism is no longer a religion, but a form of secular nationalism, culture and/or ethnicity. These, and similar approaches, are fallacious as they commit the reductionist fallacy, attempting to reduce Jewish experience to a single facet of Jewish life rather than acknowledging the multifaceted nature of Jewish historical experience and intellectual history. These views remain oblivious to the fact that Judaism, whatever else it may be, is also a religious faith that embodies distinct theological claims.

No one can deny the cultural, national, legal or social dimensions of Jewish experience. Indeed, the Jewish theologian is obliged to take these factors into account in the formulation of a theology of Judaism. However, even a cursory survey of Jewish religious literature would adduce massive evidence to affirm the existence and persistence of Jewish theological discourse throughout the long history of Judaism. To deny the existence of Jewish theology is to disregard the huge body of classical Jewish religious literature that deals explicitly and implicitly with issues of overt Jewish theological concern. To 'excommunicate' theology from Judaism is to dismiss the theological teachings of the Hebrew Bible, the Talmud, Midrash, Jewish philosophy, and Jewish mysticism. It is to disenfranchise from Jewish faith and belief its most revered expositors and practitioners, including Jeremiah, the Psalmist, Hillel, Rabbi Akiba, Saadya Gaon, Judah Halevi, Maimonides, Abraham Abulafia, Isaac Luria, the Ba'al Shem Tov, a wide variety of modern Jewish thinkers, and many others. It is to deny that Judaism is not only a way of living, but also a way of thinking.

It was the Hasidic master, Mendel of Kotzk, who said, 'It is bad enough to be in exile, but it is even worse to be in exile and not to be aware of it'. In Hasidic thought, 'exile' can mean an existential state of inauthenticity as well as geographical displacement from a historical homeland. As a community that is largely theologically illiterate, contemporary Jewry is in a state of voluntary exile, detached from the theological wellsprings of its own faith. Devoid of an anchor in the teachings and insights of Jewish religious faith as they developed throughout the centuries, contemporary Jewry is prone to identify passing social and intellectual fads, personal preferences and the proclivities of secular culture with Judaism. By so doing, individual Jews tend to forge a Judaism in their own image, a distorted facsimile of a venerable tradition that would be unrecognizable to the giants of

Jewish spirituality and thought in times past and present. As Abraham J. Heschel put it, 'Accept Judaism or reject Judaism, only do not distort it'.

Various versions of Jewish secularism articulate their positions as polemics against Jewish theological presuppositions, in an attempt to replace them with secular assumptions upon which to ground Jewish identity. Rather than refuting the existence of Jewish theology, polemics such as these in fact verify it by acknowledging Jewish theology as the object of their attack. At the opposite end of the spectrum, those who maintain from an extreme religious position that Judaism is a religion of law alone fail to appreciate that their affirmation of the divine origin of Jewish religious law (Halakhah) ultimately rests upon certain theological premises, for example, with regard to the nature of God, revelation, and Jewish peoplehood.

Though modern scholars have published many studies on the most minor and marginal episodes, communities and thinkers to be found throughout Jewish historical experience, the need remains for seminal studies on major themes of Jewish theological concern. The contemporary Jewish community supports an army of managers, administrators, fund-raisers, communal service workers, clergy and educators, but precious few theologians. A plethora of demographic and social-scientific studies is annually commissioned to determine what Jews think. Virtually none are commissioned to determine what Judaism believes. The theological wellsprings of Jewish meaning have been obscured by an obsessive preoccupation with Jewish survival. Ultimately, however, Jewish survival is vested in Jewish meaning. Only Jewish theology authentically addresses the fundamental question: survival for what purpose?

Despite efforts to marginalize or to deny the validity of the enterprise of Jewish theology, Jewish theological thinking and scholarship continue to be practised. As contemporary Jewry seeks an anchor for Jewish meaning, as contemporary Jews increasingly inquire as to what Judaism believes, as Jewish educators begin to realize that Jewish belief as well as Jewish practices should become integrated into religious-school curricula, Jewish theology will inevitably emerge from its state of 'excommunication'. This volume represents a step in that direction.

The present study collects some of my work in Jewish theological scholarship. Part One, 'Some Aspects of Jewish Theology', recalls the title of Solomon Schechter's now classic work, *Some Aspects of Rabbinic Theology*. Intended as a representative but not exhaustive investigation of some fundamental issues in Jewish theology, this section consists of ten essays. Chapter 1, 'The Nature of Jewish Theology', proposess four criteria for the formulation of a valid theology of Judaism: authenticity, coherence, contemporaneity and communal acceptance. Chapter 2, 'Jewish Theological Scholarship', offers a methodology for 'doing' Jewish theology, and examines how Jewish theological scholarship differs from academic or 'scientific' Jewish scholarship. In other words, the first two chapters examine what Jewish theology is, and how it may be practised. In effect, these chapters offer a job description of the work of the Jewish theologian. Subsequent chapters in Part One demonstrate how the nature of Jewish theology and the methodology for practising Jewish theology as given in the initial chapters may be applied to a variety of issues of theological concern.

Throughout the ages, and particularly since the Holocaust, the problem of theodicy – the persistence of evil in a world created and governed by a powerful and beneficent God – has been a major issue of Jewish theological concern. Chapter 3, 'The Perennial Problem of Theodicy', summarizes the major responses of classical Jewish theology to this problem. Chapter 4, 'Portrait of God as a Young Artist', offers a new interpretation of the biblical Flood story that can serve as a traditionally oriented, though reformulated response to the problem of theodicy. In this chapter, the notion of theology as an art form is related to the portrayal of God as an artist.

Chapter 5, 'Awe of God', deals with love, fear and awe of God in Jewish religious literature. Despite the fact that awe of God has been considered to be the primary characteristic of the religious personality throughout the history of Jewish thought, little has been written on this subject by Jewish scholars in recent decades.

Some scholars who deny the existence of Jewish theology do so because, unlike certain forms of Christian theology, Jewish theology is often not presented within a systematic framework. For such individuals, only systematic theology is true theology. However, in discussing the characteristics specific to Jewish theological discourse and thought in chapter 1, I suggest that Jewish theology has traditionally articulated concepts in terms of complementary polar opposites rather than in the definitional and systematic categories that are characteristic of western philosophy and scholastic theology. In chapter 6, 'Love and Law', I apply this suggestion to an examination of the complementary polarity in Jewish theology of love and law. Without love, Judaism is a religion without a heart. Without law, it is a body without a skeleton, an amorphous mass. This chapter also contains an overtly polemical agenda, seeking to set the record straight against those theologians and philosophers, Jewish and Christian who have perpetuated the incorrect view that Judaism is a religion of law alone, devoid of love, morality, or both. The perpetuation of this view is not only inappropriate but potentially dangerous when deployed in anti-Semitic propaganda which suggests that Judaism – and hence Jews are devoid of faith, emotion and morality.

Chapter 7, 'Philosophies of Jewish Law', presents two distinct theologies of revelation, and their implications for Jewish legal decision making, past and present. In discussing the theological foundations of Jewish jurisprudence, the inevitable nexus between Judaism as a way of thought and a way of life is established. In identifying various approaches to revelation and law with specific Jewish religious denominations or movements, the relevance of Jewish theological and jurisprudential thought to contemporary Jewish communal life is highlighted.

Jewish students of all ages study many areas of Jewish experience, but are not exposed to the fundamental theological ideas that characterize Jewish faith. The Jewish holidays, for example, are taught with thorough attention given to their related customs and ceremonies, but with little regard to the fundamental theological ideas they express, such as creation (Sabbath), revelation (Shavuot), providence (*Sukkot*), theodicy (*Tisha B'Av*), redemption (Passover), and repentance (Rosh Hashanah and Yom Kippur). Chapter 8, 'Theologies of the Jewish Holidays', explores the theological foundations of the Jewish religious festivals. How the secularization of Judaism has reshaped, and in many cases distorted the original meaning of these holidays, is also examined.

As with the celebration of the Jewish holidays, Jewish law and ethics are forms of theology in action. Chapter 9, 'Toward a Just and Compassionate Society', presents certain theological ideas as the basis for social action which are aimed at permeating society with the moral values of justice and compassion.

Theology, ethics and law coalesce in the spiritual quest. For the Jewish spiritual seeker, spirituality consists of a lifelong project to create one's life as a work of art, thereby imbuing life with meaning, direction and purpose. Chapter 10, 'Inward Journeys', presents essential features of this endeavour.

Maintaining cordial relations with other faith communities is an important item on the Jewish communal agenda. Of these, relationships with various Christian denominations have been of paramount concern, since most Jews outside of Israel reside in countries where Christianity is the dominant religion. It is therefore especially ironic that secular Jewish advocacy organizations largely control interreligious theological dialogue insofar as Jewish participation in such dialogue is concerned. In theological dialogue with theologians of other faiths, Jewish theologians are often conspicuously absent. Section Two, 'Jewish and Christian Theology', consists of three essays that address issues relating to Jewish–Christian theological dialogue.

Chapter 11, 'Toward a Jewish Theology of Christianity', introduces a Jewish theological position in respect of Christianity and certain basic Christian beliefs. Indeed, the formulation of a new Jewish theology of Christianity is not only a desideratum in and of itself, but may also be viewed as an act of reciprocity for the labours of many Christian denominations and theologians, especially during the last half-century, which have reformulated earlier Christian theologies of Judaism in a positive manner. Of these new Christian theologies of Judaism, a most significant one is that which emerges in the writings and speeches of John Paul II. Chapter 12, 'John Paul II's Catholic Theology of Judaism', reviews the late Pontiff's writings and speeches in order to formulate his positive and compelling Catholic theology of Judaism.

In medieval Jewish–Christian polemics, an item of sharp dispute was the doctrine of original sin. In Chapter 13, 'Original Sin in the Passover Haggadah?', a responsum of the twelfth-century rabbi Abraham ben David of Posquieres is analysed in terms of how it deals in a unique manner with the doctrine of original sin both in Jewish and Christian theology.

The third and final section, 'Jewish Theologians', deals with the life and work of three theologians who have had an enormous impact upon contemporary Jewish thought, and whose influence permeates the contents of this volume. Chapters 14 to 16 deal respectively with the theologians Solomon Schechter, Abraham J. Heschel, and Louis Jacobs.

Chapter 17, 'Jewish Theology in America', shows how, since the mid-nineteenth century, despite attempts to marginalize Jewish theological scholarship and thought in the United States, American Jewry has produced a number of significant theologians and theologies. This chapter and book conclude on an optimistic note regarding the future of the Jewish theological enterprise.

The studies that comprise the present volume were composed, published and revised over a period extending more than three decades. They appeared in various forms as chapters and articles in a diverse array of books and journals. Some had their genesis as oral presentations, delivered in a variety of places and before diverse audiences in North America and Europe. They have in common a reflection of my lifelong preoccupation with issues of Jewish theological concern. I am both honoured and delighted that Vallentine Mitchell has found them worthy of collection in a single volume.

Preparing this volume for publication has afforded me the opportunity not only to correct errors in my previous work, but also to revise and expand the language and ideas contained therein. In a real sense, the publication of this volume affords its contents a new lease of life – a form of literary afterlife – for materials currently out of print or tucked away in obscure and largely unavailable tomes. The following offers a genealogy of each of the chapters found below.

Chapter 1, 'The Nature of Jewish Theology', was previously published as 'An Incessantly Gushing Fountain: The Nature of Jewish Theology', in Byron L. Sherwin, *Toward a Jewish Theology* (Lewiston, NY: Edwin Mellen Press, 1991); Dan Cohn-Sherbok (ed.), *Problems in Contemporary Jewish Theology* (Lewiston, NY: Edwin Mellen Press, 1991); Elliot N. Dorff and Louis E. Newman (eds), *Contemporary Jewish Theology* (New York: Oxford University Press, 1999).

Chapter 2, 'Jewish Theological Scholarship', is a revised and expanded version of sections of Byron L. Sherwin, *In Partnership with God: Contemporary Jewish Law and Ethics* (Syracuse, NY: Syracuse University Press, 1990), chapters 1 and 12.

Chapter 3, 'The Perennial Problem of Theodicy', was first published as 'Theodicy' in Arthur A. Cohen and Paul Mendes-Flohr (eds), *Contemporary Jewish Religious Thought* (New York: Scribner's, 1987), and as 'Theodicy: Reason and Mystery' in Sherwin, *Toward a Jewish Theology*.

Chapter 4, 'Portrait of God as a Young Artist' is an expanded version of 'Portrait of God as a Young Artist: The Flood Revisited', first published in *Judaism* 33:4 (Fall 1984), and in Sherwin, *Toward a Jewish Theology*. It is published here with permission of *Judaism*.

Chapter 5, 'Awe of God', was first published as 'Fear and Awe of God', in Cohen and Mendes-Flohr (eds), *Contemporary Jewish Religious Thought*, and in Sherwin, *Toward a Jewish Theology*.

Chapter 6, 'Love and Law' is a revised version of 'Law and Love in Jewish Theology' first published in *Anglican Theological Review* 64:4 (October 1982), and is published here with permission. It was also published in Sherwin, *Toward a Jewish Theology*.

Chapter 7, 'Philosophies of Jewish Law', developed from a paper delivered at the Jewish Theological Seminary of America in 1975. It is a revised version of 'Philosophies of Law', published in Sherwin, *In Partnership with God*.

Chapter 8, 'Theologies of the Jewish Holidays', developed from a paper delivered at Chicago Theological Seminary in 1989, and is a revised version of 'Faith as Memory: Theologies of the Jewish Holidays', first published in André La Cocque (ed.), *Commitment and Commemoration* (Chicago: Exploration Press, 1994), and is published with permission of Exploration Press of Chicago Theological Seminary.

Chapter 9, 'Toward a Just and Compassionate Society' is based on a keynote address delivered in July 1994 at the annual consultation of the International Council of Christians and Jews in Warsaw, Poland, and is a revised version of 'Toward a Just and Compassionate Society', printed in *From the Martin Buber House* 22 (Winter 1995), and *Cross Currents* 45:2 (Summer 1995). It is published here with permission from *Cross Currents*.

Chapter 10, 'Inward Journeys', is based on a keynote address at the 1993 Parliament of the World's Religions in Chicago, Illinois. An earlier version, 'Inward Journeys: Life as Artform', was published in Wayne Teasdale and George Cairns (eds), *The Community of Religions* (New York: Continuum, 1996), and is published here with permission from Continuum.

Chapter 11, 'Toward a Jewish Theology of Christianity', is based upon a paper, 'Do We Believe in the Same God?', delivered in London, May 2003, at a conference on Catholic–Jewish theological dialogue, co-sponsored by the World Union of Progressive Judaism and the Holy See's Commission on Religious Relations with the Jews. Previously unpublished, it incorporates segments from Byron L. Sherwin, 'A New Jewish View of Jesus', *Journal of Ecumenical Studies* 31:3/4 (Summer 1994), and '*Corpus Domini*: Traces of the New Testament in East European Hasidism?', *Heythrop Journal* 35:3 (1994). These articles were based upon presentations delivered at conferences at the Academy of Catholic Theology in Warsaw in 1992 and 1993 and were published in Polish translation in the Academy's journal, *Collectana Theologica* 63:2 (1993) and 64:2 (1994).

Chapter 12, 'John Paul II's Catholic Theology of Judaism', is a revised version of a chapter of the same title in Byron L. Sherwin and Harold Kasimow (eds), *John Paul II and Interreligious Dialogue* (Maryknoll, NY: Orbis Books, 1999) and in Polish translation (Krakow: WAM, 2001). This essay is based on a lecture delivered in May 1995 at the Pontifical College of North America in Rome.

Chapter 13, 'Original Sin in the Passover Haggadah?' was originally published as 'Original Sin: Is it Sufficient for Us?' in the Israeli journal *Moed* 13 (2003), and is based on a presentation to the Washington, DC Board of Rabbis in April 1997.

Chapter 14, 'Solomon Schechter', is an expanded and revised version of 'The Life and Legacy of Solomon Schechter', published in Mayer I. Gruber (ed.), *The Solomon Goldman Lectures,* Volume 6 (Chicago: Spertus College Press, 1993) which was based on a lecture at Spertus Institute of Jewish Studies in Chicago, November 1992, and is published with permission of Spertus College Press.

Chapter 15, 'Abraham J. Heschel', is a revised and expanded version of excerpts from a chapter entitled, 'My Master', in Harold Kasimow and Byron L. Sherwin (eds), *No Religion is an Island: Abraham Joshua Heschel and Interreligious Dialogue* (Maryknoll, NY: Orbis Books, 1991) (Polish translation: WAM, 2005), and Byron L. Sherwin, 'Memories and Meanings of Being Heschel's Disciple', *Conservative Judaism* (Winter/Spring 1998).

Chapter 16, 'Louis Jacobs', is a revised, expanded and updated version of 'Louis Jacobs: Man of Controversy, Scholar of Distinction', *Judaism* 28:1 (Winter 1979), and is published with permission.

Chapter 17, 'Jewish Theology in America', is a revised version of 'Thinking Judaism Through: Jewish Theology in America', in Dana E. Kaplan (ed.), *Cambridge Companion to American Judaism* (New York: Cambridge University Press, 2005).

Byron L. Sherwin
Chicago, Illinois
February 2007

PART I
SOME ASPECTS OF JEWISH THEOLOGY

CHAPTER ONE

The Nature of Jewish Theology

Judaism is a way of thinking, as well as a way of living.[1] The task of Jewish theology is to establish the nature and the parameters of Jewish religious thought, to articulate coherently authentic views of Judaism, and to demonstrate how the wisdom of the Jewish religious teachings of the past can address the perplexities of contemporary Jewish existence in a manner that is compatible with the thought and life of the Jewish faith community at a given juncture in time and space. The four criteria that characterize a valid Jewish theology are identical to those of any valid theology. These are: authenticity, coherence, contemporaneity and communal acceptance.[2]

Authenticity depends upon the nature and use of sources consulted, and on the faith commitment of the individual consulting them. Coherence relates to the cohesion, clarity and communicability of a formulated theological perspective. Contemporaneity pertains to the successful application of past traditions to present situations. Communal acceptance refers to the ratification of a theological posture by committed members of a specific faith community. Should a theological stance not achieve communal acceptance, then it proves barren. When not contemporaneous, it then becomes anachronistic. If it lacks coherence, a theological position invites unintelligibility and hence proves unavailing. When a theology cannot claim authenticity, it is demonstrably spurious. Though these four criteria for theological validity apply to theology in general, what follows addresses how and why these criteria particularly relate to the formulation of a valid *Jewish* theology.[3]

Jewish theology is not a *creatio ex nihilo*. A historical tradition, an extant canon of sacred literature, and a living faith community precede each Jewish theologian's attempt to formulate a theology of Judaism. The challenge to the theologian is not to create, but to re-create tradition.[4] To use a medieval analogy, the theologian is like a 'dwarf riding on the shoulders of a giant'.[5] The giant represents the cumulative corpus of the tradition that precedes the individual theologian. This analogy indicates that the coalescence of the wisdom of the past in the giant makes his stature necessarily higher and his vista broader than that of the dwarf who represents only his own wisdom and that of his particular generation. The giant represents the summation and the quintessence of tradition. But when perched on the giant's shoulders, the dwarf gains the opportunity to see more, to exceed that which is attainable by the giant alone. Together, the giant and the dwarf guarantee the continuity and the development of tradition. Without the giant, there is no viable foundation for such development. Without the dwarf, the giant might become simply a relic of bygone days.

Tradition is a bequest of the ages available to the diligent theologian. It is a trust vouchsafed only to those who labour on its behalf. To be received, tradition must first be acquired. Study of the sacred texts is necessary, but not sufficient. As with food, the tradition must be incorporated as a part of the theologian. It is not enough to know the sacred texts. The theologian must also absorb and become absorbed by them. As Shneur Zalman of Liady wrote:

> Seeing that through the knowledge of the Torah man's soul and mind encompass the Torah and are in turn encompassed by it, the Torah is called food and the sustenance of the soul. For just as material food sustains the body and enters it and is transformed in the body into flesh and blood, by virtue of which a man lives and endures, so it is with regard to knowledge of the Torah and its comprehension by he who studies with concentration until the Torah is grasped by the mind and becomes united with it.[6]

On this view, one must consume and be consumed by the Torah, the tradition. Study of the Torah is but a means; becoming Torah is the goal. Commenting on the phrase '*ve-zot torat ha-Adam*', literally: 'and this is the Torah of man', (2 Sam. 7:19), Mordecai of Chernobyl explained it to mean that 'the man himself *becomes* the Torah'.[7]

The theologian cannot be a passive voyeur, a casual tourist surveying the landscape of tradition. The scientist, the philosopher or the historian of religion can stand outside the arena of his or her inquiry as a disinterested observer. For the theologian, however, commitment precedes inquiry. Experience of the life of faith and participation in a faith community anticipates theological investigation.[8] Only the wellsprings of individual religious commitment can generate a viable theology. Only from the passion of faith can theology emanate. Theology is passionate faith seeking understanding.

Theology is not an intellectual parlour game but the articulation of a prior commitment. Observance of the commandments is an expression of that commitment. The Jewish theologian is not only obliged to *do* what he or she *believes*, but to *believe* what he or she *does*. Halakhah (Jewish religious law) is faith in the form of deeds. Performance of the commandments represents belief articulated as action. In a sense Halakhah may be considered the 'practical theology' of Judaism, that is, Jewish theological ideas expressed as specific concrete acts. It would be an error to equate Halakhah with Jewish theology. It would also be a mistake to detach Jewish theology from Halakhah. Halakhah is predicated upon the most fundamental Jewish theological assumption: God gave the Torah to Israel. But, theological premises not only underlie Halakhah; theological ideas are also compressed within Halakhah. A task for the Jewish theologian, therefore, is: to examine and to explicate the theological underpinnings of Halakhah, to elicit the theological issues implicit within Halakhah, and to articulate the theological meaning of Halakhic observance. For the Jewish theologian, Halakhah is both *a priori* and *a posteriori*. Religious observance both precedes and flows from theological investigation.[9]

Study of the Torah, of the tradition, is a conclusion of which prior commitment is a premise. Study of the Torah without prior commitment is a conclusion without a premise, an embryo without a prior conception. Without both prior and subsequent commitment, study of the Torah is stillborn. As a Midrash observes, 'If one studies [Torah] without the intention to observe it, it is better that he had not been born ... it would have been better that he had been strangled by the placenta at birth, and had never ventured forth into the world'.[10]

The rabbis read the verse describing the Torah as an inheritance (*morashah*) of Israel (Deut. 33:4) as denoting the betrothal (*me-orashah*) of the people of Israel and of each individual Jew to the Torah.[11] As Samuel of Uceda observed, commenting upon this rabbinic text, betrothal implies commitment, and commitment grants a licence for intimacy. The person committed to the Torah, to the tradition, is granted entrée to her inner domain.[12] According to the *Zohar*, the true scholar is a lover of the Torah, invited by the Torah to penetrate her private precincts, to gain access through intimacy into her deepest mysteries, to uncover secrets she otherwise cloaks.[13] As Moses Hayyim Ephraim of Sudlykow wrote, 'When one studies the Torah for its own sake, to keep it and perform it, then he brings all his limbs close to their source whence they originated and were generated, namely the Torah ... and he becomes identical to the Torah like the unification of man and woman'.[14] Speculating further on the already mentioned rabbinic text that compares the Torah to Israel's spouse, a commentator explains this analogy to mean that the Torah is caused to conceive by the sages of Israel, thereby assuring the continuous rebirth and development of the tradition.[15]

To a lover, his or her beloved is unique. Jewish theology focuses upon the specifically unique rather than upon the scientific tendency toward generalization.[16] Jewish theology posits its own *sui generis* nature. The formative events that concern it (such as the revelation at Sinai), the corpus of sacred literature that informs it, the people of Israel who live it, and the historical experience of that people which helps to shape it, are held to be unique. Consequently, a task of the theologian is to discern the particular categories of faith and thought that characterize and are native to Judaism.

Unlike the historian of religion or the social scientist who seeks to impose imported rubrics and generalizations upon Jewish faith, experience and sacred literature, the theologian seeks to understand Judaism on its own terms, according to its own endemic categories, in its own particular language. Unlike the approach initiated by the *Wissenschaft des Judentums* (the Scientific Study of Judaism) that tried to surrender the uniqueness of Judaism to the vortex of the 'universal human spirit', that advocated the application of an objective 'value-free' universal, scientific approach to Judaism, that attempted to reduce sacred Jewish literature to belles-lettres, Jewish theology embraces Judaism in its uniqueness, on its own terms.[17] The Jewish theologian encounters Judaism as a living organism, as a beloved. The programme of the Scientific Study of Judaism, as Gershom Scholem observed, aims at 'the liquidation of Judaism as a living organism', and, as Zalman Shazar observed, its agenda inevitably leads to the 'de-Judaization of Judaism' by divesting Judaism of that which is unique to it and of that which is vibrant about it.[18]

The historian of Judaism focuses dispassionately upon the anatomy of Jewish sacred literature and historical experience, scrutinizing individual limbs. But a minute examination of individual parts tends to eclipse the vision of the whole. The theologian seeks a total gestalt, unencumbered by historical considerations: 'There is neither earlier nor later in the Torah'.[19] For the theologian, the corpus of tradition is the body of his or her beloved. The theologian strives to know the personality of his or her beloved in ways unavailable to the historian of religion. The variety of knowledge available through anatomical research is not the kind of knowledge available through an act of love.

The historian of Judaism has access to Judaism on a surface level. But licence to penetrate the deeper meaning of Judaism is vouchsafed only to one who already has received and accepted it, that is, to the theologian. As a lover of the Torah, the theologian may have an access code to the text denied to the historian of religion, to the social scientist examining Judaism, and to the historian of Jewish experience. As the Torah is *sui generis*, its knowledge gained by its lovers is also *sui generis*. According to Samuel of Uceda, on the semantic level the Torah is only truly given and only truly gives herself to her lovers.[20]

As a lover embarks upon a never-ending quest for knowledge and experience of his or her beloved, the Jewish theologian embarks on the never-ending journey toward knowledge and experience of the Torah. Though lust may be satisfied, deep abiding passionate love cannot ever truly be quenched.[21] In this regard, Samuel of Uceda noted, 'even if a person would live 2,000 years, he could not grasp its [the Torah's] totality'.[22] And as Judah Loew of Prague observed, the quest for Torah is itself Torah. A blessing praises God for allowing us to be 'preoccupied with the words of Torah' *(la-asok be-divrei Torah)*.[23] Perpetual preoccupation with the Torah is required of the Jewish theologian. Like any love relationship, a modicum of mystery must prevail to stimulate the further pursuit of knowledge of the beloved.[24] Through continuous penetration of and preoccupation with the Torah, the Jewish theologian inevitably acquires erudition and understanding.

The Jewish theologian's knowledge of and preoccupation with the Torah, coupled with the quest to understand Judaism on its own terms, grants licence to the attempt to formulate a theology of Judaism. Here 'Torah' is meant in its most generic and expansive sense: the teachings of Judaism as embodied in the literary works and oral traditions that have been held sacred by Jewish tradition.[25] In this sense, 'Torah' is the entire canon of sacred Jewish literature. At its inner core is the corpus of biblical and rabbinic literature. At its periphery are the teachings of today's Torah-scholars: 'Everything an erudite student will expound in the presence of his master was already spoken to Moses at Sinai'.[26] For the Jewish theologian, the Torah is a single corpus, one organic conceptual unit. The Jewish theologian does not approach the Torah as if it were an archaeological dig requiring stratification and identification of its individual historical layers; that is the problem of the historian of religion. The theologian, however, apprehends the Torah as a single organism, as if all of the texts that comprise it 'were uttered in a single statement'.[27]

Once vested with erudition and learning, the Jewish theologian has gained entry into the banquet hall of tradition. An immense repast is set out before the theologian. Staple servings as well as exotic offerings grace the banquet table. The variety of available servings, the presence of unusual delicacies, the richness of seasonings and garnishments, and the quality of the preparation and presentation of the menu, all reflect the theologian's breadth and depth of learning. But, despite the cornucopia that he or she encounters, the bill of fare is not without limits; the banquet table has its borders, its perimeters. Rabbinic literature compares the Torah to a 'multifaceted mirror', but the number of faces that may be reflected in the mirror, though widely diverse, nevertheless has limits: 'the Torah has seventy faces'.[28] In other words, though an expansive diversity of views characterizes the Torah, there are boundaries nonetheless. Just as the Jewish dietary laws permit a wide variety of foods to be eaten and proscribe that certain foods may not be eaten, the ideas that comprise an authentic Jewish theology and the texts that may be utilized in its formulation are diverse, but not without limits. Certain ideas, certain world views, cannot legitimately appear on the menu of Jewish theology. Jewish theology embraces a broad but finite range. Tradition itself defines its own limits. In this regard, the *Ethics of the Fathers* encourages one to plumb the depths of the Torah, but even one who is 'learned and virtuous' is enjoined from exceeding the limits, from 'revealing faces of the Torah' that contradict tradition.[29]

In order for a meal to be complete, certain courses must be eaten, certain types of foods must be consumed. As no meal can be considered complete without the consumption of certain foods, no theology of Judaism can be considered complete without the incorporation of certain ideas such as God, revelation, messiah, providence, afterlife, and so forth. As each person invited to partake of the offerings of an immense smorgasbord would emerge with a plate of food reflecting their individual tastes, so each Jewish theologian finds his or her formulation of a theology of Judaism differs from that of his or her fellow.

Though, in the final analysis, the literary resources available to each Jewish theologian are identical, the form and presentation of each individual's theology of Judaism may nonetheless differ. This is precisely why each Jewish theologian is free to compose *a* Jewish theology while no Jewish theologian can offer *the* Jewish theology. Though ultimately making use of the same raw materials, each theologian will inevitably develop them in his or her own particular manner. To be authentic, each theology of Judaism must derive from the same diverse menu; nevertheless, each Jewish theology bears the singular stamp of its composer. Just as every symphony is composed of identical notes, though the organization and presentation of these notes differs from composer to composer and from symphony to symphony, so is each authentic theology of Judaism a distinct aria of ideas. Thus, each authentic theology of Judaism simultaneously reflects the resources of a shared tradition as well as the particularity of an individual Jewish theologian and of the theology of Judaism he or she has elicited from that commonly affirmed tradition.[30]

To be authentic, Jewish theological discourse must be expressed in its own native categories, its own distinct vocabulary, and out of its own particular agenda. As Samuel S. Cohon observed, 'Attempts to cram Judaism into categories derived from other religions and theologies can lead only to grotesque results'.[31]

As members of a religious minority in a predominantly Islamic or Christian culture, inevitably influenced by western philosophical tradition, both medieval and modern Jewish thinkers have been tempted to assimilate Judaism into alien and even inimical philosophies and theologies. Indeed, the Jewish thinker may remain oblivious to the 'cultural conditioning' absorbed from his or her geographical environment, and may be led to articulate a theology of Judaism in a manner that does not cohere with authentic Jewish thought or with the inherent vocabulary of Jewish theological discourse.[32] In this regard, Solomon Schechter made a distinction between assimilating and being assimilated. An organism is able to assimilate and should assimilate that which strengthens and enriches it. However, an organism is always endangered by being assimilated into that which is inimical to it, into that which distorts its very nature.[33]

Three notions characteristic of medieval philosophical theology, derived from a profound attachment to the premises and methods of western philosophy, are often found to have been assimilated by attempts to formulate a theology of Judaism, both in the medieval and modern periods. These are: the demand for a systematic formulation of theological ideas, the perceived need to reconcile religious and philosophical truth, and the rational demonstration of the convictions that theology asserts (that is, 'natural theology').[34] Following Aristotle, who considered the validity of a system of thought as being affirmed by its logical consistency, 'systematic theology' has often been embraced as the only valid variety of theological discourse. From this perspective, if logical consistency is a requirement for theological validity, then for a Jewish theology to be valid, it has to be systematic and logically consistent within itself. Based upon these assumptions, numerous Jewish thinkers attempted to impose the rubric of Aristotelian systematic thinking upon Judaism in the attempt to articulate a valid theology of Judaism.

Though it may be described as a religious system of thought or as a coherent 'world view', Jewish theology need not be systematic in order to be valid. Neither biblical nor rabbinic literature, for example, considered the systematization of ideas either necessary or desirable.[35] System offers structure and focus, but not necessarily theological validity. System provides a finality that can prove inimical to creative theological development.[36] A demand for internal logical consistency would smother the approach of classical Jewish religious thought that tends to articulate ideas in terms of complementary polar opposites: for example., God as transcendent and immanent, human nature as simultaneously embracing both 'the image of God' as well as 'dust and ashes'.[37]

Imposing a contrived system upon reality or upon Judaism would be like trying to lay a flat grid upon the Alps. Jewish thought, especially Jewish mystical thought, perceives reality as being characterized by polarity, contradiction, tension. 'God created everything in pairs, one set against the other', says *Midrash Temurah*; in pairings such as good and evil, purity and impurity, echoes the *Zohar*.[38] 'Everything that exists in the world is either of a certain essence or of its opposite', says Judah Loew of Prague.[39] Without one entity, its polar opposite is bereft of meaning. Jewish theological discourse is at home with such 'polar' thinking. Systematic thinking in the Aristotelian and scholastic fashion is foreign to its nature and to its native manner of discourse.[40] Logic and system may be vehicles to clarity, but they are not necessarily indicative either of coherence or of truth.

As Judaism is not wedded to western philosophy, it has no endemic need to correlate or to identify its claims with those of philosophical discourse.[41] As Abraham J. Heschel observed, the categories and presuppositions that constitute the world view of Judaism are so radically different from those of the western philosophical world view that any forthright attempt to reconcile one with the other would lead inevitably to the distortion of one or the other, or both. A deformed hybrid would be the inescapable result.[42]

The assumption, made by so many medieval and modern religious philosophers, that philosophy and religion are one mouth that speaks two languages that mean the same thing, that contradictions between philosophy and religion are merely apparent, is simply a fantasy. Once philosophical truth is affirmed, and religious teaching is required to become consistent with it, the perversion of religious teachings becomes inevitable; the assimilation of religion into philosophy unavoidably ensues. Religious teachings are compelled to speak a foreign language. Gersonides, for example, insisted that any 'apparent' contradiction between the Torah and philosophy can be resolved through interpreting religious doctrine according to philosophical doctrine without 'destroying the tenets of revealed religion'.[43] Gersonides failed to appreciate, however, that conflicts between religious and philosophical doctrine can be actual and not merely apparent. He further failed to grasp how religious teachings can become distorted by subjecting them to conform to already affirmed philosophical doctrine.

Bahya ibn Pakudah expressed a typical formulation of the medieval Jewish philosophical approach when he described one who has faith only on the basis of tradition as the blind leading the blind, whereas the believer through reason is like a blind person who has learned how to see.[44] However, he neglects to consider the possibility that one who believes through reason can also be blind to truth.

While always encouraging the application of the divine gift of human reason to the quest for true belief, one nevertheless senses a hesitancy in classical Jewish thought automatically to equate the products of rationality with truth. That which is rational may neither be reasonable nor true.[45] In the quest for religious truth, rationality may become a 'dead end', or a faulty directional signal. Reason can offer acuity of vision, but it cannot grant sight itself. Reason is a necessary but not a sufficient aspect of the theological endeavour. It cannot demonstrate the validity of the convictions of theology, though it can clarify their meaning once they enter the purview of our vision. In theology, reason is a tool, a vehicle to be utilized for the clarification of what is already believed, but it is not truth personified. Like any tool, it can either improve or damage the entity to which it is applied.

Though a Jewish theology need not be systematic, correlative with philosophy, or rationalistic to be valid, it does require coherence. A lack of coherence is a danger to the formulation of a valid theology. As Louis Jacobs observes, 'loose and woolly thinking in the area of religion can lead to a glorification of the absurd … Holy nonsense is still nonsense'.[46] Though a theology can be personal and reflective of the particular style and approach of the individual theologian, it cannot become an exercise in abstract expressionism, comprehensible only to its author.

A major purpose of theological discourse is to communicate a vision, a stance, a perspective out of the collision between traditional wisdom and contemporary situations and events. A theology of Judaism that does not communicate is like a messenger who is unable to deliver the message. Such a theology proves mute and unavailing. While the theologian is not charged with the initial creation of tradition, he or she is required to re-create the tradition from the raw materials bequeathed by the past. According to a Midrashic analogy, the theologian is obliged 'to derive flour from wheat, a garment from flax'.[47] The theologian is challenged with vesting the bequest of tradition with new meaning, with liberating meanings implicit in pregnant sacred texts. The theologian is a midwife whose vocation is to bring forth new life from the womb of tradition.[48] For the Jewish theologian, erudition is a vestibule, not a final destination. Medieval Jewish writers compared the erudite scholar who had amassed much learning but who had not grasped its meaning or its implications to a 'donkey carrying books'.[49]

In medieval Jewish literature, the consonants of the Hebrew alphabet are compared to a body and the vowels to a soul.[50] Yet a Torah scroll is written only with consonants. Indeed, a vocalized Torah scroll is unfit for ritual use.[51] The Torah requires a *person* to supply the vowels, the vocalization, the soul, in order for it to become animate, alive, heard.[52] Without the person, the sacred text remains mute. Without the theologian to animate it, to provide it with a voice, tradition might otherwise remain inert. A task of the theologian is to provide the traditions of the past with a channel, with a means of speaking to the present, and with a vehicle for being transmigrated and transmitted into the future.

By providing the Torah with a voice, with animation, the theologian thereby becomes a co-author of the Torah, a collaborator with God in perpetuating and in helping to augment and to amplify in the present the voice once heard at Sinai.[53] As Meir Ibn Gabbai wrote, 'Even the sages who arise in each generation receive that which is granted from Sinai ... If new teachings [regarding the understanding of the Torah] are produced daily, this proves that the fountain [of revelation] ever gushes forth and that the great voice [from Sinai] sounds forth without interruption'.[54]

According to a Midrash quoted by Ibn Gabbai, 'Not only did all the prophets receive their prophecy at Sinai, but also each of the sages who arose in each generation received his wisdom from Sinai'.[55] As a Hasidic master put it:

> Everything depends upon the interpretation of the rabbis ... Until they had interpreted it, the Torah was not considered complete, but only half-finished; it was the rabbis, through

> their interpretations, who made the Torah whole. Such is the case for each generation and its leaders; they complete the Torah. The Torah is interpreted in each generation according to that generation's needs, and according to the soul-root of those who live at that time. God thus enlightens the sages of the generation in [the interpretation of] God's holy Torah. A person who denies this is as one who denies the Torah itself.[56]

Judah Loew of Prague observed that in the blessing over the Torah, God is not described as having *given* the Torah, but as *giving* the Torah (*notein ha-Torah*) because the Torah is continuously being given, is perpetually being revealed.[57] Judah Loew's brother, Hayyim ben Betzalel of Friedberg, said further that 'this blessing is stated all in the present tense because God is *still* giving us the Torah each day, since each person is able to introduce new meanings into it, provided they are correlative with the roots of observance and faith'.[58] As Isaiah Horowitz wrote:

> The scholars produce new words [in the understanding of the Torah] or derive them through the power of their insight. But all of it was contained in the power of that voice that was heard at the revelation; and now the time has come for them to bring it from potentiality into actuality through the efforts of their mediation ... It thus follows that while we say of God that 'He has *given* the Torah,' He can also be designated in every present time as 'the One who *gives* the Torah'.[59]

According to some of the Jewish mystics, though the Torah that God gives is the same Torah for all, each individual may understand it in his or her own particular way, according to the manner peculiar to his or her individual 'soul-root'. From this perspective, the process of the re-discovery and re-creation of the initial revelation rooted at Sinai is a profoundly personal and individual endeavour.[60] As Louis Jacobs observes, 'Every writer on the subject [of Jewish theology] can only repeat what the Jewish preachers of old were fond of saying when they squarely faced the question: Who am I to preach to others? They protested: I am speaking to myself. If others wish to overhear what I say, I cannot object'. As Jacobs further puts it, 'While the historian asks what has happened in the Jewish past, the theologian asks the more personal question: what in traditional Jewish religion continues to shape my life as a Jew in the here and now … the task [of the theologian is] discovering what it is that a Jew can believe in the present'.[61]

The individual human being is perpetually engaged in a process of self-understanding, self-discovery. The Jewish theologian is a person continuously engaged in the endeavour to understand his or her existence as a Jew. A critical component of this process is continuous understanding, discovery and re-discovery of the Torah, of that which is rooted in the initial revelation at Sinai. Once the Torah has been incorporated and assimilated into the self, the Jewish theologian's quest for understanding the Torah and his or her quest for self-understanding merge into a single endeavour. Since, as the Jewish mystics teach us, 'God, Torah and Israel are one', the quest for self and for Torah is inextricably related to the quest for the divine.[62] Thus, the Jewish theologian is engaged in the perpetual task of self-understanding within the context of the Torah – the tradition – as well as within the context of a specific moment in time and space. The theologian is charged with realizing the challenge posed by a Midrash, 'Let the Torah never be for you an antiquated decree … but as a decree issued this very day'.[63] The theologian takes inherited notes and recomposes them into a new song for his or her own age. In so doing, the theologian heeds the words of the psalmist: 'Sing unto the Lord a new song' (Ps. 96:1).

Study of the Torah aims not merely at a transmission of information to its reader, but at the transformation of that reader. The transformed and re-created reader can engender a re-created and re-imagined theology of Judaism. From this perspective, it might be more appropriate to compare theology to art rather than to science. Science can examine the physical content of a piece of art, for example, but it is incapable of elucidating its continued meaning.[64] To reduce aesthetics to subjectivity would be a mistake. Like the aesthetic dimension, the religious dimension is objectively present in the world. Like art, it requires a certain sensitivity to be appreciated and to be understood. It is objective and subjective at the same time. One must invest something of oneself to understand a great work of art. However, though one need not be an artist to be inspired by great art, one must become an artist in order to produce art. Similarly, one need not be a theologian to study or to understand the teachings of the Torah, but one must become a theologian in order to re-create Torah.

According to Scripture, Bezalel, who built the Tabernacle, was the first Jewish artist. The Talmud observes that Bezalel 'knew how to combine the letters by which the heavens and the earth were created'.[65] In other words, theological creativity derives from the ability to create new meanings from old texts. A Jewish theology offers new portraits, re-created visions, re-imagined descriptive narratives of the meaning of Judaism in general, and of specific issues of Jewish theological concern in particular. Out of the raw materials of tradition, the theologian must produce a narrative portrait of Judaism that is both authentic and communicable.[66]

While 'descriptive theology' and constructive theology would constitute the major forms of Jewish theological discourse, philosophical theology is also required. The task of philosophical theology would be to continuously refine, clarify and sharpen the focus of 'descriptive theology' in order better to convey to others the meaning of theologies composed by past and present Jewish theologians. In this view, theology operates simultaneously on three levels. The foundation level consists of the resources of sacred Jewish literature and the personal faith experiences of the individual theologian as a committed member of a faith community. The primary level consists of the descriptive but authentic reformulation in a coherent and contemporary idiom of those resources and experiences.[67] The secondary level consists of the sharpening of the focus of the vision derived from the other two levels. In this sense, philosophical theology is derivative rather than primary. 'Descriptive theology' rooted in faith and tradition remains primary. Without 'descriptive theology', philosophical theology, despite its penchant for clarity, remains a roof hanging in air, destined to collapse for lack of a foundation.[68]

Experience of the life of faith precedes theological speculation. The faith commitment and the experience of faith of the individual theologian ultimately derives from participation in a living faith community. In the final analysis, it is that faith community which will either incorporate or veto the theological views of a given theologian. Unless it acquires some form of communal acceptance, a theology of Judaism may prove to be authentic, coherent and contemporaneous, but will nonetheless remain barren and ineffectual.

Acceptance by the faith-community means inclusion into the ever-expanding canon of tradition.[69]

'Communal acceptance' does not imply acceptance by a consensus of the Jewish community as a social unit. In the biblical period, the consensus among Jews to worship the idol Baal did not mean that the authentic religion of biblical Israel was, or could ever be, Baalism, for idolatry is beyond of the boundaries of possible Jewish theological options. Rather, communal acceptance relates to acceptance by Jews who are not simply 'Jewish' by birth, but by those who constitute the believing community, the *faith* community, that is, those committed to the vocation of the people of Israel. The vocation of the Jewish people as a faith-community is divine service as understood by the Torah. As Arthur Cohen put it, 'Theology, of necessity, addresses the supernatural vocation of the Jew. When the Jewish vocation is abandoned, not theology but religious sociology takes over'.[70]

Acceptance or rejection by the majority of Jews, or by the 'organized' secular Jewish community which formulates 'Jewish' views and policies by group consensus, is irrelevant to the Jewish theologian. Such acceptance or rejection is not germane to the validity of a theology of Judaism he or she may formulate. The communal role of the Jewish theologian today is more likely to be subversive than supportive of the Jewish communal agenda. The commitment of the Jewish theologian is not organizational but theological. The theologian's ultimate obligation, like that of Judaism itself, is service to God. When the theologian perceives Jewish communal existence to be out of step with Jewish theological conviction, his or her subversive role becomes activated.

NOTES

1. On Judaism as a way of thinking, see for example, Solomon Schechter, ***Studies in Judaism*** (New York: Meridian, 1958), p.103; Solomon Schechter, ***Seminary Addresses and Other Papers*** (New York: Burning Bush Press, 1959), p.200; Abraham Joshua Heschel, ***The Insecurity of Freedom*** (New York: Farrar, Straus and Giroux, 1966), p.217; Abraham Joshua Heschel, ***God in Search of Man*** (Philadelphia: Jewish Publication Society, 1955), p.14.
2. Though these criteria for a valid Jewish theology are similar to those proposed by Jacob Neusner, my description and understanding of them differs from his. Furthermore, my proposed methodologies for composing a theology of Judaism differ substantially from those which Neusner suggests. See Jacob Neusner, 'The Tasks of Theology in Judaism', ***The Journal of Religion*** 59:1 (1979): 71–86.
3. For want of a better English word I am obliged to use the term 'theology' despite its inappropriateness when dealing with the nature and implications of Jewish faith. Etymologically,

the term means 'the study of God', or 'divine discourse'. However, Jewish teachings emphasize that the nature of God is beyond the ken of human understanding or analysis. We can only speak about the ideas, perceptions and experiences of God that we might have and that the classical sources discuss. The real subject of theology is not God per se, but the human relationship with the divine, and the nature and implications of religious faith. Compare St Thomas Aquinas, ***Summa Theologica*** I,1 where theology is considered a way of knowing God as God knows Himself.

The medieval Jewish philosophers simply translated the Greek terms that considered theology 'divine knowledge' or 'divine science' into Hebrew, for example, ***limud elohi***, ***hokhmah elohit***, ***torat ha-elohut***, ***mada ha-elohi***. In modern Hebrew, the term 'theology' (***teiologica***) is used. A viable alternative might be use of the term, '***hokhmat ha-Kodesh***', 'sacred knowledge' or 'knowledge of the sacred' suggested by Abraham Isaac Kook in ***Orot ha-Kodesh***. See Samuel S. Cohon, ***Jewish Theology*** (Assen: Royal Vangorcum, 1971), p.9.

I believe it incorrect to maintain that theology is new to Judaism. See for example, S. Daniel Breslauer, 'Alternatives in Jewish Theology', ***Judaism*** 30:2 (Spring 1981): 234 and, Cohon, ***Jewish Theology***, p.5.

4. On the issue of authenticity and tradition in Jewish theology, compare Gershom Scholem, 'Reflections on Jewish Theology', in ***On Jews and Judaism in Crisis*** (New York: Schocken, 1976), pp.261–98.
5. On the use in Jewish literature of the expression 'a dwarf on the shoulders of a giant', see Dov Zlotnick, '***Al Makor ha-Mashal ha-Nanas ve-ha-Anak ve-Gilgulav***', ***Sinai*** 77 (1975): 184–9; Hillel Levine, 'Dwarfs on the Shoulders of Giants: A Case Study in the Impact of Modernization on the Social Epistemology of Judaism', ***Jewish Social Studies*** 40:1 (Winter 1978): 68–72; Byron L. Sherwin, ***In Partnership with God: Contemporary Jewish Law and Ethics*** (Syracuse, NY: Syracuse University Press, 1990), pp.1–5.
6. Shneur Zalman of Liady, ***Lekutei Amarim [Tanya]*** (Brooklyn: Otzar ha-Hasidim, 1965), chap. 5, pp.18–19.
7. Mordecai of Chernobyl, ***Lekutei Torah*** (New York: Noble Printing Co., 1954), '***Le-Rosh ha-Shanah***', p.22b.
8. John Macquarrie, ***Principles of Christian Theology*** (New York: Scribner's, 1966), p.5; D. S. Adam, 'Theology', ***Encyclopedia of Religion and Ethics***, 12 vols. (New York: Scribner's, 1908), vol. 12, 294; Cohon, ***Jewish Theology***, p.29; Louis Jacobs, ***A Jewish Theology*** (New York: Behrman House, 1973), p.1; Bernard Bamberger, ***The Search for Jewish Theology*** (New York: Behrman House, 1978), p.5.
9. On the relationship between Jewish theologies of revelation and approaches to Jewish law, see Sherwin, ***In Partnership with God***, pp.16–47; Jacobs, ***A Jewish Theology***, pp.199–230. For a definitive study of theological issues discussed throughout the literature of Halakhic responsa, see Louis Jacobs, ***Theology in the Responsa*** (London: Routledge and Kegan Paul, 1975). In his preface, Jacobs writes, 'One result of this investigation is to give the lie to the view that Jewish theology is un-Jewish and that the Halakhist concentrates solely on the deed ignoring the beliefs that provide the deed with its sanction and infuse it with life'.
10. ***Palestinian Talmud, Berakhot*** 1:2; ***Leviticus Rabbah*** 35:7.
11. ***Berakhot*** 57a, ***Pesahim*** 49b and ***Sifre on Deuteronomy***, Meir Friedmann (ed.) (Vienna, 1865), para. 345 on Deut. 33:4.
12. Samuel of Uceda, ***Midrash Shmuel*** (Jerusalem: Brody-Katz, n.d.), pp.61a–b.
13. ***Zohar*** (Vilna: Romm, 1882), vol. 2, p.94b.
14. Moses Hayyim Ephraim of Sudlykow, ***Degel Mahaneh Ephraim*** (Jerusalem: Hadar, 1963), sec. ***Aharei***, p.175.
15. ***Sifre on Deuteronomy***, para. 345, n. 8.
16. I obviously reject that long-standing view, rooted in Aristotle and developed in medieval and modern Christian theology, that considers theology as a science. See Adam, 'Theology', pp.293–95.
17. Sherwin, ***In Partnership with God***, pp.4–8, and below, chap. 2.
18. Scholem, 'The Science of Judaism – Then and Now', in ***The Messianic Idea in Judaism*** (New York: Schocken, 1971), pp.306–7.
19. ***Pesahim*** 6b; Babylonian Talmud.
20. Samuel of Uceda, ***Midrash Shmuel***, pp.61a–b. See also, José Faur, ***Golden Doves with Silver Dots*** (Bloomington, IN: Indiana University Press, 1986), p.14.
21. In his ***Dialoghi d'Amore***, Leone Ebreo distinguishes between lust which can be satisfied and

love which cannot. Lust can be quenched while love continues to regenerate itself. See Leone Ebreo, *The Philosophy of Love*, trans. F. Friedberg-Seeley and Jean H. Barnes (London: Soncino, 1937), p.56.

22. Samuel of Uceda, *Midrash Shmuel*, p.60b.
23. Judah Loew, *Netivot Olom*, 2 vols. (New York: Judaica Press, 1969), vol.1, p.32. The blessing derives from *Berakhot* 11a.
24. Heschel, *God in Search of Man*, p.280.
25. On 'expansive' and 'restrictive' notions of 'Torah', see Abraham J. Heschel, *Torah min ha-Shamayim*, vol. 2 (London: Soncino, 1965), pp.220–64, 360–417.
26. *Leviticus Rabbah* 22:1 and discussion of this text in Heschel, *Torah min ha-Shamayim*, vol. 2 pp.236–37.
27. *Sifre on Deuteronomy*, para. 333. For parallels, see *Sifre*, Louis Finkelstein (ed.) (Berlin: Jüdischer Kulterband in Deutschland Abteilung Verlag, 1939), pp.265–66, n. 13.
28. On the Torah as a multifaceted mirror, see *Pesikta Rabbati*, Meir Friedmann (ed.) (Vienna: Herausgebers, 1880), p.100b. On the seventy 'faces' of the Torah, see *Numbers Rabbah* 13:15. See also the discussion of Moshe Idel, 'Infinities of Torah in Kabbalah', chapter in Geoffrey Hartman and Sanford Budick (eds), *Midrash and Literature* (London: Yale University Press, 1986), pp.141–57. Idel maintains that the notion that the Torah has infinite meanings was introduced with late thirteenth-century Jewish mysticism. Previously, the view prevailed that there are many but even so a finite number of meanings. On infinite meanings, see also Gershom Scholem, 'The Meaning of the Torah in Jewish Mysticism', in *On the Kabbalah and Its Symbolism* (New York: Schocken, 1965), pp.50–86.
29. *Ethics of the Fathers* 3:15. For the notion of 'principles' (*ikkarim*) as boundaries, see Julius Guttmann, 'The Principles of Judaism', *Conservative Judaism* 14:1 (Fall 1959): 1–3; Seymour Siegel, 'The Unity of the Jewish People', *Conservative Judaism* 42:3 (Spring 1990): 21–28. On 'principles' as dogmas, see Menachem Kellner, *Dogma in Medieval Jewish Thought* (Oxford: Oxford University Press, 1986).
30. As has been noted above, it is assumed that the Jewish theologian is committed to Judaism. This leads to the propriety of the theologian choosing among various theological options within the parameters of Jewish faith to design his or her own personal variation of Jewish theology. As Louis Jacobs puts it so well, 'The whole question of whether one can choose within Judaism only arises if one has first chosen Judaism'. See Jacobs, *Faith*, (New York: Basic Books, 1968), p.175.

    The approach outlined above obviates the need for the type of 'experiential' theology advocated by Breslauer, for the 'open Jewish theology' advocated by Kaufman, and for the personalist 'open traditionalism' advocated by Borowitz. Each of these authors, in my view, tend to see Jewish theology in its earlier sense as being too systematic, 'closed', and monolithic. Kaufman, for example, calls for a 'theology of clarification rather than a dogmatic [systematic] theology'. But as is discussed here, Jewish theology need not be either systematic or dogmatic. Borowitz sets up a tension between traditionalism and existentialism, between Jewish tradition and individual choice. However, once the individual can act as the ultimate arbiter of what Jewish theology may be, then the authority of tradition is undermined and a claim to authenticity becomes problematic. My contention is that the broad boundaries offered by Jewish religious literature and the absence of a central theological authority such as the Catholic Curia, provide the means for variety and multiplicity for the formulation of an authentic though 'open' Jewish theology. Moving blatantly beyond its broad parameters would deny authenticity to a theological formulation of Judaism. Just as American constitutional law cannot admit the propriety of certain concepts and options and still remain valid and authentic, a Jewish theology cannot exceed its broad boundaries and continue to remain valid and authentic. In other words, a Jew cannot formulate any theology he or she wishes and consider it a valid Jewish theology. This would invite anarchy if not heresy. See Breslauer, 'Alternatives in Jewish Theology'; William Kaufman, *Contemporary Jewish Philosophies* (New York: Reconstructionist Press, 1976), p.7; Eugene Borowitz, *A New Jewish Theology in the Making* (Philadelphia: Westminster Press, 1968), pp.208–9.
31. Cohon, *Jewish Theology*, p.43.
32. For example, despite his legion attempts to distinguish Jewish theology from Christian theology, Kaufmann Kohler's pioneering work, *Jewish Theology: Systematically and Historically Considered*, originally published in 1918 (2nd ed.: New York: Ktav, 1968), is heavily influenced by contemporary Protestant thought. Despite his insistence that Jewish theology be

systematic, he fails in the attempt to present it as such.

33. From a letter from Schechter to Max Heller, quoted in Sefton Tempkin, 'Solomon Schechter and Max Heller', *Conservative Judaism* 16 (Winter 1962): 55.
34. On the historical function and present problematics of natural theology and on the role of reason in Christian theology, see Macquarrie, *Principles of Christian Theology*, pp.39–48.
35. See Solomon Schechter, *Aspects of Rabbinic Theology* (New York: Macmillan, 1909), pp.13–14: 'The rabbis show a carelessness and a sluggishness in the application of principles which must be most astonishing to certain minds which seem to mistake merciless logic for God-given truths ... It will, therefore, suggest itself that any attempt at an orderly and complete system of Rabbinic theology is an impossible task ...'.

    On coherence without systematic thinking as a feature of rabbinic theology, see Max Kadushin, *Organic Thinking* (New York: Bloch, 1938), pp.1–3, and Kadushin, *The Rabbinic Mind* (New York: Jewish Theological Seminary, 1952), pp.11–26. According to Heschel, though rabbinic thought is not systematic, it nevertheless represents a cohesive world-view that must be elicited from the corpus of rabbinic literature. See Abraham J. Heschel, *Torah min ha-Shamayim*, vol. 1 (London: Soncino, 1962), p.viii. It is significant that Heschel translated the title of this work as '*Theology* of Ancient Judaism'. Compare Steven Schwarzschild's unsubstantiated contention that a systematic rabbinic theology is not only desirable but possible. See Menachem Kellner (ed.), *The Pursuit of the Ideal: Jewish Writings of Steven Schwarzschild* (Albany: SUNY Press, 1990), p.293, n. 64.
36. Kaufman, *Contemporary Jewish Philosophies*, p.7.
37. On polarity in Jewish thought, see Heschel, *Insecurity of Freedom*, pp.135–7.
38. See *Midrash Temurah*, in *Agadat Bereshit* (Warsaw: Levensohn, 1876), chap.1, p.49a; *Zohar* vol.2, p.69b (top). The *Zohar*'s configuration of the *sefirot* articulates the polarity of 'male' and 'female' potencies. On the critical role of polarity in the thought of Judah Loew of Prague, see Byron L. Sherwin, *Mystical Theology and Social Dissent* (Oxford: Oxford University Press, 1982), pp.70–75 and sources noted there. Compare the notions of polarity as a way to apprehending truth in Morris Raphael Cohen, *Reason and Nature* (New York: Harcourt Brace, 1931), p.165; Alan Watts, *The Two Hands of God* (New York: Collier, 1969).
39. Judah Loew, *Hiddushei Aggadot*, 4 vols. (New York: Judaica Press, 1969), vol. 2, p.89.
40. Bamberger, *The Search for Jewish Theology*, p.30.
41. In this regard, Emil Fackenheim notes, 'the attempted fusion of theology with either philosophy or science is a confusion. As regards the specific tasks of Jewish theology, it is a priori evident, not only that this is a confusion, but that it is a confusion fatal to the tasks of Jewish theology. For the categories of philosophy and science are, one and all, universal, but from such universal categories no conclusions can be derived which might be a theological justification of the particular existence of the Jewish people'. Fackenheim, *Quest for Past and Future* (Boston: Beacon, 1968), p.99.
42. Heschel, *God in Search of Man*, pp.14–15, 23 n. 8.
43. Levi ben Gershon (Gersonides), *Milhamot ha-Shem* (Leipzig, 1866), p.150. See Norbert Samuelson, 'Philosophic and Religious Authority in the Thought of Maimonides and Gersonides', *Central Conference of American Rabbis Journal* 16:4 (October 1969): 31–43. Philosophy was considered superfluous at best and an entrée to heresy at worst by many Jewish thinkers. I hope elsewhere to demonstrate that if most of medieval Jewish philosophical literature had been discarded, it would have had little substantial impact on the subsequent development of Jewish religious thought. As a largely elitist endeavour, Jewish philosophical speculation had little lasting impact on Jewish life, unlike the effect of Jewish mysticism. The criteria of acceptance by the faith community discussed below would historically disqualify much of medieval Jewish philosophical thought from claiming to be a valid expression of Jewish theology.
44. Bahya ibn Pakudah, *The Book of Direction to the Duties of the Heart*, trans. Menahem M. Mansoor (London: Routledge and Kegan Paul, 1973), p.113.
45. 'Rationality' has a wide variety of possible meanings. See Bryan Wilson, *Rationality* (New York: Harper and Row, 1971); Bamberger, *The Search for Jewish Theology*, p.4; Heschel, *God in Search of Man*, p.20; Jacobs, *Faith*, pp.41–65, 201–9.
46. Jacobs, *A Jewish Theology*, p.5.
47. *Seder Eliyahu Rabbah ve-Seder Eliyahu Zuta*, Meir Friedmann (ed.) (Vienna: Ahiyasaf, 1904), *Zuta*, chap. 2, p.172.

48. Moshe Idel, *Kabbalah: New Perspectives* (New Haven: Yale University Press, 1988), p.215.
49. On the expression, 'a donkey carrying books', see Israel Davidson, *Otzar ha-Mashalim ve-ha-Pitgamim* (Jerusalem: Mosad ha-Rav Kook, 1969), no. 2851, p.171, n. 39.
50. *Sefer ha-Bahir*, Reuven Margaliot (ed.) (Jerusalem: Mosad ha-Rav Kook, 1951), no. 115, p.51. Note Judah Halevi, *Kuzari*, trans. Hartwig Hirschfield (New York: Schocken, 1964), 4:3, p.202.
51. See e.g., Joseph Karo, *Shulhan Arukh* (Vilna: Romm, 1911), sec. *Yoreh Deah* 274:7.
52. See David ibn Zimra, *Teshuvot ha-Radbaz*, 4 vols. (Furth, 1781), vol. 3, no. 643, p.43b. See discussion in Idel, *Kabbalah*, pp.214–15, and sources noted there.
53. See, for example, the interpretation of the Talmudic phrase 'a partner in the work of creation' (*Sabbath* 10a) in the beginning of Jacob ben Asher's *Arba'ah Turim* (New York: Grossman, n.d.), sec. *Hoshen Mishpat*, where scholars of any generation who correctly interpret the Torah and declare a correct legal judgment are considered God's partners in the work of creation. On the human being as a co-author of the Torah, see Idel, *Kabbalah*, p.215.
54. Meir ibn Gabbai, *Avodat ha-Kodesh* (Jerusalem: Levin-Epstein, 1954), part 3, chap. 23, pp.85b–86a.
55. *Exodus Rabbah* 28:6; see also *Midrash Tanhuma [ha-Nidpas]* (Jerusalem: Levin-Epstein, 1964), sec. *Yitro* no. 11, p.96.
56. Moses Hayyim Ephraim of Sudlykow, *Degel Mahaneh Ephraim*, sec. *Bereshit*, p.6.
57. Judah Loew, *Netivot Olom*, vol.1, p.32.
58. Hayyim ben Bezalel, *Sefer ha-Hayyim* (Jerusalem: Weinfeld, 1968), sec. *Sefer Zechuyot*, 1:1, p.4
59. Isaiah Horowitz, *Shnei Luhot ha-Brit* (Jerusalem: Edison, 1960), vol. 1, sec. *Beth David*, pp.39a–b (pp.25b–26a in the Amsterdam edition).
60. Hayyim Vital, *Shaar ha-Gilgulim* (Jerusalem: Eshel, 1963), chap. 17, p.48; Scholem, *On the Kabbalah*, p.65 and sources noted there.
61. Jacobs, *A Jewish Theology*, pp.6, 1. As Monford Harris notes, 'an authentic Jewish theology always speaks in terms of specific historic situations'. See Harris, 'Interim Theology', *Judaism* 7:4 (Fall 1958): 305. For Harris, 'The existence in the world of Jewish existence and how each Jew is to link his private existence to Jewish existence sets into motion a *Jewish* theological enterprise' (p.302).
62. On 'God, Torah and Israel', see Abraham J. Heschel, 'God, Torah and Israel', and in his *Moral Grandeur and Spiritual Audacity* (New York: Farrar, Straus, Giroux, 1996), pp.191–208; Isaiah Tishbi, *'Kudsha Berikh hu, Oraita ve-Yisrael–had hu'*, *Kiryat Sefer* 50 (1975): 480–492, 668–74.
63. *Pesikta de-Rav Kahana*, Solomon Buber (ed.) (Lyck: Mekitzei Nirdamim, 1868), p.102a.
64. As in any analogy, there are similarities and differences between the two terms compared. In that theology demands commitment while aesthetics and art do not, the analogy cannot apply. See Bamberger, *The Search*, p.87. On Judaism as an art form, see Alan Lazaroff, 'Judaism as an Art', *Judaism* 30 (Summer 1981): 355–63; Sherwin, *In Partnership*, pp.9–15.
65. *Berakhot* 55a.
66. Compare the similar model for Christian theology advocated by Macquarrie, *Principles of Christian Theology*, p.50. I believe that while for Christian theological discourse, descriptive theology is a departure (as Macquarrie suggests), for Jewish theology it would represent continuity with the past, particularly with regard to biblical, Midrashic, Kabbalistic, and late medieval and early modern east European traditional Jewish literature.
67. On the level of 'unreflective faith', see Schechter, *Aspects of Rabbinic Theology*, p.12; Heschel, 'Depth-Theology', in *The Insecurity of Freedom*, pp.115–26.
68. This approach reflects the influence of phenomenological method with its three levels of inquiry: the pre-reflective, the descriptive and the reflective. It also reflects the influence of my mentor Abraham Heschel who utilized phenomenological method. For a similar approach utilizing phenomenological method in Christian theology, see Macquarrie, *Principles of Christian Theology*, pp.30–36. In my view, this approach merely states in another way what many Jewish thinkers have been doing throughout the ages. However, while many Jewish thinkers not profoundly influenced by Jewish philosophy developed what is called here a 'descriptive theology', Jewish philosophers utilized philosophical theology. The utilization of both would seem well advised. Cohon's observation that 'even when employing the methods of philosophy, the theologian utilizes them in a somewhat different way and with a different object in mind', is relevant here (*Jewish Theology*, p.27).

69. Faur, *Golden Doves with Silver Dots*, p.108.
70. Arthur A. Cohen, *The Natural and the Supernatural Jew* (New York: McGraw Hill, 1964), p.288. See also Cohen, 'Theology', chap. in Arthur A. Cohen and Paul Mendes-Flohr (eds), *Contemporary Jewish Religious Thought* (New York: Scribner's, 1987), pp.971–81.

CHAPTER TWO

Jewish Theological Scholarship

The perennial goal of the study of Jewish religious literature has been to preserve Judaism and to ensure its continuity. The nexus between the Jewish people and classical Jewish religious literature has been central to the survival and continuous revival of the Jewish people, of their religion, and of their literature. Much of classical western literature represents a world viewed in the third person. A goal of Jewish learning is to transform the student's perspective from the third person to the first person.[1] This goal is implicitly expressed in the Talmudic adage, 'At the beginning [the Torah] is called by the name of the Lord, but in the end it will be called by his [the student's] name'.[2] Or, as the Jewish mystics would put it, 'to be a thing is to know a thing, and to know a thing, is to be a thing'.[3]

Objective, scientific, third-person scholarship is alien to classical Jewish thinking. 'Objective' scholarship is, by its very nature, voyeuristic; it is like reading a menu with no intention of partaking of the food listed thereon. This approach results not in the assimilation of Jewish learning into the scholar's own self, but the assimilation of the object of study – in this case Judaism – into alien categories of scholarship and thought. In 1907, Solomon Schechter observed, 'there is a difference between assimilation and being assimilated'.[4] Schechter analogized *assimilating* to a person's assimilation of a steak, the individual's becoming thereby enriched and strengthened. He further analogized *being assimilated* to an individual who believes that he or she can become a cow, to an individual trying to become that which he or she is not.

The wide range of ideas present in the enormous mass of texts that comprise classical Jewish literature may be compared to a smorgasbord. The assortment of dishes served is vast, though limited. As each individual attending the repast takes an empty plate and proceeds along the table, he or she creates a combination of foods particular to his or her taste and appetite. Choices can only be made from those dishes that are on the table. Similarly, the Jewish theologian constructs his or her own collage of Judaism or of a particular issue or problem of Jewish theology, ethics, or law from the menu at hand. The menu derives from the smorgasbord of ideas and statements contained in classical Jewish literature.

'Just as each blow of a hammer strikes forth many sparks, so a single verse [of the Torah] unfolds into many meanings'.[5] However multivalent these interpretations are, they are not without limit. The rabbinic view that there are 'seventy faces' of the Torah indicates that the interpretation and the exposition of Judaism embraces a wide but finite range. The tradition itself defines these limits. The scholar who goes beyond them forfeits his or her place within the ongoing development and growth of Jewish tradition. In this regard, the *Ethics of the Fathers* condemns even one who is 'learned in the Torah and virtuous' when he or she 'reveals faces of the Torah that contradict tradition [Halakhah]'.[6] *Peshat* (the literal or contextual meaning of a text) that cannot be legitimately assimilated into the corpus of tradition should not be incorporated into the corpus of Jewish theological scholarship.[7]

As the artist gathers his or her materials to create an *objet d'art*, so does the theologian collect his or her texts to blend them into a portrait of the subject at hand. Like the culinary artist, the theological scholar must be concerned with what has been chosen and placed on the serving platter and with the manner of its presentation. The manner of presentation must be coherent. A primary goal of theological scholarship is transmission, which requires clarity as well as authenticity.

Jewish theological scholarship must be faithful to the past while being pertinent to the present. In the words of a Midrash, 'Let the Torah never be for you an antiquated decree but as a decree issued this very day'.[8] As a vital link between the past and the future, it must be well forged to ensure that it attains transmission. On occasion, the claims of tradition will be demonstrated to be at odds with the agenda and with the value system of the contemporary Jewish community. When such is the case, Jewish theological scholarship discloses its 'subversive' role, that is, its task to make contemporary Jewish existence correlative with Jewish tradition.

In the final analysis, Jewish scholarship is a seance. It provides a vehicle for the past to commune with the present. In this regard, a Talmudic adage states that when one quotes a tradition in the name of a sage, one should at the same time be able to sense his presence.[9] Jewish theological scholarship aims at making our ancestors our contemporaries so that they may share their problems with us and so that we may share our problems with them.

In 1905, Solomon Schechter wrote, 'It is one of the great tragedies of modern Judaism that it knows itself so little'.[10] Similarly, in 1958, Abraham Heschel observed, 'Judaism today is an unknown religion. The vital issues it raises, the sublime views it discloses, the novel goals it points to are forgotten. We have failed to learn how much Judaism has to say to the mind, to the soul.... Judaism is a source of cognitive insight, a way of thinking, not only an order of living'.[11] One may suggest that much of the vast corpus of Jewish scholarship produced since 1905 or 1958 has not significantly altered the pertinence of these observations.

The approach to Jewish theological scholarship that informs this work has been inspired by the vision offered by Solomon Schechter, Abraham Joshua Heschel and Louis Jacobs. [Chapters on each of these significant thinkers will be found below.] In their writings, Schechter, Heschel and Jacobs applied the wisdom of the past to the contemporary issues that confronted them. In his own unique way, each drew from the vast mass of Jewish texts of all past generations to formulate and to recreate an authentic yet novel approach to conceptual, ethical and social problems that he perceived to be of contemporary concern. As Heschel wrote, 'After the Holocaust, Jewish scholarship should be devoted to that which advances Judaism'.[12]

Jewish Scholarship

'If the earlier scholars were like angels, then we [later scholars] are like human beings. However, if the earlier scholars were like human beings, then we are like asses'.[13] This Talmudic adage articulates the notion of progressive decline, which is assumed by much of classical Jewish literature.[14] From this perspective, the further we move away from the revelation at Mount Sinai chronologically, the weaker our spiritual and intellectual abilities become. The opposite notion was introduced into Jewish intellectual and religious life by nineteenth-century modern Jewish scholarship (*Wissenschaft des Judentums*) and by early Reform Judaism. In this view, Jewish history and experience (to be understood in Hegelian terms) demonstrate the gradual, inevitable progress of the spiritual and intellectual nature of Judaism and of the Jewish people. From this perspective, the later is always better. The closer we draw to the future messianic age, the stronger our spiritual and intellectual prowess becomes.[15]

Neither the self-deprecation of the first approach nor the triumphalism of the second is conducive to the creative development of a vibrant tradition such as Judaism. The first perspective leads to the stifling of growth, to the view that 'the new is taboo'.[16] The second perspective subverts the very notion of tradition by denying its authority and hence its validity as a source of perennial wisdom and truth. This doctrine of 'progressive revelation' seems to imply that moderns are in many ways spiritually and intellectually superior to Isaiah, Rabbi Akiva and Moses Maimonides, that God withheld certain insights from our ancestors in order to vouchsafe them to us.

The collision between these two perspectives of inevitable recession and supersession may be cushioned, though not prevented, by evoking the analogy of 'a dwarf riding on the shoulders of a giant'. Commonly attributed to the seventeenth-century scientist, Sir Isaac Newton, this expression seems to have been coined by the twelfth-century French philosopher, Bernard of Chartres.[17] The thirteenth-century Italian Halakhist, Isaiah di Trani, appears to have been responsible for its incorporation into Jewish writing. In subsequent Jewish literature, this term is frequently found.[18]

The comparison of the cumulative corpus of past tradition to a giant and of the contemporary scholar to a dwarf satisfies the traditional conviction that no single individual – no matter how gifted or learned – can approach the stature of the cumulative wisdom of the tradition. This view protects the tradition from the subversion of the work of earlier authorities by that of later scholars. Once the dwarf climbs the body of the giant and stands on his shoulders, the dwarf supersedes the giant both in height and in visual perspective. In other words, the view of the later scholar may be accepted as valid without casting aspersions upon the authority or competence of earlier scholars, even while assuming the intrinsic superiority of those earlier scholars.

In his commentary to the Mishnah, the late sixteenth-century

Talmudist, Abraham Azulai, discussed the analogy of the dwarf and the giant:

> For the modern is like a dwarf and the ancients are like giants but because the modern is later, he is like a dwarf riding the shoulder of a giant who can see at a distance farther than the giant. And so it is with the modern who may be unable to attain what the ancient had attained, but being later and having had the benefit of the knowledge and great wisdom of the ancients, then, if he himself should discover something new, be it but a trifle, he will certainly with that trifle contribute more wisdom than they; even though his own wisdom would have been naught had he not the benefit of their wisdom.[19]

The doctrine of regressive authority condemns later scholars to the lower and very narrow perspective of a dwarf. The doctrine of progressive authority maintains that the giants of the past were dwarfs compared to the giants of today. The notion of the dwarf riding on the shoulders of a giant claims that the coalescence of the wisdom of the past in the giant makes the stature of the giant necessarily higher and his vista broader than that of the dwarf, who represents only the wisdom of his own generation. However, it also maintains that, by climbing upon the giant's shoulders, the dwarf can exceed that which is attainable by the giant alone.

The regressive view stifles the dwarf's potential. The progressive view pretends that dwarfs are giants. The third view organically links the dwarf to the giant, to the benefit of both. Furthermore, it may well be that the dwarf is not a dwarf at all but only appears to be a dwarf when measured against the enormous stature of the giant. Separated, the giant and the dwarf are destined each to his own individual fate. Together, the giant and the dwarf guarantee both the perpetuation and the development of tradition.

Tradition is a living force that animates and informs the present. Tradition is that which assures the continuity of creativity. Without the dwarf, tradition is like a giant, a relic of bygone days. However, without the giant, there is no viable foundation for future creativity, development, and growth. Without the giant, the dwarf either stands tied close to the ground or is transfixed in mid-air, waiting to fall into an abyss.

The giant would be unwise to be threatened by what the dwarf might achieve. Indeed, he should be grateful to the dwarf for expanding his purview. The dwarf should be grateful to the giant, for without the giant the vision of the dwarf would remain severely limited. Once perched on the giant's shoulders, the dwarf must overcome the temptation of forgetting that he is not a giant, but a dwarf riding on the shoulders of a giant. It is further incumbent upon the dwarf to know the giant well. What the dwarf will be able to see depends upon the nature of the giant and where the giant will carry him.

How should the dwarf relate to the giant who bears him on his shoulders? What should the dwarf search for as he surveys the panorama from his elevated perch? Questions such as these can serve as indicators to help establish an appropriate programme for contemporary Jewish theological scholarship.

It would be tragic if the dwarf, once elevated onto the giant's shoulders, was found to suffer from myopia. It would be equally unfortunate if the dwarf discovered that his peripheral vision was severely impaired. Yet, much of contemporary 'scientific' Jewish scholarship seems to suffer from restricted peripheral vision. Scholars seem prone to overspecialization in minute sub-areas of Jewish studies without surveying the breadth of classical Jewish sources. Some limit their scholarly investigations to specific texts, written in specific lands during specific periods. A paradigmatic feature of modernity, this tendency toward specialization gives licence to scholars to know more and more about less and less. Commenting on what he calls the 'barbarism' of specialization, the Spanish philosopher José Ortega y Gasset has written the following with specific regard to the modern scientist:

> He is one who, out of all that has to be known in order to be a man of judgment, is only acquainted with one science, and even of the one only knows the small corner in which he is an active investigator. He even proclaims it as a virtue that he takes no cognizance of what lies outside the narrow territory specially cultivated by himself, and gives the name 'dilettantism' to any curiosity for the general scheme of knowledge ....The specialist 'knows' very well his own tiny corner of the universe; he is radically ignorant of all the rest ....We shall have to say that he is a learned ignoramus.[20]

The 'Scientific' Study of Judaism

By analogizing modern Jewish scholarship to modern science, the founders of *Wissenschaft des Judentums* predetermined the direction toward overspecialization that contemporary 'scientific' Jewish scholarship has taken. By trying to make Jewish scholarship scientific and objective, even 'value-free', they placed the giant in the laboratory and did not climb upon his shoulders. They transformed the giant into a dwarf by degrading the exalted status he once had enjoyed.

The founders of *Jüdische Wissenschaft* reduced sacred Jewish literature to belles lettres.[21] The unique nature and meaning that classical Jewish literature held, particularly for Jews, was now surrendered into the vortex of the 'universal human spirit'. The dwarf had climbed off the giant's shoulders and was now preparing to lock the giant in a laboratory to await vivisection. In this regard, Gershom Scholem described the programme of the *Wissenschaft des Judentums* as 'the liquidation of Judaism as a living organism' and its adherents as 'academic morticians'. Scholem's words remind one of Moritz Steinschneider's quip that modern Jewish scholars 'have only one task left: to give the remains of Judaism a decent burial'. Similarly, Zalman Rubashov (Shazar) described Leopold Zunz's programme for the scientific study of Judaism as an agenda aimed at the 'de-Judaization' of Judaism.[22]

While Jewish tradition always emphasized the nexus between thought and action, theory and practice, modern 'scientific' Jewish scholarship severed that relationship. For the first time, Jewish learning and Jewish life and faith became related by chance, rather than by necessity. Whereas in the past, the life of the Jewish scholar fell under the provenance of the text, now the life of the text came under the control of the scholar. No longer bearing the dwarf on his shoulders, the giant was now led about by the dwarf, drawn to places alien to his nature.

Scientific objectivity rather than the continuity of tradition has become the primary feature of the new Jewish learning. Consequently, an unprecedented fissure emerged in the world of Jewish scholarship. For the first time, the products of Jewish scholarly investigation have become detached both from the internal dynamic and organic development of Jewish religious faith, and from contemporary Jewish communal concerns and spiritual needs.

Much of contemporary Jewish scholarship seems to have abandoned its history by casting its destiny with secular academe. How well the giant will fare in this alien environment remains obscure. Whether the continuity of the tradition of Jewish learning can prevail remains uncertain.

Historical scholarship became the means by which the dwarf would examine and analyze the giant. Classical Jewish learning perceived the giant as an organism requiring growth and development. Modern Jewish scholarship compares the giant to an archaeological dig and seeks to stratify and identify its layers. Traditional Jewish learning sought a total gestalt, unencumbered by historical considerations: 'There is neither earlier nor later in the Torah'.[23] Modern 'scientific' Jewish learning has sought to examine each of the giant's cells individually in an elusive search for his essence. As the leading nineteenth-century Jewish historian Heinrich Graetz put it, 'the totality of Judaism is only recognizable through its history; in history the whole essence, the sum of its powers must be made explicit'.[24] Nevertheless, minute examination of the parts tends to eclipse a vision of the whole. The historical quest becomes an end in itself. As Leo Baeck observed, 'History began to mean more than the content'.[25] The study of the anatomy of the giant became more important than the personality of the giant. For the first time in Jewish experience, Jewish historiography became divorced from Jewish collective memory. Ironically, this new approach to the Jewish past represents a decisive break with the Jewish past.[26] Though admirable in itself, the awakening of Jewish historical consciousness has led to the anaesthetizing of the Jewish religious consciousness.

Despite its self-proclaimed identification with objective, 'value-free' universal science, the original agenda of the *Wissenschaft des Judentums* was closely tied to a subjective, particular, value-laden agenda: Jewish scholarship was to serve as a strategic tool to further the integration of the Jews into the socio-political life of the nations in which they resided. *Jüdische Wissenschaft* was not an intellectual parlour game; it was the avant-garde of a particular ideology inextricably related to the crisis of Jewish social and political emancipation and to the struggle to attain it.[27] In a sense, this massive effort to bring about the emancipation of the Jews led to the emancipation of Judaism from its traditional moorings. The giant was surgically transformed – cut down in size with his features re-formed. By casting the history, religion, literature, and institutions of the Jewish people into western academic categories, the very tradition that these scholars wished to preserve was distorted beyond recognition.

The introduction of the chronological axis into Jewish learning made the enterprise of dating classical Jewish texts into a critical obsession. This approach proves valuable in elucidating the contextual meaning of classical texts and of demonstrating the historical development of the tradition. This endeavour parallels efforts characteristic of scholarship in the humanities and the social sciences. One might even argue that this approach is a modern form of the age-old quest for the *peshat*, the literal and contextual meaning of an examined text.[28] However, though the *peshat* may be necessary and even desirable, it never can be adequate. It offers an important perspective, but by its very nature, it is one-dimensional. The giant, however, is multidimensional. The text is 'a multifaceted mirror which reflects the subject from every side'.[29] Abraham Isaac Kook compared the Torah to a mirror in which each succeeding generation observes its own particular reflection. The mirror always remains the same, but the reflections cast into it perpetually change. The task of the dwarf is not to convert the mirror into a window, thereby becoming an impassive voyeur gazing at the past, but to seek his own reflection mirrored in the eyes of the giant. *Wissenschaft des Judentums* smashed the mirror and placed the giant under glass for objective study.

To establish the *peshat*, substantial effort has been invested in discovering a *Grundtext*, an exact primary text for subsequent scholarly investigation. Modern Jewish scholarship has made prodigious contributions in providing reliable readings of primary texts. The danger, however, occurs when finding the correct reading stifles the quest for the text's meaning. In this regard, it is told that a famous Jewish theologian once received a small package in the mail. The package contained a newly published scholarly work on the Talmud that he had long awaited. Written by a leading Talmudic scholar, this volume already had been heralded by reviewers as a definitive work. The theologian's hands shook with anticipation as he withdrew the book from its wrapping. Feverishly, he turned the pages until he came to a commentary on a passage in the Mishnah that had perplexed him for many years. Anxiously, he began to read the great Talmudist's commentary, hoping for a resolution to his perplexity. He read, 'The word "*betulah*" ["virgin"] in this passage appears written with the letter "*vov*" in fourteen consulted manuscripts, and without the letter "*vov*" in twelve other manuscripts consulted by this commentator. From this careful investigation one may conclude that whether the correct reading is with or without a "*vov*" is uncertain'. The theologian sighed heavily and muttered to himself, 'Does the virgin really care whether she has kept or whether she has surrendered her "*vov*"?'

It is also told that, when a certain Lithuanian rabbi was a young scholar, he began a project that would engage him for the remainder of his life. Convinced that Moses Maimonides was a paragon of consistency, he set out to prove that Moses Maimonides never contradicted himself. The young scholar spent five years studying Maimonides' vast corpus of writings. He diligently recorded the numerous contradictions in Maimonides' work. He then spent the next ten years demonstrating that the contradictions in Maimonides' writings were merely apparent contradictions rather than actual contradictions and that his theory regarding Maimonides' total consistency was both accurate and true. At the conclusion of this decade of scholarly work, he had proven to his satisfaction that all of the apparent inconsistencies in Maimonides' writings were capable of resolution – all but one, which continued to perplex him for many years.

On the day before his death, the scholar resolved the final apparent inconsistency, and he died a happy man, content that he had proved his theory that Maimonides was a model of logical consistency. When he arrived in heaven, the scholar was informed by one of the angels that he could speak to any individual in heaven with whom he wished to speak. The scholar, needless to say, asked to speak to Maimonides. When he appeared, Maimonides asked the scholar why he wished to speak specifically to him. The scholar told Maimonides about his life's work. Maimonides was curious, and he asked the scholar to quote the two texts that took him so many years to resolve logically. The scholar proudly quoted the texts from memory. Maimonides thought for a moment and said, 'That was no problem at all. The *Grundtext* you used contained a misprint!'

While the thrust of modern Jewish scholarship is largely directed toward discovering the *peshat* of the text, that is, its proper reading and its contextual meaning, a feature of the sources it seeks to examine is their denial of the ultimate importance of contextual meaning and of the presupposition that a one-dimensional meaning is preferable to a multidimensional exegesis. The *Zohar*, for example, reminds us not to confuse the 'outer garb' of the text with its body, soul, or essential meaning.[30] Those who take the text seriously cannot take it only literally.

The chronological axis characteristic of modern 'scientific' Jewish scholarship embodies an assumption that appears incompatible with traditional or classical Jewish scholarship. The latter assumes that the classical texts must be explained and interpreted as if they constituted a single conceptual unit. They are to be treated synchronically rather than diachronically or chronologically. While useful within the parameters of its own programme, the chronological axis of modern Jewish scholarship represents an intrusion upon the conceptual presuppositions and the native value system of classical Jewish scholarship.[31] The *peshat* it offers may prove irrelevant (as well as irreverent) from the perspective of traditional Jewish self-understanding. The goal of traditional Jewish learning is not simply to preserve and to transmit, but also to generate and to re-create new meaning from the text. From this perspective, one is obliged not only to receive, but also to return what one has received in a new and even altered form. As a Midrash observes, 'The Holy One gave the Torah to Israel like wheat from which to derive fine flour, or like flax from which to make a garment'.[32] To paraphrase a rabbinic proverb, 'One who says "I have only the text," does not have even the text'.[33]

Both the diachronic and the synchronic axes are necessary for a total view of Judaism. The diachronic axis is eminently necessary to understand the context of Jewish texts and institutions. However, the diachronic approach, characteristic of the *Wissenschaft des Judentums* and of much of subsequent Jewish scholarship, is in the final analysis, external to Judaism. It is about Judaism; it is not Judaism.[34] It is scholarship about Judaism rather than Jewish scholarship. What is advocated here is a programme for contemporary Jewish theological scholarship aimed at the perpetuation and the continuous re-creation of Judaism. In this sense, the dwarf desires to help the giant grow so that the vista from his shoulders may be even more elevated than before.

Engaging the Tradition

As already stated, *Jüdische Wissenschaft* tried to embody scientific objectivity and a 'value-free' approach to Judaism. In his 1822 essay, 'On the Concept of a Science of Judaism', Immanuel Wolf, one of the founders of the *Wissenschaft des Judentums*, described the following as being characteristic of the new Jewish learning:

> It treats the object of study in and of itself, for its own sake, and not for any special purpose or definite intention. It begins without any preconceived opinion and is not concerned with the final result. Its aim is neither to put its object in a favorable, nor in an unfavorable light, in relation to prevailing views, but to show it as it is. Science is self-sufficient ... It therefore needs to serve no other purpose than its own.[35]

One may not only reject the position that perceives Jewish learning primarily and exclusively as a scientific endeavour, one may also contend that even in science there is no 'immaculate perception', and that to assume such is to perpetuate an 'immaculate deception'. Texts cannot be read with complete objectivity or conceptual innocence. The reader brings himself or herself *to* the text, or even *into* the text. The Hebrew word for 'ark' is the same as the Hebrew word for 'letter', *teivah*. According to Hasidic sources, like Noah, one must enter the *teivah*.[36] The goal of Jewish theological scholarship is not simply to see the text, 'pure and chaste from afar', but to enter and to become the text. As Judah Loew of Prague observed, the goal of the scholar is not to study the Torah, but to become the Torah. The ideal Jewish scholar is the Torah incarnate, a literally meant 'embodiment' of the text.[37] By becoming the text, the dwarf becomes part of the giant.

Jewish mystics perceived study of the Torah as a vehicle toward establishing a nexus between its author, its text, and its interpreter. Study thereby becomes not only a conduit toward union with God but a means of merging the scholar and the text. The Hasidic master, Moses Hayyim Ephraim of Sudylkow, the grandson of the Ba'al Shem Tov, compared the act of study to the love act: 'When a man studies the Torah for its own sake, to keep it and to perform it, then he brings all his limbs close to their source whence they originated and were generated, namely to the Torah ... and he becomes identical with the Torah in a unification and in a complete union, like the unification of man and woman'.[38] Furthermore, the Hasidic sage, Mordecai of Chernobyl, took the Scriptural phrase '*ve-zot torat ha-adam*' [literally: 'and this is the Torah of man'] (2 Sam. 7:19) to mean that 'the person himself becomes the Torah'.[39]

The purpose of Jewish theological scholarship is to advance the value system embodied in the Jewish texts and institutions it studies. For Jewish theological scholarship, unlike for *Judische Wissenschaft*, Judaism is the subject of study, not an object to study. Therefore, a primary item on the agenda of Jewish theological scholarship must be the identification of a particularly Jewish way of thinking and of the value system expressed by it. Rather than import foreign categories to Judaism or impose them upon Judaism, one must first discern the authentic endemic categories of Judaism. Seen from this perspective, Jewish theological scholarship is self-reflective. It is a perpetual exercise in self-examination, self-clarification, and self-understanding.[40]

It may be more appropriate to study Judaism artistically than scientifically. Jewish religion and the cultivation of its moral virtues may be compared to an art. Study of Jewish texts may be compared to the study of artistic works. Science can examine the physical content of a piece of art, for example, the paint, the wood of a sculpture, but it is incapable of elucidating its continued meaning. It is the quest for meaning that drives the Jewish theological enterprise.

To reduce aesthetics to subjectivity would be a mistake. Like the aesthetic dimension, the religious dimension is objectively present in the world. Like art, it requires a certain sensitivity to be appreciated and to be understood. It is objective and subjective at the same time. One must invest something of oneself to understand great art. One need not be an artist to appreciate great art. However, one must be an artist to be inspired by art to create art. Similarly, in literature, virtually all great writers have been great readers. Literature is a process of reimagination and re-creation.[41] The process of literary development is often furthered by a series of intentional and unintentional 'misreadings'.[42] Indeed, unless one can entirely and accurately discern the initial meaning and intention of an author or artist, every reading becomes a misreading. The history of classical Jewish literature may be understood as a continuous process of a creative misreading of the primary text, the Torah. Indeed, the tradition of *keri* and *ketiv* (write this, but read that) illustrates how to misread the text to elicit its proper meaning.[43] Seen from this perspective, contextual reading is important, but not crucial. Viewed in this manner, Jewish theological scholarship is better analogized to artistic rather than to scientific study. The task is to continue the process of the creative misreading of the text within the parameters of the value system that teaches us how to relate to the text in the first place. In this way, the continuity of tradition is assured. Through a genuine appreciation of the text, one expands and amplifies its meaning. A dialogue is thereby created between the author and the reader. Through the process of interpretation, the reader becomes a co-author, a collaborator in the artistic endeavour.

A Torah scroll contains only consonants; it has no vowels. According to Jewish law, a vocalized Torah scroll is invalid for ritual use.[44] It is the reader who provides the vowels, the vocalization of the text. The medieval kabbalistic work *Sefer ha-Bahir* compares the consonants to a body and the vowels to a soul.[45] The sixteenth-century Halakhist, David ibn Zimra, noted in a responsum (a legal decision) that 'vocalization is like a commentary to the written Torah'.[46] By giving vocalization to the text, the reader animates and interprets the text, giving it life, allowing it to be spoken, heard, and understood. According to Maimonides, the Israelites who stood at Sinai heard 'the great voice [of God], but not the articulations of speech'. It was Moses who conveyed the Torah 'with the articulation of the letters'.[47] The unvocalized word of God invites human articulation and vocalization.

According to David ibn Zimra, the Torah may be read according to its 'spiritual' meaning and according to its 'concrete' meaning. Put another way, the scholar cannot be content with only discovering the text's concrete meaning, its contextual meaning. The scholar is obliged to make audible and explicit the otherwise mute and inaccessible meaning of the text. The task of the scholar is to liberate some of the reservoir of implicit meaning pregnant within the text. The scholar is a midwife whose task is to bring forth new life from the womb of tradition. The scholar's duty is to try to penetrate the text's inexhaustible meaning. In ibn Zimra's words:

> I found a document written by one of the earlier sages, and I do not know his name. [He taught that one should] know that because the vocalization is the form and the soul of the letters, the scroll of the Torah is not vocalized. It embodies in all its aspects [literally: 'faces'] all of the profound paths. All of these may be expounded in each individual letter: faces within faces, mysteries within mysteries. No limits are known to us ... If the scroll had been vocalized, then it would have a limit and a perimeter ... It could [then] not have been interpreted except in accordance with the specific vocalization of the word ... This is why our sages said, 'There are seventy faces to the Torah'.[48]

Though much of modern Jewish scholarship has been preoccupied with establishing a correct *Grundtext* as the necessary prerequisite for locating its *Grundbedeutung* (its original contextual meaning), a number of classical Jewish writers denied that access to an original and accurate *Grundtext* of the most primary of all Jewish texts – the Torah – has been granted to us. In this regard, Levi Yitzhak of Berdichev, the nineteenth-century Hasidic master, taught that between the black letters of the Torah there are white spaces that contain invisible letters currently unknown to us. These blank letters will, however, become known to us in the messianic age. Knowledge of these letters will alter the present reading of the text and consequently our understanding of it. Other Jewish mystics taught that the eternal 'essential' Torah is never revealed. It remains in its purely spiritual form, an eternal citizen of the divine realm. The form in which we have the Torah is a corrupt, imperfect form. According to the *Sefer ha-Temunah*, for example, the Torah assumes different forms in various aeons. The text we have is not the correct text; it is the version of the text appropriate for our particular age. In our aeon, the Torah is in exile, in an alienated state. A version of this teaching is that the Hebrew alphabet properly consists of twenty-three rather than the twenty-two letters we currently assume it has. The complete actualized text of the Torah embodies this missing letter. When this letter is revealed in the future and each of its proper appearances in the Torah is discerned, the text will be correct, and only then will the proper reading of the text and its meaning be determined.[49] It was apparently the belief that no present text of the Torah is the actual and correct one that led Judah

Loew of Prague to offer a legal ruling – in opposition to most Halakhic authorities – that a Torah scroll with a scribal defect may be used in the synagogue. For Loew, no Torah scroll contains the absolutely correct primal text.[50]

According to Scripture, the first set of tablets given to Moses was written with 'the finger of God'. It contained the text in its purely spiritual and essentially correct form. The second set was written by Moses at God's command. This version of the Torah, now in our possession, represents the humanly edited and transmitted version of the originally divine text. When the first set of tablets was broken, 'the letters engraved upon it flew heavenward'.[51] They have not been returned. With the second set, our set, the process of the humanization of the Torah begins. Once the human process of acceptance, transmission and 'publication' commences, the Torah that we have 'is no longer in Heaven' (Deut. 30:12) but falls under the province of the continuous process of human interpretation and even misinterpretation. Once surrendered into human hands and accepted by them, the Torah takes on a life of its own. Now, its readers become its co-authors and its interpreters.[52] Its readers become writers who convey its meaning.

The nexus between the book and the 'people of the book', between the giver and the recipient of the Torah, establishes the parameters for interpreting the text. On the level of *peshat*, anyone has access to the text; however, participation on the semantic level, licence to penetrate and to re-create the deeper meaning of the text, presupposes the commitment of a person who has received and has accepted the Torah. As the *Zohar* teaches, only the lover of the Torah will be vouchsafed its most intimate disclosures, meanings, secrets. Only the scholar who is in love and who 'makes love' with the Torah is a 'true adept in the Torah, a "master of the house."'[53] The uncommitted voyeur may grasp the *peshat* but not the essential meaning of the Torah, that is, of Jewish tradition. In this view, Jewish theological scholarship presumes Jewish commitment.

To make love to the Torah it is necessary to disrobe it. In Hebrew, the word '*peshat*' comes from the root '*P-Sh-T*', which also means to 'strip' or to 'divest'. According to Jewish mystics, the true *peshat* of the text is not its literal, plain, or contextual meaning but its divested, unclad, hidden spiritual meaning.[54] The true meaning of the text must always elude the scholar who identifies the text with its appearance, who seeks the apparent rather than the concealed *peshat*. Only in the act of making love to the Torah, by one committed to it, can its true meaning and nature be discerned.

The *Ethics of the Fathers* states, 'Beloved are Israel, for they were given a precious object [the Torah]. A special love was shown them in that they were given a precious object. As it is written (Prov. 4:2): I have given you good doctrine; forsake not My Torah'.[55] In his commentary on this passage, the sixteenth-century scholar, Samuel of Uceda, observed that:

> only to Israel it [the Torah] was given as a gift and not to others ... The intention [of the text under discussion] is that to the sages and to [the people of] Israel was given [the licence] to interpret [the Torah] and to explain it, and that is evident from the verse: I have given you good doctrine ... I gave it to you to interpret ... I have given this gift to Israel alone ... [It is] an inheritance [*morashah*] [through which I (God)] became betrothed [*me'urasah*] to you. No other man can be involved with a woman once she has become betrothed ... This may have been the intention of the men of the Great Assembly who established the blessing of the Torah which reads 'who has chosen us from among all peoples and gave us the Torah', meaning that an unconditional gift was given to us to explain and to interpret as we desire. It was given to us alone, and not to any other people.[56]

Elsewhere, Samuel of Uceda noted, 'even if a person would live 2000 years, he could not grasp its [the Torah's] totality, for it is without end or limit ... One must take delight in knowing about that which one does not yet know'.[57] The quest for Torah is itself Torah.

The task of Jewish self-understanding is never-ending, perpetual. As Judah Loew of Prague reminds us, a blessing describes God as 'one who gives the Torah' (*notein ha-Torah*). As Loew observes, 'that is to say, You give the Torah each day'. As Loew further reminds us, another blessing praises God for allowing us to be 'preoccupied with the words of Torah' (*la-asok be-divrei Torah*).[58] The agenda for Jewish theological scholarship requires learning to be a continuous preoccupation not a hobby. It requires involvement; it presumes commitment.

Features of Jewish Theological Scholarship

What is recommended here is that contemporary Jewish theological scholarship embody the following features:

1. Its purpose should be Jewish self-understanding. As such, it should utilize Jewish categories and should embrace a Jewish value system.
2. It should be a part of, rather than a departure from, classical Jewish scholarship. It should be predicated upon the analogy of a dwarf riding upon the shoulders of a giant.
3. It should perceive its task as the reformulation (not the reformation) of Judaism. It should aim at reimagining and re-creating Judaism for its own age. It should cast a renewed image in the mirror of tradition.
4. The Jewish theologian should be committed not only to scholarship but to Judaism as well. While availing himself or herself of the findings of historians, philologists, and other scholars, his or her point of departure must be the intersection of the past with the present. While the historian focuses attention upon the past, and while the sociologist may focus attention on the present, the Jewish theological scholar focuses upon the interaction of the past and the present. Ultimately, the Jewish theologian's problem is a personal one: What in classical Judaism can shape my life as a Jew in the present? How can the traditions of the past be brought to bear on the problems of the present?
5. Neither Jewish theological scholarship nor Jewish theologians can divorce themselves from Jewish observance or from Jewish life. As a Talmudic text and its Midrashic variants put it, 'If one studies [Torah] without the intention to observe it, it is better that he had not been born ... it would have been better had he been strangled by the placenta at birth, and had never ventured forth into the world'. Quoting this text, the medieval Spanish scholar, Jonah Gerondi, relates it to the verses in Hosea (8:12) – 'The many teachings I [God] wrote for him, have been treated as something alien', and in Jeremiah (8:8c,d) – 'Assuredly, for naught has the pen laboured, for naught the scribes'.[59] Another Midrashic text describes the scholar who refuses to apply what he knows to ameliorating social problems within the Jewish community as a destructive individual. '"But the man of separation

overthrows it" (Prov. 29:4) – this refers to a sage who knows Halakhah, Midrash and Haggadah, to whom widows and orphans go to plead their cause, but who excuses himself with the plea, "I am engaged with my studies and have no leisure." To him God says, "I regard you as if you have destroyed the world.'"[60]

6. Jewish theological scholarship should be understood not primarily as the 'science of Judaism', but as a Jewish art form. As such, it is an aesthetic as well as a religious and intellectual undertaking. It embraces the objective quest for truth and the subjective search for meaning.

   According to Scripture, Bezalel, who built the tabernacle, was the first Jewish artist (Exod. 35:30–35). The Talmud observes that Bezalel 'knew how to combine the letters by which the heavens and the earth were created'.[61] In other words, artistic creativity derives from the ability to create form and meaning from the otherwise lifeless letters of the text. The vocation of the Jewish theologian is to vocalize the text, to transmute old words into new meanings.

   Like the artist who transforms the raw materials of nature into something more than they had been, the Jewish theologian is one who takes the raw materials conveyed through revelation and inherited from tradition and re-creates them. The theologian refuses to allow tradition to become inert. He or she transmits and transports tradition from the past into the present. The theologian's task is to provide tradition with a voice, but that voice must speak in a contemporary idiom.

7. The Jewish theological scholar should contribute not simply to an understanding about Judaism but to Judaism itself. As the dwarf riding on the giant's shoulders, he or she sees a horizon that the giant does not imagine. It is the theologian's task to guide the giant's movements toward that horizon. It is the vocation of the Jewish theologian to discern where the giant – where Judaism – has come from, where it now is, and to where it must proceed. However, before the dwarf can become a pioneer for the giant, he first must become his heir. To become his heir, he or she must attempt to be at home in all areas of Jewish learning. He or she cannot specialize in a limited area of Jewish scholarship. He or she must know the giant well, from head to toe.

8. Because the materials the Jewish theologian uses are bequeathed by tradition, what is formulated becomes an organic extension of the past and is therefore authentic. Because the theologian chooses which inherited texts to present, interpret, and express, the work thereby formed is uniquely his or her own.

The tradition is a body of inherited wisdom and experience. The task of the theologian is to give it a soul so that it may transmigrate from the past into the present, to invest the bequest of tradition with extended meaning. The theologian is perpetually confronted with the challenge of liberating the implicit meanings pregnant in sacred texts. By recreating the tradition, the Jewish theological scholar can become a co-author of the Torah, a co-creator with God of the tradition.

In the final analysis, an evaluation of the validity of the theologian's labours is governed by four criteria. The first is authenticity: that the texts utilized in composing a theological or ethical portrait of a specific issue are drawn from the tradition and are interpreted in a manner consistent with the tradition. The second is contemporaneity: the theologian's task is to apply old texts to contemporary situations, to give a modern voice to ancient and medieval texts. Though there must be continuity with the past, there must also be meaning for the present. The third is coherence and clarity, without which theological discourse is reduced to a personal exercise in unintelligible abstract expressionism. The fourth is communal acceptance: the validity of the artistic work of the theological scholar is ultimately determined by its ability to communicate a present vision of the past and by the acceptance of that vision by his or her faith community. Ultimately, the community of Jews committed to Judaism and not academe determines the disposition of the products of Jewish theological scholarship.

If the theologian's portrait is not authentic, it is fallacious. If his or her portrayal of a theological or moral issue is not contemporary, it is anachronistic. If the theologian engages in a form of expression meaningful only to himself or herself, or if his or her faith community cannot identify with what is offered, then his or her work may be authentic and aesthetic, but barren.

Medieval Jewish scholars compared the erudite scholar who has amassed much book learning but who has not grasped its contents to 'a donkey carrying books'.[62] Erudition is a prerequisite not a destination. Once he or she has amassed knowledge, the theologian must be prepared to apply that knowledge to the problems at hand. From the wealth of inherited tradition, the theological scholar should be able 'to derive flour from wheat, a garment from flax'.

About those who seek sustenance at the smorgasbord of Jewish learning, one may again turn to the Talmud:

> If someone tells you, 'I have laboured but not found,' do not believe him.
>
> If he says, 'I have not labored, but I have found,' do not believe him.
>
> But, if he says, 'I have labored and I have found,' then believe him.[63]

NOTES

1. Jose Faur, 'Some General Observations on the Character of Classical Jewish Literature', *Journal of Jewish Studies* 38:1 (Spring 1977): 31–36; Erich Auerbach, *Mimesis*, trans. Willard Trask (Princeton: Princeton University Press, 1968), pp.11–23.
2. *Avodah Zara* 19a. See also *Kiddushin* 32a: 'Indeed the Torah is his [the scholar's]'.
3. Solomon Schechter, *Seminary Addresses and Other Papers* (New York: Burning Bush Press, 1959), p.111.
4. From a letter from Schechter to S. Heller dated 1 February 1907.
5. *Sanhedrin* 34a.
6. *Ethics of the Fathers* 3:15.
7. Compare David Weiss Halivni, *Midrash, Mishnah and Gemara* (Cambridge, Mass.: Harvard University Press, 1986), pp.103–13. Weiss notes the attempt of Samuel ben Meir (Rashbam) and others to discover the *peshat* of biblical verses. However, as Weiss also admits (pp.112–15), the approach of Samuel ben Meir and other early medievals who sought the *peshat* independent from its Halakhic application or from rabbinic exegetical interpretation was discontinued in subsequent Jewish tradition. Furthermore, as Weiss also notes, Samuel ben Meir did not apply the quest for the *peshat* in his Talmudic commentaries. Weiss further notes (p.108) that Talmudic literature continuously warned against scholarship unrelated to action. As Louis Jacobs notes in his review of Weiss' book, the sages did not seek the 'plain' meaning of the text, but the 'true' meaning as defined by the parameters of tradition. See Louis Jacobs, 'Jews and Law', *Judaism* 37 (Spring 1988): 246–47. See also Jose Faur, *Golden Doves with Silver Dots* (Bloomington, IN: Indiana University Press, 1986), pp.xv–xvi, 123–24.
8. *Pesikta de-Rav Kahana*, Solomon Buber (ed.) (Lyck: Mekitzei Nirdamim, 1868), 12:12, p.102.
9. *Palestinian Talmud*, *Kiddushin* 1:7.
10. Solomon Schechter, *Studies In Judaism: Second Series* (Philadelphia: Jewish Publication Society, 1908), p.156.
11. Abraham J. Heschel, *The Insecurity of Freedom* (New York: Farrar, Straus and Giroux, 1966), p.217.
12. Abraham J. Heschel, *The Circle of the Ba'al Shem Tov*, Samuel H. Dresner (ed.) (Chicago: University of Chicago Press, 1985), p.xxiv.
13. *Shabbat* 112b.
14. Louis Jacobs, *Theology in the Responsa* (London: Routledge and Kegan Paul, 1975), p.131.
15. Louis Jacobs, *A Jewish Theology* (New York: Behrman House, 1973), p.202. This notion of 'progressive revelation' (where , the most recent is the most true) was central to the supers-

essionist claim of Christianity with regard to Judaism. It was later used by Islam with regard to Christianity and Judaism. Subsequently, it was used by Bahai to apply to Judaism, Christianity and Islam. Apparently for this reason, the doctrine of 'progressive revelation' was not a feature of classical Jewish theology. Early Reform Judaism, clearly influenced by Protestant Christianity, applied this concept in its attempt to justify theologically its reforms of traditional Judaism.

16. Louis Jacobs, *A Tree of Life* (New York: Oxford University Press, 1984), pp.255–56. In the nineteenth century, this view was expressed by Moses Schreiber as part of his attack on Reform Judaism.
17. On Bernard of Chartres, see Fredrick Copleston, *A History of Philosophy: Medieval Philosophy, Part 1* (New York: Image Books, 1962), pp.190–203.
18. On the use in Jewish literature of the expression 'a dwarf riding on the shoulders of a giant', see Dov Zlotnick, *'Al-Makor ha-Mashal ha-Nanas ve-ha-Anak ve-Gilgulav'*, *Sinai* 77 (1975): 184–89; Hillel Levine, 'Dwarfs on the Shoulders of Giants: A Case Study in the Impact of Modernization on the Social Epistemology of Judaism', *Jewish Social Studies* 40:1 (Winter 1978): 63–72; Israel Ta-Shema, *'Halakhah ke-Batrei'*, *Shenaton ha-Mishpat ha-Ivri* 6/7 (1979/1980): 418–22. The source for the statement is Isaiah di Trani in his collected response, *Teshuvot ha-Rid*, Abraham Wertheimer (ed.) (Jerusalem: Machon ha-Talmud ha-Yisraeli ha-Shalem, 1967), no. 67, p.302.
19. Cited and translated in Dov Zlotnick, 'The Commentary of Rabbi Abraham Azulai to the Mishnah', *American Academy of Jewish Research Proceedings* 40 (1973): 163–64.
20. José Ortega y Gasset, *The Revolt of the Masses* (New York: W.W. Norton and Co., 1957), pp.110–12.
21. Lionel Kochan, *The Jew and His History* (Chico, CA: Scholars Press, 1985), p.66.
22. Gershom Scholem, 'The Science of Judaism – Then and Now', in *The Messianic Idea in Judaism* (New York: Schocken, 1971), pp.306–7; see also Scholem, *'Mi-Tokh Hirhurim al Hokhmat Yisrael'*, in Ezra Spicehandler and Jakob Petuchowski (eds), *Perakim ba-Yahadut* (Jerusalem: Newman Publishing House, n.d.), pp.312–27.
23. *Pesahim* 6b. For a discussion of the meaning of this term in rabbinic theology, see Abraham J. Heschel, *Torah min ha-Shamayim*, vol. 1 (London: Soncino, 1962), pp.199–202. For a discussion of this term and its relevance to contemporary Jewish scholarship, see Faur, *Golden Doves with Silver Dots*, pp.xi–xv.
24. Quoted in Kochan, *The Jew and His History*, p.81.
25. Ibid., p.136, note 41.
26. Yosef Hayyim Yerushalmi, *Zakhor: Jewish History and Jewish Memory* (Seattle, WA: JUniversity of Washington Press, 1982), p.93.
27. Ibid., pp.84–85; Max Wiener, 'The Ideology of the Founders of Jewish Scientific Research', *YIVO Annual* 5 (1950): 195; Michael Meyer, *The Origins of the Modern Jew* (Detroit: Wayne State Press, 1967), p.175; Ismar Schorsch, *Jewish Reactions to German Anti-Semitism* (New York: Columbia University Press, 1972), p.43.
28. Ismar Schorsch, *Thoughts from 3080* (New York: Jewish Theological Seminary, 1988), p.28.
29. *Pesikta Rabbati*, Meir Friedmann (ed.) (Vienna: Herausgebers, 1880), chap. 21, p.100b.
30. *Zohar* (Vina: Romm, 1882), vol. 3, p.152a.
31. Faur, *Golden Doves*, p.xv.
32. *Seder Eliyahu Rabbah ve-Seder Eliyahu Zuta*, Meir Friedmann (ed.) (Vienna: Ahiyasaf, 1904), *Zuta*, chap. 2, p.172.
33. *Yevamot* 109b.
34. Faur, *Golden Doves*, p.xvi.
35. Immanuel Wolf, 'On the Concept of a Science of Judaism', Lionel Kochan, trans. *Leo Baeck Institute Yearbook* 2 (1957): 201.
36. *Tza'avat ha-Rivash* (Cracow: n.p., 1896), p.96.
37. Judah Loew, *Netivot Olom* (New York: Judaica Press, 1969), sec., *Netiv ha-Torah*, chap. 8, p.34; Byron L. Sherwin, *Mystical Theology and Social Dissent: The Life and Works of Judah Loew of Prague* (New York: Oxford University Press, 1982), p.140; Moshe Idel, *Kabbalah: New Perspectives* (New Haven, CT: Yale University Press, 1988), pp.243–47.
38. Moses Hayyim Ephraim of Sudlykow, *Degel Mahaneh Ephraim* (Jerusalem: Hadar, 1963), sec. *Aharei*, p.175.
39. Mordecai of Chernobyl, *Likkutei Torah* (New York: Noble Printing Co., 1954), sec. *Le-Rosh ha-Shanah*, p.22b.

40. Abraham J. Heschel, *God in Search of Man* (Philadelphia: Jewish Publication Society, 1955), pp.8–10.
41. Alan Lazaroff, 'Judaism as an Art', *Judaism* 30:3 (Summer 1981): 355–63.
42. Harold Bloom, *Kabbalah and Criticism* (New York: Seabury, 1975).
43. *Soferim*, chap. 7.
44. See the discussion and sources cited in Faur, *Golden Doves*, pp.11, 135–36.
45. *Sefer ha-Bahir*, Reuven Margaliot (ed.) (Jerusalem: Mosad ha-Rav Kook, 1951), no. 115, p.51. See also Judah ha-Levi, *The Kuzari*, Harry Slonimsky, trans. (New York: Schocken, 1964), 4:3, p.202; *Zohar*, vol. 1, p.15b.
46. David ibn Zimra, *Teshuvot ha-Radbaz*, vol. 3 (Furth: n.p., 1781), no.643, p.43b. Menahem Zioni, *Commentary to the Torah* [Hebrew] (Lwow: Nissim Zis, 1882), p.2b.
47. Moses Maimonides, *Moreh Nevukhim* (Jerusalem: n.p., 1960), Book 2, chap. 33, p.71a.
48. David ibn Zimra, *Teshuvot ha-Radbaz*, p.43.
49. See Gershom Scholem, 'The Meaning of the Torah in Jewish Mysticism', in *On the Kabbalah and its Symbolism*, trans. Ralph Mannhein, (New York: Schocken, 1965), pp.81–82.
50. Judah Loew, *Tiferet Yisrael* (New York: Judaica Press, 1969), chap. 67, p.205; Sherwin, *Mystical Theology and Social Dissent*, p.42. On the theological premises of this Halakhic problem, see Abraham J. Heschel, *Torah min ha-Shamayim*, vol. 2 (London: Soncino, 1965), pp.364–67.
51. *Pesahim* 87b. There is a rabbinic tradition that the entire Torah was written on the tablets, see Heschel, *Torah min ha-Shamayim*, vol. 2, pp.348–50.
52. *Bava Metzia* 59a–b.
53. *Zohar*, vol.2, p.94b
54. Moshe Idel, *Kabbalah: New Perspectives*, pp 239, 399 n. 184.
55. *Ethics of the Fathers* 3:19.
56. Samuel of Uceda, *Midrash Shmuel* (Jerusalem: Brody-Katz, n.d.), pp.61a–b.
57. Ibid., p.60b.
58. Judah Loew, *Netivot Olom*, p.32. These blessings derive from *Berakhot* 11a.
59. See Palestinian Talmud, *Berakhot* 1:2; *Leviticus Rabbah* 35:7, and Jonah Gerondi, *Sha'arey Teshuvah* (Jerusalem: Eshkol, 1978), 2:13, p.42.
60. *Exodus Rabbah* 30:13.
61. *Berakhot* 55a.
62. On this expression, see Israel Davidson, *Otzar ha-Meshalim ve-ha-Pitgamim* (Jerusalem: Mosad ha-Rav Kook, 1969), no. 2851, p.171, n. 39.
63 *Megillah* 6b.

CHAPTER THREE

The Perennial Problem of Theodicy

'Theodicy' is a term attributed to the philosopher, Gottfried Wilhelm Leibniz. In his 1710 treatise, *Theodicy: Essays on the Goodness of God, the Freedom of Man and the Origins of Evil*, Leibniz attempted to reconcile his well-known claim that ours is 'the best of all possible worlds' with the observation that evil is a feature of human experience. Leibniz derived the term 'theodicy' from the Greek '*theos*', God, and '*dike*', justice. 'Theodicy' refers to the defence of God's justice and righteousness in the face of the fact of evil.

In Western philosophy and theology, discussion of theodicy, the problem of evil, often relates to the attempt to reconcile three premises:

1. God is good, benevolent.
2. God is omnipotent, all powerful.
3. Evil is real.

These premises assume that if evil is real, God, being benevolent, would not want evil to occur, and, that, being omnipotent, God could prevent evil from happening. David Hume, the eighteenth-century British philosopher, put it this way: 'Epicurus' old questions are yet unanswered. Is he [God] willing to prevent evil, but unable? then he is impotent. Is he able, but not willing? then he is malevolent. Is he both able and willing? whence then is evil?'[1] Hume was correct to argue that these questions remain unanswered, for as Nahmanides observed, the problem of evil is 'the most difficult matter which is at the root both of faith and of apostasy, with which scholars of all ages, peoples and tongues have struggled'.[2]

Theological and philosophical attempts to resolve the problem of theodicy often concentrate upon modifying, redefining or denying one or more of the three premises: God is good; God is omnipotent; evil is real.

The first premise, that God is good, raises the question both of the origin and of the continued existence of evil. If God is good, why is there evil: Whence is there evil? In the history of Jewish theological speculation, a variety of responses to these questions emerged and developed. Three examples follow.

God being good, by nature and by definition, cannot be associated with evil. Therefore, since God could not be the author of evil, the source of evil must be other than God.

While it is God's nature to be totally good, it could not also be the nature of the world to be totally good. For the good to have meaning in the world, for the good to be recognizable and identifiable in the world, requires that evil be present. For example, for the good to be chosen and to be realized logically and morally demands the availability of its opposite. Free choice of the good would be meaningless in a world without evils.

God is good, but God is also partly evil, actually or potentially. If creation requires both good and evil to be complete, then to be complete God also must contain elements of evil as well as good. Since 'perfection' in Hebrew is *sheleimut*, wholeness, completeness, for God to be perfect in this sense, would require God to be complete, embracing qualities both of good and of evil.

The first position, that God, being good, could not therefore be the source of evil, takes on a variety of forms in Jewish theological literature. One view maintains that 'nothing evil dwells with God',[3] that 'evil does not descend from Above'.[4] This claim leads some to maintain that since God is good, and since creation is 'very good' (Gen. 1:31), and that since 'everything God does is for the good',[5] the agent through whom evil enters existence must be a being other than God, a being capable of moral choice and of doing evil, That is, the human being. In this view, evil enters existence and is perpetuated through the human being's misuse of freedom, through the human being's introduction of the evil of sin into the world. By identifying evil with human sin, by 'explaining' evil as punishment for sin, human deeds rather than God's actions become the catalyst for evil's presence in the world. God's goodness seems thereby preserved.

By linking both natural and moral evil in the world to human sin (see for example, Lev. 26:14–17, 20, Deut. 11:13–17, 18), Scripture attempts to 'explain' human suffering and natural catastrophe as necessary correlatives of divine justice. Theodicy appears alleviated by interpreting evil as a by-product of human deeds, and as a proper expression of divine justice. For Scripture, God's benevolence is inseparable from God's justice. For God to reward evil and to punish righteousness would be a violation of God's nature, justice, and goodness. For Scripture, divine benevolence requires divine justice, but it also entails divine mercy in mitigating the severity of punishment (for example, Exod. 32:11–14, 34:6–10).[6]

The theory of 'divine retribution' that maintains that sin requires punishment and that righteousness demands reward is the most representative and the most prevalent response throughout the history of Jewish theological speculation to the problem of evil and human suffering. Individual affliction, natural catastrophe, and national disaster were pervasively interpreted as punishment for sin. Introduced and reiterated in numerous scriptural texts, this approach was reaffirmed throughout post-biblical Jewish literature. The representative rabbinic position is that of Rabbi Ami: 'There is no death without sin, no suffering without transgression'.[7]

The inclusion in traditional Jewish liturgical texts of divine retribution as the predominant explanation for evil and suffering, particularly for national Jewish tragedies, reflects the status of divine retribution as a virtually codified Jewish theodicy. The *musaf* ('additional') liturgical prayers for festivals, for instance, consider the exiled status of the Jewish people as punishment for sin: 'Because of our sins, we were exiled from our country and removed far away from our land'. Throughout the liturgical lamentations (*kinot*) on *Tisha B'Av*, ancient and medieval national catastrophes are often related to divine retribution. In a *kinah* (pl.: *kinot*) by Abraham ibn Ezra, for example, the author bluntly stated, 'the Sanctuary was destroyed because of our sins, and because of our iniquity our Temple was burnt down'.[8] In the 'Elegy on the Martyrs of York' by the twelfth-century Joseph of Chartres, the attempt of the victims of York to preserve divine justice by means of their own martyrdom is depicted: 'The judgment of their Creator they accepted, but they did not break off God's yoke; they justified the righteousness of the Rock, whose work is perfect'.[9]

In situations where the sins of the afflicted individual were clearly not consistent with the degree of suffering visited upon him or her, the doctrine of divine retribution was broadened in an attempt to accommodate experience to theology. This conceptual expansion takes three major forms: 'horizontal', 'vertical', and eschatological. 'Horizontal' divine retribution holds that a given individual or group may be afflicted for the sins of another individual or group. The 'corporate personality' of the Jewish people, which assumed the moral responsibility of the group for each individual member, and of each individual member for one another, led to the view that the group may suffer for the sins of an individual member of the group. A Scriptural example is the episode of Achan (Josh. 7), and a Talmudic example is the story of how Jerusalem was destroyed because of one man's mistreatment of another.[10]

Deutero-Isaiah's portrayal of the 'suffering servant' articulates the notion of 'horizontal' retribution. Identified by both medieval and modern scholars with the people of Israel, the 'suffering servant' takes on suffering for the iniquities of all the rest of the peoples of the world so as to allow them access to God and to eventual redemption (see Isa. 53–54).[11] Other rabbinic and medieval sources maintain that righteous individuals may suffer for the sins of others.[12]

'Vertical' divine retribution holds that individuals may be punished for the sins of their forebears. Lamentations (5:7) puts it best, 'Our fathers sinned and are no more, and we must bear their iniquities'.[13] Not only punishment for sin but also reward for the righteousness of previous generations was an essential feature of the notion of 'vertical' divine retribution (for example, Exod. 20:5, 24:7).[14] A final feature of this notion is that not only may descendants be rewarded and/or punished for the deeds of their ancestors, but that forebears may also be punished for the deeds of their progeny, at least until a child reaches the age of majority.[15]

Jewish eschatology embraces three ideas: messianic redemption, resurrection of the body, and the World-to-Come. All three are related to the notion of delayed, yet assured, divine retribution. The observed clash between theological assumptions regarding God's justice, and observations of the prospering of the wicked (Jer. 12:2, Job 21) and of the suffering of the righteous, led to a merging of the idea of divine retribution with eschatological expectations. Justice denied in this world, it was claimed, would be assured in the future, that is, the messianic future, and/or the time of bodily resurrection, and/or the World-to-Come.

This statement from *Midrash on Psalms* presents a typical rabbinic and medieval view: 'In this world the righteous are smitten, but in the World-to-Come they will have firm footing and strength'[16] In the succinct words of the Jewish philosopher, Saadia Gaon, 'the prophets, peace be upon them, were all agreed upon this: that the reward for a man's behaviour is not meted out in this world but is only given in that which comes after it'. For Saadia, divine retribution in the afterlife is not only a doctrine of scriptural origin, but is also one of 'logical necessity'.[17] Furthermore, the idea of transmigration of souls maintained that justice denied in one lifetime would be compensated for in the next lifetime. The Kabbalists employed the notions of transmigration of souls and reincarnation in their multifaceted attempts at formulating a variety of theodicies.[18] Finally, with regard to the messiah and divine retribution, it should be noted that in late rabbinic and medieval Jewish literature, the biblical figure of the 'suffering servant' was transmuted into the figure of the suffering messiah, who takes on sufferings for the sins of others.[19]

Though the doctrine of divine retribution achieved almost dogmatic status, it was unable to fulfil the quest of many for a satisfactory theodicy. Too much suffering by the righteous remained unexplained. Too much reward of the wicked remained unaccounted for (Jer. 12:2, Job 9:24). Were the tradition assured that divine retribution was properly operative, were it adequately convinced of the validity of the doctrine of divine retribution to explain all varieties of evil, it would not have sought nor would it have posited alternative explanations for human suffering. Furthermore, the forthright rabbinic claim that 'there is death without sin and suffering without transgression' undermines the fundamental assumption upon which the doctrine of divine retribution rests.[20]

With attempts to formulate a theodicy in the wake of the European Holocaust, the doctrine of divine retribution as an acceptable response to catastrophe has come under severe criticism. Jewish theologians now almost unanimously reject divine retribution as a viable post-Holocaust theodicy. What sin, they query, with regard to the Holocaust, could justify such massive, devastating punishment? And, even if such a sin could be identified, what kind of sadistic, cruel God emerges, capable of inflicting such horrible punishment? Theologians such as Eliezer Berkovits and Emil Fackenheim find it unacceptable and 'obscene' to apply the doctrine of divine retribution to the Holocaust in an attempt theologically to explain the deaths of over a million Jewish children.[21]

Divine retribution may serve as a viable theodicy to explain some evil and some suffering, but it is clearly inadequate to explain satisfactorily all evil and all suffering. By assigning the origin and the perpetuation of evil to human beings, it attempts to disassociate God from evil. Even if it is correct to claim that human beings engender evil, the doctrine of divine retribution is not correct in its desire to separate God from evil and suffering. It cannot escape the assertion that while God may not actually have created evil, God nevertheless must have created the potential for evil, otherwise evil could not have come to be. Furthermore, the doctrine of divine retribution, if assumed to be valid and properly operative, may adequately defend the claim that God is just, but it does not seem sufficient to defend an affirmation of a single divine being who is exclusively good and removed from all evil. To distance God from evil and suffering is to distance God from creation and creatures. Maimonides' claim that God's self-sufficiency and perfection exclude the possibility of God's relationship with things of time and space, that is, with God's creation and creatures, may be philosophically compelling, but it is a theological absurdity when applied to a living faith.[22]

As has been discussed above, the theory of divine retribution rests on the assumption that human beings, and not God, are responsible for introducing and for perpetuating the existence of evil in the world. Despite this attempt to preserve God's pristine goodness, it is clear that in a monotheistic faith, the one God must be the source of all, including evil. For some, evil does not represent the human perversion of a world perfectly created by God. Rather, evil is viewed as having been created by God. Evil is considered an element endemic to creation: 'Is it not from the mouth of the Most High that good and evil come?' (Lam. 3:38). 'I form light and darkness; I make good and evil; I the Lord do all these things' (Is. 45:7, see Job 2:10, Eccl. 7:14). These texts form the foundation of a theodicy that maintains that evil exists because it serves the good, that to expect God to produce the good without the evil upon which it depends is to demand a logical and an ontological impossibility. Without evil, good would be unrecognizable and unattainable. Free moral choice between good and evil would become unrealizable.

This view maintains that a polarity of opposites characterizes everything in creation. Only God remains beyond all dichotomies. Everything else, particularly good and evil, each exist as a member of a pair of opposites. The existence of one necessarily implicates the existence of the other. The *Sefer Yetzirah*, for example, states: 'God has set each thing to correspond with another; the good against the evil, and the evil against the good'.[23] From this perspective, the existence of evil flows not from the essential nature of God, but from the nature of creation and from the nature of the creative process. In the sixteenth century, the Lurianic Kabbalists further developed this approach. Similarly, some modern theologians refer to the evil element, the random and irrational factor built into the fabric of creation, and call it – the 'dysteleological surd'.[24]

Lurianic Kabbalah describes destruction, evil and imperfection as necessary aspects of the process of creation.[25] In this view, God cannot create without destroying, not because God is essentially imperfect, but because it is an essential feature of the creative process to include destruction, and because creation, by its very nature, must be imperfect; creation must embody dichotomies such as good and evil. Further, that creation embodies evil as well as good also derives from the empirical observation that evil is a component of created existence. In the Lurianic view, though God (*En Sof* – the infinite divinity) is perfect in essence, God must nevertheless will to relinquish absolute perfection in order to act as a creator.

The Lurianic doctrine of *zimzum* (divine contraction) has God withdraw into Himself, thereby corrupting essential perfection, as the initial step in the process of creation. Furthermore, the Lurianic concept of 'the breaking of the vessels' teaches that there is an initial flaw in creation, and that this cosmic flaw reaches back to the creative process itself. Through the process of *tikkun* (restoration), the human creature can repair the flaws which form part of the initial fabric of creation.[26] A feature of this view is that human actions can amplify through sin and can reduce through righteousness the flaws that are built into creation. From this position, a conceptual jump can be made from the affirmation of a perfect God who compromises His perfection in order to become a creative God, to the claim that the elements of good and evil embedded in creation reflect parallel components in the nature of the Creator. While the Lurianic mystics envisaged the continuous purging of the implicitly evil element in the Godhead as a central scene in the divine drama, the earlier Kabbalistic text, *Sefer ha-Bahir*, explicitly states, 'there is in God an attribute that is called evil'.[27] Scripture, rather than the *Sefer ha-Bahir*, may be the earliest source of the claim that in a monotheistic faith, evil as well as good, must ultimately be referred back to God. Reflecting upon such biblical episodes as God's unfathomable and unexplained attack on Moses (Exod. 4:24), some modern biblical scholars maintain that biblical theology holds that the single God must embrace a polarity of good and evil, of the benevolent and the demonic, of the merciful and the sinister.[28]

To affirm that the divine nature includes tendencies toward good and evil, toward creativity and destruction, when translated into ethical or theological terms would mean that God performs both acts of virtue as well as sinful deeds. In a Talmudic text God is described as having made a flawed creation, as having unjustifiably punished a creature – the moon – and as having 'sinned'. Even more remarkable is this text's assertion that human beings may act to atone for God's 'sin'.[29] In this view, evil is an ontologically necessary component of existence, and perhaps even a theologically necessary feature of the divine. Rather than concluding that the necessary existence of evil leads inescapably to nihilism and despair, and rather than perceiving the human condition as one of random victimization, this position asserts to the contrary that the human person may become an active protagonist in the ongoing battle to contain and to control the evil element within the self and within the world. This approach aims at reducing the power of evil in the self, in the world, and even within God, by means of redemptive deeds. This approach perceives evil to be a fact of life, a feature of existence to be reckoned with, rather than a problem to be solved. Bordering on the pragmatic, this position affirms concrete redemptive human action rather than abstract theological speculation as the most effective attempt at a theodicy.

In the preceding discussion of the first assumption that leads to an attempt at a theodicy, that is, the assumption that God is good, a number of ways in which some Jewish theological sources relate to the assumption of divine omnipotence have already been presented. Nevertheless, a number of further observations regarding the relationship of divine omnipotence to the problem of evil bear mention. Though most of the medieval Jewish philosophers stressed divine omnipotence as a crucial feature of a self-sufficient, perfect God, the notion of divine omnipotence seems either unknown or irrelevant to biblical and rabbinic theology. Certainly, biblical and rabbinic sources discussed the 'power' of God, but omnipotence, as it was understood by many of the Jewish philosophers, does not seem to have been a characteristic of Jewish thought until the Middle Ages, probably through Islamic philosophical influence.

The understanding of the divine nature, reflected throughout Scripture, particularly in the classical prophetic writings, and amplified in rabbinic literature, particularly in texts where God is denoted by '*Shekhinah*', emphasizes divine pathos and not divine omnipotence.[30] In this view, God is a participant in human suffering and a victim of moral evil.[31] From the assumption that God is not omnipotent, that God is affected by evil human deeds, flows the claim that God's power in the world is contingent upon the nature and the quality of human acts. Thus, 'anthropodicity' replaces theodicy as the issue at hand. Rather than trying to justify God's deeds and evil human deeds that God might prevent, the problem becomes the justification of human deeds vis-à-vis other people and vis-à-vis God.

A number of rabbinic and Kabbalistic texts are oblivious to the problem of how to reconcile divine omnipotence with the existence of evil. They rather assume that God, not being omnipotent, relies upon human efforts to increase what power God does have. Human deeds can serve either to enhance or to reduce divine power in the world. Evil in the world becomes a reality for human beings to ameliorate by means of sacred deeds, rather than a concept to be made consistent with the doctrine of divine omnipotence. Those Midrashic and Kabbalistic sources that describe the divine reliance upon human beings took seriously and literally the statement in Psalms (68:35): 'Give strength to God'. For example, a Midrash reads: 'Hence Moses' plea: "And now, I pray thee, let the strength of the Lord be enhanced" (Numb. 14:17) ... When men do not do God's will, then, if one dare say such a thing, "The Rock that begot you, you weakened" (Deut. 32:18) ... Whenever Israel does the Holy One's will, they enhance the power of the Almighty'.[32] In the words of the *Zohar*, 'The Holy One, as it were said: When Israel is worthy below My power prevails in the universe; but when Israel is found to be unworthy she weakens My power above'.[33]

Regarding the third assumption upon which the problem of theodicy historically rests, i.e., that evil is real, a variety of views are found throughout Jewish theological literature. These views come in three major forms: denial, redefinition, and confrontation. For those, like Maimonides, who affirmed God's goodness and omnipotence, the most promising path to an intellectually viable theodicy is to deny the claim that evil is real. For Maimonides, 'all evils are privations', that is., evil is non-existent, non-being, a privation of the good, a state in which the good is absent. For Maimonides, what are perceived as evils by human beings are sufferings that come upon them because of human actions that represent privations of knowledge or privations of virtue.[34] Furthermore, Maimonides understood human suffering as a correlative of human free choice. 'It is because of our own deficiencies that we lament and call for aid. We suffer because of evils that we have produced ourselves of our free will; but we attribute them to God'.[35]

Maimonides attempted to reconcile divine omniscience and omnipotence with free will by claiming that divine foreknowledge of human deeds cannot be construed as a cause of human deeds. More recent theological speculation has maintained that free will is a precarious gift God must give human beings to allow them to be truly human, that is, free moral agents. In this view, God chooses to limit divine power so that humans may exercise their freedom. Evil then becomes the price that humans must pay and that God must tolerate.[36] This approach may be useful with regard to some manifestations of evil, but with regard to catastrophic events such as the Holocaust, it fails. If God is assumed omnipotent and if miracles are assumed possible, then God's lack of intervention to prevent massive catastrophes remains unexplained.

A second approach deals with evil by maintaining that what may appear to be evil is really not evil but good, when seen from an alternate perspective. Here evil and suffering are virtually redefined as being good. One example of this approach found in rabbinic literature and in the medieval literature of Jewish martyrology is that 'suffering is precious',[37] that 'one should be happier with suffering than with good',[38] that what seems evil 'is also for the good'.[39] The assumption upon which this seemingly masochistic view is based is that suffering atones for sins committed in this world so as to free one from punishment for sin in the next world. Rooted in the doctrine of divine retribution, this view fails to reconcile the necessity of severe human suffering with the alleged goodness and mercy of the divine.

A further example of the approach that attempts to neutralize the reality of evil appeals to the finiteness of the human being when compared to the infinity of God (Job, chaps. 38, 39). Seen from God's panoramic view, what appears to us as evil, may not be so. Further, since it is beyond the ken of human ability to understand the ways of God, what we experience as evil may actually be a fulfilment of God's purpose and must therefore be good. Though an appeal to divine knowledge and to divine mystery may intellectually satisfy some, it cannot serve to explain suffering to the afflicted. A final example of this approach sees suffering as pedagogic rather than punitive, and therefore as ultimately good (Ps. 73, 119:67, Prov. 3:12).

An additional approach, that of confrontation, posits the existence of evil, affirms the presence of undeserved suffering, and calls God to account regarding it. This approach provides no theodicy, but it offers a scream of frustrated protest toward a God who appears apathetic, who seems to be acting contrary to God's covenantal commitment, and in contradiction to the divine qualities of justice and of mercy. Abraham's cry, 'Shall the judge of all the earth not do justice?' (Gen. 18:25) echoes down through the ages (see also Hab. 1:1–3, Jer. 12:2, Job 21:7, Ps. 22:2). Aware that 'the earth is given into the hand of the wicked' (Job 9:24), advocates of this view challenge God to reconcile their observation with God's claim that the world is 'very good' (Gen. 1:31). Believing in God in spite of God, they cajole God to emerge from God's silence.[40]

One must finally conclude that the many attempts at a theodicy betray the impossibility of formulating a conceptually acceptable solution to the problem of evil, a solution that would also prove acceptable to the afflicted victim. Certainly the Holocaust demonstrates that there can be no 'final solution' to the problems engendered by that event, especially not a theological one. The Talmud quotes Moses as asking

God, 'Lord of the Universe, why is it that some righteous people prosper and others are in adversity; some wicked men prosper and others are in adversity?'[41] The only acceptable answer is that theology can provide responses to evil but not solutions, for in the final analysis, 'it is not in our power to understand either the suffering of the righteous or the prosperity of the wicked'.[42]

NOTES

1. David Hume, *Dialogues Concerning Natural Religion* (New York: Hafner, 1966), p.66.
2. Moses Nahmanides, *Kitve Rabbenu Moshe ben Nahman*, 2 vols, Charles B. Chavel (ed.) (Jerusalem: Mosad ha-Rav Kook, 1963), vol. 1, p.193.
3. *Midrash on Psalms* [Hebrew], Solomon Buber (ed.) (Vilna: Romm, 1891), sec. 5:7, p.27b.
4. *Genesis Rabbah* 51:3. See also *Berakhot* 60b; *Genesis Rabbah* 3:6. 5:5.
5. *Berakhot* 60b.
6. See God's 'prayer' in *Berakhot* 7a.
7. *Sabbath* 55a.
8. *Kinot*, A. Rosenfeld (ed.) (London: n.p., 1965), p.38.
9. See *Kinot*, p.168.
10. *Gittin* 55b–56a.
11. Rashi to Isaiah 53; Joseph Klausner, *The Messianic Idea in Israel*, trans. William F. Stinespring (New York: Macmillan, 1955), pp.161–63.
12. *Pesikta de-Rav Kahana*, 2 vols. Bernard Mandelbaum (ed.) (New York: Jewish Theological Seminary, 1962), 26:11, vol. 2, p.399.
13. *Yalkut Shimoni*, 2 vols. (New York: Pardes, 1944), sec. *Ruth*, no.600, vol. 2, p.1040; *Sabbath* 32b.
14. Solomon Schechter, *Aspects of Rabbinic Theology* (New York: Macmillan, 1909), pp.170–99.
15. *Genesis Rabbah* 63:10 which is the basis of the traditional blessing releasing a father from responsibility for the deeds of his son at the occasion of the son's Bar Mitzvah. For further discussion of the theological implications of this blessing, see Byron L. Sherwin, *In Partnership with God: Contemporary Jewish Law and Ethics,* (Syracuse: Syracuse University Press, 1990), p.161, and sources noted there.
16. *Midrash on Psalms* 1:20, p.11b; *Rosh ha-Shanah* 16b–17a, *Hagiga* 15a, *Kiddushin* 40b, *Genesis Rabbah* 9:8, 33:1.
17. Saadya Gaon, *The Book of Beliefs and Opinions*, trans. Samuel Rosenblatt (New Haven: Yale University Press, 1948), sec. 9:2, pp.327–30.
18. Nahmanides on Job 33:3 in Chavel (ed.), vol. 1, p.101 and p.101 n. 30. On the nature and development of this idea in Jewish mysticism, see Gershom Scholem, 'Gilgul: The Transmigration of Souls' in *On the Mystical Shape of the Godhead* (New York: Schocken, 1991), pp.197–251.
19. *Pesikta Rabbati*, Meir Friedman (ed.) (Vienna: Herausgebers, 1880), chap.37, p.162b.
20. See Rabbi Simeon ben Eleazar's statement in *Sabbath* 55b and compare with Rabbi Ami in *Sabbath* 55a. The text confirms Rabbi Simeon ben Eleazar's view.
21. Eliezer Berkovits, *Faith after the Holocaust* (New York: Ktav, 1973), p.89.
22. Moses Maimonides, *Guide of the Perplexed*, trans. Shlomo Pines (Chicago: University of Chicago Press, 1963), 1:52, p.117.
23. *Sefer Yetzirah* (Jerusalem, 1968), sec. 6:2, p.59b. See also '*Midrash Temurah*' in Adolph Jellinek (ed.), *Beit ha-Midrash*, 6 vols. (2nd ed.: Jerusalem: Wahrmann, 1967), vol. 1, pp.106–14.
24. The term 'dysteleological surd' was coined by Edgar S. Brightman, *A Philosophy of Religion* (New York: Prentice Hall, 1940). See the discussion of this term in Geddes MacGregor, *Introduction to Religious Philosophy* (Boston: Houghton Mifflin Co., 1959), pp.255–6.
25. For rabbinic precedents of this view, see e.g., *Genesis Rabbah* 9:2, and the sources collected by Abraham Heschel in his *Torah min-ha-Shamayim*, vol. 1 (London: Soncino, 1962), pp.90–2.

26. Louis Jacobs, *Seeker of Unity* (New York: Basic Books, 1966), pp.49–64 and sources noted there.
27. *Sefer ha-Bahir*, Reuven Margaliot (ed.) (Jerusalem: Mosad ha-Rav Kook, 1951), para. 162, p.71.
28. Helmer Ringrenn, *Israelite Religion* (Philadelphia: Fortress Press, 1966), p.73.
29. *Hullin* 60b. See also chapter 4 below.
30. Abraham J. Heschel, *The Prophets* (Philadelphia: Jewish Publication Society, 1962) and his *Torah min-ha-Shamayim*, vol. 1, pp.65–92.
31. *Megillah* 29a; *Hagiga* 15b; *Mekhilta de Rabbi Yishmael*, Hayyim Horovitz and Israel Rabin (eds) (Jerusalem: Wahrmann, 1960), chap. 14, sec. *Bo*, p.52.
32. *Pesikta de-Rav Kahana*, 25:1, vol. 2, p.380.
33. *Zohar*, vol. 2, p.65b.
34. Maimonides, *Guide*, 3:10, pp.438–40.
35. Maimonides, *Guide*, 3:12, p.443.
36. Eliezer Berkovits, *God, Man and History* (New York: Jonathan David, 1959), p.79.
37. *Sanhedrin* 101a.
38. *Sifrei – Devarim* [*Sifre on Deuteronomy*], Louis Finkelstein (ed.) (Berlin: Jüdischer Kulterband in Deutschland Abteilung Verlag, 1939), para. 32, p.56.
39. *Taanit* 21a.
40. *Mekhilta de Rabbi Yishmael*, sec. *Be-Shalah*, chap.8, p.142.
41. *Berakhot* 7a.
42. *Ethics of the Fathers* 4:5.

CHAPTER FOUR

Portrait of God as a Young Artist

> What I have built I am breaking down and what I have planted I am plucking. (Jer. 45:4)

Unlike the world that the Flood destroyed, the biblical account of the Flood was not created *ex nihilo*. In the biblical era it was believed that a great flood had occurred in the distant past. It was further known that the cultures that had preceded and/or were contemporaneous with biblical Israel had composed certain myths, like the Epic of Gilgamesh, to explain why and how the Flood had happened.[1] Like other preserved versions of ancient accounts of the Flood episode, the biblical version endeavours retroactively to explain what was believed already to have taken place. Like other reports, the biblical narrative may be read as a short historical novel that embellishes a well-known historical event with an imposed, if not a contrived, plot which differentiates the biblical account from other ancient accounts, for example, the Gilgamesh Epic.

The plot of the biblical story of the Flood seems simple enough. Human sin has escalated to the point of no return. Corruption is rampant, and the severity of the situation demands extreme measures. Radical sin requires punishment and excludes the possibility of repentance and of consequent forgiveness. There is but one viable option – destruction. God destroys the world with water, but one family is saved, the family of Noah, the righteous person of his generation. It is Noah's virtue that saves his family from extinction. When the Flood subsides, God begins again; the world is re-created. Noah is the new Adam, the new ancestor of humankind.

Modern biblical scholars and educators, in their reflections upon the Flood story, often draw parallels and demarcate contrasts between the story of Noah and of Utnapishtim, the 'Babylonian

Noah', whose tale is found in the Epic of Gilgamesh. Those who utilize this approach are quick to indicate that in the Epic the flood is the product of divine caprice rather than of divine justice. God brings the Flood to render justice, while the Babylonian gods bring the flood for no apparent reason, except, perhaps, to eliminate the noisy racket that people make while the gods are trying to sleep. Furthermore, God saves Noah because of his righteousness, because God is just, and because Noah deserves salvation. On the other hand, the Babylonian gods plan to save no one – righteous or wicked. Utnapishtim is saved secretly by one of the gods – Ea, the god of wisdom – but for no apparent reason, certainly not because of his virtue. On the basis of such comparisons and contrasts, the conclusion is reached that the 'pagan' gods of Babylonia act out of caprice and without reason, while the God of Scripture acts out of justice, with reason.[2] Thus, while the storyline of the biblical account has many similarities with that of the Babylonian version, the respective plots are markedly different, expressing radically different theologies, severely diverse world views.

Seemingly unaware of other ancient versions of the flood story, the rabbis, in their commentaries on the biblical Flood story, certify the biblical version's account of the plot and strengthen it. They amplify the corruption of Noah's contemporaries that justified God's bringing the Flood and they elaborate upon Noah's righteousness which justified his being spared from the destruction wrought by the Flood. For example, the rabbis endow Noah with messianic qualities. He is born uncircumcised like the expected Messiah, and, like the Messiah his real name is Menahem. In his youth, he, like the expected Messiah, restores the world to the state of perfection it enjoyed before Adam's fall. In Noah's later life, when human beings begin to sin increasingly, he, like the later prophets of Israel, is described by the rabbis as one who exhorts the people to repent so as to annul the divine decree of destruction. But, their sins multiply, and the punishment of annihilation becomes inevitable.[3]

It would seem that the biblical text, rabbinic exegesis of the biblical text, and cross-cultural studies of the text all yield the identical plot: God is just, the people were irredeemable sinners; Noah was righteous. Therefore, God saved Noah and destroyed everyone (and everything) else as punishment for radical unrepentant sin. The text seems unproblematic. The plot seems simple enough. The ancient and modern commentaries seem to be fortifying and amplifying the plot as it is stated. But, is it so simple? Is the usual reading of the story acceptable? Is another reading possible, or even desirable?

The central theological problem which this plot evades is the problem of theodicy. As applied to the Flood story, the question is whether or not God was truly justified in annihilating the world and humankind by bringing the Flood. Neither the biblical narrative itself nor the rabbinic commentaries on it raise this question. They assume that the punishment fits the crime, that God acted justly. For example, according to a Midrash, God's works are perfect. God did not create people wicked or righteous; they become so. Therefore, even if God annihilates the wicked, as in the case of the Flood, one must not question God's actions.[4] No one questions God's justice in bringing the flood, certainly not Noah – the silent witness-survivor. Despite Noah's silence, and despite the Midrashic exhortation not to question God's actions, questions are, nonetheless, in order.

The doctrine of divine retribution is a central assumption of biblical and subsequent Jewish theology.[5] Sin requires punishment; virtue promises reward. The Flood story articulates this theological position: Noah is saved because of his virtue; others are destroyed because of their corruption. Yet, is there a sin or a cumulative group of sins that could justify the almost total annihilation of the human species? And, if such sins exist, what kind of God could be merciless enough, cruel enough, to destroy the human race for committing them? The biblical text implies that the sins were indeed heinous enough to require such punishment. The rabbinic commentaries rest content that the sins they identify with the Flood generation, lawlessness, murder, idolatry, sexual perversion and witchcraft would surely justify God's actions.[6] Nevertheless, one may question whether God's action can be justified, and whether trust, faith and love in a God who would exact such a terrible punishment can still be maintained. The question of whether an alternative plot to the Flood story might be extracted from the text needs to be examined.

A world-wide holocaust by water rather than by fire, the Flood, like the European Holocaust, cannot theologically rest well with the argument of divine retribution. Theologians of the Holocaust, the

'Final Solution to the Jewish Problem', almost unanimously reject divine retribution as a viable theological explanation for the Holocaust. Consequently, they seek alternative explanations and articulate alternative responses.[7] Similarly, theologians of the Flood, the 'Final Solution to the Human Problem', should seek alternative explanations to divine retribution. As descendants of the survivors of the Flood, 'post-Flood theology' must concern us.

The text's account of God's decision to destroy creation may be read in at least two ways: one would identify human corruption as the cause of God's decision to destroy the world by water. This, as was noted above, is the usual reading of the text. However, another reading of the text would place the primary reason for God's decision not in God's disappointment with human beings, but rather in God's self-disappointment.

God's decision may have been more directly evoked by regret and sorrow (Gen. 6:6) with His own actions, with His own 'experiment', than with the deeds of those whom God had created. The verse in which God announces His intentions reads, 'I will blot out from the earth the humans whom I have created – humans together with creeping things and birds of the sky; for I regret that I made them' (Gen. 6:7). God's decision to destroy not only human beings, but also animals, insects, reptiles and birds, seems in this verse to be caused more by God's own dissatisfaction with His abilities as a creator, than with the sins of any of the species He had created. In this text, God may be exhibiting Freudian projection: God is unhappy with what He had done, depressed regarding what had happened to creation, to His 'experiment', and so God decides to destroy it and to start anew with Noah.[8] However, in order to rationalize this radical decision, God must put the blame somewhere else; God must find a reason other than divine failure in order to justify such actions. God locates that reason in human sin. Human beings will pay the price for God's mistake. God convinces Himself (and readers of the biblical text) that the real reason for the Flood is human corruption when, in fact, human corruption is but an after-the-fact rationalization of God's decision, already made, to destroy the world because God is unhappy with His own work, with His own creations. Unless one argues, as do the rabbis, that the animals also 'sinned' and required punishment, it would not follow that human sin requires the obliteration of *all* life, rather than just of human life.

From this line of interpretation it would seem that God's decision to destroy the world does not have human sin as its *primary* cause. Rather, the *primary* cause of this decision is God's unhappy realization that He had failed as a creator. Human sin emerges either as a secondary cause of this decision, a rationalization after the fact to 'justify' this decision; or, as the catalyst which provokes God's awareness of His failure as a creator and frustration as an artist.

After the Flood, God observes that evil is part of human nature (Gen. 8:21). But, if this was known to God at the outset, how can human evil justify the divine decision to destroy humankind (Gen. 6:5)? Perhaps because it was not human corruption that led to God's decision to obliterate the world, but rather, God's realization that creation was not what God had hoped it would be. Humankind turned out differently than God had expected. The plot of God's novel failed to follow the original outline.[9] The characters God created took on a life of their own. They began to interpret the script in their own way. The actors in the drama started to improvise. The players on the stage made God aware of the flaws in His work. And so, though God's endeavour was a 'commercial success' it was a 'critical failure', and God decides to close the play, to destroy the script, and to start all over again. The divine director cancels the actors' contracts and destroys the scenery.

Every artist, 'every creator painfully experiences the chasm between his inner vision and its ultimate expression', Isaac Bashevis Singer wrote. God, Singer maintained, is no different. Like a novelist discontented with the story he has written, like a playwright unhappy with his play once it is staged, like a painter dissatisfied with a portrait, God is drawn to destroy His handiwork, as a prelude to beginning anew.[10] Like an artist venting passionate, destructive rage at a failed creation rather than at himself, God vents self-disappointment at the world. The product of artistic creation is made to pay the price for the artist's disappointment with the way it turned out. God's world emerges flawed. The execution of the plan was not congruent with the initial design. For the sake of the artist's self-esteem, the creation must be destroyed. Before he can start anew, the artist must wipe the palette clear. Before God can re-create the world, God must destroy the world. God's mistake, and not human sin, ultimately condemns the world to destruction. Artistic rage and not divine justice brings about the destruction.

God, the creator, the artist, is not the God of the medieval Jewish philosophers. This is not the static omnipotent God of the Jewish Aristotelians. Rather, here is a God of pathos and of passion, a being capable of artistic proclivities such as anger and rage, imagination and fantasy, a God who makes mistakes and tries to rectify them. Creation entails destruction; rectification necessitates destruction and renewal. Contrary to popular belief, such a portrait of God is not alien to Jewish theological speculation.

The medieval philosophers press hard to convince us that God must be perceived as a rational, statically perfect being devoid of emotion or of pathos. To ascribe emotion or error to God is, in their view, a mistaken apprehension of the divine that borders on heresy. To be sure, this approach offers a rationalistic view of God, of the world God created, and of ourselves. The human being, created in God's image, is a rational being; the human being, following this Aristotelian claim, is the 'rational animal'. The world is a rational place, following rational laws of cause and effect. In such a world, divine retribution functions with the certainty, the consistency and the rationality of any of the laws of nature. Evil is punished and virtue is rewarded with the same predictable regularity as the sun's rising and the seasons' changing in their ordained sequence.[11] Evil is the product of human deeds; to imply that God has any relationship to evil is to impugn divine perfection.

Such a portrait of reality is very comforting. To live in a rational world, governed by a rational God with fellow humans who think and act rationally, means that everything is 'in order' and 'under control'. Everything is predictable, reasonable. But where do evil, trauma and tragedy fit in to this portrait of reality? How can the rationalist explain the existence of meaningless tragedy, of irrational catastrophe? The answer is: he cannot. As Dostoyevsky observed in *The Brothers Karamazov*, all the wisdom of all the philosophers cannot explain to a mother why she has lost a child. Or, as David Hume reminded us, 'Epicurus' old questions are yet unanswered. Is he willing to prevent evil, but unable?, then he is impotent. Is he able, but not willing? then he is malevolent. Is he both able and willing? whence then is evil?'[12] In other words, the problem of theodicy rests upon three assumptions: God is benevolent. God is omnipotent. Evil is real. Not willing to compromise God's perfection by questioning divine benevolence or omnipotence, rationalistic theologians have tended to confront the problem by defining evil out of existence. 'Evil', they claim, is the 'privation of the good', a non-entity.

In order to maintain this rationalistic, mechanistic view, evil is either defined away into oblivion, or human beings are identified as its cause, or both. As the product of human sin, evil is explicable, rational. It is the effect of an identifiable cause. Evil which appears to have no identifiable cause appears to be irrational, and, therefore, it must be explained and defined away. Either there is a cause (perhaps, known only to God) but we remain unaware of it; or evil is relegated to being an apparency rather than a reality.

The linguistic and the intellectual acrobatics of these philosophers seem to be a means for defending the notion of divine perfection and divine rationality, a way of getting God 'off the hook' for meaningless suffering and for absurd tragedy. It seems that, to these thinkers, protecting the perfection of God and reaffirming the rational quality of existence is more crucial than forthrightly confronting the problematic existence of inexplicable evil and of pervasive human tragedy. The dysteleological surd – the factor within existence which has no purpose or meaning – cannot be integrated into their neatly systematic apprehension of reality, and, therefore, must be swept under the theological rug in order to maintain the notion of a statically perfect and rigidly rational God.

The dominant Jewish theology of divine retribution that describes God as a celestial accountant tabulating up our debits and our credits in order to determine whether it is 'cost effective' to maintain us, pervades biblical, rabbinic and liturgical texts. Though based upon a rationalistic assumption, though positing a cause and effect relationship between sin and punishment in an almost scientific manner, this theology must be severely questioned when it is so facilely applied to enormous human catastrophes such as the European Holocaust and the biblical Flood. From this perspective, God brings the Flood because human beings are morally bankrupt; it is no longer rational to sustain the human species. An alternative theology, however, would portray God as a creative artist who has successes and failures, triumphs and mistakes, who acts with irrational passion as well as with rational method.

It is no more anthropomorphic to portray God as a frustrated artist than it is to portray God as a totally rational being. All concepts of God, deriving as they do from the human mind and heart, are necessarily anthropomorphic. Indeed, one might suggest that some so-called anthropomorphisms may in fact be theomorphisms.[13] Both our rational nature and our artistic nature may be reflections of God's nature within us, rather than projections of our nature onto God. Scripture describes us as having been created in the divine image and likeness. Yet, the second commandment of the Ten Commandments forbids us from making an image of God. Nevertheless, God breaks His own law in creating us. God creates an image and a likeness of Himself. Is God guilty of anthropomorphism; or, is God expressing a theomorphism?

Nahman of Bratslav translated the verse, 'Let us make man in our image and likeness (*kidemutenu*) (Gen. 1:26)', as 'Let us make man endowed with an imagination'.[14] In medieval Hebrew, *ha-koah ha-medameh* is the term used to denote the imaginative faculty of the human soul, the human imagination. In Nahman's view, the essential human trait is imagination, creativity, fantasy. This essential human attribute reflects an attribute of the divine nature. What we know of God to this point (i.e., Gen. 1:26) in the biblical narrative – that God is a creator, would support the portrayal of the essence of human nature as a reflection of the divine attribute of imagination, and of creativity. Like God, we can be rational beings, but, like God, we can be simultaneously creators, artists, imaginative and irrational beings.

Being of a creative and an artistic temperament, we, like God, share the frustrations endemic to artistic creativity. Like God, we are susceptible to the foibles and to the mistakes endemic to the artistic process. Like God, we become aware of the fact that destruction is part and parcel of the process of creation. As an omnipotent, rational, 'divine dictator', as a 'celestial accountant', God cannot afford to make mistakes, to err; otherwise, God's nature would be irredeemably compromised. As an artist, however, God must make mistakes. God must destroy as part of the process of creating. Even God cannot make an omelette without breaking the eggs. As an artistic creator, it is consistent with God's nature to make mistakes, to fail and to begin again.

The notion of God as an artist who fails, as a creator who makes mistakes, is found in rabbinic literature and is amplified by Jewish mystical literature.[15] A midrash describes God as continuing to create and to destroy worlds until God manages to create one with which He is sufficiently satisfied: 'The Holy One, blessed be He, went on creating and destroying worlds until He created this one and declared – This one pleases Me; those did not please Me'.[16] Thus, God's destruction of the world by the Flood, the destruction of a creation with which God is not satisfied, has precedent. Reflecting upon this Midrash, Isaac Bashevis Singer observed:

> God was for me an eternal belle lettrist. His main attribute was creativity … .I quoted to myself that passage from the Midrash that says God created and destroyed many worlds before He created this one. Like my brother and myself, God threw His unsuccessful works into the wastebasket. The flood, the destruction of Sodom, the wanderings of the Jews in the desert, the wars of Joshua, these were all episodes in a divine novel, full of surprise and adventure'.[17]

Some rabbinic sources contend that not only is God a fallible creator, but that God's mistakes require rectification by means of the destruction of that which God created with an original flaw, and, that God, the creator, is also God, the destroyer. Furthermore, these sources maintain that God's act of destruction is sinful, that in destroying what He created, God sins! Finally these texts take the radical theological position that human beings can take actions which atone for God's sin. God needs us to redeem His sins. In the Talmud, for example, we read:

> Rabbi Simeon ben Pazzi pointed out a contradiction [between the verses]. One verse says, 'And God made the two great lights' (Gen. 1:16), and immediately the verse continues, 'The greater light [the sun] … and the lesser light [the moon]'. The moon said unto the Holy One, blessed be He, 'Sovereign of the Universe! Is it possible for two kings to wear one crown?' God answered, 'Go then and make yourself smaller'. 'Sovereign of the Universe!', cried the moon, 'Because I have suggested that which is proper must I then make myself smaller?' … On seeing that it [the moon] would not be consoled, the Holy One, blessed be He, said, 'Bring an atonement for Me for making the moon smaller'. This is what is meant by

> Rabbi Simeon bar Lakish when he declared, 'Why is it that the he-goat offering offered on the new moon is distinguished in that there it is written concerning it "for the Lord" (Numb. 28:15)?' Because the Holy One, blessed be He, said, 'Let this he-goat be an atonement for Me for making the moon smaller'.[18]

The Lurianic Kabbalah describes destruction, evil and imperfection as necessary aspects of the process of creation. God cannot create without destroying, not because God is necessarily imperfect, but because it is the nature of the creative process to include destruction, and, because a creation by its very nature must be imperfect. In the Lurianic view, God (*En Sof*) must relinquish absolute perfection in order to become a creator.

The Lurianic doctrine of *zimzum* (divine contraction) has God withdraw into Himself, go into 'exile' into Himself, thereby corrupting God's initial, absolute perfection, as the first step in the process of creation. Furthermore, the Lurianic concept of 'the breaking of the vessels' teaches that there is an initial flaw in creation, and that this cosmic flaw reaches back to the divine creative process itself. And, the Lurianic idea of the *parzufim* (divine faces) relates to the re-creation which must follow the 'breaking of the vessels'. As in the Talmudic text just noted, the Lurianic Kabbalah provides human beings with a role in rectifying God's mistakes, of atoning for the destruction that God implants within the process of creation. Human deeds can reorganize the *parzufim*, as a part of the process of *tikkun*, the repair of the flaws that form part of the initial fabric of creation.[19]

To return to our initial question of whether God's actions in bringing the Flood were justifiable, we must conclude that God's actions were not justifiable, but they are understandable. No parent is justified in murdering his children, no matter what gap exists between the parent's expectations and plans for the child and the actual behaviour of the child. One may argue that no great artist or novelist has the right to order his or her creations destroyed, denied to posterity. For example, we laud Max Brod's refusal to obey Kafka's wish that all his manuscripts be burned. We condemn Gauguin's burning of his own paintings. Once the creation leaves the hand of its creator it enjoys a life of its own. To destroy it is murder. For God to have destroyed creation cannot be justified. In destroying His creatures God is guilty of a crime of passion, of murder, of sin. God's actions are inconsistent with a theology that holds God to be essentially benevolent and omnipotent, yet merciful. For such a theology, the choice is a cruel God of retribution or a theodicidal dilemma. However, with a theology of a God both of method and madness, of rationality and passion, of benevolent intent and artistic temperament, His actions may be unjustifiable, but they become more comprehensible.

The perception of God as being irrational as well as rational, a passionate creator as well as a celestial accountant, represents not merely an alternative theology, but, also, an alternative anthropology. If we accept the biblical claim that human beings are created in the divine image, then our perception and our understanding of that image must affect our image of humankind and our self-image as well. If that image embraces the creative capacity, including the capacity to re-create the world, then one sees how ethics and theology are ultimately intertwined. If we strive for *imitatio Dei*, if we strive to imitate God in our actions, then our vision of God must be both theologically feasible and morally defensible.

An alternative anthropology based upon an alternative theology must have a human as well as a divine model for human behaviour, particularly for human behaviour in response to evil. Is the Noah of the Flood story such a model, or should one look elsewhere?

The biblical text describes Noah as 'righteous in his generation' (Gen. 6:9). The Flood story suggests that it was his righteousness that saved Noah and his family from annihilation. Nevertheless, some of the rabbis are quick to categorize Noah's righteousness as a relative rather than as an absolute virtue. Noah, they indicate, was 'righteous in his generation', a generation that was corrupt. However, had he lived in Abraham's generation, his righteousness would have been inconsequential.[20] Furthermore, according to Rashi, the phrase 'Noah walked with God' (Gen. 6:9) means that 'Noah needed God to support him (in righteousness) while Abraham strengthened himself and walked in his own righteousness by himself (that is, by his own efforts)'.[21] In other words, Noah 'walked *with* God' while Abraham walked *before* God (Gen. 24:40), Abraham was a pace-setter, an initiator, his 'own man', independent, while Noah was passive, dependent, requiring support. Indeed, the very name, 'Noah', relates to the Hebrew word *nah*, to rest. Noah literally epitomized passivity. The rabbis' verdict is that compared to Abraham, Noah was a person of little consequence.

God announces the destruction of the world to Noah and he fails to respond. Passively, without a murmur, without a word, without protest, Noah obeys in acquiescent compliance. Perhaps he thought that any questioning of God, any defiance of God, might endanger his life and that of his family. No taker of risks, no man of action or of initiative, Noah accepts God's decree, passively, meekly. His relationship with God is a conspiracy of silence. Noah's silence buys his survival. Noah's silence represents his consent to the divine decree. By his silence, Noah becomes God's 'silent partner', God's co-conspirator in the annihilation of humankind. Perhaps God chooses Noah for his weakness, for his passivity, for his silence. Noah fits God's needs. Noah is the ideal accomplice.

Were Abraham there then, God would not have chosen him. Abraham, who challenges God's plan to destroy Sodom and Gomorrah, would not have remained silent. Abraham would have spoken up. Abraham would have protested. 'Shall not the Judge of all the world do justice?' (Gen. 18:25), Abraham would have said. Interestingly enough, commenting on the verse, 'Shall not the Judge of all the world do justice?', a Midrash has Abraham appeal to God not to destroy Sodom and Gomorrah on the grounds that such a destruction would violate the promise God made to Noah after the Flood: '(Abraham pleaded): "You have sworn not to bring a deluge to the world. Would you evade Your oath? Not a deluge of water will you bring but a deluge of fire? Then You have not acted according to Your oath! If You desire absolute strict judgment, the world cannot endure, yet You would hold the cord by both ends, desiring both the world and absolute judgment."'[22] Had Abraham been there rather than Noah, he might not have prevailed in the end, but he would not have allowed God to destroy without a struggle, without a word. No wonder that the rabbis judge Noah as being inconsequential when compared to Abraham.

Two biblical characters are saved by an ark *(teivah)*. The term *teivah* is used in Scripture only with regard to these two: Noah and Moses (Exod. 2:3, 5). Unlike Noah, Moses would not have acquiesced to God's decree to destroy the world. Moses would not have remained silent. In Genesis, God announces the Flood with the words, 'I will blot out (*emheh*) from the earth the humans I have created' (Gen. 6:7). *Emheh* means to 'blot out', 'to erase', 'to rub out'. Like an enraged mafioso God decrees that humankind must be 'rubbed out'. Those who obey God's laws are spared. God demands that we do things His way; otherwise, he'll 'rub us out'. 'Whosoever has sinned against Me, him I will blot out of My book' (Exod. 32:33).

When God decrees the 'rubbing out' of all life with the Flood, Noah is silent. When God decrees the destruction of Israel for their building the Golden Calf, Moses contends with God. Noah says nothing. Moses says, 'Forgive their sin, and if not, rub *me* out *(maheini)* from the book you have written' (Exod. 32:32). In the story of the Flood, God regrets *(va-yenaheim)* creating humankind. Noah does not try to convince God to repent of His regret or of His decree. God proceeds to destroy. Even after the flood, the promise of devastation now a reality, Noah remains the silent survivor. God regrets creating humankind, but never admits regret at destroying the world with water, and Noah never attempts to evoke divine regret.

God offers Moses a similar arrangement to that which He offered Noah. When Israel is corrupted by the sin of the Golden Calf, God announces that He will destroy the people, leave Moses as the sole survivor, and make him the parent of a new people (Exod. 32:10). But Moses, unlike Noah, is unwilling to accept the offer. Unlike Noah, Moses refuses to remain silent. Unlike Noah, Moses risks God's wrath, and unlike Noah he speaks up in protest. Noah acquiesces before God while God acquiesces before Moses. God 'regrets' His having created human beings and destroys them in Noah's presence. But Moses admonishes God and convinces Him to 'regret' His decision and to relent of His plan to destroy the people (Exod. 32:12, 14).

The term *va-yenaheim* can be translated 'repented' as well as 'regretted'. Noah lets God sin and God remains unrepentant of having destroyed the world. Moses cajoles God into repenting of the sin God intended to commit, but which Moses convinces God not to commit. Moses sets the pattern for future generations of prophets and sages. Noah passively accepts God's decree. Moses protests to avert God's decree. Both Noah and Moses are called *zaddik*, righteous.[23] Yet, only one – Moses – would meet the criterion set down by this rabbinic text: 'God says, "I rule mankind. Who rules Me? – the *zaddik*. For I make a decree, and he annuls the decree."'[24] The prophetic credo is not 'Thy kingdom come, Thy will be done' but rather 'Thy kingdom come, Thy will be *changed*'. For the prophet, sin is not irredeemable. The final verdict can always be appealed and reversed. Even when God is justified, divine justice remains open to question.

To summarize: The generally accepted plot of the biblical story of the Flood is open to question and to examination. The applicability of the doctrine of divine retribution to the Flood is at least as problematic as its applicability to the European Holocaust. Therefore, an alternative theology may be sought, an alternative view of God to the one which underlies the idea of divine retribution may be formulated. The view introduced above is that the Flood was not primarily engendered as punishment for human sin, but rather that the primary cause of the Flood was God's dissatisfaction with Himself and with the world He had created. Furthermore, once the doctrine of divine retribution is no longer seen as a factor in God's destruction of the world by water, an alternative theology to that which perceives God as a God of justice, retribution and rational action is required. Such a view of God, such an alternative theology, would portray God as being both rational and irrational, sometimes justified in His deeds and sometimes unjustified. Such an alternative theology would opt for a God of passion and pathos, a God who is primarily a creative artist rather than a calculating accountant.

In this alternative account of the Flood narrative, God is an artist disappointed with His own creation who destroys His creation out of the passion of dismay and frustration. God is an artist who knows that in order to re-create, the palette must first be cleared, who understands that renewed creation often requires the destruction of what had initially been created. Noah, passive and acquiescent by nature, is the perfect accomplice for such a God. Noah does not challenge God's intention to destroy the world. The price Noah pays for survival is silence. The story of the Flood is the story of a conspiracy between God and his silent accomplice, Noah.

NOTES

1. See the summaries of the ancient Near Eastern accounts of the flood in Alexander Heidel, *The Gilgamesh Epic and Old Testament Parallels* (Chicago: University of Chicago Press, 1963); Samuel Noah Kramer, *Sumerian Mythology* (New York: Harper and Row, 1961), pp.97–8; and Nahum M. Sarna, *Understanding Genesis* (New York: Schocken Books, 1966), pp.37–63.
2. Ezekiel Kaufmann, *The Religion of Israel*, trans. and abridged by Moshe Greenberg (Chicago: University of Chicago Press, 1960), pp.21–102.
3. Louis Ginzberg, *Legends of the Jews*, 7 vols, (Philadelphia: Jewish Publication Society, 1968), vol. 1, pp.146–57 and sources noted in vol. 5, pp.167–74.
4. *Sifrei – Devarim*[*Sifrei on Deuteronomy*], Louis Finkelstein (ed.) (Berlin: Judischer Kulterband in Deutschland Abteilung Verlag, 1939), para. 307, p.344.
5. Solomon Schechter, 'The Doctrine of Divine Retribution in Rabbinic Literature' in *Studies in Judaism* (New York: Meridian, 1958), pp.105–23; Arthur Marmorstein, *The Doctrine of Merits in Old Rabbinic Literature* (2nd ed.: New York: Ktav, 1968); Robert Gordis, *The Book of God and Man* (Chicago: University of Chicago Press, 1965), pp.135–56; and Byron L. Sherwin, 'Theodicy: Reason and Mystery', *Central Conference of American Rabbis' Journal* 18:3 (1971):62–76.
6. Ginzberg, *Legends of the Jews*, vol. 5, p.173 n. 17.
7. Byron L. Sherwin, 'Jewish and Christian Theology Encounters the Holocaust' in Sherwin and Susan Ament (eds), *Encountering the Holocaust* (Chicago: Impact Press Inc., 1979), pp.407–42.
8. On creation as an experiment that failed, see the science fiction story, 'The Cunning of the Beast' by Nelson Bard in M. Mohs (ed.), *Other Worlds, Other Gods* (New York: Avon, 1971), pp.19–39.
9. On the analogy of creation with a book which God has composed, see Zadok ha-Kohein of Lublin, *Zidkat ha-Zaddik* (New York: n.p., 1947), p.46a, 'God composed a book which is the world, and He wrote a commentary on it which is the Torah'. The idea of the world as God's book is also found in Gersonides' *Commentary on the Torah*, on Exod. 33.
10. Isaac B. Singer, *Gifts* (Philadelphia: Jewish Publication Society, 1985), p.11.
11. Hans Kelsen, 'Causality and Retribution', *Journal of the Philosophy of Science* 8 (1941): 533–56, also in his *Society and Nature* (Chicago: University of Chicago Press, 1943).
12. David Hume, *Dialogues Concerning Natural Religion* (New York: Hafner, 1966), p.66. See also the discussion of theodicy in the previous chapter.
13. On biblical anthropomorphism see Abraham J. Heschel, *The Prophets* (Philadelphia: Jewish Publication Society, 1962), pp.270–78, and Moshe Greenberg, 'Anthropomorphism in Ezekiel', in Monford Harris (ed.), *Perspectives in Jewish Learning*, vol. 1 (Chicago: Chicago College of Jewish Studies Press, 1965), pp.1–11.
14. Arthur Green, *Tormented Master: A Life of Rabbi Nahman of Bratslav* (University, Alabama: University of Alabama Press, 1979), pp.341–44.
15. The theme of God as an artist is found in a poem by the ninth-century Hebrew poet, Amittai ben Shephatiah. However, he depicts God as an artist who creates without flaw: 'God is an awesome artist who can shape form within form, flawless and perfect in all dimensions'. This poet contrasts the perfection of God's artistic works with the imperfection of artistic works by human beings. See Amittai ben Shephatiah, 'God the Artist', in T. Carmi (ed. and trans.), *The Penguin Book of Hebrew Verse* (New York: Penguin, 1981), p.240. For the Hebrew original, see Yonah David (ed.), *The Poems of Amittay* [Hebrew], (Jerusalem: Achshav, 1975), pp.20–24. According to the medieval ethical treatise, *Sefer ha-Yashar*, God is an artist whose work cannot be duplicated by human beings, but whose work should be emulated by them. See *Sefer ha-Yashar: The Book of Righteousness*, trans. Seymour J. Cohen (New York: Ktav, 1973), pp.18–19.
16. *Genesis Rabbah* 3:7, 9:2; *Midrash Tehillim* [*Midrash on Psalms*], Solomon Buber (ed.) (Vilna: Romm, 1891), 34:1, p.123a.
17. Singer, *Gifts*, p.11.
18. *Hullin* 60b. See the discussion in Abraham J. Heschel, *Torah min ha-Shamayim*, vol. 1 (New York: Soncino, 1962), pp.87–90.
19. For an excellent summary of the Lurianic view, see Louis Jacobs, *Seeker of Unity* (New York: Basic Books, 1966), pp.49–64. As Gershom Scholem has observed in this regard, 'The

question of why God did not create a perfect world, Himself being perfection, would have seemed absurd to the kabbalists of the Lurianic school: a perfect world cannot be created, for it would then be identical to God Himself, who cannot duplicate Himself, but only restrict Himself. The naive expectation that God would reproduce Himself is alien to the kabbalists'. Scholem, *On the Mystical Shape of the Godhead* (New York: Schocken, 1991), p.84.

20. *Sanhedrin* 108a.
21. Rashi on Gen. 6:9.
22. *Genesis Rabbah* 49:9.
23. On the Jewish tradition of protest against God, see Byron L. Sherwin, 'The Impotence of Explanation and the European Holocaust', *Tradition* 12:3–4 (Winter 1972):101–4 and Abraham J. Heschel, *Torah min ha-Shamayim*, vol. 2 (New York: Soncino, 1965), pp.306–8.
24. *Moed Kattan* 16b.

Awe of God

'The Torah is of no use to an individual but for *yirat shamayim* [fear or awe of Heaven, that is, of God], for it [*yirat shamayim*] is the very peg upon which everything hangs'.[1] This observation of the medieval ethical treatise *Orhot Zaddikim*, reaffirms the perspective of Hebrew Scripture that considers *yirat shamayim* to be the essential attitude that characterizes the religious personality. The term *yirei shamayim* (those who have awe of God) is used in Hebrew, like the term 'God-fearing' is used in English, to refer to persons of religious faith and moral virtue. In Judaism, the religious person is not characterized primarily as a 'believer' who assents to a given creed, as in other religions. Rather, the religious person is depicted as one who has *yirat shamayim* or *yirat ha-Shem*, fear and awe of God. Indeed, *yirat shamayim* is almost a synonym for 'religion'.

Though Scripture considers love as the primary attitude of God vis-à-vis human beings, *yirah* is Scripture's primary attitudinal requirement for human beings in their relationship with God. The obligation for one to have *yirah* of God is stated many more times in Hebrew Scripture than is the requirement for one to love God. Scripture identifies *yirah* of God with religious commitment. For example, when Jonah states that he is a 'Hebrew', he explains that to mean that he is one who has '*yirah* of the God of Heaven' (Jon. 1:9). The opening verse of the Book of Job describes Job as 'blameless and upright; he had *yirah* of God and shunned evil' (Job 1:1; see also Gen. 22:12, 42:18). Proverbs characterizes the righteous as those who have *yirah* of God (Prov. 10:27, 14:27, 19:23). *Yirah* of God is inextricably related by Scripture to moral action. *Yirah* of God is considered by Scripture to be the essential ingredient for a life of happiness and virtue (Ps. 112:1, Prov. 19:23).

Yirah of God engenders moral and even courageous behaviour (Exod. 1:21). *Yirah* of God also serves as the ultimate justification for moral behaviour. One should treat one's fellow in a particular manner because one has *yirah* of God (Gen. 42:18, Lev. 19:14, 32, 25:27, 36, 43). Conversely, *yirah* of God is described as a necessary and a sufficient means of dissuading immoral behaviour (Gen. 20:11, Exod. 20:17, Mal. 3:5, Prov. 8:18, 14:27, 16:6, Neh. 5:15, 2 Chron. 5:15). Implicit in these texts is the expectation that fear of God's punishment and/or awe of God's majesty provides fundamental motivation for a life of moral rectitude. Other texts explicitly regard longevity as a reward that can be anticipated by those who live a life motivated by *yirah* of God. Finally, for Scripture, *yirah* of God ensures not only moral rectitude but also wisdom (Job 28:28; see also Isa. 11:2, Ps. 111:10, Prov. 2:9, 9:10, 15:33).

The term *yirat shamayim* is of rabbinic (and not biblical) origin. The Bible uses direct terms such as *yirat Elohim* or *yirat Adonai* to denote fear or awe of God. In biblical Hebrew, the term *yirah* denotes 'fright', or 'fear' and 'awe' or 'reverence'.[2] It also can denote anxiety, as in Genesis 26:24 which may be translated 'Do not be anxious, for I [God] am with you' (see also Gen. 15:1, Isa. 41:10, Jer. 1:8). In rabbinic Hebrew and in rabbinic literature, the semantic and conceptual features of *yirah* of God were expanded. Discussion of *yirah* of God in rabbinic literature focuses around two issues: the distinction between fear and awe of God, and the relationship between *yirah* of God and love of God. These two issues also provide much of the agenda for medieval Jewish literature's further analysis and amplification of the notion of *yirah* of God. Though Scripture does not distinguish between fear of God and awe of God, rabbinic literature initiates a discussion that attempts to differentiate between these two distinct attitudes, denoted by the identical word. Furthermore, while Scripture clearly subordinates love of God to *yirah* of God, rabbinic literature resists considering the matter as being closed.

These two issues are implicitly raised in the following early rabbinic statement of Antigonus of Sokho in which the term 'fear of Heaven' (here: *mora shamayim*) is used for the first time: 'Be not like servants that minister to the master for the sake of receiving reward ... and let the fear of Heaven be upon you'.[3] The implication here is that a servant who serves without expectation of reward serves out of love of the master, i.e., of God. In this view, love and *yirah* of God are inextricably intertwined.[4] Furthermore, Antigonus of Sokho's characterization of *mora shamayim* as being properly separated from the expectation of reward for virtue, and by implication, from the expectation of punishment for sin, establishes the basis for later explicit distinctions in medieval Jewish literature between two disparate connotations of *yirah* of God: fear of God, that is, of God's punishment for sin, and awe and reverence of God's majesty.

That the term *yirat heit*, fear of (punishment for) sin, begins to appear in rabbinic literature, seems to indicate the beginning of an implicit distinction between fear of God and awe of God. *Yirah* of God, understood as fear of punishment, was clearly an undesirable, though not a completely unacceptable attitude, according to rabbinic theology. As a prophylactic measure to prevent sin, fear of God served a function.[5] However, as a basis for religious life, fear of God could not be deemed as being preferable.

It may well be that the association of *yirah* of God with the principle of divine reward and retribution encouraged some rabbinic authorities to elevate love of God over *yirah* of God, in a blatant reversal of the biblical view that considered *yirah* of God to be supreme. It is therefore ironic that the rabbis, while elevating love over *yirah*, link reward both to love and to *yirah*. For example, *Sifrei on Deuteronomy* states, 'Act out of love, for the Torah distinguishes between one who acts out of love and one who acts out of *yirah*'.[6] 'In the former case reward is doubled and redoubled'.[7] Whether the motivation for serving God is the promise of reward or selfless devotion, the Talmudic rabbis clearly opt for love over *yirah*. This representative rabbinic view is epitomized by the statement of Simeon ben Eleazar: 'Greater is he who acts from love than he who acts from *yirah*'.[8] Summarizing the rabbinic consensus, Solomon Schechter observed, 'it is known that the rabbis always elevated actions motivated by love over actions motivated by *yirah*'.[9]

Implicit within the aforementioned statement of Antigonus of Sokho is the understanding that *yirah* of God and love of God are inseparable. Later rabbinic sources make this notion explicit by affirming authentic *yirah* of God to have love of God at its source.[10] The distinction between *yirah* as fear and *yirah* as awe that begins to emerge in rabbinic literature becomes clear and explicit in medieval Jewish literature. The debate as to whether *yirah* or love of God is granted priority reverberates throughout Jewish medieval philosophical, legal, mystical and ethical literature.

Among medieval Jewish philosophers, Bahya ibn Pakudah, Abraham ibn Daud, Moses Maimonides and Joseph Albo speculated about the meaning of *yirah* of God. For Bahya ibn Pakudah, *yirah* is the necessary prerequisite for and the proper conduit to love of God. Bahya distinguished between a lower and a higher form of *yirah*. The lower form is not fear of God per se, but fear of God's punishment for sin. The higher form is reverence and awe of God, and of God exclusively. It is this variety of *yirah* that inevitably transmutes into love of God.[11] The twelfth-century Jewish philosopher, Abraham ibn Daud, distinguished between two varieties of *yirah*: 'awe of greatness' and 'fear of harm'. For Ibn Daud, the former is clearly the desirable of the two varieties. Ibn Daud defined 'awe of greatness' as an attitude that makes one aware of 'one's deficiencies in relation to the object of one's awe, that is, God'. Like other medieval authors, Ibn Daud related *yirah* to a feeling of 'embarrassment' before God.[12]

In his *Guide of the Perplexed*, Moses Maimonides clearly endorsed awe of God as a necessary but insufficient expression of divine worship. For Maimonides, awe of God ensures right action and moral perfection which constitute the necessary prelude to the more desirable attitude of love of God. Love of God leads to right thinking and to the higher level of intellectual perfection.[13] In his earlier *Commentary to the Mishnah* and *Book of the Commandments*, Maimonides assigned value to fear of God when it serves as a means of stimulating religious observance.[14] However, in his subsequent legal code, *Mishneh Torah*, Maimonides relegated fear of God, i.e., fear of God's punishment for sin, as being an 'improper manner of serving God. One who serves in this manner serves from fear. This is not the standard set by the prophets and the sages'. For Maimonides, only if service from fear becomes a conduit for service from love, can it retroactively claim any validity.[15]

Maimonides' discussion of the well-known Talmudic statement, 'Everything is in the hands of Heaven, except *yirat shamayim*' bears mention.[16] In one of his responsa, Maimonides interpreted this statement to mean that the word 'everything' refers to the natural order of things, but not to human deeds. Moral choice remains the provenance of human beings.[17]

The discussion of *yirah* of God in Joseph Albo's fifteenth-century philosophical work, *Sefer ha-Ikkarim*, is more reminiscent of Ibn Daud than of Maimonides.[18] Like Ibn Daud, Albo clearly distinguished between *yirah* as fear of harm and *yirah* as awareness of human deficiency when standing in awe of God's sublimity. Unlike Maimonides, Albo did not condemn fear of punishment, but considered it as a first necessary step toward awe of God. For Albo, fear of God aims at the physical nature of human beings, while awe of God relates to the higher spiritual aspects of the human personality. Following Scriptural precedent, though in opposition to Maimonides, Albo described *yirah* of God, rather than love of God, as being the conduit to wisdom.

Besides Maimonides, other medieval Halakhists discussed *yirah* of God. For example, the thirteenth-century *Sefer ha-Hinukh*, ascribed to Aaron ha-Levi of Barcelona, defines *yirah* of God primarily in terms of fear of God's punishment. As in Maimonides' earlier writings, this work stresses the value of fear of God as a catalyst for religious observance, and counts fear of God among the 613 commandments of the Torah.[19] This text also observes that fear of God, like love of God, is one of a severely limited number of the commandments that must be practised at all times by everyone.

The fourteenth-century code of Jacob ben Asher, and Moses Isserles' glosses to the sixteenth-century code *Shulhan Arukh*, begin by stressing *yirah* of God, and not love of God, as the primary religious attitude upon which divine worship and observance of Jewish law rests. These codes further insist that only *yirah* of God, and not social pressure, is a viable reason for religious observance.[20] That these codes open with a discussion of *yirah* of God rather than with a discussion of love of God, is indicative of a reluctance on the part of a considerable number of legal, ethical and Kabbalistic writers to tacitly affirm the supremacy of love of God over *yirah* of God.

Yirah of God is a subject widely discussed in medieval Jewish pietica and ethical literature. *Yirah* of God is often described in such texts as being essential in the quest for piety. For example, the *Sefer Hasidim* of Judah the Pious directly claims that 'the root of piety is *yirah*'. The *Sefer Hasidim* further defines *yirah* of God as an attitude that leads one to suppress one's natural appetites and desires. Proof of possessing *yirah*, is the individual's ability to withstand a trial of faith. The more severe the trial, the greater the *yirah*. More than fear of punishment, *yirah* of God is characterized as the fear of not being able to withstand God's trials; it is fear of not loving God adequately.[21] For Eleazar of Worms, love of God is an essential aspect of *yirah* of God, rather than the opposite, as many of the Talmudic rabbis would have it.[22]

In Bahya ben Asher's thirteenth-century ethical-homiletical treatise *Kad ha-Kemah*, *yirah* of God is characterized as 'the foundation of the entire Torah ... the root of all the commandments'. Like Ibn Daud and Albo, Bahya ben Asher held that fear of God's punishment inevitably leads to the awareness of God's majesty. Nevertheless, following Talmudic precedent, Bahya ben Asher insisted that *yirah* itself is insufficient unless it includes love of God. Love is clearly the supreme desideratum in divine worship.[23] In opposition to Maimonides and like Albo, Bahya ben Asher identified true wisdom with *yirah* of God, rather than with love of God. A similar approach is also taken in the *Orhot Zaddikim*.[24] Following Talmudic precedent, *Orhot Zaddikim* finds scholarship uninformed by *yirah* of God to be a crippled variety of knowledge, intellectual attainment devoid of wisdom.[25]

Orhot Zaddikim also distinguishes among three varieties of *yirah*: fear of social disapproval; fear of punishment, that is, fear of harm to oneself; awe of God's greatness. Because awe is rare and difficult to achieve, the author, like a number of sources already mentioned, considered fear of punishment to be acceptable in Halakic terms, though theologically not a desirable motivation for divine worship. Despite the significance attached to *yirah* of God by this author, he nevertheless followed earlier precedents by describing *yirah* as a rung on the ladder of ascent toward the higher rung of love of God. Finally for this text, echoing *Sefer Hasidim*, the highest variety of *yirah* is actually intertwined with love: '"Serve the Lord with *yirah*" (Ps. 2:11), that is, fear of losing God's love ... Thus, this fear is really love'.[26]

Sefer ha-Yashar, an ethical treatise traditionally ascribed to Jacob ben Meir (Rabbenu Tam), and probably written in the thirteenth century, sees *yirah* as the necessary by-product of love of God, but considers fear of God in itself inadequate. *Yirah* is 'not the service of the truly pious, but of the wicked or of the nations of the world'. Furthermore, according to this work, fear of God offers an opportunity for self-knowledge. 'By doing God's will and by fearing God, we will come to recognize who we are and what our lives are'.[27]

Extensive discussion of *yirah* of God is also found in Moses Hayyim Luzzatto's eighteenth-century ethical tract *Mesillat Yesharim: The Path of the Upright*.[28] Luzzatto distinguished between two varieties of *yirah* of God: fear of punishment, and a sense of awe. Fear of punishment, a universal trait, is easy to attain, and is rooted in self-interest. A sense of awe, though difficult to attain, evidences both moral perfection and the acquisition of wisdom. Fear of punishment 'can be experienced at all times' and is characteristic of the masses, while awe of God is a rare commodity, characteristic of the saintly scholar.

The medieval Jewish mystical tradition reaches no consensus as to whether *yirah* or love of God is the higher spiritual trait. The *Zohar*, in opposition to many earlier Jewish philosophical and Kabbalistic sources, identifies religious consciousness with *yirah* of God. While identifying both *yirah* and love with various pairs of the divine emanations (*sefirot*), the *Zohar* consistently equates *yirah* with the higher emanations.[29]

The *Zohar* distinguishes among three varieties of *yirah*.[30] Of these three varieties only one is deigned to be true and proper. The first variety is fear of physical punishment in this world for oneself and for one's family. The second is fear of punishment in the World-to-Come. Neither is considered genuine *yirah* of God. These are 'evil fears' as opposed to the third variety which is 'holy fear'. This third valid variety of *yirah* is characterized by awe of God's majesty and is inevitably intertwined with selfless love of God. Thus, for the *Zohar*, love is a byproduct of true *yirah*. But, *yirah* is the foundation, not only of love of God, but also of faith and of all of creation.[31]

In his mystical-ethical writings, Judah Loew of Prague, rejected the view of the *Zohar* that elevates *yirah* over love of God. Judah Loew returned to a position that considers awe of God to be inferior to love of God. For Loew, awe is a necessary step in preparing the individual for communion with the divine, which is the result of love of God. Awe guarantees the prerequisite wisdom and the prerequisite self-abnegation that are the premises upon which love of and communion with God are predicated.[32]

The most comprehensive discussion of *yirah* of God in Jewish literature is found in the opening section, consisting of fifteen chapters, of Elijah de Vidas's sixteenth-century mystical-ethical treatise *Reshit Hokhmah*. Like Judah Loew, de Vidas considered *yirah* to be the necessary prerequisite for the higher attitude of love of God. De Vidas expanded upon earlier distinctions between fear of sin and awe of God. Developing earlier Kabbalistic notions of sin, de Vidas placed considerable significance on fear of sin, since sin affects not only the human self, but the Godhead as well. For de Vidas, fear of sin is not simply motivated by a fear of self-harm, but by a fear of causing a flaw in all of the 'worlds' that are placed between us and the divine. Indeed, for de Vidas, fear of sin entails fear of disrupting the flow of divine grace to our world, of disturbing the balance of the *sefirot*, and of causing injury to the *Shekhinah*. For de Vidas, as for Luzzatto, fear of sin is a necessary spur directed at the coarser features of the human personality. The coarser the person, the more fear of sin is required. Like Luzzatto, de Vidas reserved the higher *yirah*, awe of God, for the saintly and for the wise. In the course of his discussion, de Vidas transmits a manuscript on the tortures of hell (*Massekhet Gehinnom*) that contains typical medieval descriptions of the tortures reserved for those who were devoid of fear of sin during their lifetimes.[33]

Though the earlier distinction between fear and awe was perpetuated by the *Musar* (Ethics) movement that arose in nineteenth-century Lithuania, this movement strongly emphasized fear of punishment as the primary means to human self-development, and as a necessary prophylactic measure against improper behaviour.[34] In eighteenth- and nineteenth-century Hasidic thought, fear of punishment for sin receives less emphasis, and fear of punishment in hell is absent. Hasidic literature perpetuates the distinction between a lower and a higher variety of *yirah* of God. Levi Yitzhak of Berditchev, for example, considered the 'lower' to be both a prelude for and a conduit to the 'higher'. For Levi Yitzhak, echoing Judah Loew, awe of God means the surrender of self-awareness in response to the majesty of God.[35] The first Hasidic author, Jacob Joseph of Polnoyye, identified the 'lower' *yirah* with outward expression and the 'higher' *yirah* with the inwardness of the soul. He proceeds to address the long-standing problem of the prioritization of *yirah* and love of God by asserting that, at a high level of inwardness, *yirah* and love of God coalesce into one and become inseparable and indistinguishable, thus obviating the need to prioritize one over the other.[36]

Despite the considerable discussion of *yirah* in classical Jewish literature, modern Jewish thinkers have largely ignored the notion of *yirah* of God. An exception is Morris Joseph who is unique in that he stresses fear of God as a concept with modern relevance in that it may still serve as a powerful motive for engendering responsible moral behaviour.[37]

Abraham Joshua Heschel offered a short phenomenological analysis of *yirah* in *God in Search of Man*. Heschel stressed the role of awe as a prerequisite for faith, and discussed the interrelationship between awe and wisdom.[38] Louis Jacobs offers informative and erudite analytical essays on *yirah* of God in *Jewish Values* and in *A Jewish Theology*. Jacobs correctly observes that religion devoid of *yirat shamayim* tends to become reduced to a comfortable sentimentality.[39]

NOTES

1. *Orhot Zaddikim*, trans. Seymour J. Cohen (New York: Feldheim, 1960), p.590.
2. Mayer I. Gruber, 'Fear, Anxiety and Reverence in Akkadian, Biblical Hebrew and other Northwest Semitic Languages', *Vetus Testamentum* 40:4 (October 1990): 411–23.
3. *Ethics of the Fathers* 1:3.
4. Compare Ben Sira 2:16.
5. *Nedarim* 20a.
6. *Sifrei–Devarim* [*Sifre on Deuteronomy*], Louis Finkelstein (ed.) (Berlin: Jüdischer Kulterband in Deutschland Abteilung Verlag, 1939), para. 32, p.54.
7. *Seder Eliyahu Rabbah*, Meir Friedmann (ed.) (Vienna: Ahiyasaf, 1904), pp.140–41.
8. *Sota* 31a.
9. *Avot d'Rabbi Nathan*, Solomon Schechter (ed.), (2nd ed., New York: Feldheim, 1967), p.26 n. 11; compare p.26 text and p.26 n. 10; See also Adolph Buchler, *Studies in Sin and Atonement* (London: n.p., 1928), pp.118–75; Ephraim E. Urbach, *Emunot ve-Deot Hazal* (Jerusalem: Magnes, 1971), pp.348–70.
10. *Tosefta Sota* 6:1; *Sota* 31a in the name of Rabbi Meir.
11. Bahya ibn Pakudah, *The Book of Direction to the Duties of the Heart*, trans. Menahem M. Mansoor (London: Routledge and Kegan Paul, 1973), pp.432–7.
12. Abraham ibn Daud, *Emunah Ramah* (Frankfurt: n.p., 1852), p.100.
13. Moses Maimonides, *Guide of the Perplexed*, trans. Shlomo Pines (Chicago: University of Chicago Press, 1963), 3:52, pp.629–30. See also Maimonides, *Mishneh Torah-Sefer ha-Mada*, sec. *Hilkhot Yesodei ha-Torah*, 2:1, Saul Lieberman (ed.) (Jerusalem: Mosad ha-Rav Kook, 1964), 2:1, p.99.
14. Maimonides, *Commentary to the Mishnah* [Hebrew], Joseph Kapah (ed.) (Jerusalem: Mosad ha-Rav Kook, 1965), on *Ethics of the Fathers* 1:3, pp.267–88. Maimonides, *Sefer ha-Mitzvot*, Joseph Kapah (ed.) (Jerusalem: Mosad ha-Rav Kook, 1971), sec. 'Positive Commandments', no. 4, p.60.
15. Maimonides, *Mishnah Torah-Sefer ha-Mada*, sec. *Hilkhot Teshuvah*, 10:1, 2,5.
16. *Berakhot* 33b.
17. Maimonides, *Responsa* [Hebrew], Aaron Freimann (ed.) (Jerusalem: Mekitzei Nirdamim, 1934), no.345, pp.309–310. See also *Niddah* 16b.
18. Joseph Albo, *Sefer ha-Ikkarim: The Book of Principles*, 6 vols., trans. and ed. Isaac Husik (Philadelphia: Jewish Publication Society, 1946), vol. 3, chaps. 31–33, pp.291–304.
19. *Sefer ha-Hinukh* (Jerusalem: Eshkol, 1946), no. 432, p.268. For precedents for this view, see Rashi to *Megillah* 25b and *Midrash Tenaim*, Zvi Hoffmann (ed.) (Berlin: nN.p., 1908), p.260.

20. Jacob ben Asher, *Arba'ah Turim* (New York: Grossman, n.d.), sec. *Orah Hayyim* 1:1; Joseph Karo, *Shulhan Arukh* (Vilna: Romm, 1911), sec. *Orah Hayyim* 1:1.
21. *Sefer Hasidim*, Reuven Margaliot (ed.) (Jerusalem: Mosad ha-Rav Kook, 1960), nos. 12–13, pp.62–63.
22. See *Sefer Raziel* (Amsterdam, 1701), p.7b.
23. Bahye ben Asher, *Kad ha-Kemah* (Lwow, 1892), secs. *Ahavah*, *Yirah*, pp.5–8, 97–98.
24. *Orhot Zaddikim*, pp.590–629.
25. See *Sabbath* 31a–b; *Yoma* 72b, *Pesahim* 22b, *Exodus Rabbah* 30:14.
26. *Orhot Zaddikim*, pp.121, 129.
27. *Sefer ha-Yashar: The Book of the Righteous*, trans. Seymour J. Cohen (New York: Ktav, 1973), pp.34–35, 50–51.
28. Moses Hayyim Luzzatto, *Mesillat Yesharim: The Path of the Upright*, trans. Mordecai M. Kaplan (Philadelphia: Jewish Publication Society, 1936), pp.12, 310–16, 422–23.
29. See Isaiah Tishbi, *Mishnat ha-Zohar*, vol. 2 (Jerusalem: Mosad Bialik, 1961), pp.293–5.
30. *Zohar* (Vilna, 1882), vol.1, pps. 11b–12a.
31. See also *Ecclesiastes Rabbah* 3:14,1.
32. Judah Loew, *Netivot Olom*, 2 vols. (London: Judaica Press, 1969), vol. 2, pp.20–37.
33. Elijah de Vidas, *Reshit Hokhmah*, 3 vols., Hayyim Joseph Wildman (ed.) (Jerusalem: Or ha-Musar, 1984), vol. 1, pp.245–59.
34. Isaac Blazer in Dov Katz, *Tenuat ha-Musar*, 4 vols. (Tel Aviv: Menorah, 1973), vol. 2, pp.260–273.
35. Levi Yitzhak of Berditchev, *Kedushat Levi* (New York: n.p., 1962), sec. *Ekev*, pp.876–86.
36. Jacob Joseph of Polnoyye, *Toledot Yaakov Yosef*, 2 vols. (Jerusalem: Sifrei Musar va-Hasidut, 1961), sec. *Ekev*, vol. 2, pp.628–32.
37. Morris Joseph, *Judaism as Creed and Life* (New York: Bloch, 1903), pp.112–26.
38. Abraham J. Heschel, *God in Search of Man* (Philadelphia: Jewish Publication Society, 1955), pp.73–9.
39. Louis Jacobs, *Jewish Values* (London: Vallentine Mitchell, 1960), pp.31–50; Jacobs, *A Jewish Theology* (New York: Behrman House, 1973), pp.174–182.

CHAPTER SIX

Love and Law

> The Holy One, blessed be He, said, 'When you stood at Mount Sinai and received the Torah, I wrote that I love you, as it is written, "it was because the Lord loved you"' (Deut. 7:8).[1]

Jewish theology is a palace of faith and conviction grounded in revelation, and forged by tradition. Engendered by divine providence and love, carefully crafted by human intuition and intellect, and honed by history and experience, the theological edifice of Judaism rests upon three firmly planted pillars: God, Torah and Israel.[2] The underlying foundation which supports and binds these three fundamental theological non-negotiables of Judaism is the awareness of the commitment to an eternally binding covenant between God and the people of Israel.

According to the Talmud, the covenant compacted between God and Israel at Sinai is the raison d'être not only for the creation of the people of Israel, but also for the creation of the world. The Talmud reports that, 'the Holy One, blessed be He, stipulated with the Works of Creation and said thereto: If Israel accepts the Torah [at Sinai] you shall continue to exist, but if not, I shall revert you back to chaos and to void'.[3] Without the revelation at Sinai, creation is revealed to be a purposeless venture. Without the covenant, Jewish existence is a conclusion without a premise, a fallacy. At Sinai, the three foci of Jewish theological concern converge at one time, in one place. At Sinai, *God* gives the *Torah* to *Israel*.

Rabbinic tradition likens the theophany at Sinai to a wedding. According to one tradition, the people of Israel were married to the Torah at Sinai.[4] According to a second tradition, at Sinai, God, the bridegroom, is wedded to Israel, the bride: '"On the day of his espousals" (Song of Songs 3:11). This alludes to the revelation at Sinai which was, as it were, a wedding ceremony [between God and Israel], as is borne out by the text, "Betroth them today and tomorrow"' (Exod. 19:10).[5] The Torah serves as the 'marriage contract' that eternally binds the bridegroom and the bride together.[6] As a *contract*, the Torah is a legal document that states the mutually accepted duties and responsibilities of the two parties to the agreement. However, as a *marriage* contract, the Torah is a document attesting to the love that obtains between God and Israel. Thus, while it embodies a legal element, the Torah is not simply law; rather it embraces a polarity of love *and* law.

To the dispassionate reader, a marriage contract might appear a dry legalistic document, but to the bridegroom and the bride it represents an expression of their love, a concretization of their commitment. To those who attend a wedding, the liturgy may sound unduly encumbered by legalistic jargon. However, the bridegroom and the bride hear the legal wording of the marriage service as a song echoing their mutual love. At Sinai, the Torah – the marriage contract between God and Israel – was presented. Some read it and hear its melody of love; others, however, see only law but remain deaf to its message of love.[7] Commenting on the biblical account of the giving of the Torah at Sinai, the Ba'al Shem Tov offered the following analogy in the form of a story:

> A musician was playing at a wedding celebration at a local inn. His music so enraptured the people that they were driven to dance. Then a deaf man who could not hear the music happened to pass the inn. As the fiddler stood in the corner, the man did not see him. As he was deaf, he did not hear the music. Looking through the window, all he saw were people jumping up and down. 'Madmen, all madmen', he muttered and went his way.[8]

Those who have identified the Torah with law alone, those who portray Judaism as a religion obsessed with law to the exclusion of love and emotion, fail to hear the music. Like the deaf man in the tale, they perceive acts of celebration as acts of madness. But, to those who hear the music, observance of the laws of the Torah is an expression not simply of obedience to God, but also of love for the

Giver of the Torah. Observance of the law is a free expression of joy and not a spiritually crippling manifestation of servitude. Observance of the commandments is not a curse from which the Jew needs to be redeemed, but a blessing which makes one worthy of being redeemed.[9]

Though made at one time, at one place, the covenant is binding upon all Jews for all time, at all times in all places. As a husband and wife must perpetually renew their love, must continually recommit themselves to the pledge made on their wedding day, as love must be continually revitalized lest it be taken for granted, lest it dissolve into habit, so must the original covenant between God and Israel continually be reaffirmed both in the life of the people of Israel as well as in the life of each member of the people of Israel.

Scripture reports occasions at which Israel renewed the covenant with God originally made at Sinai.[10] The liturgies of various Jewish festivals of the year offer opportunities for the renewal of the commitment to the covenant.[11] Events in the life cycle of the individual Jew such as circumcision (Hebrew: *brit*, covenant), bar/bat mitzvah, marriage, and so forth, offer opportunities for the individual Jew to renew the pledge his or her ancestors had made long before. Each day, with each prayer service, an opportunity for reaffirmation is offered. In this vein, Mendel of Kotzk once said: The liturgy refers to the Pentecost festival (*Shavuot*) as 'the time of the giving of the Torah'. Why is it not called 'the festival of the *receiving* of the Torah?' For if Israel had not accepted the Torah, there would be no occasion to celebrate. And, as is the wont of Hasidic masters, he answered his own question, saying: The reason is because the Torah was given only once – at Sinai. But, it cannot be received only once; otherwise, it would be forgotten. It must be received continuously, daily. Festivals in the Jewish calendar and liturgies recited throughout the year give expression to the fact that the events of the past, such as Sinai, have an undiminished importance for each generation. Through one's daily re-acceptance of the Torah, the Jewish past becomes the Jewish present. Events in the life of one generation become contemporary events in the lives of each subsequent generation.

Describing the arrival of Israel at Sinai for its wedding with God, Scripture records, 'In the third month after Israel had departed Egypt, on *this* day they came to the wilderness of Sinai' (Exod. 19:1). Should not the verse read 'on *that* day' rather than 'on *this* day?', asked the rabbis. The commentaries observe: '"On this day" was written rather than "on that day" [to teach] that the words of the Torah should be new to you, as if God gave them to you today'.[12] Similarly, the Hasidic master, Abraham Joshua Heschel of Apt, said: 'Everyone is told to consider himself to be standing at Mount Sinai, to receive the Torah. For to human beings, there are past and future events, but not for God; day in and day out God gives the Torah, and day in and day out one may receive the Torah'.[13]

Before beginning to recite the daily morning prayer, the observant Jew dons the prayer shawl and phylacteries (*tefillin*). As one does so, one recites a verse from Hosea (2:21–22) that recalls the espousal of Israel to God at Sinai:

> I betroth you to Me forever.
> I betroth you to Me in righteousness, with justice,
> with loving kindness and with mercy.
> I betroth you to Me with faithfulness and you shall love the Lord.

The liturgy of the daily morning service commences with an assurance of God's endless love. The liturgy of the evening service reconfirms that theme while providing a reminder of the nexus between love and law. God's law is a token of God's love. The evening liturgy reads: 'With great love have You loved the people of Israel, teaching us Your Torah and Your commandments, Your statutes and Your judgments. Blessed are You, O Lord, who loves Your people Israel'.

Each act the observant Jew performs in the course of the day is accompanied by a blessing, when rising from sleep, eating, and so on. Many of these blessings take the following form: 'Blessed are You, our God, King of the Universe, who has sanctified us (*kideshanu*) with His commandments and commanded us to...'. A long-standing tradition maintains that the Hebrew word *kideshanu* – 'who has sanctified us' – can also be translated as 'who betroths us to Himself'. Thus, by observing the commandments, by obeying God's laws, each person, in each act, may become betrothed to God.

As was noted above, one tradition compares the revelation at Sinai to a wedding between God and the people of Israel. However, a second tradition analogizes the Sinaitic theophany to a marriage between the Torah and the people of Israel. Rabbinic literature as well as Jewish mystical tradition describes the Torah as the betrothed of Israel: 'Moses commanded us the Torah, an inheritance [*morashah*] of the congregation of Jacob (Deut. 33:4)'. The rabbis comment, 'Do not read the word as *morashah* – as an inheritance – but as *me'orasah* – as a betrothal'.[14]

God, the father, gives His daughter, the Torah, as a bride to the people of Israel.[15] The presence of the Torah in the life of Israel guarantees the perpetual presence of God in the life of Israel. In this regard, the rabbis offered the following parable:

> Once there was a king who had an only daughter whom another king married. When the latter wished to return to his country and take his wife with him, the father said, 'My daughter whom I have given you in marriage is my only child. My love for her is great. I cannot depart from her. Yet, I cannot ask you not to take her to your realm. It is now her proper home. Permit me this one request. To whatever distant place you take her now to live, always have a chamber ready for me that I may dwell with you and with her. For I can never consider really leaving my daughter'. So God said to Israel: 'I have given you a Torah from which I cannot really part. I cannot tell you not to receive it in love. Yet, I request only this. Wherever you go with it, make Me a house wherein I may sojourn'. As it is written, "Let them make Me a sanctuary so that I may dwell among them"' (Exod. 25:8).[16]

As the 'daughter' of God, the Torah is both apart from and a part of its parent. In God's giving the Torah to Israel, part of the Giver is given with the gift.[17] The Torah is Israel's beloved, Israel's spouse, the touchstone of meaning for Israel's life. As the rabbis put it, 'When a man loves the Torah, he loves life itself. Thus Scripture says, "Enjoy life with the wife you love" (Eccles. 9:9)'.[18] The place of the Torah in the life of Israel guarantees the perpetual presence of God in the history of Israel. The presence of the Torah binds God to Israel and Israel to God. It is through his or her observance of the commandments of the Torah that the Jew binds himself or herself to God through the Torah. God's Torah is the law of God's love. Israel's obedience to God's will manifests their love of God's law.

The observance of God's law is the Jew's primary way of manifesting his or her love for God. Both the words 'religion' and 'legal' derive from the identical Latin root *ligo* which means 'to be bound'. Observance of the law binds us to God. Observance of the commandments is religion in action, 'practical theology'. Levi Yitzhak of Berditchev said, 'The word *mitzvah* – commandment – means "to bind," which is to say, he who properly performs a *mitzvah* binds himself to the Creator'.[19] The law is a means of establishing the bond between God and Israel, and not an end in itself. The law is a path, not a destination. Jewish law – *Halakhah* – comes from the verbal root of 'go', not from the verbal root of 'arrive'.

As God cannot be separated from Israel, and as neither can be separated from the Torah, the Torah cannot preserve its nature either without love or without law. Without love, the Torah is a body without a soul. Without law, the Torah is a bodiless, vagabond spirit. The portrait of Torah that equates Torah with law alone paints only half a face of its subject. The Septuagint's translation of 'Torah' as '*nomos*' – law – gave rise to a tradition of misunderstanding both of the nature of the Torah in Judaism, and, consequently, of the nature of Judaism in its entirety. Despite the claims of those who equate Judaism with legalism, Judaism has never been exclusively a religion of law.[20]

The claim that Judaism is totally a religion of law to the exclusion of love, faith and morality, is simply neither historically nor theologically defensible. The claim found in Christian theology that the laws of the Torah are superseded and therefore obsolete has helped engender tragic results throughout Jewish history. Kant's equation of Judaism with law alone led him to the conclusion that Judaism was at best a-moral, at worst immoral. This conclusion led Kant to call for the 'euthanasia of Judaism', an idea that was translated into social and political policy by Nazi Germany during the European Holocaust.[21]

The supersessionist idea found in Christian theology in effect denigrates both the people of Israel and the Torah of Israel.[22] Consequently, such notions denigrate the God of Israel. To insult one's wife is to besmirch her husband. To insult a child is to insult its parent:

> A parable: Once a king had a daughter. He built her palaces with many halls. His decree went forth: Whosoever is granted

> an audience with my daughter is considered as being in my presence. Whosoever dares to insult my daughter, it is as if he insulted me.[23]

In Jewish tradition, *Shavuot* is celebrated as the anniversary of the giving of the Torah at Sinai.[24] It is not surprising therefore that liturgical texts for that festival reflect a vision of Sinai as the occasion at which the people of Israel became eternally wedded to the Torah. Nor is it surprising that the liturgy articulates the view that celebration of *Shavuot* provides an opportunity for renewing that marriage, for reaffirming that commitment.

In many Sephardic congregations, before the Torah is read during the mourning liturgy for *Shavuot*, a ***ketubah le-shavuot*** – a marriage contract for *Shavuot* – is read. This document is modelled after the traditional Jewish marriage contract, the ***ketubah***. The various versions of this document describe the solemnizing of a marriage between the Torah, the bride, and the people of Israel, the bridegroom. As father of the bride, God gives as dowry the 613 commandments of the Torah. As 'best man', Moses presents a gift to the groom of the Sabbath and the festivals. Some versions describe God and Moses as signatories to the original marriage contract while others have the heavens and the earth as witnesses to the original document. A second practice developed under the influence of the late medieval mystics, provides for the reading of a marriage contract which describes God as the bridegroom, the people of Israel as God's bride, and the Torah as the dowry presented to the bride on the wedding day.[25]

Following the text of the traditional Jewish marriage contract, this liturgical version of the marriage contract between God and Israel does not simply purport to attest to the love between God and Israel. It also – as does any contract – unequivocally states the legal obligations attendant upon the two parties to the agreement. The people agree to express their love for God by observing the commandments of the Torah, by upholding God's law. God, in turn, agrees to extend perpetual providential care over the people, and commits Himself to be bound by the promises made to His people.

When two parties enter into a legal agreement there is an expectation that each party will uphold its respective obligations under the agreement. However, as is often the case, parties to an agreement violate its stipulations. Initial expectations are tempered by mutual disappointments. When Israel violates its duties and obligations under the covenant, God invokes His justice. By transgressing the conditions of its marriage contract with God, by violating the law, Israel becomes liable to divine justice and judgment. For example, as the Talmud compares Sinai to a wedding between God and Israel, so it extends the analogy to compare the building and worshiping of the Golden Calf to harlotry, to a blatant disregarding of Israel's marriage vows: 'Shameless is the bride that plays the harlot within her bridal chamber'.[26] Under such circumstances the law might require divorce, the annulment of the marriage, the cancellation of the covenant. But such is not the case. Because the covenant is eternal, and because God is bound to the covenant, the covenant endures, the marriage remains in force. Because the covenant embraces love as well as law, God's mercy tempers God's justice. The spirit of God's love hovers over God's law. At first, God wishes to enforce His law to the letter: 'I will judge you as women who break wedlock and shed blood are judged and I will bring upon you the blood of fury and jealousy' (Ezek. 16:38). But, in the end, God's love prevails over His law:

> For thus says the Lord God, I will deal even with you as you have done, who has despised the oath in breaking the covenant. Nevertheless, I will remember my covenant with you in the days of your youth, and I will establish with you an everlasting covenant. And I will establish my covenant with you, and you shall know that I am the Lord, that you may remember … that I have forgiven you all you have done, says the Lord God (Ezek. 16:59–63).

According to the Talmud, God obeys His own laws, even the laws regarding prayer. God prays. And what is God's prayer?: 'May it be My will that My mercy may suppress My anger, and that My mercy may prevail over My [other] attributes, so that I might deal with My children in the attitude of mercy, and on their behalf, stop short of the limit of strict justice'.[27]

As was just noted, rabbinic sources depict God as obeying His own laws. In other words, God is considered to be a 'person' in

Jewish law, 'enjoying rights, being subject to obligations, and heeding His own precepts, in relationships with His creatures'.[28] This rather startling notion is established in the Talmud: 'Rabbi Lazar said: A human king issues a decree and he may choose to obey it or he may choose to have only others obey it. Not so the Holy One, praised be He. When God issues a decree, God is the first to obey it, as it is stated, "And they shall observe My observances, I am the Lord," that is, I am He who is first to observe the commandments of the Torah'.[29]

As a person under the law – albeit His own – God may be called to account for His apparent failure to honour the legal obligations to which He committed Himself. As Israel is liable to God for its violations of the covenant, so is God liable to Israel for His violations of the pact made with the people.

Throughout the massacres and pogroms that punctuate Jewish history, Jews have dared to suggest – and to claim – that God has failed to uphold His duties and obligations under the covenant. Human suffering may be justified by human sin, and punishment may be the price Israel pays for its failure to fulfil its part of the pact with God. Nevertheless, so much suffering, so many tragedies, so many hosts of martyrs, so many oceans of blood, so many streams of tears, so many stacks of corpses, could not possibly be the products of divine justice. The nightmare of Jewish history seems to conflict with the promise of divine providence, with God's proclivity toward justice, with God's attribute of mercy. Abraham's cry, 'Will the Judge of all the earth not do justice?' (Gen. 18:25) – echoed throughout the centuries. The rabbis read the verse in Exodus (15:11): 'Who is like unto You among the mighty (*elim*) O Lord?' and commented, 'Read not *elim* (mighty) but *elmim* (silent). Who is like unto You among the silent, O Lord – seeing the suffering of His children and remaining silent?'[30]

This tradition of Jewish 'protestantism' was begun by Abraham, the first Jew, and was perpetuated by his descendants. The covenant requires, the law demands, that God act with justice. For God to act otherwise, means that God is in breach of contract. When God acts otherwise, God may be called to account. The prophet Jeremiah questions God's justice: 'Why does the way of the wicked prosper?' (Jer. 12:1). The prophet Habakkuk indicts God for perverting His own justice, for misusing judgment, for manifesting apathetic silence instead of providential concern: 'Lord, how long shall I cry and You will not hear, even cry out to You of violence and You will not save ...The wicked encompass the righteous, wrong judgment proceeds ... Wherefore do You hold Your tongue when the wicked devours the person more righteous than he?' (Hab. 1:1–3).

When did Habakkuk say this? A Midrash offers this response:

> Habakkuk drew a figure of a circle and stood in the middle of it and said to the Holy One, blessed be He, 'Master of the Universe, I shall not stir from this place until You declare to me how long You will continue to show forbearance to the wicked in this world.' The Holy One, blessed be He, replied, 'You have cried to Me but you have not doubted Me. As you live, I shall answer you and cause you to understand. I show forbearance to the wicked in this world so that they may come back to Me in repentance and their willful sins will then be reckoned as unwitting sins ...' When the Holy One lets the righteous envision the trials that are to come upon Israel, the righteous stand up and protest to Him.[31]

As one is required to bear witness before God, so may one bear witness against God. Only after Jacob struggles with the divine is he called 'Israel', which means 'to wrestle with God'. Israel is a people by virtue of its eternal struggle with God to make God remain faithful to His law, to the covenant.

Of those in the annals of Jewish history, the individual most closely identified with reminding God to be faithful to His own justice is the Hasidic master, Levi Yitzhak of Berditchev. In this regard Rabbi Barukh, the grandson of the Baal Shem Tov, is reputed to have said:

> According to Rabbi Levi Yitzhak of Berditchev the Holy One, blessed be He, has not done justice to even a single Jew. [Reflecting on the analogy of Sinai with a wedding between God and Israel,] Levi Yitzhak once observed: 'Master of the World, the sages and prophets of old speak of the covenant at Mount Sinai as a marriage between God and Israel. But what kind of marriage is it? Israel brought great *yihus* (nobility, family status, genealogy) to the marriage, for are we not the children

> of the patriarchs, Abraham, Isaac and Jacob? But what *yihus* did You bring Lord? Who were Your ancestors? You brought wealth to the marriage – that was Your part of the bargain, as it is written of You, 'Mine is the silver and the gold' (Hag. 2:8). Therefore, Master of the World, open up Your vast treasure house for us, ease our pressing needs, and act like the one to whom all the world belongs![32]

On another occasion, commenting on the verse, 'they stand this day for Your judgments, for all things are Your servants' (Ps. 119:91), Levi Yitzhak explained: '"They stand this day for Your judgment," that is, the children of Israel, the people You have chosen, the people who fulfill Your law, they stand this day – if one may utter it – to judge You! ... they judge You for that which they bear – wicked and cruel decrees, pogroms and persecutions, poverty and sorrow – all of which has come upon us because "we are your servants"... [Therefore] our judgment is that You must redeem us without delay'.

God is bound to observe His own law. The law is 'You shall not afflict the orphan' (Exod. 22:21). Levi Yitzhak prayed, 'Master of the World, law after law, prohibition after prohibition You have given in Your Torah that one should not afflict an orphan. And we have observed Your laws all these years, caring for orphans with tender mercy and with great sacrifice. But, Lord, are we too not orphans? Is Israel not an orphan today? Is it not written, 'We are become orphans with no father' (Lam. 5:3)? Where then is Your mercy? Why do You not obey Your own law and care for us, and redeem us?'

It was Levi Yitzhak who brought God to trial: 'Good morning to You, Lord, Master of the Universe, I, Levi Yitzhak, son of Sarah, of Berditchev, I come to serve You with an indictment (*din Torah*) on behalf of Your people, Israel'. Bringing God before the bar of justice was not uncommon amongst the Hasidic Jews of nineteenth-century eastern Europe.[33] Nor was it uncommon among Jewish inmates of the Nazi death camps during the Holocaust. An account of one such trial is related in Elie Wiesel's novel, *Gates of the Forest*:

> In a concentration camp, one evening after work, a rabbi called his colleagues and convoked a special court. Standing with his

> head held high before them, he spoke as follows: 'I intend to convict God of murder, for He is destroying His people and the Law He gave them from Mount Sinai. I have irrefutable proof in my hands. Judge without fear or sorrow or prejudice. Whatever you have to lose has long since been taken away'. The trial proceeded in due legal form, with witnesses for both sides with pleas and deliberations. The unanimous verdict: 'Guilty'.[34]

Though details of the covenant are violated throughout history – both by Israel and by God – the covenant remains intact; the marriage endures. Like a human husband's anger against his spouse, God's anger against Israel flows from disappointment with Israel. Divine anger is an expression of frustrated love. Similarly, the Jew's protests against God emanate from a need to believe in God in spite of God. Such protests are expressions of frustrated faith and disappointed love. One should not confuse momentary tensions within a relationship with an abrogation of that relationship. Friction between true lovers cannot last. The passion of anger is inevitably replaced by the passion of mutual devotion. Israel repents of its transgressions and God repents of His indiscretions, and transmutes divine wrath into love: 'The Lord repented. Concerning this it shall not be, said the Lord' (Amos 7:3). 'For a small moment I have forsaken you, but with great love I shall gather you. In a little wrath I hid My face from you for a moment; but with everlasting love will I have mercy on you, says the Lord, your redeemer ... My love will never depart from you, neither shall My covenant be removed' (Isa. 54:4, 5–10).

Memories of past association dissolve disappointment and rage. 'I remember the devotion of your youth, your love as a bride', God says to Israel (Jer. 2:2). And in his daily prayers, the Jew reminds himself, 'You shall love the Lord your God with all your heart, with all your soul, and with all your might' (Deut. 6:5). God promises to 'remember His covenant forever, the word He pledged for a thousand generations' (1 Chron. 16:15). And in gratitude, the Jew prays to God, 'Blessed are You, O Lord, who remembers the covenant'. The covenant between God and Israel is eternal. Though it may be breached, it cannot be abrogated. Though its stipulations may be violated, the marriage contract cannot be annulled. Despite tensions, the marriage persists; despite strains, the covenant endures; despite times of mutual disappointment, the devotion is unyielding.

According to the rabbis, God the lover, God the redeemer, is not Himself truly redeemed until final redemption has been achieved for His beloved. God the bridegroom is unredeemed until His bride is granted redemption. Linked to Israel by law, bound to Israel by love, God and Israel wait together for the final redemption which both have faith will one day come.

'A parable: Once a prince was betrothed to a princess. A certain day was appointed for festivities before the wedding. The prince was looking forward to his wedding joy, and the princess was looking forward to her wedding joy ... So does the Holy One, blessed be He, look forward for redemption for Israel, and Israel awaits redemption for the Holy One, blessed be He'.[35]

NOTES

1. *Exodus Rabbah* 32:2.
2. Abraham J. Heschel, *Moral Grandeur and Spiritual Audacity* (New York: Farrar, Straus, and Giroux, 1996), pp.191–208.
3. *Shabbat* 88a. See Emil Fackenheim, 'Can There be Judaism Without Revelation?' in *Quest for Past and Future* (Boston: Beacon, 1968).
4. On the analogy of Sinai with a wedding between Israel and God's 'daughter', the Torah, see: *Exodus Rabbah* 30:5, 33:7; *Song of Songs Rabbah* 8:11; *Pesikta de Rav Kahana*, 2 vols, Bernard Mandelbaum (ed.) (New York: Jewish Theological Seminary, 1962), 12:11, 19, vol. 1, pp.210–11, 217. The medieval Jewish mystics analogized Sinai to a wedding between God and the Torah. See *Zohar* (Vilna: Romm, 1882), vol. 1, p.8a. The mystic who studies the Torah the entire night of the Pentecost festival is compared to the 'best man' at the wedding. On 'sacred marriage' rituals practised by the medieval Jewish mystics, see Gershom Scholem, *On the Kabbalah and its Symbolism* (New York: Schocken, 1965), pp.138–46.
5. *Numbers Rabbah* 12:8. See also: *Ta'anit* 26b, *Song of Songs Rabbah* 3:11, *Exodus Rabbah* 52:5, *Numbers Rabbah* 12:8, *Midrash Tanhuma*, 2 vols, Solomon Buber (ed.) (Vilna: n.p., 1885), *Exodus*, sec. *Pekuday* 8, vol. 2, p.67a, and *Numbers*, sec. *'Bamidbar'* 5, p.3a; *Pesikta de Rav Kahana* 1:3, 22:5, vol. 1, pp.7, 329; *Pirke de Rabbi Eliezer* (New York: Ohm, 1946), 41, p.97b. For Scriptural roots of the portrayal of Israel as God's bride, see Isa. 62:5, Jer. 2:1–3, Hos. 2:16–18, Ezek. 16, 23. Some scholars understand certain biblical festivals as having been observed originally as celebrations of a sacred marriage between God and Israel. See Helmer Ringrenn, *Israelite Religion* (Philadelphia: Fortress, 1966), pp.190, 198–99. See p.197 on the Song of Songs as being rooted in the idea of a sacred marriage. This was the interpretation of the Song of Songs ascribed both by subsequent Jewish and Christian exegetes.
6. See *Deuteronomy Rabbah* 3:12 where the Torah is described as the marriage contract between God and Israel written by Moses. See also Jacob Petuchowski, *Ever Since Sinai* (New York: Scribner's, 1961), pp.1–25; Samuel H. Dresner and Byron L. Sherwin, *Judaism: The Way of Sanctification* (New York: United Synagogue, 1978), pp.103–125. The question of the eternality of the covenant, of the marriage between God and Israel, is a theological non-negotiable in Jewish theology. This issue was a point of dispute between Jews and Christians in

medieval polemics, Jewish theologians claiming that the marriage is eternal, Christian theologians claiming that God had divorced Israel for faithlessness and had married another wife, the Church. For some discussion of these matters in sixteenth-century Jewish literature, see Byron L. Sherwin, 'In the Shadows of Greatness: Rabbi Hayyim ben Betsalel of Friedberg', *Jewish Social Studies* 37:1 (1975): 56–9; Byron L. Sherwin, *Mystical Theology and Social Dissent* (Oxford: Oxford University Press, 1982), pp.85–8.

7. On the Torah as a song, see for example, *Midrash on Psalms*, Solomon Buber (ed.) (Vilna: Romm, 1891), 119:41, p.249b: 'David said, "Oh how I love Your Torah" (Ps. 119:97) ... It is always with me. I have not neglected it at all. And because I have not neglected it, it has been to me not a burden, but a song'.
8. Moses Hayyim Ephraim of Sudylkow, *Degel Mahaneh Ephraim* (Jerusalem: Hadar, 1963), sec. *Yitro*, p.111.
9. On observance as joy, see Solomon Schechter, *Aspects of Rabbinic Theology* (New York: Macmillan, 1909), pp.148–70. Paul's denigration of the Torah as the law of slavery and as a curse is in direct contradiction to the Jewish view of the Torah and its laws.
10. On biblical sources for the renewal of the covenant, see Josh. 24:22–27, 2 Kings 23:3–4, Neh. 9:32–37, 10:1.The term 'before the Lord' when discussing the covenant, refers to the renewal of the covenant.
11. Ringrenn, *Israelite Religion*, p.193.
12. Rashi to Exod. 19:1 paraphrasing *Berakhot* 63b, 'The Torah is as beloved every day to those who study it as the day it was given from Mount Sinai'. See also Rashi to Deut. 11:13 and 26:16. Note *Midrash Tanhuma*, sec. *Ki-Tavoh* 3, vol. 2, p.23b.
13. See Martin Buber, *Tales of the Hasidim*, trans. Olga Marx (New York: Schocken, 1948), p.116.
14. *Berakhot* 57a.
15. See *Pirke de Rabbi Eliezer*, chap. 41 which compares God to the father of the Torah, the Torah to a bride, and the people of Israel to the bridegroom who is wed to his bride at Sinai.
16. *Exodus Rabbah* 33:1.
17. 'Ordinarily, when a man buys an article in the market, is he then able to acquire its owner, too? But the Holy One, blessed be He, gave the Torah to Israel and said to them: You are taking Me, as it were! Hence the verse, "that they take Me an offering" (Exod. 25:2)'. *Exodus Rabbah* 33:6.
18. *Midrash on Psalms* 119:41, p.249b.
19. Levi Yitzhak of Berditchev, *Kedushat Levi* (Jerusalem: Mosad l'Hotza'at Sifrei Musar va-Hasidut, 1958), p.33; Eugene Kullman, '*Tikvah* and *Mitzvah*', *Conservative Judaism* 10:4 (Summer 1956): 34–95.
20. Heschel, *God in Search of Man* (Philadelphia: Jewish Publication Society, 1955), pp.320–30.
21. Note Samuel Sandmel's observation, 'It is somewhat strange to Jewish ears to hear Catholics with their elaborate canon law, or Anglicans with theirs, or Methodists with their Discipline, ascribe to Jews exclusively a tendency equally persistent in themselves ... Denomination after denomination in Protestantism has extolled Paul for breaking the shackles of narrow legalism; and denomination after denomination has felt compelled to devise its own, equally necessary legalism'. See Samuel Sandmel, *A Jewish Understanding of the New Testament* (New York: Ktav, 1974), p.167. Sidney Ayinn, 'Kant on Judaism', *Jewish Quarterly Review* 59 (July 1968):9–23. On Kant, Hegel and Toynbee, see Nathan Rotenstreich, *The Recurring Pattern: Studies in Anti-Judaism in Modern Thought* (London: Weidenfeld, 1968).
22. On the social and historical implications of the supersessionist doctrine, Franklin Littell, *The Crucifixion of the Jews* (New York: Harper and Row, 1975); Rosemary Ruether, *Faith and Fratricide* (New York: Seabury, 1974).
23. *Midrash Tanhuma [ha-Nidpas]* (Jerusalem: Levin-Epstein, 1964), sec. *Pekuday'* 4, p.134a.
24. In Scripture, Pentecost is only a harvest festival unrelated to the theophany at Sinai, see Exod. 23:16, 34:22, Numb. 28:26. It seems that after the destruction of the Second Temple in the first century, it became more closely identified as the anniversary of the revelation at Sinai. On the Pharasaic identification of Pentecost with the time of the giving of the Torah, see Louis Finkelstein, *The Pharisees*, 3 vols. (Philadelphia: Jewish Publication Society, 1968), vol. 1, pp.115–18.
25. Philip Goodman, *The Shavuot Anthology* (Philadelphia: Jewish Publication Society, 1974), pp.96–101,156–57.
26. *Sabbath* 88b.

27. *Berakhot* 7a.
28. Moshe Silberg, *Talmudic Law and the Modern State*, trans. Ben Zion Bokser (New York: Burning Bush Press, 1973), pp.1, 8.
29. *Palestinian Talmud*, *Rosh ha-Shanah* 1, 3a.
30. *Mekhilta de Rabbi Yishmael*, Hayyim Horovitz and Israel Rabin (eds) (Jerusalem: Wahrmann, 1960), p.142.
31. *Midrash on Psalms* 77:1, p.172a.
32. Citations from Levi Yitzhak: Samuel H. Dresner, *Levi Yitzhak of Berditchev* (New York: Hartmore House, 1974), pp.77–90.
33. Jiri Langer, *Nine Gates to the Chassidic Mysteries* (London: Clarke, 1961), pp.130–32. The source of this seems to be Abraham Hayyim Michaelson (ed.), *Sefer Ohel Elimelekh* (Jerusalem: N.p., 1968), p.18b.
34. Elie Wiesel, *Gates of the Forest* (New York: Holt, Rinehart and Winston, 1966), p.197.
35. *Midrash on Psalms* 14:6, pp.57b–58a.

CHAPTER SEVEN

Philosophies of Jewish Law

To attempt to understand Halakhah, Jewish religious law, one must confront the theological premises that give it life and meaning, direction and purpose. Halakhah articulates the *mitzvot*, and the *mitzvot* – the commandments – assume a *metzaveh* – one who commands.[1] God is the one who commands, and revelation is the event through which those commands are conveyed. The Torah is the record and the product of the revelatory event. The Torah, the giver of the Torah, and the recipient of the Torah become bound together in a covenant by means of the revelatory event. In a sense, Halakhah is a form of 'applied theology' or 'practical theology'; it is theology in practice.

Both a philosophy of Jewish law and a process for making halakhic decisions ultimately rest upon specific theologies of revelation. A review of the relevant literature seems to indicate that two distinct theologies of revelation, characteristic of classical Jewish theology, have engendered two distinct philosophies of Halakhah and two distinct correlative approaches to the process of Halakhic decision making. For reasons that are clarified below, one of these approaches may be called 'the monologic view', and the other may be called 'the dialogic view'.[2]

The Monologic View

The monologic view is grounded in a particular understanding of the revelatory experience and of its products: Torah and *mitzvot*. According to this view, revelation is a monologue of God; the Torah and its commandments are imposed upon passive recipients; there is no human element either in revelation or in the products of revelation.

The classical Talmudic expression of the monologic view is the following account of the revelation at Mount Sinai: 'The Holy One, blessed be He, overturned the mountain [Mount Sinai] on them [Israel] like an [inverted] cask and said to them: If you accept the Torah it is well; if not, here shall be your burial place'.[3] Thus, revelation and its products – Torah and commandments – are imposed upon the people of Israel. The people have little choice but to accept the commandments of God. There is no dialogue; there is only a divine monologue. In the late Middle Ages, this text was interpreted to mean that God chose Israel for reasons known only to God; Israel did not initially freely choose God. The text was interpreted by means of a blunt analogy: God *raped* Israel; the covenant binding God to Israel was forced upon a reluctant people. Israel was coerced into passively accepting the covenant and its laws.[4]

The monologic view rejects the possibility of all but a passive role for the recipient of revelation. Even the prophet is but a passive vessel in the revelatory experience. Though the voice may be the voice of the prophet, it is really God who is speaking, utilizing the prophet's voice. The prophet is oblivious to his own prophesying. This view, for example, interprets the verse in Psalms, 'My mouth shall speak the praise of the Lord' (Ps. 145:21), to mean, 'My mouth only produces the words of the *Shekhinah* ... One who has reached this stage is a man who is no more than a channel through which the words of the Most High flow'.[5] When the prophet prophesies, he is unaware of what he is doing.[6] He is completely passive. God uses the organs of his body without his knowledge or consent. In the words of Philo of Alexandria, 'Nothing of what he says will be his own, for he that is truly under the control of divine inspiration has no power of apprehension when he speaks. He only serves as a channel for the insistent words of Another's prompting ... His organs of speech, mouth and tongue are wholly in the employ of another'. Both Philo and the Targum (the Aramaic rendition of Scripture) follow the view that the prophet is but a passive recipient of revelation. He may interpret what he receives to the people;[7] however, he may not supplement the message he has received. He enters into no dialogue with God.[8] In this view, the role of the prophet is compared to the role of a stenographer: God dictates and the prophet records.[9]

This view of revelation maintains that the Torah and its commandments are the dictates of God. As such, they can neither be questioned nor changed. They are only to be obeyed. The human being worships God, as a servant obeys his or her master, in passive obedience.

In medieval Jewish philosophy, the notion of the immutable nature of the Torah came to be considered a principle of Jewish faith. As God who gave the Torah is immutable and static, that is, perfect, so must the Torah have these qualities. As God is the source of truth, and the Torah is the repository of truth, its commandments must be objectively true and unchanging.[10] As truth is objective and monolithic, so must the commandments be monolithic. There can be but one Halakhic option. Truth is either/or; plurality of truth cannot exist. Truth must be exclusive; there can be only one correct answer to each question, specifically to each Halakhic question. For many medieval Jewish philosophers, truth and perfection went hand-in-hand. God is perfect, hence static. The Torah is perfect and true; ergo, it must be static. The Torah represents the divine will; therefore, for the Torah and its commandments to change would imply a change within God, which would entail compromising the perfection of God. God's will – as expressed in the Torah and its commandments and as articulated by Halakhah – cannot change, according to this view. For it to do so would imply a lack of divine perfection; to do so would imply that the Torah and its commandments are lacking perfection.

The view that Halakhah is objectively true and therefore static, apparently led Moses Maimonides and others to attempt to systematize and codify this objective truth. Since Halakhah is objectively true and immutable, there can be but a single correct Halakhic response to a given Halakhic question. Halakhah can only be monolithic; it cannot be pluralistic, since plurality in a Halakhic decision would imply a plurality of truths. The attempt made by Maimonides and others to codify Jewish law may be interpreted as an attempt to express the monolithic nature of Halakhah in a systematic form. In this view, just as revelation is monological and monolithic, devoid of any human (subjective) element, so must Jewish law – which expresses the concrete manifestation of revelation – have this quality. Those who attempted to codify Jewish law consciously defend the notion of law by objective standard rather than admit the presence of a subjective or social element in Halakhic decision.

As Maimonides' philosophical magnum opus was meant as a guide for the philosophically perplexed, his legal code, the *Mishneh Torah*, was intended as a guide for the Halakhically perplexed. In his philosophical works, Maimonides attempted to remove the impediments and confusions from one seeking philosophical certainty. In the *Mishneh Torah*, Maimonides attempted to remove the confusions from one seeking halakhic truth. He claimed to have extracted the Halakhah concerning each issue from the confusing maze of the Talmudic dialectic and from the labyrinth of post-Talmudic Halakhic literature. Holding to a monolithic view of the Halakhah, Maimonides was unwilling to admit the possibility of a plurality of Halakhic options. He claimed to have discovered the singularly valid Halakhah.

Just as Maimonides claimed to have reconstructed the certainties of Jewish philosophical speculation in *The Guide of the Perplexed*, so in the *Mishneh Torah* did he claim to have reconstructed the Halakhic certainties known by former generations. For Maimonides, the 'severe vicissitudes' of the 'exile' caused both philosophical and Halakhic certainty to have been lost. Maimonides, therefore, attempted to recover these lost certainties.[11]

In later attempts at codification, the concept of law by objective standard was reiterated. For example, in the sixteenth century, Joseph Karo consciously attempted to defend the notion of law by objective standard rather than admit the presence of a subjective element in the very code he composed. Though not consistent in practice with the plan he outlined in theory, Karo embraced a methodology that would guarantee automatic, objective decision on a given issue. Karo is, therefore, a representative of the trend that holds Halakhah to be autonomous and considers the process of Halakhic decision to embody a logic of its own.

As a commentator, Joseph Karo was bold, resourceful, and innovative; as a personality, he was saintly; but as a codifier, he was self-effacing. At least theoretically, Karo followed a methodology in his code that excluded the codifier – namely, himself – from the process of codification. His plan of self-effacement in his own code was not simply an expression of humility; it was part of his attempt to strip legal decision of its subjective element by making it solely dependent upon an objective standard and an objective methodology. For Karo, the objective standard was the consensus of the majority view of three scholars whom Karo considered the authoritative codifiers who preceded him: Isaac Alfasi (Rif), Moses Maimonides (Rambam), and Asher ben Yehiel (Rosh). The objective methodology Karo purported to employ virtually eliminated any subjectivity on the part of the codifier. All the codifier needed to do was find a consensus amongst the triumvirate just noted, or an agreement of any two of them, and that view was *the* Law.[12] Karo assumed that the attempts at codification produced by these three individuals represented the summary and quintessence of all that had gone before.[13] Therefore, while commenting upon the codes, one is free to examine and identify earlier sources; however, in the process of adjudication, the codes are to be considered as having superseded previous views, in that the codes represent the quintessence of all previous traditions and views. As the process of codification progressed, less and less text came to represent more and more of what came before. Whereas Karo's adjudication took into consideration the three great codifiers who preceded him, Halakhists who succeeded him had only one code – Karo's view – from which to adjudicate. By eliminating options for decision by means of codification and standardization, Halakhah became monolithic. One searched for *the* Halakhah, now clearly stated in the codes.

As part of his involvement with codification, the sixteenth-century Polish scholar Moses Isserles, advocated another criterion that served to stifle creative thought in Halakhic decision making and to obviate change on the basis of any factor, including contemporary social conditions and well-established past precedent. This element served to make the peculiar and particular the standard. Responses to particular problems or specific conditions in specific communities might become frozen as standard and as a precedent for future decisions. This element is Isserles' adaptation of the principle of 'following the most recent authorities' (*Halakhah ke-batre'ei*).[14] The adaptation of this approach, together with the process of codification, all but eliminated the possibility for the dynamic process of Halakhic decision to proceed.

For Moses Isserles, the most recently accepted view became standard. For Joseph Karo, the majority or consensus of three previous authorities automatically determined the law. Legal decisions became the product of an autonomous inner dynamic rather than an expression of law as a developing organism informed by socio-economic and historical factors. Accepted by individuals in subsequent generations, the approaches of Karo and Isserles, duly codified and frozen, led Jewish law to atrophy. The weight of whole traditions against 'the most recent authority' or against a paragraph in the *Shulhan Arukh* did not disconcert subsequent rabbinical figures. While recognizing that a trend a thousand years in the making may have been overturned by a comparatively recent decision and that the long-standing trend is more representative than the 'recent' decision, some modern Halakhists hold fast to Isserles' rule and timidly forbid themselves from overturning past individual authorities, even though that individual had overturned long-standing precedents and even though that precedent may simply represent a response to a particular social or historical situation.

From the notion of *halakhah ke-batre'ei* it is but a small jump to the notion of *gadol ha-dor* or *gadol be-Yisrael*. Once it can be presumed that final authoritative Halakhic decision making is vested in the most recent precedent, it is but a minor step to proceed to the idea that Halakhic authority may become vested in a single contemporary scholar in whom the entire Torah is virtually embodied. In this view, the *gadol be-Yisrael*, the great Halakhic authority, through constant Torah study, acquires a guaranteed authoritative response to every question and every situation. This person is presumed to make decisions inspired by God and free of error. He is not necessarily required to justify his views with reasoned argument or with adequate documentation from classical sources. Halakhah, thereby, becomes vested in a person rather than in a process. To be sure, it is difficult to find support in Halakhic sources for such an oracular view of the nature of Halakhic decision making.[15]

In recent times, these attitudes have come to characterize much of Orthodox Judaism. Grounded in an essentially fundamentalist theology, assuming a monologic theory of revelation, many contemporary spokespersons of Orthodox Judaism assume themselves to be in particular possession of the authentic, 'Torah-true' Halakhah. The codes, specifically the *Shulhan Arukh*, are considered authoritative. The Halakhah is considered divine and objectively true. The power to discern Halakhah is by means of consulting the code, and if such consultation is not fruitful, Isserles' standard of *halakhah ke-batre'ei* may be invoked. Though these methods theoretically prevail, in actual practice, the specific individual – the *gadol be-Yisrael* – who represents the quintessence of the tradition, who has mastered the methodology for Halakhic decision, is consulted. Thus, a prevalent view in Orthodox Judaism today is this first view – the monologic view – which seeks a single, irrefutable Halakhic decision.

The monologic view assumes that truth is regressive; that is, the further we get from the revelation at Mount Sinai by the passage of time, the further we get from the source of truth. This notion of historically degenerating truth finds its classical expression in the Talmudic citation: 'If the earlier scholars were like angels, we are like men; if they were like men, we are like asses'.[16] Thus, the authority of a *tanna* (an early Talmudic sage) is greater than any *amora* (a later Talmudic sage) simply because he lived at a time period closer to the revelation at Mount Sinai; the authority of an *amora* is greater than that of the *ga'onim* (post-Talmudic sages) for the same reason, and so on. In this view, since we are further from the truth than any previous generation, we are less competent at Halakhic decision than any previous generation. Therefore, we have to rely upon a book, a code, or a person that represents the quintessence of all that has gone before, and we are unable, therefore, to make any legal innovations. This rejection of the right to legislate or to make innovations is crystallized in the statement of the nineteenth-century Halakhist, Moses Schreiber: '*Hiddush assur min ha-Torah*' ('the new is taboo').[17]

One may note an implicit inconsistency in this approach. On the one hand, the most recent (or even contemporary) Halakhic authority is considered authoritative; on the other hand, truth and Halakhic authority are considered historically regressive. To claim that recent or current authorities represent the quintessence of all of that which came before does not alleviate this contradiction.

In the writings of Samson Raphael Hirsch, considered by many to be the 'father of modern orthodoxy', one finds a clear articulation of the monologic view. For Hirsch, revelation was understood to be the direct communication of the divine will. The role of the people is purely passive. They are merely the recipients of the divine commands, which, according to Hirsch, are as immutable as the laws of nature. As Hirsch considered revelation to be a monologue, he maintained that the products of revelation – Torah and commandments – are devoid of any human element. His fundamentalism was grounded in his view of revelation as a monologue.

His view of the static and unchanging nature of Halakhah was rooted in an essentially monologic view of revelation and a monolithic view of Halakhah.[18]

In more recent years, this approach was espoused by Joseph B. Soloveitchik. For Soloveitchik, Halakhic truth is objective in its nature. Halakhic truth is *a priori*. It exists independently of subjective or social concerns or realities. Halakhic truth is like mathematical truth and may be known with mathematical certainty. The function of the halakhist is not to discover but to uncover what is implicit. The Halakhist may not legislate, may not develop the law; the Halakhist may only elicit the inherently presumed truth of the law. Trained in the proper methodology, the Halakhist, of necessity, will elicit the correct conclusion in Halakhic decision. In this view, Halakhah is an *a priori* system of categories with an internal logic of its own. These categories may direct human affairs but must not be influenced by them. A particular Halakhic decision will be the same whether it is made in response to a specific social or individual human condition or whether it is simply a theoretical exercise. The Halakhah, being totally of divine origin, must be objective and autonomous, for only that which is objectively true may be constant and true in an absolute sense. The law proceeds on its own course, unaffected by social or intellectual fashion, unencumbered by any subjective disturbance.[19]

The Dialogic View

From its earliest to its most recent expression, the monologic view emphasizes the possibility of only a single Halakhic response to each Halakhic question. It is grounded in a monologic understanding of revelation. It encourages the need for Halakhic certainty through the compilation of codes of law considered to be both authoritative and binding. It seeks certainty by means of localizing and centralizing Halakhic authority in a code of law or in an individual whose views concerning the interpretation of law are considered singularly valid and binding. In contrast, the dialogic view understands revelation to be a dialogue between God and human beings. It assumes the presence of a human element both in the revelatory event and in the products of revelation – the Torah and its commandments.

The understanding of revelation as a dialogue and of the recipient of revelation as a partner in revelation is deeply rooted in biblical, rabbinic, and post-Talmudic literature. In contrast to the monologic view of the revelation at Mount Sinai, which understands the Torah to be imposed upon Israel, the dialogic view is that Israel freely accepted the Torah with the words 'we shall observe and we shall understand' (Exod. 24:3). From this perspective, revelation consists of two components: the giving of the Torah by God (*matan Torah*) and the receiving of the Torah by Israel (*kabbalat ha-Torah*). Without the second component, revelation is meaningless, devoid of impact. It is Israel's willingness to enter into the covenant, to enter into dialogue with God, that is essential to the revelatory event.[20] Revelation consists of a divine initiative and a human response, of God's commandments and of Israel's acceptance of those commandments. In this view, the Torah and its commandments are not imposed upon Israel. Rather, they are offered to Israel. The revelatory event is only complete when the Torah and its commandments are ratified by the people of Israel.

A Talmudic expression of the dialogic view of revelation is the interpretation of the verse in Proverbs (1:8): 'Hear, my son, the instruction of your father, and forsake not the teaching (*torat*) of your mother', where 'father' is said to refer to God, and 'mother' is said to refer to the community of Israel (*Knesset Yisrael*).[21] In this view, the Torah is revealed directly by God as well as through the community of Israel. Torah is the product of an ongoing dialogue between God and Israel. Accordingly, the dialogic view perceives the prophet as a 'partner in the work of revelation'. An example of this perspective is the text, 'Rabbi Judah says: ... the Holy One, blessed be He, said to Moses: Behold, I shall speak to you and you shall answer me'.[22]

The view that revelation is a dialogue between God and human beings, that there is a human element in the Torah, that the Torah contains the word of God but is not in its totality the word of God, led to a re-evaluation of the nature of the Torah in the medieval Jewish mystical tradition. The monologic view, which in medieval Jewish philosophy embraced the notion of the immutable Torah, was re-examined by the Jewish mystics who claimed that the Torah as it exists in its essential form, in the supernal world of the *sefirot* (divine potencies), is beyond human apprehension. In this world, they claimed, we only know the Torah in the form in which it appears to us. This form, necessarily adapts the characteristics of this world, specifically imperfection, change, and flux.

The idea that the Torah and its commandments, as we know them, are not objectively and absolutely true and static is an insight nurtured and developed in the Jewish mystical tradition. According to the *Sefer ha-Temunah*, the form that the Torah takes in this world is conditioned by the nature of the historical aeon that exists at present. Thus, while the essence of the Torah in the supernal realm is static, its form in our world is determined by the conditions of our world.[23] According to the *Zohar*, the Torah adopts a form peculiar to this world to become operative in this world.[24] According to Judah Loew of Prague, the commandments of the Torah will prevail for historical and for messianic times but will become obsolete in the spiritual dimension of the World-to-Come; the commandments are the matter of which the Torah is the form. They are accidental, while it is essential. Manifest in this world, the Torah must express itself in terms alien to its nature. Essentially supernatural, the Torah, as manifest in this world, must adapt characteristics that reflect the natural world of time, of history, of space, and of social conditions.[25]

According to the Lurianic mystics, the position of the philosophers – specifically Maimonides – that held the Torah as we know it to be perfect, immutable, and static, is grounded in an assumption that must be denied. As noted, the idea of the immutable, static Torah had assumed that nothing imperfect could emerge from God, who is static and perfect. The Torah, therefore, it was claimed, must be immutable, static, and perfect since it came from God. Under the impact of natural catastrophes, historical traumas, and moral evil, the Lurianic mystics rejected this assumption. The imperfect world, the world saturated with evil did emerge from the perfect God for reasons unfathomable to humans. The logical extension of this view is that the Torah too is imperfect in this world. The Torah is affected by conditions of this less-than-perfect world.[26] It must, therefore, deal with less-than-perfect human institutions. It must even deal with morally dubious human institutions, such as slavery.

According to Judah Loew of Prague, Moses had to break the first set of tablets because it represented the essential Torah, which cannot function in this imperfect world. A second set of tablets, embodying laws operative in this world, was needed. Imperfect laws are required in an imperfect world.[27] By their nature, God's laws in the natural, human world must be imperfect. They cannot be immutable, static, or objectively true. Being laws in history for human beings, they must inevitably embody a human, social, and historical element.

The view that the Torah embraces a human as well as a divine element precludes a fundamentalist position. The claim that the Torah, as it exists in this world, is not static and immutable, allows for the claim that revelation is continuous. From this perspective, change and development of the manifestation of the Torah in this world does not impugn divine perfection and does not imply a change in the divine will that compromises divine perfection. It only asserts that, while the Torah in essence may be immutable and represents absolute truth, the Torah as it is represented in this world is subject to the changes, developments, and vicissitudes of this world.

According to the dialogic view, the 'essential' Torah may reside in some supernal realm and may exhibit a static state of being; however, as manifest in this world, it is subject to continuous development and never-ending interpretation. Already in rabbinic literature, the notion that the Torah, being no longer in heaven, is subject to human interpretation, was stressed.[28] This ongoing process of interpretation was understood to be divinely sanctioned and even divinely inspired. The continuous development of the 'raw materials' of the revelatory experience by human beings was perceived as a fulfillment of a divine mandate and as an expression of the ongoing nature of revelation and of interpretation.

According to a Midrash, 'The Holy One, blessed be He, gave the Torah to Israel like wheat from which to derive fine flour or like flax to make a garment'.[29] In other words, the record of revelation – the sacred texts – are to be refined and developed by human effort. The human element is required to make the Torah whole (*shalem*). For the monologic view, the Torah is static, perfect. This view expresses a Greek philosophical notion of perfection. The dialogic view expresses a classical biblical and rabbinic view of perfection. Wholeness, completeness (*sheleimut*) is perfection. For the dialogic view, it is the continuous interaction of human beings with the Torah that makes the Torah whole, complete, perfect. It is through the continuous development and interpretation of the Torah that an event meant for all times (the revelation of the Torah at Mount Sinai) can speak at any time.

Just as God summons the prophet to be a partner in the ongoing process of revelation, God invites the Halakhist to become a partner in the ongoing processes of creation and revelation.[30] According to a Midrash, 'Not only did all the prophets receive their prophecy from Mount Sinai, but also each of the sages that arose in every generation received his [wisdom] from Mount Sinai'.[31] Commenting on the verse, 'According to the law which they shall teach you, and according to the judgment they shall tell you, you shall do'. (Deut. 17:11), Judah Loew of Prague noted, 'All that they [the sages] teach you are permitted to do, do it – for thus God commanded you'.[32]

Without the active presence of the human element, the Torah would be mute. God's word would be bereft of a presence in God's world. According to one commentator, the Torah is described as Israel's spouse because it is caused to conceive by the sages of Israel. In this way, the continuous birth and development of tradition are assured.[33] From the human perspective, truth is relative. For human beings, the truth is that the truth cannot be known, including the truth of the Torah.[34] As the early twentieth-century philosopher, Franz Rosenzweig, observed, truth is a noun only for God, for man it is but an adjective.

For God, contradictory opposites can be equally true. For human beings, however, a choice between alternatives must be made:

> The masters, the disciples of the wise, sit in manifold assembly and interpret the Torah – some pronouncing things permitted, some pronouncing the identical things forbidden. Should one ask: How in these circumstances shall I learn Torah, that is, how shall I learn what is the law?, one should answer him with the verse – 'All is given by one Shepherd' [Eccles. 12:11] – which means, One God gave them, one Leader uttered them, from the mouth of the Lord of all creation did they come. As it is written, 'God spoke *all* these things' [Exod. 20:1].[35]

Perhaps in the celestial realm, truth is absolute and monolithic. However, in the terrestrial realm, truth is not monolithic but is manifest in a plurality of modes. The human task is to apply what we can know to what we should do. The human concern is not with absolute truth but with applied truth, with operative truth. A 'heavenly voice' may inform us that contradictory views on the identical subject may both be true, may both be 'words of the living God', but the Halakhah for a specific issue or in a specific situation must be one way or the other; it cannot be both ways. Before truth can be implemented, a decision among options, even among equally valid options, must be made.[36]

Though truth through revelation is provided, human discretion in concrete situations is required.[37] Though two equally valid options may be provided, and though they both may be true 'words of the living God', only one can be appropriately applied to a specific situation at a given time and place. As Rashi (Shlomo Yitzhaki) explained, in such a case, 'there is no falsehood. Each view is true from its own perspective. "These and these are the words of the living God." In other words, at certain times this one applies, and at other times that one applies, for the change of times and of conditions determines which option applies to the situation at hand'.[38]

Once it leaves the celestial realm and becomes a citizen of the terrestrial realm, the future development of the Torah becomes vested in responsible human hands. The administration and the interpretation of the revealed word and will of God subsequently fall to human stewardship. Discerning the meaning of the Torah and explicating the truth of the Torah become the provenance of the responsible application of human knowledge and wisdom. According to a rabbinic text, when Moses requested Halakhic certainty, God responded by indicating that there can be no a priori certainty in Halakhic matters. God reminded Moses that the Torah contains multifaceted meanings and that the application of one or more of those possible meanings to a specific situation is vested in the majority view of the sages of each generation.

> The words of the Torah are not given as clear-cut decisions. For with every word which the Holy One spoke to Moses, and offered him forty-nine arguments by which a thing may be proven clean, and forty-nine other arguments by which the same thing may be proven unclean. When Moses asked:

> 'Master of the Universe, in what way shall we discern the true law?' God replied: 'The majority is to be followed [Exod. 23:2], that is to say, when a majority says it is unclean, it is unclean; when a majority says it is clean, it is clean'.[39]

In the commentaries to this text, God is quoted as saying to Moses, 'Were I to reveal to you the Halakhah, there would be no subsequent interpretation of the Torah. The process of interpretation would be stifled from the outset'.[40] As Rabbi Yannai said, 'Had the Torah been given in the form of incisive legal decision, we would have no leg upon which to stand',[41] which means, 'the Torah could never be established, for the Torah needs to be interpreted in various ways, all of which are the words of the living God'.[42]

In a similar vein, the fifteenth-century Spanish philosopher, Joseph Albo, observed, 'The law of God cannot be perfect so as to be adequate for all times, because the ever new details of human relations, their customs and their acts are too numerous to be embraced in a book. Therefore, Moses was given orally certain general principles, only briefly alluded to in the Torah, by means of which the wise men in every generation may work out the details as they appear'.[43] Consequently, the Halakhist's task is not to encapsulate the law in codes, not to fossilize the law in immutable *a priori* categories; the obligation of the Halakhist is to ensure the ongoing dynamic development of the law, to cause the 'sprouting of branches from roots'.[44] In other words, God does not reveal Halakhic decisions but Halakhic possibilities. The task of the sages of each generation is to discern Halakhic decisions for their own generation from among these many possibilities.

Because the dialogic view assumes the impossibility of knowledge of absolute truth in this world, it can embrace the notion that truth may take a plurality of equally valid forms. Only truths, and not *the* truth, can be vouchsafed to human beings. Consequently, Halakhic truth is never *a priori*, but is always *a posteriori*. Halakhic truth is evident in a variety of modes. The process of Halakhic decision making does not aim at discerning absolute truth but endeavours to posit the product of the dialogue between God's word and God's world, between divine revelation and human intelligence. This product cannot claim to be objectively true. It can only claim to be true within the confines of the human condition and within the parameters of specific historical conditions. As Aryeih Leib Heller, in his nineteenth-century commentary to the *Shulhan Arukh*, pointed out, 'The Torah was not given to the angels. It was given to human beings who possess intelligence. He gave us the Torah in conformity to the ability of the human mind to decide, even though it may not be the truth [objectively speaking], only that it be true according to the conclusions of the human mind ... Let truth emerge from the earth [Ps. 85:12], that is, the truth as the sages decide using human intelligence'.[45]

Codification

For a Halakhic decision to be reached, for a choice to be made in a specific situation from equally valid Halakhic options, the availability of those options have to be preserved. The process of codification tended to preclude all options but one. Codification tended to prune the tree of Halakhah rather than to encourage the sprouting of already-existing or of new branches. The monologic view, that seeks Halakhic certainty, that tries to establish objective Halakhic truth, encourages codification. The dialogic view, which assumes equally valid plural modes of Halakhah, rejects the claim of the codifiers that Halakhah can be expressed in absolute terms in binding and authoritative codes of Jewish law. Advocates of the monologic view consider codification an urgent desideratum aimed at establishing Halakhic certainty. Advocates of the dialogic view consider codification to be a danger to the diversity, the flexibility, and the creativity endemic to the very nature of Halakhah, and to the nature of the process of Halakhic decision making. While the monologic view aims at arriving at Halakhic certainty, by means of codifying Jewish law, the dialogic view strives to keep open the gates of Halakhic possibility. The opposition of advocates of the dialogic view to the codification of Jewish law is one characteristic of this endeavour.

Those who opposed codification (especially the *Mishneh Torah* and the *Shulhan Arukh*) did so for one or more of the following reasons.[46] First, the codes attempt to establish a single Halakhic view as *the* final Halakhic position on a given issue. The codes attempt to eliminate the possibility of equally legitimate and defensible Halakhic options. They attempt to make Halakhah monolithic. Second, the codes either claim or are understood to claim to represent the quintessence of the entire Halakhic tradition that preceded them. Their presumption of binding authority is grounded in that claim.

Those who opposed codification rejected the attempt to mould Halakhah into an exclusivist, monolithic structure. They maintained that the codes may claim to be the quintessence of the entire Halakhic tradition which preceded them, but in actuality that claim is fallacious. The codes are, therefore, neither authoritative nor binding. Though the codes merely express the predispositions of their respective authors in Halakhic matters, they attempt to establish a single Halakhist's interpretation as the Halakhic norm.

There is not, nor can there be, universal agreement with the author of a given code. This tenet is self-evident, given the existence of equally authoritative precedents on many Halakhic issues, and this has also become evident by the proliferation of various codes, each holding views in opposition to those maintained by other codes. The codes may claim to utilize an objective methodology in arriving at Halakhic decisions; but a close examination of the codes and of the responsa written by the authors of the codes clearly demonstrates that the codifiers often departed from their own purportedly objective methodologies. The codes, therefore, may claim to have removed the subjective concerns of their authors as a factor in Halakhic decision, but in actuality they did not do so. Thus, the codes represent the proclivities of their respective authors and should not be considered as binding.

Opponents of codification, advocating the dialogic view, maintained that, because the codes only represent their individual author's view, they threaten to establish their author's view as the norm, should the codes become accepted as the basis for Halakhic decision. This situation might eventually result in having a weak precedent or a minority precedent used by a codifier or the codifier's view unfounded in any precedent, becoming a precedent for future decisions. Furthermore, that most of the authors of the codes failed to justify their positions by identifying their sources calls the validity of their views into question. Their approach tends to exacerbate rather than to ameliorate the quality of halakhic decision. Halakhic decision of the codifiers cannot be accepted on faith. The documentation and the reasoning processes underlying their views must be made evident before one can seriously consider their views as being possibly correct.

Opponents of the codes also claimed that in establishing a single Halakhic option as the only halakhic option, the codes minimize the importance of local custom as a proper source for halakhic decision. In this expression of the dialogic view, the people have a role in 'making' Halakhah by means of the development of custom. Codification would eliminate custom as a basis for a number of equally acceptable Halakhic options. Finally, opponents of the codes maintained that the codes could not and should not be considered authoritative for the reasons already stated. The codes are merely an individual author's compilation of his or her views.[47] The codes are simply *guides*; they are not binding. As guides to Halakhic decision they may be consulted along with other sources. They only supplement, but do not supplant or replace, Halakhic decision.

As noted, the second claim levelled against the codifiers is that codification is intrinsically inimical to the Halakhic process. By taking a single precedent and elevating it into a norm, the codifiers disregard other equally valid precedents and even reject stronger precedents than the one they may be inclined to accept. Should the codified view become the norm, Halakhic judgments other than their own, though firmly rooted in precedent, would become disenfranchised in future Halakhic decisions. The historical and social conditions prevalent at the time of the codifier might become the basis for Halakhic decision at *all* later times and places. This undesirable result of codification, the opponents of codification maintained, must be contested.[48]

The opponents of codification perceived the codes as a threat to competent yet independent Halakhic decision. Once the codes are accepted, they claimed, scholars will become reluctant to oppose them. The Halakhic scholar will be replaced by a code, even though the particular scholar may be a superior Halakhist to the author of a specific code. Furthermore, as codification makes the law 'popular' and accessible to the masses, laypeople will read the codes and make Halakhic decisions for themselves based upon the views expressed in the codes. Thus, the authority of local scholars will be undermined. People will consult the codes rather than the scholars. Rabbis will rely upon the codes rather upon earlier sources, and the masses will be led to err. The quality of Halakhic scholarship among the rabbinate will suffer. A leading advocate of this position was the sixteenth-century Polish Halakhist, Solomon Luria. In opposition to Moses Isserles, he wrote, 'You [Isserles] wonder by what warrant I am empowered to bring certainty into the law. You impugn my authority to disagree with the codifiers. It is knowledge of the law which invests me with the prerogative to take issue with the halakhists and to expose their errors'. Elsewhere, Solomon Luria wrote, 'I shall acknowledge my error only in the event that you prove my decisions are not founded in the Talmud, or that my line of reasoning is not supported by the early *ga'onim*'.[49] In a similar vein in thirteenth-century Spain, Nahmanides (Moses ben Nahman), expressed this view in his glosses to Maimonides' *Sefer Ha-Mitzvot*:

> Notwithstanding my ardent desire to be a disciple of the earlier authorities, to establish and maintain their views, to [adorn myself] by making their [views] a gold chain about my neck and a bracelet upon my hand, I shall not serve them as a 'donkey carrying books'. I shall explain their methods and appreciate their value, but when their views cannot be comprehended by me, I shall debate before them in all modesty, I shall judge according to what appears best in my eyes ... for God gives wisdom in all times and in all ages.[50]

By opposing the claim that the codes are authoritative and binding, advocates of the dialogic view allow for the possibility of a subjective and a social element in Halakhic decision. In their view, the subjective element was especially important to prevent codification from stifling the dynamics of the halakhic process. The presence of the subjective element in Halakhic decision assured the possibility for continuous creative development of Halakhah. According to the Hasidic master Israel of Rhyzen, 'Why does the Torah have five books while the *Shulhan Arukh* consists of only four books? Where is the missing part of the law? – The missing part is the person. For, without the subjective human element, the Halakhah is incomplete'.

Because it assumed that the Halakhah is neither autonomous nor objectively true in any absolute sense, the dialogic view remained open to Halakhic flexibility and diversity. The acceptance of plural modes of Halakhic truth made possible and desirable the inclusion of historical, moral, social and economic factors in the process of

Halakhic decision making. As a result, the Halakhic scholar was permitted and encouraged to apply his learning and experience as well as his best personal judgment in reaching Halakhic decisions. Unlike the monologic view that seeks to eliminate the Halakhist and the external conditions characteristic of his time and place from the process of Halakhic decision, the dialogic view deems the personal judgment of the Halakhist, and the historical, social and economic conditions out of which that judgment came, to be crucial and necessary factors in the process of Halakhic decision making.[51] A review of the relevant literature demonstrates that an awareness of the need to integrate these factors into the Halakhic process has always been characteristic of Jewish legal tradition.

Custom

To accept and to advocate the inclusion of custom into a legal structure is to accept social factors as a basis for law and to enfranchise the people with a role in the initiation and development of law. From the perspective of the monologic view, this possibility is unacceptable and undesirable, as it threatens to undermine any view of the autonomous nature of Halakhah. To admit sociological factors as viable elements in Halakhic decision making is also in conflict with the monologic perspective because it would impose external factors upon the self-contained inner dynamic of Halakhic decision making. From the dialogic perspective, however, custom plays a crucial role in the development of Halakhah, for it articulates the necessarily dialogical role that the people are encouraged to play both in the revelatory experience and in the development of subsequent tradition. Precisely because the existence of a variety of equally valid customs articulates the notion of plural modes of Halakhic truth, the dialogic view embraces and encourages the initiation and the development of customs.

The problem of the relationship between custom and law in Jewish jurisprudence has a long and complicated history.[52] Nevertheless, one may distinguish among three attitudes related to this issue. The first attitude is that custom is inimical to law and that, when law clashes with custom, law always prevails; legal development must proceed oblivious to custom. This position is embraced by many advocates of the monologic view. The second attitude is that custom is a variety of law, and as such, it cannot clash with law. This position is held, for different reasons, both by advocates of the monologic and of the dialogic views. The third attitude is that custom can suspend and replace law in certain circumstances. This, essentially, is the position of the dialogic view.

Advocates of the monologic view largely sought to diminish the role of custom and to reject the claim that custom could triumph over law. For example, in one text, the twelfth-century Halakhist and grandson of Rashi, Jacob Tam (Rabbenu Tam), chided his colleagues for defending a custom as a replacement for an established law. He wrote, 'Even a proper custom does not uproot a law'. In this text, he also reminded his reader that the Hebrew letters of the word '*minhag*' (custom) are the same letters that when read backwards spell '*gehinnom*' (hell).[53]

The idea that custom is a variety of law was held by advocates of both the monologic and the dialogic views. For advocates of the monologic view, such as Moses Maimonides, only universally accepted, long-standing customs that did not impinge upon established legal precedent seemed to be considered in this regard.[54] Custom, for Maimonides, was a tightly circumscribed element that, in very specific circumstances, may become part of the law, part of Torah. For advocates of the dialogic view, however, custom is law, custom is Torah: '*minhag avoteinu, torah hu*' ('the custom of our forefathers is Torah').[55]

In a number of his responsa, the late thirteenth-century Spanish Halakhist, Asher ben Yehiel (Rosh), maintained that, in certain circumstances, '*minhag okeir et ha-halakhah*', ('custom uproots the law'), even when the law is of scriptural origin or of rabbinic decree (*takkanah*).[56] Similarly, the thirteenth-century German Halakhist, Meir of Rothenburg (Maharam), is quoted by a later source as having said, 'The customs of the community are Torah, even when such customs abrogate Halakhah'.[57] According to the twelfth-century French Halakhist, Abraham ben David (Rabad) of Posquieres, 'The only guiding principle we have is the custom of the people'.[58] The claim that 'the custom of our forefathers is Torah' harks back to the earliest forefathers, the biblical patriarchs. A Midrash notes, 'Rabbi Shimon bar Yohai said: Do not change the customs instituted by our forefathers, the biblical patriarchs'.[59]

Rabbi Jonathan found support for the validity of custom in the verse, 'Hear, my son, the instruction of your father, and forsake not the instruction (*torat*) of your mother' (Prov. 1:8).[60] Because custom derives specifically from one's own forebears, Nahmanides elevated the authority of custom by linking it to the commandment to honour one's parents.[61] The opinion that custom can supersede or replace law, in certain circumstances, has its roots in a statement found in the Palestinian Talmud: '*minhag me'vatteil halakhah*' ('custom abrogates law').[62] Consideration of the implications of this statement in Talmudic and medieval Jewish literature led to the establishment of certain parameters for the application of this principle. It was generally agreed, for example, that custom could supersede law in commercial matters and in most civil matters but not in the category of law known as 'the forbidden and the permitted'.[63] Nevertheless, advocates of the monologic view attempted to restrain the intrusion of custom into all areas of law.

Despite these efforts at constraint, the acceptance of custom as a law-making force in commercial matters opened a door for it to infiltrate and to influence change in other areas, such as laws related to marriage. While marriage laws clearly fell under the category of 'the forbidden and the permitted', there were certain commercial and civil documents and transactions connected to marriage, such as the dowry. The interpenetration at these points, between marriage law and commercial law, offered an entrée for custom to move into areas beyond that in which it was originally assigned propriety. From playing a tangential role in these expanded areas of its original purview, custom began to play a major role in almost all areas of Jewish law. From a limited role in commercial matters related to marriage, custom began to play a central role in introducing major changes with regard to Jewish marriage, for example, the prohibition of polygamy, the prohibition of concubinage, the fusing of the two ceremonies of *eirusin* (betrothal) and *kiddushin* (marriage) into one. In addition, social and economic conditions clearly play a role in these innovations, and in spite of the prohibition against following gentile practices (*hukkat ha-goy*), it is clear that gentile concepts and practices influenced these changes in Jewish law and practice.[64] Moreover, one should note that, without the notion of custom, the Jewish marriage would have no meaning.

A term often used to denote a law that has its origin in custom is the Hebrew word '*dat*'. In this regard, it is relevant to note that marriages are solemnized 'according to the *dat* of Moses and of

Israel'. In other words, a Jewish marriage comes into being because it is in accordance with the custom of the people of Israel. Even in the area of criminal law custom played a role. Though the Talmud established the rule that the punishment for defaming the character of another is corporal punishment in the form of whipping (stripes), this rule was abandoned when local practice had rejected its observance. In such a case, one is obliged 'to follow the [local] *takkanah*, and not to follow the Talmudic law'.[65]

A further principle that was generally accepted regarding custom was that custom may be invoked only to make the observance of the law more stringent but never to justify making it more lenient.[66] There was apparently a fear that if custom could replace any law, the intrusion of custom into law would eventually lead to the progressive abolition of all stringent laws. The fifteenth-century north African Halakhist, Solomon ben Simeon Duran (Rashbash), wrote, 'Were we to abolish laws prohibiting certain things as a result of the [contrary] *minhag*, then one by one all prohibitions would become permitted, and the whole of the Torah set at naught'.[67]

Notwithstanding this attempt to restrict the impact of custom, once it was deigned to have a role in legal decision, the dimensions of its influence broadened; the gates of restriction slowly opened. For example, Abraham ben David of Posquieres maintained that, while custom could not override a biblical prohibition, it could override a rabbinic prohibition. This position substantially broadened the power of custom in altering existing law and practice.[68] Once the place of custom in influencing law was established, the entire range of *halakhah* eventually became its domain.

That popular practice serves as the final arbiter where the law is uncertain is already established by the Talmud: 'Whenever the law is uncertain insofar as the court is concerned, and you do not know what one should do [literally: 'the state of the law'], go out and see how the people conduct themselves, and do likewise'.[69] However, it is clear that, historically, the role of custom was not limited to arbitrating conflicting legal opinions. Custom emerged as an independent law-creating force, sometimes overriding or supplanting existing legal precedent, and sometimes creating law *ex nihilo*. Particularly in the area of liturgy, the dynamism of legal creativity rooted in custom becomes evident.[70]

Customs initiated by local communities frequently became widely accepted practices; for example, mourner's Kaddish, *yahrzeit*, bar mitzvah, and breaking a glass at weddings.[71] Subsequently, rabbinic authorities searched the sources to find 'precedents' upon which to 'hang' them, and to justify their place in Halakhah.[72] If sources were unavailable, a presumption was made that they were once available but are presently obscured. For example, in his discussion of the practice of wearing a certain kind of sleeve on the Sabbath and holidays, the seventeenth-century German rabbi, Joseph Yuspa Hahn, in his *Yosif Ometz*, articulated this attitude when he wrote, 'All the customs of our ancestors are Torah. What we do not know can be accounted for as being due to the limitation in our own knowledge or the loss of earlier books during the persecutions that befell our leaders of blessed memory'.[73]

Once entrenched, custom was difficult to uproot. As Moses Isserles put it, 'One must never abolish any custom or scoff at it for it was not fixed without a purpose'.[74] Or, as Jacob ben Asher's fourteenth-century code, the *Arba'ah Turim*, succinctly states, 'it is forbidden to alter the customs of our forefathers'.[75] Moreover, custom not only stimulated the creation of laws but also reflected the abolition of established laws, as evidenced by the people's custom not to observe them. In other words, by ignoring certain laws, the people, in effect, legislated them out of existence. Those seeking to justify such neglect are wont to quote the Talmudic adage, 'Go out and see what people do'.[76]

Debate about the place of custom in Halakhah and about the role of the people in the creation of Halakhah extended into the modern period. In modern times, advocates of the monologic view have taken the position that custom plays no role in Halakhah, while advocates of the dialogic view argue for the place of custom in the Halakhic process. In the nineteenth century, the leading protagonists on this question were Samson Raphael Hirsch and Zacharias Frankel. The former is generally considered the father of neo-Orthodoxy, while the latter is considered the ideological parent of Conservative Judaism.

Hirsch stressed the direct communication of the divine will. The role of the people is purely passive. They are merely the recipients of the divine will. The source of all Jewish law is God's monologue rather than being an interaction between the human and the divine. Hence, custom, which represents the active and dynamic contribution of the people, could not be admitted as a valid source for Halakhic decision. Expressing the dialogic view, Frankel claimed that the people play an active role in the birth and development of Halakhah. This role is evidenced by the continual development of customs spontaneously created by the people. In Frankel's view, the people have a part to play in the process by which the laws, rooted in custom, become as binding as the word of God.[77]

According to early conservatives, who embraced the dialogic view and who articulated the concept of 'Catholic Israel'(*kelal Yisrael*), the law is embodied in the people; it is, therefore, neither progressive nor regressive. It continually develops as the people develop; it reflects the community out of which it emerges, out of the Jewish community, out of 'Catholic Israel'.[78] When this idea of 'Catholic Israel' was originally formulated, the majority of Jews were observant. It was offered as an alternative to the innovations made by Reform rabbinic synods and to the claim that the *Shulhan Arukh* was the ultimate Halakhic authority. Despite the impact this contention made and the option it offered, the idea of 'Catholic Israel' created more problems than it solved. It suggests that law is determined by the majority view among the people. As has been noted many times, this idea of 'Catholic Israel' if applied to the biblical period would mean that at the time of the biblical prophet Elijah, when most of the Jews worshipped Baal and only the minority worshipped God, the religion of Israel was in effect Baalism.[79] Thus, while this notion may have served a purpose in the times of Frankel and Solomon Schechter in their opposition to early reform, at a time when 'Catholic Israel' was religiously observant, it cannot be expressed with the same kind of force today when most Jews are not religiously observant. One would have to conclude that, if one were to assert this view today, it would follow that observance of the Sabbath and dietary laws, for example, ought to be abandoned simply because the majority of Jews today do not observe these traditions. Thus, Frankel's notion that 'Judaism is the religion of the Jews' is one fraught with difficulties.[80]

The redefinition of 'Catholic Israel' by Robert Gordis and others in the 1940s and 1950s is also beset with difficulties. These individuals have suggested that 'Catholic Israel' does not refer to all Jews, only to the majority of those Jews concerned with Jewish religious tradition and committed to its observance.[81] The problem with this claim is that, if this redefinition (by leading spokespersons for Conservative Judaism) were accepted by the Conservative Jewish movement, it would mean an implicit suggestion for its own dismantling since the majority of observant Jews today are not to be found within the ranks of Conservative Judaism but in the ranks of Orthodox Judaism. Thus, if 'Catholic Israel' in this definition primarily implies those drawn from the ranks of the Orthodox, the Conservative movement would become obliged to let orthodoxy decide what Jewish law and practice ought to be. Obviously, Conservative Judaism could not accept this posture, which would entail its dissolution. One may suggest, therefore, that the idea of 'Catholic Israel', as Frankel and Schechter employed it and as Gordis reinterpreted it, requires some rethinking. The concept of '*Catholic* Israel' as opposed to '*Reform* (as in 'Protestant') Israel' is no longer relevant. 'Catholic Israel', referring to the majority of Jews being Halakhically observant at present, is no longer accurate. Changes in social and historical circumstances which initially encouraged the articulation of the notion of 'Catholic Israel' have now weakened its impact as an idea useful in polemics. Nonetheless, certain aspects of the idea may still be effectively employed in the area of Jewish law. Specifically, 'Catholic Israel' may be reinterpreted as a concept denoting the social factor in the development of Jewish religious law. Though not the single determinant in the Halakhic process, 'Catholic Israel', so defined, represents *a* major source of Halakhic development and legislation.

The dialogic view recognizes that extra-Halakhic factors, such as social factors and conditions articulated as customs, have played and may continue to play a central role in Halakhic decision making. Similarly, the dialogic view recognizes that economic factors have played and may continue to play a decisive role in altering existing Halakhic norms and in establishing new ones. In addition, 'legal fictions' were often employed, and may be continued to be employed, to maintain the illusion that the requirements of law were being maintained while the actualities of practice were being altered. Examples of well-established legal fictions include the 'sale' of *hametz* (leaven) to non-Jews during Passover, the justification of a salaried rabbinate, the collection of interest on borrowed principal, the Jewish use of gentile wine (*stam yeinam*), and the rulings regarding *hefseid merubeh* (substantial financial loss) and *bateil b'shishim* in the context of the dietary laws.[82]

The obligation to consider the economic implications of Halakhic decisions, especially in the area of 'the forbidden and the permitted', was stated by the thirteenth-century French Talmudic commentator Menahem Meiri. 'It is improper for a sage to be excessively pious, seeking overmuch to be stringent and discovering justifications for it. He should rather consider the financial loss [involved]. For the Torah itself took this factor into consideration'.[83] Throughout the Middle Ages, Halakhic authorities provided justification for practices engendered by changing social, economic, and historical conditions, even in cases in which such practices conflicted with legal precedent of Talmudic or even of biblical origin.[84] Legal casuistry was often utilized to disguise such Halakhic alterations.

Changes of climatic conditions also served as a basis for changes in Halakhah. For example, Talmudic law established an unequivocal rule requiring one to eat and sleep in the *sukkah* (booth) during the Festival of Booths (*Sukkot*). However, because of the frequently unfavorable climatic conditions in northern countries, as in Poland, the custom to eat but not to sleep in the *sukkah* arose and subsequently became a sanctioned practice.[85] Because of cold weather, people kept a fire burning in their homes during the Sabbath. Occasionally, the fire spread, causing a threat to property. Despite Talmudic prohibitions against extinguishing a fire on the Sabbath where property is endangered, this prohibition was disregarded. The position of the thirteenth-century German Talmudic commentator, Mordecai ben Hillel, is instructive in this regard. He wrote, 'Nowadays, it is the practice in the majority of lands to put out a fire on the Sabbath, but this practice cannot be based upon any precedent ... [This practice is prohibited by Talmudic law and] there is no clear permission to allow this'.[86]

Rabbinic Legislation

The place of social, economic and other factors in modifying or altering practices required by legal precedent led to their role in establishing new practices, many of which were subsequently translated into law. The legal principle of 'nowadays' (*ha-idna*) articulated the view that new conditions require new legal rulings. Only the dialogic view could justify these possibilities. Furthermore, the institution of various forms of rabbinic legislation (*takkanot*) often derived from practices that originated in popular or local customs (especially community *takkanot*, *takkanot ha-kahal*).[87] Advocates of the dialogic view encouraged and defended these developments as legitimate expressions of social creativity and of historical and socio-economic influences on the continuing creation of Jewish law.

Codification aims at making the legal process self-sufficient, autonomous. However, for a legal system to develop throughout the ages, provision for legislation is necessary. In Jewish law, legislation takes the form of *gezerot* and *takkanot*.[88] Such legislation may be perceived as the second area (custom, being the first) where subjective elements enter into legal decision. A *gezera* is a restriction added by the sages to safeguard the observance of scriptural law. Such *gezerot* were even considered so important as to override a positive commandment of the Torah. For example, the shofar (ram's horn) is not sounded on Rosh Hashanah when it occurs on the Sabbath lest it lead to an infraction of a Sabbath ordinance, despite the fact that blowing the shofar on Rosh Hashanah is established by biblical command.[89]

Because of the difficulties attendant upon annulling past *gezerot*, some medieval Halakhists denied themselves the right to make new restrictions of this sort and retroactively restrict the making of *gezerot* to the Talmudic period.[90] One may use this position to defend two suggestions. First, that Halakhists today not be concerned with making *gezerot*, that is, with encumbering future generations with additional restrictions. Secondly, if one assumes that the authority to legislate *gezerot* is limited to the Talmudic period, then Halakhic decisions of the post-Talmudic period purporting to be *gezerot* would be denied that status. They would remain Halakhic options rather than difficult-to-repeal *gezerot*. But what about *gezerot* of the Talmudic period, such as those regulating relationships between Jews and Gentiles?

The effective repeal of such *gezerot* by means of the process of legal interpretation and not by simply claiming them 'invalid' may be accomplished. The successful medieval attempts to repeal strictures – economic and social – in the area of Jewish–Gentile relationships might stand as a model of repeal by means of interpretation. Consciously drawing a distinction between conditions of the rabbinic period and their own age, some medieval Halakhists, such as Menahem ha-Meiri, redefined 'Gentiles' to exclude Christians, thereby opening up the possibility for socio-economic relationships.[91] Hence, through exegetical exercises and by the process of interpretation, social and economic realities can influence the repeal of standing legislation in general and of the *gezerot* of earlier generations in particular. What is suggested is that present and future attempts to repeal standing *gezerot* on the basis of certain social, economic, or moral criteria should be modelled after the manner in which such repeals were affected by medieval scholars, specifically in the area of Jewish–Gentile relationships.

The second variety of halakhic legislation relates to *takkanot*. A *takkanah* is a new regulation instituted to cope with a new socioeconomic or historical situation or to improve compliance with existing Halakhah. Thus, a *takkanah* (pl.: *takkanot)* may either add new Halakhic restrictions or remove past restrictions. It may either expand or contract the scope of existing law. The goal of a *takkanah* is stated by the meaning of the term itself – 'to set aright'. While *gezerot* may be properly said to have ceased with the close of the Talmudic era, most authorities concur that *takkanot* extend from the Talmudic era into and throughout the Middle Ages and down to the present. One may distinguish, however, between *takkanot* of the Talmudic era and *takkanot* of subsequent times. A *takkanah* of the Talmudic era, generally speaking, was universally recognized by all Jewish communities, whereas a *takkanah* of post-Talmudic origin is usually applicable only with regard to a specific constituency.

Probably the best known post-Talmudic *takkanah* is the one attributed to the late-tenth, early eleventh-century rabbinic leader, Gershom of Mainz (called Rabbenu Gershom, the Light of the Exile), that banned polygamy among Ashkenazic Jews. It is now generally agreed that monogamy, established as the norm by this *takkanah*, was not an innovation he introduced but an established social practice of European Jewry in his time, which required a basis in legislation. In this case, as well as others, the *takkanah* represents the intrusion of socio-economic realities into the law. In the case of the ban on polygamy, the custom of the people became the basis for this *takkanah*. In this instance, we have an example of custom serving as the basis for legislation and rabbinic authority ratifying this legislation, which is an example of what was discussed above regarding custom and law. Monogamy became customary. Though rabbinic authority might have prevented custom from becoming law by invoking a veto based upon the idea that monogamy, since it rejects biblical precedent, is *minhag ta'ut* (mistaken custom) or, *hukkat ha-goy* (a custom derived from gentile influence) – certainly an accurate claim in this instance – rabbinic authority nevertheless decided to ratify this custom into practice.[92]

Thus a *takkanah* may simply formalize in law that which is already standardized in practice. Rabbinic judgment, albeit a subjective criterion, ultimately determines whether common behaviour becomes law. It is suggested that, in its application to specific problems, the *takkanah* be sparingly used. Indeed, even the *takkanah* regarding polygamy could have been avoided and the same aim as that intended by the *takkanah* accomplished by means of standardizing a 'monogamy clause' in the *ketubah* (marriage contract), as *genizah* fragments indicate was done in medieval Egypt.[93] One must sparingly use *takkanah* as one must sparingly use the constitutional amendment process in United States law. There is a danger of abuse. There is a danger of social whim becoming standardized through legislation, making enforcement and repeal difficult. The quick pace of changing contemporary conditions must be carefully considered before *takkanah* is undertaken. One must decide whether the particular social trend is worthy of being translated into law. One must evaluate a potential *takkanah*'s impact upon the rest of the legal system. One must consider how it will be interpreted by members of the lay community. Finally, one ought to be convinced that the social situation occasioning the *takkanah* will be of some considerable duration.

It is suggested that the idea of the post-Talmudic *takkanah* be somewhat reinterpreted along the following lines: whereas post-Talmudic *takkanot* were made for specific geographically cohesive communities, contemporary *takkanot* may be made for a specific 'community' or constituency not necessarily of the same *geographical* locale but having in common the recognition of an identical source of Halakhic authority. Thus, one might consider members of certain synagogal organizations to be members of the same 'community', though not in a geographical sense. *Takkanot* made by those considered the rabbinic authorities for that 'community' could be considered *takkanot* relevant only to that specific Jewish *community*. Secondly, it is suggested that a limit be placed upon the duration of ***takkanot***, for example, seven years. If the ***takkanah*** takes root, it will become standardized and need not be reasserted. It will become normative. If the ***takkanah*** does not take root, it will simply expire.[94] When the Halakhist 'legislates', when he 'makes' a ***takkanah***, the people serve as the final power of veto. They decide whether his or her view will be accepted into practice. When the people generate 'new law', the scholar's ***takkanah*** represents a ratification of 'legislation' by the people.[95] In the former case, the scholar interprets the 'written law' to extend the 'oral law'. In the second instance, the 'oral law' emerges first, retroactively seeking an anchor in the 'written law'.[96]

Conclusion

One might conclude that the monologic view, representative of contemporary Orthodox Judaism, is a theologically authentic expression of an historically defensible philosophy of Jewish law. However, as the preceding discussion demonstrates, the dialogic view, representative of the ideology of classical Conservative Judaism, is also a theologically authentic and an historically defensible philosophy of Jewish law. Though both of these approaches are theologically authentic and historically defensible, what remains to be determined is which of the two is more conceptually and pragmatically preferable. A number of arguments can be adduced to demonstrate how and why the dialogic view is the more desirable of the two.

According to the dialogic view, the Torah in its supernal essence may be static and perfect, but as it exists in this world, it takes on characteristics of this world, such as imperfection and change. The second set of tablets is all we have; the first set, representing the essential Torah, could not coexist with the terrestrial realm. This second set of tablets, this Torah, is neither perfect nor entirely divine, but is the word of God set down by human hands. In a sense, the monologic view tries to pretend that the original set of tablets never was shattered, that the Torah in our possession is the supernal, perfect, completely divine word of God, represented by the first set of tablets.

The thrust of historical research conclusively demonstrates that Jewish law is a continually developing, dynamic entity, characterized by constant elaboration, often brought about by changing social, economic and other factors. These findings accord with the position represented by the dialogic view. The claim of the monologic view that Halakhah is static, autonomous, and monolithic, that it is grounded in *a priori* truth, that it proceeds oblivious to subjective factors or to socio-economic conditions and developments, cannot be defended, either historically or on the basis of an appeal to Halakhic literature itself, as many of the sources noted above clearly demonstrate. Ultimately, the monologic view cannot be verified; it can only be taken on faith. It cannot account for the plurality of Halakhic views that have always abounded; nor can it account for the continuing changes in Jewish law occurring even today, even those that are accepted by the Orthodox Jewish community.[97]

In the nineteenth century, Jewish orthodoxy opposed many alterations then being introduced into Jewish law on the grounds that they were based upon extra-Halakhic categories, such as *hukkat ha-goy* (the following of Gentile practice).[98] In this regard, it should be noted that the interpenetration of the Jewish and non-Jewish communities had already stimulated countless changes in Jewish practice in times past, for example, monogamy, which became part and parcel of accepted Jewish practice. Furthermore, for Orthodox Judaism to challenge innovations based on extra-Halakhic categories such as *hukkat ha-goy* begs the question. Indeed, the very term "orthodox" is not a Jewish one, and the use of it by Orthodox Judaism could itself be considered from a Halakhic perspective as an articulation of *hukkat ha-goy*.[99] That Jewish orthodoxy itself could not function were it to operate consistently within the scope of the monologic view is evident from many examples that might be presented, but let one example suffice.

Without the acceptance of economic considerations and custom as bases for Halakhah, the contemporary rabbinate, including much of the Orthodox rabbinate, would not be able to function. The institution of a professional, salaried rabbinate in effect abolishes and supersedes unequivocal, firm precedent to the contrary.[100] Furthermore, the very basis for contemporary Halakhic authority, strongly defended by orthodoxy, is rabbinic ordination. However, it is clear historically that the rabbinic ordination of today is not that which was originally instituted in Talmudic times. It is instead based upon a custom with medieval roots. Hence, the very Halakhic authority that is used by advocates of the monologic view

– which denies the Halakhah-creating prerogative of custom – actually itself derives from custom.[101]

The attempt of the monologic view to vest halakhic decision in the codes or in the *gedolei ha-dor* cannot be defended. The claim that the authors of the codes and the *gedolei ha-dor* represent objectively true Halakhah – devoid of any subjective element – is not conceptually, historically or psychologically viable. As discussed above, neither the authors of the codes nor the contemporary *gedolei ha-dor* represent total objectivity. For instance, if the Halakhic process is an objective one akin to mathematics, then why does two plus two always equal four, while various Halakhists purporting to utilize identical methods and sources conflict with one another?

Neither a code of law nor a *gadol ha-dor* can serve as the final basis for Halakhic decision. Careful research into the development of a particular problem in the Jewish legal tradition would have to be undertaken. In the words of Judah Loew of Prague, to adjudicate decisions in Jewish law, not the 'signs' (*simanim*) of the codes, but the sources of the totality of Halakhic tradition must be consulted.[102] To make decisions in Jewish law, an examination into the development of a specific problem ought to be made. The views on all sides of the question, as they have appeared and reappeared down through the ages, should be identified. Once the plurality of trends on a given subject has been sorted out, these trends are to be examined in relation to the current social mood. If the current social climate and an identifiable trend in the Halakhic literature on a given subject agree, despite Halakhic norms currently in force, then the past trend may influence a change in current Halakhah.

Finally, it would be a mistake to claim, as do many contemporary advocates of the monolithic view within Orthodox Jewry, that the dialogic view – as it has been articulated by the founders of Conservative Judaism – is deviationist or anarchistic. That it is not deviationist, that it is representative of a firmly entrenched position within the history of Jewish theology and law, has been demonstrated in this chapter. That it is not anarchistic is clear from a consideration of a system of checks and balances that is endemic to the philosophy of law represented by the dialogic view. According to this system of checks and balances, the rabbis have the authority to veto specious practices developed by the people. On the other hand, by being unable to abide by decrees of the rabbinic authorities, the people may exercise a veto of their own. In the words of the Talmud, 'No decree may be imposed upon the community, unless a majority of the community is able to abide by it'.[103]

This interaction between the creativity of the people and the responsibility of the rabbinate allows for innovation and change without anarchy. When the spontaneity of the people embellishes the fabric of Halakhah, such creativity is to be encouraged. But when popular practice threatens to alter Halakhic essentials, when it promises to change the very nature of Halakhah, the rabbinic prerogative of veto should be invoked. As Asher ben Yehiel stated, 'one must not alter custom ... but if a custom is observed in various places, and in observing this custom one commits a sin, one must alter the custom, even if prominent scholars observed it'.[104] Furthermore, both in the areas of custom and *takkanah*, additional safeguards within this system of checks and balances may easily be introduced and implemented.

Before concluding, the exclusion of a consideration of Reform Judaism from the preceding discussion should be explained. To be valid, a theologically authentic and a historically defensible philosophy of Jewish religious law must be drawn from the sources that represent classical Jewish religious thought. Just as Jewish law, to remain authentic, cannot legislate fundamental practices out of existence, Jewish theology cannot arbitrarily dispense with fundamental beliefs. Among the fundamental beliefs of Judaism insofar as Jewish law is concerned, is the assumption that Halakhah is binding. By its denial of this claim, Reform Judaism moves itself beyond the boundaries of theologically or historically authentic Judaism.[105] The same could be said about current trends in Conservative Judaism where the binding quality of Jewish law is denied. Indeed, it would be difficult, if not impossible, for members of any community to speak meaningfully about a philosophy of law for that community unless the binding quality of that law upon that community is first assumed.

While the monologic and the dialogic views differ substantially, both are nevertheless defensible within the context of classical Jewish history, theology and tradition. The same cannot be said of the attitudes toward Jewish law that are representative of Reform Judaism and of some strands in the Conservative movement. Historically, one of the distinctions that differentiates between

Orthodox, Conservative and Reform Judaism is the following: Orthodox Judaism holds that both Halakhah and the codes are authoritative and binding; classical Conservative Judaism maintains that while Halakhah is binding, the codes are not, but represent precedents and guides to be used in Halakhic decision making; Reform Judaism maintains that neither the codes nor the Halakhah are binding.[106]

The monologic view, that vests Halakhic decision making in a central authority, be it a code or a person, requires no system of checks and balances. The dialogic view insists that a system of checks and balances between subjective judgment and objective precedents, between the creative spontaneity of the people and the responsible utilization of authority by the rabbinate, is necessary for dynamic Halakhic creativity and for preventing religious anarchy. The dialogic view maintains that 'the life of law has not been logic; it has been experience' (Oliver Wendell Holmes). It maintains that law reflects the human condition and must be infused with a human element. However, the dialogic view also realizes that law cannot relinquish its very nature by degenerating into pure subjectivity, by becoming *Gefühlsjurisprudenz* (law by sentiment) as advocates of Reform Judaism and increasing numbers of advocates of Conservative Judaism seem to suggest.[107]

In the Talmud, there is a case of a scholar who was called '*hakham*' (wise man), but was not called 'rabbi'.[108] Discussing this text, the nineteenth-century scholar, Joseph Hayyim of Baghdad, made this distinction between two forms of Halakhic decision making, which relates to the distinction between the monolithic and the dialogic views. In the first form, the Halakhist collects all available sources, weighs the pros and cons, and arrives deductively at a rule to be followed. This process, for Joseph Hayyim, exemplified the *hakham* who is not called 'rabbi'; it represents the necessary but insufficient Halakhist. Such an individual is insufficient as a Halakhist because he merely collects and sifts material, thereby arriving at a final ruling; but that ruling is not original; it is that of the authorities on which the *hakham* relies. On the other hand, the complete Halakhist, who also merits being called 'rabbi', collects and sifts past precedents and arrives at a final ruling that brings into play his intellectual skills, individual judgment, and personal creativity as applied to his knowledge of the law.[109]

The monologic view is admirable in its attempt to formulate a foolproof method for Halakhic decision making. Unfortunately, it is an impossible goal to attain. In the final analysis, Halakhic decision making, like all legal deliberation, is subject to subjective human judgment and open to human error. For the dialogic view though, it is precisely the opportunity to relate God's word to God's world, the challenge to apply judgment to learning and experience to scholarship, that characterizes the ongoing dialogue that commenced at Mount Sinai.

NOTES

1. See Franz Rosenzweig, *On Jewish Learning* (New York: Schocken, 1955), p.122, 'Only in the commandment can be the voice of him who commands be heard'.
2. The distinction between the 'monologic' and 'dialogic' approaches stated here is similar to the distinction made by Chaim Tchernowitz in his *Toledot ha-Poskim*, vols. 2 and 3 (New York, n.p., 1947). Tchernowitz identified two trends which he called 'the expansive trend' and the 'restrictive trend'. The former is roughly equivalent to the dialogic view that opposed codification while the latter is roughly equivalent to the monologic view that favoured codification. Though Tchernowitz's monumental work has been consulted in the preparation of the current discussion, it has not influenced the development of its ideas. The present discussion focuses on the relationship of theological views to philosophies of Jewish law, an issue that was not central for Tchernowitz.
3. *Shabbat* 88a.
4. The eternality of the covenant, of the enduring 'marriage' between God and Israel, is a theological non-negotiable in Jewish theology. This issue was a point of dispute between Jews and Christians in medieval theological polemics, Jewish theologians claiming that the marriage is eternal and unconditional and Christians claiming that God had divorced Israel for faithlessness and had taken another wife, the Church,as the 'New Israel'. In an apparent response to this Christian theological challenge, Jewish theologians sought a scriptural precedent for a marriage that could not be ended with a divorce. They found such an example in Deut. 21:10–14, with regard to a woman who had been raped and then married. Judah Loew of Prague and his brother, Hayyim ben Betzalel of Friedberg, utilized this motif both as a justification of the eternality of God's covenant with Israel and as an example of the coercion of Israel into the covenantal relationship. See Byron L. Sherwin, 'In the Shadows of Greatness: Rabbi Hayyim ben Betsalel of Friedberg', *Jewish Social Studies* 37:1 (1975): 56–7.
5. This citation is from the works of Uziel Meisels, a disciple of the Hasidic master Dov Baer, the Maggid of Mezeritch. The translation is that of Louis Jacobs in his *Hasidic Prayer* (New York: Schocken, 1972), p.122. On this theme, Abraham J. Heschel, *Torah min ha-Shamayim,* vol. 2 (London: Soncino, 1965), pp.215–17, 264–67, 335–37, 344–48.
6. *Midrash Tehillim* [*Midrash on Psalms*], S. Buber (ed.) (Vilna: Romm, 1891), 90:4, p.194.
7. The Targum translates '*navi*' (prophet) as '*meturgemanakh*' (interpreter). See *Targum Onkeles* and Rashi to Exod. 7:1, in standard editions of Hebrew Scripture with commentaries.
8. Abraham J. Heschel, *The Prophets* (Philadelphia: Jewish Publication Society, 1962), pp.335–37. Harry Wolfson, *Philo* (Cambridge, MA: Harvard University Press, 1947), vol. 2, pp.22–43.
9. See *Baba Batra* 15a; *Sifrei–Devarim* [*Sifrei on Deuteronomy*], Louis Finkelstein (ed.) (Berlin: Jüdischer Kulterband in Deutschland, 1939), para. 357, p.427.
10. Louis Jacobs, *Principles of the Jewish Faith* (New York: Basic Books, 1964), pp.302–7.
11. Moses Maimonides, *The Guide of the Perplexed*, trans. Shlomo Pines (Chicago: University of Chicago Press, 1963), 'Introduction to Book Three', pp.415–16; Maimonides, *Mishneh*

Torah, Saul Lieberman (ed.) (Jerusalem: Mosad ha-Rav Kook, 1964), 'Introduction', pp.13–14.

12. Joseph Karo, *Beit Yosef, 'Introduction'* in *Jacob ben Asher, Arba'ah Turim* (New York: Grossman, n.d.), sec. *Orah Hayyim*, unpaginated introduction.
13. See the extensive discussion in Isadore Twersky, 'The *Shulhan Arukh:* Enduring Code of Jewish Law', *Judaism* 16 (1967): 141–59.
14. On this principle in Jewish law, see discussion and sources noted in Menahem Elon, *Ha-Mishpat ha-Ivri* (Jerusalem: Magnes Press, 1973), vol. 1, pp.232–36, and, *Encyclopedia Talmudit* (Jerusalem: Talmudic Encyclopedia Publishing, 1984), vol. 9, pp.141–45. On Moses Isserles' use of this principle, see Elon, p.235; Twersky, 'The *Shulhan Arukh*', p.147, and, Asher Siev, *Rabbi Moses Isserles* [Hebrew] (New York: Yeshiva University Press, 1972), pp.158–59.
15. Louis Jacobs, *A Tree of Life* (New York: Oxford University Press, 1984), p.77; Alan J. Yuter, '*Mehizah*, Midrash and Modernity', *Judaism* 28(1979): 147–59; Ze'ev Falk, *Law and Religion* (Jerusalem: Mesharim Publishers, 1981), pp.142–43, 148.
16. *Shabbat* 112b.
17. Moses Schreiber, *Sefer Hatam Sofer* (Vienna: n.p., 1892–1895), secs. *Orah Hayyim*, no. 28, *Yoreh Deah*, no. 19.
18. See the discussion of Hirsch in Louis Jacobs, *Principles of the Jewish Faith*, pp.291–315; Louis Jacobs, *A Jewish Theology* (New York: Behrman House, 1973), pp.215–18; Isaac Heinemann, *Ta'amei ha-Mitzvot be-Sifrut Yisrael* (Jerusalem: n.p., 1956), vol. 2, pp.91–161.
19. Joseph B. Soloveitchik, '*Ish Ha-Halakhah*', *Talpiot* 1 (1944):651–734. See also his 'The Lonely Man of Faith', *Tradition* 7 (Summer 1965): 5–67; and his *The Halakhic Mind* (New York: Macmillan, 1986). For a presentation and analysis of Soloveitchik's views, see e.g., Lawrence Kaplan, 'The Religious Philosophy of Rabbi Joseph Soloveitchik', *Tradition* 14 (Fall 1973): 43–65. For a brutal critique of Soloveitchik's view, see e.g., Ze'ev Falk, *Law and Religion*, pp.156–64; Jacob Agus, *Guideposts in Modern Judaism* (New York: Bloch Publishing Co. 1954), pp.37–44. It is noteworthy that the attempts of Soloveitchik's grandfather, Hayyim Soloveitchik of Brisk, to impose his 'method' on Halakhah and the correlative attempt to analogize Halakhic method with scientific method were condemned by early twentieth-century Orthodox Halakhists for 'bringing a foreign spirit into the Oral Law and of causing more harm than good'; see sources quoted by Jacobs, *A Tree of Life*, pp.59–60.
20. Abraham J. Heschel, *God in Search of Man* (Philadelphia: Jewish Publication Society, 1955), pp.259–61. These two perspectives on revelation, monologic and dialogic, passive and participatory, are identified by Heschel as being characteristic of the schools of Rabbi Akiva and Rabbi Ishmael respectively. According to Heschel, Rabbi Akiva considered the prophet a passive recipient of revelation while Rabbi Ishmael considered the prophet an active partner in the revelatory experience; see Heschel, *Torah min ha-Shamayim*, vol. 2, pp.264–99.
21. *Berakhot* 35a.
22. *Mekhilta de Rabbi Yishmael*, Jacob Lauterbach, ed. and trans. (Philadelphia: Jewish Publication Society, 1933), sec. *Ba-Hodesh*, chap. 2, p.207.
23. See the comprehensive article by Gershom Scholem, 'The Meaning of the Torah in Jewish Mysticism', in *On the Kabbalah and its Symbolism*, trans. Ralph Manheim (New York: Schocken, 1965), pp.32–87.
24. *Zohar* (Vilna: Romm, 1882), vol. 3, p.152a.
25. Byron L. Sherwin, *Mystical Theology and Social Dissent* (Oxford: Oxford University Press, 1982), pp.70–82.
26. This notion is developed further by David Weiss-Halivni, 'Revelation and *Zimzum*', *Judaism* (Spring 1972): 205–11.
27. Sherwin, *Mystical Theology*, pp.121–22.
28. *Baba Metzia* 59b.
29. *Seder Eliyahu Rabba ve-Seder Eliyahu Zuta*, Meir Friedmann (ed.) (Vienna: Ahiyasaf, 1904), sec. *Zuta*, chap. 2, p.172.
30. See *Shabbat* 10a, and Jacob ben Asher, *Arba'ah Turim*, sec. *Hoshen Mishpat*, beginning.
31. *Exodus Rabbah* 28:6; see also *Midrash Tanhuma [Ha-Nidpas]* (Jerusalem: Levin-Epstein, 1964), sec. *Yitro*, no. 11, p.96.
32. Judah Loew, *Gur Aryeih* (Jerusalem: Yahadut, 1972), vol. 5, p.83.
33. See *Sifrei–Devarim* [*Sifrei on Deuteronomy*], Meir Friedmann (ed.) (Vienna: n.p., 1865), no. 345, n. 8.

34. Moses Nahmanides, *Kitve Rabbenu Moshe ben Nahman* [*Commentary to the Torah*], Charles B. Chavel (ed.) (Jerusalem: Mosad ha-Rav Kook, 1959), sec. 'Introduction', vol.1, p.3.
35. *Hagiga* 3b.
36. *Erubin* 13b.
37. Commentary of Samuel ben Meir (Rashbam) to *Baba Batra* 130b, 131a, in standard editions of the Talmud.
38. Rashi to *Ketubot* 57a, in standard editions of the Talmud.
39. *Midrash on Psalms* 12:4, p.54.
40. *Midrash on Psalms* 12:4 is a variant of *Palestinian Talmud*, *Sanhedrin* 4:2. This citation is derived from the commentaries to the latter text, Moses Margaliot's *P'nei Moshe* and Jacob David of Slutzk (Ridbaz), in standard editions of the Palestinian Talmud.
41. *Palestinian Talmud*, *Sanhedrin* 4:2.
42. Moses Margaliot's eighteenth-century commentary, *P'nei Moshe* to *Palestinian Talmud, Sanhedrin* 4:2. Also see Yom Tov ibn Asevelli (Ritba)'s fourteenth-century commentary, *Hiddushei ha-Ritva* to *Erubin* 13a, in standard editions of the Talmud.
43. Joseph Albo, *Sefer ha-Ikkarim – The Book of Principles*, ed. and trans. Isaac Husik, (Philadelphia: Jewish Publication Society, 1930), vol. 3, p.203. See also, Nahmanides, *Kitve Rabbenu* [*Commentary to the Torah*], vol. 2, p.376 on Deut. 6:18, and, Vidal Tom Tov of Tolosa's fourteenth-century commentary *Maggid Mishnah* on Maimonides' *Mishneh Torah* (New York: Friedman, 1963), *Sefer Kinyan*, sec. *Hilkhot Shekheinim*, 14:5. One may detect the influence of Aristotle who claimed that 'law is always a general statement'; see Aristotle, *Nichomachean Ethics* 5.10.4, 1137b, and *Politics* 3, chap. 15, para. 4, 1286a.
44. Responsum no.97 of Abraham the son of Maimonides, quoted in Elon, *Ha-Mishpat ha-Ivri*, p.345.
45. Aryeh Leib Heller's nineteenth-century commentary, *Ketzot ha-Hoshen*, on Karo, *Shulhan Arukh – Hoshen Mishpat* (Lwow: n.p., 1888), 'Introduction'. See also, Louis Jacobs, 'Rabbi Aryeh Laib Heller's Theological Introduction to his *Shev Shema Tata*', *Modern Judaism* 1 (September 1981): 184–217, and, Tchernowitz, *Toledot ha-Poskim*, vol.3, pp.246–52.
46. For literature on this problem, see Elon, *Ha-Mishpat ha-Ivri*, pp.938–1213; Tchernowitz, *Toledot ha-Poskim*, vol. 3; Isaac Zev Cahana, *Mehkarim be-Sifrut ha-Teshuvot* (Jerusalem: Mosad ha-Rav Kook, 1973), pp.8–96; Siev, *Rabbi Moses Isserles*, pp.268–96; Byron Sherwin, 'In the Shadows of Greatness', pp.43–47; Sherwin, *Mystical Theology*, pp.178–80; Isadore Twersky, *Rabad of Posquieres* (Cambridge: Harvard University Press, 1962), pp.128–98; Elliot Dorff and Arthur Rosett, *A Living Tree* (Albany: SUNY Press, 1988), pp.366–402.
47. The idea that the codes were written as private compilations for their authors meant for their personal use only and not for widespread distribution was noted by Hayyim ben Betzalel of Friedberg and his brother Judah Loew of Prague. In a letter to Joseph ibn Aknin, Maimonides noted that his original intention in composing his code was to have a compilation of Halakhic views only for his own private use; see Moses Maimonides, *Kovetz Iggrot ha-Rambam*, 2 vols. (1859; reprint, Jerusalem, n.p., 1967), vol. 2, p.30c.
48. According to Judah Loew, it is better that one – even a novice in Halakhah – make a faulty decision based upon a review of Talmudic and other sources than make a correct decision based only upon the codes; see Judah Loew, *Netivot Olom*, (New York: Judaica Press, 1969), sec. *Netiv ha-Torah*, chap. 15, p.69. See also Asher ben Yehiel, *She'eilot u-Teshuvot ha-Rosh* (Jerusalem: n.p., 1965), 31:9, p.31a. Judah Loew's view is in direct conflict with that of the early twelfth-century Spanish halakhist Joseph ibn Migash, who greatly influenced Maimonides. According to ibn Migash, it is preferable to make an incorrect decision based on the codes – especially if one is a novice in Halakhah – than to try to make a decision based on complicated Talmudic sources; see Joseph ibn Migash, *Responsa* [Hebrew] (Jerusalem: Gitler, 1959), no. 114, p.17.
49. See Solomon Luria, *Yam Shel Shlomo* (Stettin: Shrenzel, 1861), sec. *Baba Kamma* 8:72, 2:5; Solomon Luria, *Responsa* [Hebrew] (Lublin: n.p., 1774), no. 16. Simon Horwitz, *The Responsa of Solomon Luria* (New York: Bloch, 1968), p.14. See also, Moses Isserles, *Responsa* [Hebrew], Asher Siev (ed.) (Jerusalem: n.p., 1970), no.6.
50. Nahmanides, *Commentary to Maimonides' Sefer ha-Mitzvot* [Hebrew], printed in Moses Maimonides, *Sefer ha-Mitzvot* (Jerusalem: Levin-Epstein, 1965), 'Introduction', p.3. This translation is from Twersky, *Rabad*, pp.217–18.
51. For contemporary attempts to articulate philosophies of Jewish law that approximate what is termed here the 'dialogic view', see Eliezer Berkovits, *Not in Heaven* (New York: Ktav,

1983), especially chapter two; Jacobs, *Tree of Life*; Eliezer Berkovits, *Ha-Halakhah: Koha ve-Tafkidah* (Jerusalem: Mosad ha-Rav Kook, 1981).

52. On custom (*minhag*), see Elon, *Ha-Mishpat ha-Irvi*, pp.713–67; Menahem Elon, '*Minhag*', *Encyclopedia Judaica*, Cecil Roth (ed.) (Jerusalem: Keter, 1971); Cahana, *Mekhkarim be-Sifrut ha-Teshuvot*, pp.108–17; Burton Leiser, 'Custom and Law in Talmudic Jurisprudence', *Judaism* 20 (1971): 396–403; Joseph Kalir, 'The Minhag', *Tradition* 7 (1965): 89–95; Chaim Tchernowitz, *Toledot ha-Halakhah* (New York, n.p., 1945), vol. 1, pp.144–51; Alexander Guttmann, '*L'She'eilat ha-Yahas Minhag-Halakhah be-Tekufat ha-Talmud*', *Bitzaron* (1946): 192–99; Joel Roth, *The Halakhic Process* (New York: Jewish Theological Seminary, 1986), pp.205–31.

53. Joshua Boaz, *Shaltei ha-Gibborim* to the Mordecai, in standard editions of the Talmud, '*Gittin*', para. 444, where a responsum of Jacob Tam of Orleans is recorded.

54. See Moses Maimonides, *Hakdamah le-Peirush ha-Mishnah*, Mordecai Rabinowitz (ed.) (Jerusalem: Mosad ha-Rav Kook, 1961), sec. 5, p.41; Maimonides, *Mishneh Torah – Sefer Shofetim*, sec. *Hilkhot Mamrim*, 1:2–3, 2:2–5. In his discussion of custom in the *Mishneh Torah*, Twersky notes, 'Inasmuch as he [Maimonides] envisaged his code as fulfilling a universal role, his standards had to transcend localism or nativism'. See Isadore Twersky, *Introduction to the Code of Maimonides* (New Haven: Yale University Press, 1980), p.127; also see pp.124–34 on Maimonides' treatment of custom. In considering custom as a variety of law and not as an extra-legal entity, Maimonides may have been influenced by the Greeks; see Boaz Cohen, *Law and Tradition* (New York: Ktav, 1969), p.47, n. 27. Blackstone, in his classification of British law, also considered custom a variety of law. See also Benjamin Cardozo, *The Nature of the Judicial Process* (New Haven: Yale University Press, 1921), pp.58–60. It is perhaps ironic that had Isserles' glosses containing Ashkenazic custom not been incorporated into the printed text of the *Shulhan Arukh*, Karo's code would not have gained universal Jewish acceptance. In a sense, this consideration for custom furthered the aims of codification.

55. Moses Isserles in the name of the late-thirteenth-century Halakhist, Jacob Moelin (Maharil), in his glosses to Karo, *Shulhan Arukh*, sec. *Yoreh De'ah* 376:4, in standard editions of the *Shulhan Arukh*; Judah Loew, *Netivot Olom*, sec. *Netiv ha-Avodah*, chap. 7, p.97; Jacob ben Asher, *Arba-ah Turim*, sec. *Orah Hayyim*, para. 619 (end); see para. 551 (end): 'It is forbidden to alter the custom of our forefathers'. See also *Tosafot* on *Menahot* 20b, in standard editions of the Talmud. Note, Moses Isserles, *Responsa*, no. 20, p.130; no. 51, p.250; no. 132, p.512.

56. Asher ben Yehiel, *She'eilot u-Teshuvot ha-Rosh*, no. 101:1, p.94, with regard to giving 'stripes' for defamation of character. See also *Kiddushin* 28a.

57. See the responsum of the thirteenth-century German Halakhist, Samson ben Zadok Duran, *Responsa Tashbeitz* [Hebrew] (Lwow: n.p., 1891), 2:63. See also Isserles, *Responsa*, no. 19, p.127, 'Even in times of persecution, custom should not be altered'. Isserles, in this responsum, referred to the fifteenth-century Halalkhist Joseph Colon, *Responsa Maharik* [Hebrew] (Venice, 1519), '*Shoresh*' no. 9, '*Anaf*' no. 3, who says, 'We follow custom even if it means going against the law, for custom is established according to the sages of the place'.

58. Cited in Twersky, *Rabad of Posquieres*, p.241.

59. *Midrash Mishlei*, Solomon Buber (ed.) (Lwow: n.p., 1893), 22:38, p.47a.

60. *Pesahim* 50a; see also Asher ben Yehiel, *Arba'ah Turim*, sec. *Orah Hayyim*, para. 551.

61. See Tchernowitz, *Toledot ha-Halakhah*, vol. 1, p.145.

62. *Palestinian Talmud – Baba Metzia* 7:1; *Palestinian Talmud – Yebamot* 12:1. See also *Soferim* 14:8: 'People have adopted the following procedure, that is, that no ruling is authoritatively laid down unless a custom has been definitely established. As regards the sayings of the rabbis that a custom abrogates a law, it applies to a custom that has no support from the Torah and is therefore an error in judgment'.

63. See Elon, *Ha-Mishpat ha-Ivri*, pp.724, 738, 739. On the influence of custom over law in the area of communal taxation, see Karo, *Shulhan Arukh*, sec. *Hoshen Mishpat*, para. 163, and the long discussion there in Abraham Zevi Eisenstadt's nineteenth-century commentary, *Pithei Teshuvah*, nos. 1, 16; see also Elon, *Ha-Mishpat ha-Ivri*, pp.746–49. On other commercial areas, see Steven M. Passamaneck, *Insurance in Rabbinic Law* (Chicago: Aldine Publishing Co., 1974), pp.170–71. For examples, see Isserles, *Responsa*, no. 20, p.130; no. 51, p.250.

64. Zev W. Falk, *Jewish Matrimonial Law* (New York: Oxford University Press, 1966), pp.1–86; H. J. Zimmels, *Ashkenazim and Sephardim* (Oxford: Oxford University Press, 1958), pp.6, 166–81.

65. Asher ben Yehiel, *She'eilot u-Teshuvot ha-Rosh*, no. 101:1, p.94.
66. Moses Maimonides, *Mishneh Torah – Sefer Zemanim*, sec. *Hilkhot Shevitat Assor*, 3:3; Maimonides, *Teshuvot ha-Rambam* (Tel Aviv: Mekitzei Nirdamim, 1934), nos. 25, 33, pp.22, 30.
67. Solomon ben Simeon Duran, *Responsa Rashbash*, nos. 419, 562, cited in Cahana, *Mekhkarim be-Sifrut ha-Teshuvot*, p.115.
68. Abraham ben David of Posquieres (Rabad)'s gloss to Maimonides, *Mishneh Torah – Sefer Zera'im*, sec. *Hilkhot Ma'aser Sheini*, 1:3, in standard editions of the *Mishneh Torah*.
69. *Palestinian Talmud – Peah* 7:5 end, *Palestinian Talmud – Ma'aser Sheini* 5:2 end, *Palestinian Talmud – Yebamot* 7:3; *Berakhot* 45a, *Erubin* 14b, *Menahot* 35b, *Pesahim* 54b. Note that in the Palestinian Talmud the citation ends with the injunction, 'and do likewise', unlike the Babylonian Talmud which just recommends surveying popular practice. Thus, for the Palestinian Talmud, custom is more a law-making force than it is for the Babylonian Talmud. On the role of custom in arbitrating legal decisions, Asher ben Yehiel, *Sh'eilot u-Teshuvot ha-Rosh*, no. 55:10, p.53: 'As the Palestinian Talmud teaches – when the Halakhah is uncertain, follow custom. This means that if there is an uncertainty, and it is unclear according to whom the Halakhah is to be decided, observe the common practice, that is, follow custom. One may rely on the fact that if notable [Halakhists] practice this custom, it must be in accordance with Halakhah'.
70. Elon, *Ha-Mishpat ha-Ivri*, p.738; Zimmels, *Ashkenazim and Sephardim*, pp.109–15; Herman Pollack, *Jewish Folklore in Germanic Lands* (London: MIT Press, 1971), especially pp.125–26, 167–68. Liturgical changes inspired by the Kabbalah were introduced, especially in the late Middle Ages and by the Hasidim; see Jacobs, *A Tree of Life*, pp.82–91, and *Theology in the Responsa* (London: Routledge and Kegan Paul, 1975), pp.123, 183, 334–7.
71. Solomon B. Freehof, 'Ceremonial Creativity Among the Ashkenazim', *Jewish Quarterly Review*, 75th Anniversary Volume (1967): 210–14.
72. The Talmud describes the many laws derived from scant scriptural reference as 'mountains hanging by a hair', see *Hagiga* 10a–11a.
73. Cited in Pollack, *Jewish Folklore in Germanic Lands*, p.161. For a similar view, see Moses Schreiber, *She'eilot u-Teshuvot Hatam Sofer* [Hebrew] (Vienna: n.p., 1883–1895), sec. *Yoreh De'ah*, no. 191, p.74a, and *'Orah Hayyim'* no. 51, p.186; H. J. Zimmels, 'The Significance of the Statement "We are not acquainted anymore,"' in *Leo Jung Jubilee Volume* (New York: n.p., 1962), pp.223–35.
74. Karo, *Shulhan Arukh*, sec. *Orah Hayyim*, 690:17; see commentary there of Judah Ashkenazi, *Be'er Heitev*, n. 15.
75. Jacob ben Asher, *Arba'ah Turim*, sec. *Orah Hayyim*, para. 551 end.
76. Jacobs, *A Tree of Life*, p.228.
77. Jacobs, *Principles of the Jewish Faith*, pp.297–8.
78. The influence of German romantic philosophy upon proto-Conservative nineteenth-century Jewish thought is clearly evident. See Mordecai M. Kaplan, *Greater Judaism in the Making* (New York: Reconstructionist Press, 1960), pp.354–57; David Rudavsky, 'The Historical School of Zecharia Frankel', *Jewish Social Studies* 5 (1963): 224–44.
79. Schechter often used the term 'Catholic Israel', which seems to have been coined by Isaac Leeser.
80. Jacobs, *Principles of the Jewish Faith*, pp.297–298.
81. Robert Gordis, 'Authority in Jewish Law', *Proceedings of the Rabinical Assembly* 8 (1941–1944): 78–81.
82. To my knowledge, Louis Ginzberg was the first modern Jewish scholar to examine the role of economics in Jewish law. His investigations, however, were largely limited to the Talmudic period. See Louis Ginzberg, 'The Significance of Halacha for Jewish History', in his *On Jewish Law and Lore* (New York: Atheneum, 1970), pp.77–127. Ginzberg was followed in this approach by Louis Finkelstein and others. On the role of economic conditions in Halakhic decision making in the medieval period, see Jacob Katz, *Exclusiveness and Tolerance* (New York: Schocken, 1962), pp.3–67. The first important precedent regarding economic considerations and Halakhic change was probably the *prosbul*; see *Mishnah*, *Shevi'it* 10:3–4, *Gittin* 36a–b.

    The institution of a legal fiction providing for the sale of *hametz* (unleavened bread) to a non-Jew during Passover seems to have originated as a result of economic conditions in late medieval central Europe where Jews in the business of manufacturing liquor from grains could not economically survive divestment of their stock of grain during Passover. This practice, apparently introduced for a specific commercial group, at a specific historical time, led to a popular and common practice in subsequent periods. See Joel Sirkes' seventeenth-century commentary, *Bayyit Hadash*, to Jacob ben Asher, *Arba'ah Turim*, sec. *Orah Hayyim* 448:1, in standard editions of the *Arba'ah Turim*. It may be noted that the use of legal fictions was more prevalent among Ashkenazic than Sephardic Jews.

On the clash between Judah Loew and Moses Isserles on the question of whether economic factors can play a role in Halakhic decision making, particularly on the issue of Jewish use of gentile wine, see Sherwin, *Mystical Theology*, pp.94–102. Loew opposed the intrusion of economic considerations into Halakhic decision making, while Isserles was a leading advocate of considering economic conditions in the process. For example, on Isserles' use of the principle of *hefseid merubeh*, see his glosses to Karo, *Shulhan Arukh*, sec. *Yoreh De'ah*, 31:1, 32:5, 35:5. Isserles even permitted Jewish peddlers to sell Christian religious items. For other discussions of economic considerations in legal decision, see Zimmels, *Ashkenazim and Sephardim*, pp.54, 199–200, 207–17, and Solomon Zucrow, *Adjustment of Law to Life in Rabbinic Literature* (Boston: Stratford, 1928), pp.54–74, 75–100.

83. Menahem Ha-Meiri, *Beit ha-Behirah – Hullin* (Jerusalem: n.p., 1970), p.164.
84. The idea that changed conditions lead to changed laws crystallizes in the notion of '*ha-idna*', 'nowadays'. See especially *Tosafot* to *Beitzah* 6a. Also see discussion and sources noted in Immanuel Low, '*Ha-Iddana*', *Hebrew Union College Annual* 11 (1936): 193–206. There was a belief that even human nature and anatomy changed. For example, it was believed that in ancient times children matured more quickly than in medieval times, and were able to propagate at the age of eight. See *Tosafot* to *Sanhedrin* 69a, Meir Schiff's commentary to *Sanhedrin* 69a, in standard editions of the Talmud, and Solomon Luria, *Yam Shel Shelomo*, sec. *Baba Kamma* 7:37.
85. *Mishnah, Sukkah* 2:1; Isserles' gloss to Karo, *Shulhan* Arukh, sec. *Orah Hayyim*, 639:2.
86. See *Mishnah, Shabbat* 16:1; *Shabbat* 116a, and Mordecai ben Hillel to *Shabbat*, no. 393, in standard editions of the Talmud.
87. On *Takkanot ha-Kahal*, see Isaac Levitas in *Encyclopedia Judaica*, entry '*Takkanot*'.
88. On *gezerot* and *takkanot*, see Elon, *Ha-Mishpat ha-Ivri*, pp.367–713.
89. *Rosh ha-Shanah* 29b.
90. Asher ben Yehiel, *Tosafot ha-Rosh* (in standard editions of the Talmud) to *Shabbat* 164a, writes: 'Behold I am amazed at how the *gaonim* could innovate a *gezerah* after Rav Ashi completed the Talmud'. See *Encyclopedia Talmudit*, vol. 5, pp.530–40.
91. Katz, *Exclusivness and Tolerance*, pp.24–36.
92. See for example, the custom of *kapparot*. Though many authorities opposed it and even condemned it as a pagan custom, it was nonetheless retained. See Karo's *Beit Yoseif* to Joseph ben Asher, *Arba'ah Turim*, sec. *Orah Hayyim*, 605.
93. Mordecai Friedman, 'The Monogamy Clause in Jewish Marriage Contracts', *Perspectives in Jewish Learning*, Volume Four, Nathaniel Stampfer (ed.) (Chicago: Spertus College of Judaica Press, 1972), pp.20–40.
94. Compare Cardozo, *The Nature of the Judicial Process*, p.178: 'What is erroneous is pretty sure to perish. The good remains the foundation on which new structures will be built. The bad will be rejected and cast off in the laboratory of the years'.
95. Maimonides, *Mishneh Torah – Sefer Shofetim*, sec. *Hilkhot Mamrim*, 2:6–7.
96. The claim that aspects of the 'oral law' might have preceded the 'written law' is presented by Yehezkel Kaufmann in his *Toledot ha-Emunah ha-Yisraelit* (Tel Aviv: Mosad Bialik, 1966), especially vol. 8, p.346. What Kaufmann claims about the development of Jewish law in its earliest epoch is at least equally true of later eras.
97. On the whole question of plural modes in Halakhah see Jakob Petuchowski, 'Plural Modes within Halakhah', *Judaism* 19 (Winter 1970): 77–90, and the rejoinder by Walter Wurzburger, 'Plural Models and the Authority of Halakhah', *Judaism* 20 (Fall 1971): 390–96; Eugene Borowitz, 'Subjectivity and the Halachic Process', *Judaism* 13 (Spring 1964): 211–20, and Jacob B. Agus, *Dialogue and Tradition* (New York: Abelard Schuman, 1971), pp.555–61.

The clear divergence between the monologic and the dialogic views as expressed respectively by advocates of Orthodox and Conservative Judaism is apparent in the following excerpt from an evaluation of the Conservative *Beit Din*'s decision concerning the role of women by a leading spokesperson for American Orthodox Judaism. He begins by quoting the statement of the chairman of the Rabbinical Assembly's Committee on Jewish Law and Standards, which accompanied the decision on women. 'The approach to Jewish law in Conservative Judaism has always been to change existing norms where they do not further ethical or spiritual values. When an existing norm reflects a world-view or social situation that no longer exists, then the Halakhah is modified'. The spokesperson for Orthodox Judaism responds as follows: 'These sentiments belie a lack of recognition of the fact that Halakhah possesses an enduring validity which, while applicable to changing circumstances, is not subject to change by lobbying or by the exertion of pressure in any guise or form ... Normative Judaism teaches that Halakhah is not derived from any temporal "world view" or "social situation" but expresses the transcendental view of the Divine Lawgiver'. See J. David Bleich, 'Women in a *Minyan*?' *Tradition* 14 (1973): 117.

Orthodoxy would be unable, for example, from the perspective of the monologic view, of justifying such recent innovations as proclaiming Israel Independence Day as a religious holyday that sets aside certain observances of *sefirah* (the spring mourning period) and introduces new liturgical elements. Yet it does so.

98. *Eleh Divrei ha-Brit* (Altona: n.p., 1819).
99. Jacobs, *A Tree of Life*, p.243.
100. On the institution of a professional, salaried rabbinate, see Jacobs, *A Tree of Life*, pp.148–50 and sources noted there.
101. See Isserles' gloss to Karo, *Shulhan Arukh*, sec. *Yoreh De'ah*, para. 242:12. Note, Zimmels, *Ashkenazim and Sephardim*, p.273. Compare Sherwin, *Mystical Theology and Social Dissent*, pp.167–68; R. J. Zwi Werblowsky, *Joseph Karo* (Philadelphia: Jewish Publication Society, 1977), pp.122–7. See also J. Newman, *Semikah* [*Ordination*] (Manchester: N.p., 1950).
102. Judah Loew, *Netivot Olom*, sec. *Netiv ha-Torah*, chap. 15.
103. *Baba Kamma* 79b, *Horayot* 3b. See *Palestinian Talmud, Shabbat* 1:4: 'Every decree which is decreed on the community, but which is not accepted by the majority of the community, is no decree'.
104. Asher ben Yehiel, *She'eilot u-Teshuvot ha-Rosh*, no. 55:10, p.53. See also *Pesahim* 56a and *Tosafot* to *Baba Batra* 2a. Compare Maimonides, *Responsa*, no. 25, p.22.
105. In recent years, the liberal wing of Conservative Judaism has also taken the position that Halakhah is not binding but is only a guide to religious observance. Those who have taken this view have thereby rejected the ideology of the founders of Conservative Judaism and have embraced the ideological position characteristic of Reform Judaism.
106. As far as I know, the first person to call himself a 'Conservative Jew' was a rabbi from Vienna named Szanto. He attended the 1871 Augsburg Synod at which the question of whether the composition of a new *Shulhan Arukh* was desirable was discussed. The Orthodox position clearly was that the *Shulhan Arukh* is legally binding and authoritative and need not be replaced. The Reform position was that Halakhah is not binding, and therefore any code is altogether unnecessary. Szanto, however, identified himself as a 'Conservative Jew', which he defined as one who holds that Halakhah is binding but the codes are not authoritatively binding. He therefore spoke against the composition of a new code. See David Philipson, *The Reform Movement in Judaism* (New York: Macmillan, 1907), pp.452–53. This position was also endorsed by Boaz Cohen in 'The *Shulhan Arukh* as a Guide for Religious Practice Today', in his *Law and Tradition*, pp.62–100. This represents a rejection by Cohen of his earlier view (1935) that held the codes to be binding, see his *Law and Tradition*, p.59. In the 1880s, the Conservative camp was divided between those who accepted Halakhah and the codes as binding and those who accepted *halakhah* as binding but not the codes. The former group, represented by individuals such as Sabato Morais, eventually joined the orthodox camp, while the latter group, represented by individuals such as Alexander Kohut, stayed in the conservative camp and helped it develop during its critical period of reorganization. See Moshe Davis, *The Emergence of Conservative Judaism* (Philadelphia: Jewish Publication Society, 1963), pp.231–39. Before the Conservative–Reform split, the reason why Orthodoxy opposed the position that considered the codes no longer binding is understandable as it was often tied together with a rejection of Talmudic authority.
107. Cardozo, *The Nature of the Judicial Process*, p.106. The quote from Holmes is cited from his *The Common Law*; see Cardozo, *The Nature of the Judicial Process*, p.33.
108. *Baba Metzia* 85b–86a.
109. See Louis Jacobs, 'Rabbi Joseph Hayyim of Baghdad', in Arthur Chiel (ed.), *Perspectives on Jews and Judaism* (New York: Rabbinical Assembly, 1978), p.191.

CHAPTER EIGHT

Theologies of the Jewish Holidays

Losing one's memory means losing one's mind. To remember is to re-mind. Bereft of certain remembrances, one becomes dismembered from the divine, from one's own self, from one's past, from one's faith -community.[1]

For Judaism, faith is memory; recall of the past is a call to faith in the present. As Abraham Heschel has written:

> When we want to understand ourselves, to find out what is most precious in our lives, we search our memory ... That only is valuable in our experience which is worth remembering. Remembrance is the touchstone of all actions. Memory is a source of faith. To have faith is to remember. Jewish faith is a recollection of that which happened to Israel in the past ... Recollection is a holy act: we sanctify the present by remembering the past.[2]

No absolute command to believe is given in Hebrew Scripture. Rather, memory of events, of experiences, is prescribed. The handing on of the faith tradition from generation to generation is vested in the transmission of experienced events through memory. For example, a verse in Deuteronomy (4:9) reads: 'Take heed to yourself diligently, lest you forget the things your eyes saw, and lest they depart from your heart all the days of your life, make them known to your children and your children's children'. The prophets of Israel did not formulate creedal propositions. Rather, they offered memories of moments illuminated by the divine presence. They did not enjoin the people to define God, but to witness the divine presence in history. God asked Israel to be a people of witnesses to God (Isa. 43:10), not a committee of definers of God.

In his classic work *Kuzari*, the medieval poet and philosopher, Judah Halevi, observed that the Ten Commandments do not begin with a creedal proposition, but with a memory of an experienced event: 'I am the Lord your God who brought you out of the land of Egypt, out of the house of bondage' (Exod. 20:1). For Halevi, faith is rooted in the memory of events. Tradition's task is to transmit experience as memory.[3] Memory makes the past present, the future possible. The foundation for faith in the present is forged by the perpetuation of certain memories of the past. As Deuteronomy (32:7) tells us: 'Remember the days of old, consider the years of ages past; ask your father, he will inform you, your elders, they will tell you'.

Observance of many Jewish feasts and fasts offers a prime example of the nexus between faith and memory. Already in the biblical period, the process of transforming the nature festivals of Mesopotamia into commemorations of remembered events in Israel's history had begun.[4] For example, the festival of *Aviv* (Spring) was transformed into Passover, a festival commemorating the Exodus from Egypt (Exod. 13, Deut. 16:3). By the first century, it seems that the nature festivals of Mesopotamia's polytheistic and pagan cult had been re-formed to comply with the monotheistic and demythologized features of Israelite faith. Nature-festivals were celebrated as harvest festivals, with recognition of divine grace through sacrifice and celebration at the Temple in Jerusalem as a major motif. Commemoration of historical events was present, but not yet dominant. However, after the destruction of the (Second) Temple, the motif of memory and commemoration prevailed. Once severed from their land and from the Temple cult, the Jews focused upon the historical features of the festivals. Indeed, in the diaspora, even the Land of Israel and the Temple cult entered the orbit of the people's cherished memories.[5]

Rabbinic Judaism transformed Israelite faith into a based on history religion. The memories of Israel's past were firmly embossed upon the festivals that comprised the Jewish liturgical year.[6] As the eminent Jewish historian, Salo W. Baron, put it: 'It is well known, for instance, that the ancient Israelite festivals were taken over from the earlier cultures of Canaan and Babylonia. But in each case ancient Judaism changed the fundamental meaning of the festival first by adding to it, then by substituting for its natural an historical interpretation'.[7]

Similarly, as Heschel observed:

> To Israel the unique events of historic time were spiritually more significant than the repetitive processes in the cycle of nature, even though physical sustenance depended upon the latter. While the deities of other peoples were associated with places or things, the God of Israel was the God of events: the Redeemer from slavery, the Revealer of the Torah, manifesting Himself in the events of history rather than in things or places.[8]

Remembrances of the formative events in Israel's biblical past—the Exodus from Egypt and the revelation at Sinai – became prominent features of holy day observance. For example, the summer harvest festival, *Shavuot*, or Pentecost, designated by Scripture as the 'feast of ingathering' the wheat harvest and the summer fruits (Exod. 34:22, Numb. 28:26) became identified by the rabbis as the anniversary of the revelation of the Torah at Sinai.[9] The Jewish liturgy identifies this festival as 'the time of the giving of the Torah'.

The association of *Sukkot*, the Feast of Booths, (Lev. 23:34) with the fall harvest was overshadowed by its identification with the booths in which the Israelites dwelt during their sojourn in the wilderness after the liberation from Egypt (Lev. 23:41–43). Though both the agricultural and the historical origins of this festival are stated by Scripture, the historical meaning subsequently became dominant. The 'booth' was now more closely identified with historical memory of the desert experience, and less strongly identified with the booths in which the field workers would dwell during the harvest. Here, too, nature gave way to history.

On Passover, the memory of the Exodus became the central motif. The Sabbath, the day of rest, is also associated with the Exodus. Slaves have no Sabbath. According to a verse in Deuteronomy (5:15), one should observe the Sabbath as a means of remembering Egyptian slavery and the liberation from bondage. Though the Sabbath is also a commemoration of creation, the link with the memory of freedom from slavery provided an experiential referent that a focus on creation could not offer: that Israel participated in the Exodus, but only God witnessed the creation of the world. The Jewish liturgy for the Sabbath preserves referents both to the Exodus and to Creation.[10]

Holy days such as Purim – the Feast of Lots, Hanukkah and

Tisha B'Av (the ninth day of the Hebrew month of Av, a day of national mourning) – had clear historical references from the outset of their celebration. Purim refers to the events narrated in the biblical story of Esther. Hanukkah refers to the liberation from oppression by Syrian Hellenists. *Tisha B'Av* is linked to the destruction of the Temple in Jerusalem as well as to other tragedies in Jewish history.[11] Even the apparently a-historical occasion of the Jewish New Year (*Rosh ha-Shanah*), denoted by Scripture as a Day of Remembrance (Lev. 23:24) (though the object of remembrance is not stated) is described by the Talmudic rabbis, and later by the liturgy, either as the anniversary of the creation of the world or as the anniversary of the creation of the first human being.[12]

Reflection upon the role of remembrance in the Jewish liturgical year yields a variety of insights into the nature of Jewish faith. Because faith is articulated as memory, and because memory of the formative events of ancient Jewish history is identified with the Jewish holy days, it should not be surprising to find that central concepts of Jewish theological concern are associated with the religious festivals. Thus, the structure of Jewish theology is not systematic, but liturgical. As the nineteenth-century rabbi, Samson Raphael Hirsch, put it, the Jewish liturgy is Judaism's catechism. Celebration of the Jewish festivals conveys the Jewish theological agenda. For example, Passover relates to redemption, Pentecost to revelation, *Sukkot* (the Feast of Booths) to divine providence, Sabbath to creation, *Tisha B'Av* to theodicy.[13]

Theological concepts and concerns are not permitted to remain abstract propositions. Rather, they are communicated as specific memories through festivals of celebration and remembrance. For Judaism, theological concepts never atrophy into abstract creeds because they are continuously being vocalized through deeds. The function of rituals associated with the various Jewish holy days is to internalize in the life of each member of the people the memory of an event in the life of the people. Consider, for example, this citation from the Passover Haggadah:

> In each generation, each individual should consider himself or herself as if he or she was redeemed from Egypt, as it is said, 'It is because of what God did for *me* when *I* went free from Egypt' (Exod. 13:8). For the Holy One redeemed not only our

ancestors, but *us with them*, as it is said, 'God took *us* out of there to bring us to the land promised to our ancestors' (Deut. 6:23). Therefore, we must ... praise God who ... took *us* from slavery to freedom.[14]

The liturgy for the Seder, the Passover meal, is called Haggadah, 'telling'. This relates to the biblical injunction to pass down memories of experiences to one's children: 'You shall tell to your child on that day: It is because of what the Lord did for me when I went free from Egypt' (Exod. 13:8). History is remembered; it is retold; but it is not re-enacted. Tradition is passed down by the telling within linear time. Re-enactment, on the other hand, aims at obliterating time. The goal in Jewish ritual is to remember and not to re-enact an event.[15] The uniqueness of the event can be recited, but not repeated. However, what can be re-enacted is the *meaning* of the event. Indeed, for the tradition to continue, for the story to have perpetual and perpetuated meaning, it must be internalized.[16]

By the internalization of memory through ritual, we become our ancestors' contemporaries. Present and past converge at the moment of celebration and commemoration. Memory is the stimulus, and, ritual and liturgy are the vehicles that bind past and present, ancestor and descendant, ancient experience and contemporary faith. The expectation that commemoration of the Exodus would bring about a personal as well as a communal experience of liberation is expressed by the Hasidic master, Nahum of Chernoble. He suggests that two types of liberation are necessary for Passover observance to be considered complete. One type celebrates the liberation of Israel from Egypt. The second type is the liberation of each person from that particular thing that enslaves him or her. Unless the individual liberates himself or herself from his or her own particular Egypt, the celebration of Passover is not complete.[17]

The Hebrew word for memory is *zakhar*. But memory does not merely signify mental recall, it includes a call to action. Not affirmation of dogmas, but evocation of deeds, is the meaning of this term. Liturgy and ritual serve as vehicles to prevent memory from deteriorating into an abstract reminiscence. Remembrance through observance of the festivals suppressess the proclivity toward abstract theological speculation, toward intellectual voyeurism devoid of commitment. As Abraham Heschel put it, 'An esthetic experience leaves behind the memory of a perception and enjoyment; a prophetic experience leaves behind the memory of a commitment'.[18]

In his analysis of the syntax of the word *zakhar,* 'remembrance', in Hebrew Scripture, the biblical scholar J. Pedersen observed that *zakhar* does not refer to an 'objective memory image of some thing or event, but that this image is called forth in the soul and assists in determining its action ... Therefore, *zakhar* may also mean to begin an action, to proceed to something, as when Elihu says, "Proceed (*zekhor*) to magnify God's work, which people sing of" (Job 36:24)'.[19]

This understanding of *zakhar* as memory pregnant with action, as memory as a directional signal for the performance of particular deeds, is found in a variety of classical Jewish sources. For example, in the first Hasidic book, the *Toledot Ya'akov Yosef,* Jacob Joseph of Polnoyye wrote: 'In every place in Scripture where one finds the commandment to remember, one is commanded to perform a specific deed whereby one links memory to action, as in the commandment of the fringes (see Numb. 15:37–41) and those like it which are like a knot [on one's finger to remind one] not to forget [to do something]'.[20]

Memory is a call to action, to commemoration. However, the call is directed to those who share a memory of an event. For example, the command to commemorate the Exodus is addressed to those who experienced it. As the text in Exodus reads:

> This day shall be for you one of remembrance; you shall celebrate it as an institution for all time (Exod. 12:14) ... Remember this day, on which you went free from Egypt, the house of bondage, how the Lord freed you from it with a mighty hand; no leavened bread shall be eaten (Exod. 13:3) ... And you shall explain it to your son on that day: It is because of what the Lord did for me when I went free from Egypt' (Exod. 13:8; also see Deut. 16:1–8).

In this view, participation in the life of the community is a prerequisite for commemorating events in the history of that faith-community. For example, the Passover liturgy tells of four sons. Of these, the wicked son asks: '"What does this ritual mean to you?" (Exod. 12:26), that is, to you and not to him. Since he excludes himself from the community and denies God's role in the Exodus, you should confront him and say: "This is done because of what God did for me when I went out of Egypt" (Exod. 13:8). For me and not for him. Had he been there he would not have been redeemed'.

Rejection of the memories bequeathed to us is a form of spiritual self-disinheritance. One can only pity the person who fails to hear the melody of memory. In this regard, commenting on the biblical description of the revelation of the Torah at Sinai, the Hasidic master, Moses Hayyim Ephraim of Sudlykow, told this tale:

A certain man played so exquisitely on a violin that anyone who heard his playing could not be restrained from dancing. The closer one was to the sound of the music, the stronger the urge to dance and the greater one's pleasure and joy from the music. Once, a deaf person came around. He did not see the person playing the violin, and because he was deaf, he could not hear the music. All he saw were people dancing in joy and ecstasy. He muttered to himself, 'They are mad. They are mad'.[21]

Participation in the life of a faith-community means participation in its memories. It entails being able to discern the nuances of its medley of memories. To participate means to act, to observe, to celebrate. Memories are pregnant with action. Memories that do not stimulate action are stillborn. For Judaism, there is no faith without correlative deeds, without observance of ritual and law (Halakhah).

The continuity of a faith community depends upon its ability to perpetuate its memories. Memory is then simply the retelling of what we once knew, of what we once experienced. According to a midrash, the souls of all future generations of Jews stood at Sinai with the generation of the Exodus to receive the Torah. The Hasidic master, Elimelekh of Lizensk, once said, 'I not only remember the giving of the Torah at Sinai, I even remember who stood next to me then and there'.[22] More recently, an Israeli newspaper told the story of two strangers who meet on a crowded bus in Tel Aviv. One says to the other, 'Don't I know you from somewhere?' The other facetiously says, 'Maybe we stood together at Sinai'. The more friendly stranger holds out his hand and says, 'You must be right. How have you been all of this time?'

Tradition is selective in terms of which memories of which events it seeks to emphasize and to perpetuate. Consequently *Heilsgeschichte* ('sacred history') and not *historische Wissenschaft* ('scientific history') determines the contours of memories of past events, and selects which memories are to play a role in the liturgical life of the faith community. The works that constitute the sacred canon, rather than archaeological discoveries or the claims of extra-canonical works or the products of philological-historical method, decide how the past is to be understood by, and transmitted to, the future. Thus, though memory engenders faith, faith shapes memory. Faith forms memory by selecting the significant, by determining what is to be remembered, and how it is to be remembered. Faith forms and transforms memory. Memory both stimulates and transmits faith.

The demilitarization of Jewish memory by rabbinic tradition may serve as an example of how faith shapes memory. For instance, there are no Jewish festivals commemorating military victories. Joshua's defeat of the Canaanites, David's conquest of Jerusalem, and Samson's victory over the Philistines, have no liturgical referents. What about Hanukkah, The Festival of Lights? Is Hanukkah not rooted in the memory of the military victories of the Maccabees? Do not the Books of the Maccabees and Josephus recount these military victories and relate them to Hanukkah? They do. However, this is not the story tradition sought to remember.

The story of the military victory of the Maccabees is not preserved in Jewish canonical literature. The books of the Maccabees are outside the canon. They are apocryphal, non-canonical. The Talmudic discussions of Hanukkah focus on the miracle of the single cruse of oil in the desecrated Temple that lasted eight days rather than one day.[23] Hanukkah became a festival of lights, not of fights. The liturgy recalls those who remained faithful to the Torah in times of oppression, rather than the military exploits of the Maccabees. Indeed, God – and not the Maccabees – is described as the one who vanquishes the enemy.[24] The liturgy focuses on the miracle not on the military, on divine providence and not on successful military strategies. Indeed, classical Jewish religious literature stresses the ideological rather than the military conflict in its discussion of Hanukkah.[25] The emphasis is upon the battle of ideologies – Judaism vs. Hellenism, totalitarianism vs. liberty – and not upon the battle of armies.

While memory is a dominant theme in the celebration of the Jewish festivals, expectation also plays a role. In linking memory to expectation, past and future converge in the present. For example, the ram's horn (*shofar*) blown on the Jewish New Year is as much a reminder of the blasts characteristic of the expected messianic redemption as they are of the recalled revelation at Sinai. The redemption from Egypt is the precedent upon which faith in the final messianic redemption is predicated. Here one encounters a polarity between memory and expectation, between remembrance of historical events and hopes for a time that brings history to its eschatological conclusion.[26] For example, the Sabbath is a commemoration both of the beginning and of the end. It is both a remembrance of creation and a 'foretaste of the World-to-Come'.[27] Or, as Martin Buber said, 'He who does not himself remember that God led him out of Egypt, he who does not himself await the Messiah, is no longer a true Jew'.[28]

While memory of past events serves as a call to action, so does the evocation of other types of remembrance. For example, the biblical injunction of remembrance regarding the New Year has no specific historical referent. A verse in Leviticus (23:24) reads: 'In the seventh month, on the first day of the month, you shall observe a complete rest, a sacred occasion commemorated with loud blasts'. Although, as was noted, some rabbinic and liturgical texts relate the New Year to the creation of the world or to the creation of the first human being, and though others relate the 'loud blasts' to the revelation at Sinai, still other sources posit additional referents. Some texts relate remembrance to the demand that the individual remember his or her sins, his or her covenantal commitment, and seek reconciliation with the divine through repentance. The blast of the ram's horn may be compared to an alarm clock, awakening the awareness of the need for self-scrutiny and self-improvement. Other texts, particularly liturgical ones, interpret the biblical call to remembrance as a call to God to recall the steadfast faith of one's ancestors and to apply their merit to the penitent's deficit of good deeds. One asks God to remember him or her with grace and forgiveness when determining one's fate on the basis of an evaluation of one's deeds.[29]

The Hebrew word *zakhar* means not only 'memory' but 'male'. This observation was utilized by the medieval Jewish mystics to provide the celebration of the Jewish holy days with an additional level of meaning. For the Kabbalists, the main purpose of human action is not anthropocentric but theocentric. They developed ideas found in earlier rabbinic texts that considered human actions as opportunities for rectifying and repairing the shattered cosmos, and more particularly the Godhead itself. For the Jewish mystics, each act has the ability either to help further to fragment or to unify the divine, either to accelerate or to retard the messianic advent. For the Kabbalists, human action has theosophical-theurgic implications and effects.[30] According to these Jewish mystics, there are 'masculine' and 'feminine' elements within the Godhead, the *sefirot*. Human actions may affect the desired reunification and harmony of these elements; or, they may bring about an undesirable disaffection and conflict between these elements. Observance of the laws and commandments stimulates harmony, while sin increases disharmony.

The medieval Jewish mystics both amplified the meaning of already existing rituals related to holy day observance and introduced new rituals for holy day observance. Many of these relate to the goal of inducing harmony between the 'male' and 'female' features of the divine personality. A paradigmatic example relates to Sabbath observance.[31] In the version of the Ten Commandments found in Exodus (20:8), one is enjoined to 'remember' the Sabbath day. Here we have the word *zakhor* which the Kabbalists understood as a double entendre, referring both to remembrance and to maleness. In the Deuteronomic version of the Ten Commandments, the command is to 'observe' or to 'guard' (*shamor*) the Sabbath day (Deut. 5:12). The medieval Kabbalistic text, *Sefer ha-Bahir*, observes: 'Why is it said: "Remember the Sabbath" and "Observe the Sabbath?" "Remember" ("*zakhor*") refers to the male ("*zakhar*") and "observe" refers to the female'.[32]

According to the Kabbalists, the goal of Sabbath observance is to bring about the reunification of the male and female aspects of the divine.[33] In Kabbalistic literature, one encounters similar views regarding the meaning of observance of the other Jewish holydays.[34] The *zivvuga kaddisha* – 'sacred coupling' (in the parlance of the *Zohar*) has certain similarities with hierogamy or *hieros gamos* known in other religious traditions.[35] However, one can detect a different focus in kabbalistic texts. Though many other traditions portray the 'sacred marriage' as an imitation of the divine coupling, the kabbalists perceived humanly performed sacred deeds as stimulating the divine coupling. For the kabbalists, human activity – particularly sexual activity

– is theurgic and not imitative. The goal of the Kabbalist is not to mimic but to transform the divine. By effecting a re-union of the male and female elements of the divine through the performance of sacred deeds related to holy day observance, the individual celebrant stimulates the influx of divine blessing into the world.

By adding this layer of meaning upon the observance of the Jewish holy days, the Kabbalists provided a rubric of meaning that might be applied even to those holydays unrelated either by history or interpretation to memories of past events. One example is the celebration of the New Moon, a festival related not to history but to nature, to a cyclical event rather than to linear time. The moon is related by the Kabbalists to the *Shekhinah*, the feminine aspect of the divine. The goal is to liberate the Moon/*Shekhinah* from exile, and to restore her to her original fullness. The liberation of the moon from her cosmic exile would then be reflected in the end of Israel's terrestrial exile, which is identified with the advent of messianic redemption.[36] Thus while the medieval Kabbalists shifted the focus of holy day observance from the anthropocentric to the theocentric, from memory to theurgy, they did not abandon the focus on history. Indeed, a central goal of the Kabbalists was to encourage through observance the acceleration of history towards its eventual messianic climax.

Before concluding this discussion of the Jewish holy days, reference should be made to a number of contemporary trends of understanding and observing the Jewish festivals. Each generation of Jews has perceived a contemporary meaning in the paradigms of the past embodied in the holy days. Indeed, the continuity of tradition has largely been assured by the ability of each generation to perceive its contemporary situation in the mirror of tradition. As Abraham Isaac Kook put it, 'The Torah is like a mirror. Like a mirror, the Torah always stays the same, but each generation sees its own reflection, a different reflection, in the same mirror'.

Throughout the generations, in many different lands, the Passover paradigm of captivity and freedom, or the Hanukkah paradigm of religious oppression and subsequent liberation, was perceived in terms of past as prologue, memory of the past as contemporary experience. Each generation identified a contemporary figure with Haman, a demagogue desiring the annihilation of the

Jewish people. Torquemada, Chemelnitzki and Hitler were perceived as contemporary reincarnations of Haman, the perennial archenemy of the Jews. The festival of Purim serves as an annual reminder that a Haman lurks waiting to attack in each generation. The constant hope is that as Haman was defeated so will be his later incarnations. According to a Midrash, 'Rabbi Nathan said: Haman came to serve as a reminder for all generations, as it is said, "These days of Purim should not fail from among the Jews, nor the memory of them perish from their descendants (Esther 9:28)."'[37]

The two formative events for contemporary Jewry are the Holocaust and the establishment of the State of Israel. Response to these events by world Jewry has led to a number of significant changes in the celebration of the Jewish liturgical year. One example is the initiation of new Jewish holy days, such as *Yom ha-Atzma'ut* (Israel Independence Day), *Yom ha-Shoah* (Holocaust Memorial Day), and, primarily in Israel, *Yom Yerushalayim* (Jerusalem Day) celebrating the reunification of Jerusalem during the 1967 war.[38] That new Jewish holy days have been established for the first time in hundreds of years demonstrates the profound significance afforded to the events they commemorate. That these holy days have received the endorsement and encouragement of much of the Orthodox rabbinate, a group largely ideologically resistant to change and innovation, is significant. Nonetheless, a number of problematic issues with regard to these new holy days merit mention.

One such issue is the introduction into the Jewish liturgical year of celebrations of military victories as such. Though David's conquest of Jerusalem did not lead to the establishment of a commemorative festival, the 1967 reunification of Jerusalem did. This is but one indication of how the demilitarization of the Jewish liturgical year imposed by rabbinic and medieval tradition is currently being uprooted and reversed. This new approach to telling and remembering Jewish history and to celebrating certain events that comprise it has led to a retelling of past events, a revisaging of memory, a restructuring of the meaning of the Jewish liturgical year. As Liebman and Don-Yehiya have observed correctly, in their insightful study *Civil Religion in Israel*, there must be an inevitable clash between traditional Jewish symbols and values and those of Israel's 'civil religion': 'The symbols and values, expressed in traditional forms, conflict with the needs and values of the modern state'.[39]

One example of the transformation of the traditional focus of festival observance and meaning relates to Hanukkah. Originally a 'minor' holiday in the Jewish liturgical year, it has become in recent generations a major festival. In America, this seems to have occurred because Jews felt a need to have a counterpart to Christmas. This is especially ironic because Hanukkah, which celebrates the refusal of the Jews to acculturate into the dominant Hellenistic culture, has been magnified under the influence of the dominant Christian culture in America. In Israel, this seems to have occurred because Hanukkah could be easily reinterpreted to conform with the dogmas of the civil religion of the State of Israel.

As was noted above, the Talmudic rabbis and the medievals largely demilitarized Hanukkah. The war of the Hasmoneans was given little emphasis, while the miracle of the oil and the re-dedication of the sanctuary were stressed. Indeed, Hanukkah means 'rededication'. The clashes on the battlefield were minimized; the clash of ideologies – Judaism vs. Hellenism – was emphasized. When the liturgy speaks about the Maccabean triumph, it assigns the victory to divine intervention rather than to military acumen. However, in the civil religion of Israel, the military victory becomes the central motif. A religious holiday is transformed into a primarily national holiday. The Maccabees and not God are awarded the victory. The rededication of the Sanctuary is all but forgotten. Not divine redemption but self-redemption through military skill is stressed. This is ironic, given the fact, for example, that the prophetic reading (*haftarah*) for the Sabbath of Hanukkah ends with the words, 'Not by might, nor by power, but by My spirit – says the Lord of hosts' (Zech. 4:7).

The Maccabees are presented not as fighters for religious freedom or for the preservation of Jewish religious life and thought, but as patriots, as guerillas rebelling against military occupation and national subjugation.[40] The past is viewed as a prologue: the I.D.F. (Israel Defence Forces) are considered the Maccabees of our generation. The victory of the Maccabees over the Syrians becomes the precedent for the defeat of Syria in modern Israel's wars. The past is understood in terms compatible with the realpolitik of today's Middle East conflict.

Even *Yom ha-Shoah* has been given a military focus. In Israel, the official name of this commemoration is *Yom ha-Shoah ve-ha-Gevurah*

– the 'Day of Holocaust and Heroism', with increasing importance being afforded Jewish armed resistance during the Second World War. The Warsaw Ghetto uprising is now often perceived in Israel as the prelude to the formation of the Israel Defence Forces, as a paradigm for Jewish responses to Nazism rather than as an exception.[41] It is further significant that commemoration of the Holocaust was not subsumed under previously established Jewish holy days commemorating national disasters, such as the Ninth of Av (*Tisha B'Av)*, the day commemorating the destruction of the Temples and numerous other catastrophes. This may be grounded in the perception of the Holocaust as a unique, unparalleled and incomparable event in Jewish experience. Nevertheless, the choice of 27 Nissan as the date for *Yom ha-Shoah* is curious since there is no significant referent for that date in the annals of the history of the Holocaust. While some associate that date with the Warsaw Ghetto uprising, the date of *Yom ha-Shoah* does not exactly coincide with any significant date related to the uprising. What is also noteworthy is that the Ninth of Av does in fact coincide with a significant date in Holocaust history; namely, the initiation of the use of the gas chambers at Treblinka (which, unlike Auschwitz, was almost exclusively involved with the mass murder of Jews to the exclusion of members of other national or religious groups).[42] In this regard, one may speculate that the relationship on the calendar between *Yom ha-Shoah* and *Yom ha-Atzma'ut* (the latter occurs a week after the former) articulates a major dogma of the 'civil religion' of Israel, and of the 'civil religion' of American Jewry; namely, linking the Holocaust to the emergence of Israel, death to rebirth, murder to resurrection.[43] In a sense, the relation of *Yom ha-Shoah* to *Yom ha-Atzma'ut* (Israel Independence Day) might be interpreted as a Jewish parallel to Good Friday and Easter.

In the United States, growing concern for ecological issues, and in Israel the 'civil religion' have encouraged a shift of focus from history back to nature with regard to the observance of certain Jewish holy days. For example, Zionist ideology's emphasis upon the rebuilding of the land of Israel through agricultural development predictably led to the return to the biblical or even the pre-biblical view of the holy days as being primarily nature festivals. Particularly among the 'secular' Israelis, this has brought about a de-sacralization, even a 're-paganization' of the Jewish festivals.[44] Furthermore, as was already noted, the remilitarization and nationalization of the meaning of traditional Jewish holy days, has inevitably led to their de-theologization.

In my view, the growing secularization of Judaism, evident in contemporary interpretations of the Jewish festivals, poses a profound threat to the continuity of Jewish faith. Theological concepts endemic to Jewish faith are being ignored or forgotten. Traditional memories are being cast into oblivion, or recast beyond recognition. Religious festivals are being purged of their religious meaning. Nationalistic themes are replacing theological motives. It is therefore not surprising that a demographic study found that in the United States 95 per cent of those surveyed who identified themselves as Jews did not see commitment to Judaism as *the* essential component of their Jewish identity.[45]

Jewish continuity is in danger because of a progressive amnesia from within the Jewish community. As Abraham Heschel put it, 'We are like messengers who have forgotten the message'. The late Nobel laureate for literature, Isaac Bashevis Singer, used to say that Jews suffer from many diseases, but amnesia is not one of them. However, I am afraid he was wrong.[46] Unless Jews recapture and preserve their memories, they will do to themselves what massacres, pogroms and Holocaust were unable to accomplish – to obliterate Judaism, to make of it a forgotten memory. Again, to quote Heschel: 'The tasks, begun by the patriarchs and prophets and continued by their descendants, are now entrusted to us. We are either the last Jews or those who will hand over the entire past to generations to come. We either forfeit or enrich the legacy of the ages ... We of this generation are still holding the key [to the sanctuary hidden in the realm of spirit]. Unless we remember, unless we unlock it, the holiness of the ages will remain a secret of God'.[47]

NOTES

1. According to Hasidic theology, each Jew is *aiver ha-Shekhinah*, a 'limb of God', a 'divine member'. This is similar to the Catholic idea that in being part of the Church, one is part of the *Corpus Christi*, the Body of God. Dismemberment means separation from the divine. For Judaism, remembrance is an entreé to re-memberment. See Byron L. Sherwin, '*Corpus Domini*: Traces of the New Testament in East European Hasidism?', *Heythrop Journal* 35:3 (1994): 267–80, and chap. 11 below.
2. Abraham Joshua Heschel, *Man is Not Alone* (Philadelphia: Jewish Publication Society, 1951), pp.162–3.
3. Judah Halevi, *Kuzari*, trans. Hartwig Hirschfield, (New York: Schocken, 1964), 1:21–26, pp.46–47.

4. Helmer Ringgren, *Israelite Religion* (Philadelphia: Fortress Press, 1966), p.51.
5. I deliberately have chosen not to discuss the celebration of the festivals in biblical times, such as those connected with the Temple cult or those that may have predated the Temple cult. Nor have I chosen to discuss the various intriguing theories regarding biblical 'enthronement' or 're-enactment' rituals, many of which have been put forth by the 'Swedish School' of modern biblical scholarship. Though it has often been said, it is nonetheless necessary to state again that Judaism is not equivalent to Hebrew Scripture. Rather, Judaism is how Jewish tradition interpreted Hebrew Scripture. Consequently, the focus of my attention is on the meaning of the Jewish holy days within the context of classical Jewish religious interpretation, primarily during the Talmudic and medieval periods.
6. On the festivals in rabbinic literature, George Foot Moore, *Judaism* (Cambridge: Harvard University Press, 1927), vol. 2, pp.40–69, esp., p.48.
7. Salo W. Baron, *A Social and Religious History of the Jews*, vol. 1 (New York: Columbia University Press, 1952), p.5. For a more popular view, see Hayyim Schauss, *The Jewish Festivals* (New York: Union of American Hebrew Congregations, 1938), pp.43–44.
8. Abraham Joshua Heschel, *The Sabbath* (New York: World, 1963), p.63. Compare this discussion to Eliade's paradigm of the 'archaic man' who refuses 'to accept himself as a historical being, his refusal to grant value to memory and hence to the unusual events'. Mircea Eliade, *Cosmos and History* (New York: Harper, 1959), p.85. On the 'God of the Jewish people ... who carelessly intervenes in history, who reveals his will through events', see p.104. also Mircea Eliade, *The Sacred and the Profane* (New York: Harper, 1961), p.110, 'For Judaism, time has a beginning and will have an end. The idea of cyclical time is left behind'. See also Monford Harris, 'History, Memory, Action', *Conservative Judaism* 26:4 (Summer 1972): 58–63.
9. *Pesahim* 68b; *Exodus Rabbah* 31:16. In the *Guide of the Perplexed*, trans. S. Pines (Chicago: University of Chicago Press, 1963), Book 3, chap. 43, Maimonides succinctly states, 'The Pentecost is the day of the giving of the Torah'. See Louis Finkelstein, *The Pharisees* (Philadelphia: Jewish Publication Society, 1966), pp.115–18.
10. See the *kiddush* (blessing over wine) for the Sabbath.
11. *Taanit* 26b, 29a. Traditions also relate *Tisha B'Av* to events such as Moses' shattering of the Ten Commandments, the destruction of the fortress at Betar, and the expulsion of the Jews from Spain in 1492, that is, August 2, 1492, which corresponded that year with *Tisha B'Av*.
12. On *Rosh ha-Shanah* as Adam's 'birthday', see *Leviticus Rabbah* 29:1; as the birthday of the biblical patriarchs, see *Rosh ha-Shanah* 10b. The liturgy for *Rosh ha-Shanah* (*musaf-amidah* prayer) states, 'Today is the birthday of the world'. This also seems to be based on *Rosh ha-Shanah* 10b.
13. Three Jewish thinkers who relate fundamental ideas of Jewish theology to the holy days are the fifteenth-century Spanish commentator, Isaac Arama, the sixteenth-century mystic, Judah Loew of Prague, and the early twentieth-century German philosopher, Franz Rosenzweig. And see Isaac Arama, *Akedat Yitzhak* (Pressburgh: N.p., 1849), Sermon No. 67, p.99b. Arama relates six theological concepts to the festivals listed in Lev. 23: Sabbath–creation, Passover–God's power, *Shavuot*–revelation, *Rosh ha-Shanah*–providence, Yom Kippur – repentance, *Sukkot* – immortality. See the discussion of Arama by Menahem Kellner, *Dogma in Medieval Jewish Thought* (New York: Oxford University Press, 1986), pp.159–61. On Judah Loew, see Byron L. Sherwin, *Mystical Theology and Social Dissent* (New York: Oxford University Press, 1982), pp.39–40. Rosenzweig relates the Sabbath and the 'pilgrimage festivals' to creation, revelation and redemption. See Franz Rosenzweig, *The Star of Redemption*, trans. William H. Hallo, (New York: Holt, Rinehart & Winston, 1970), pp.308–28.
14. This text in the *Haggadah* is based on *Mishnah*, *Pesahim* 10:5, 6. See the insightful analysis by Baruch M. Bokser, *The Origins of the Seder* (Berkeley,CA: University of California Press, 1984), pp.86–87.
15. See the illuminating study by Monford Harris, 'The Passover Seder: On Entering the Order of History', *Judaism* 25:2 (Spring 1976): 167–74.
16. Certain Jews, such as Yemenites and Russian Caucasians, do 're-enact' the Exodus as part of their Passover observance. However, this is an ethnic curiosity rather than a normative practice.
17. Menahem Nahum of Chernoble, *Ma'or Einayim* (Jerusalem: Ma'or Einayim 1966), sec. *Tzav*, pp.130–1.

18. Abraham Joshua Heschel, *God in Search of Man* (Philadelphia: Jewish Publication Society, 1955), p.212.
19. Johannes Pedersen, *Israel: Its Life and Culture* (Oxford: Oxford University Press, 1926), vol. 1, pp.106–107.
20. Jacob Joseph of Polnoyye, *Toledot Ya'akov Yosef* (Jerusalem: Ha-Motzad L'Hotza'at ha-Musar ve-Ha-Hasidut, 1967), sec. *Mattot*, p.598. See also, *Zohar* (Vilna: Romm, 1882), vol. 3, p.93b.
21. Moses Hayyim Ephraim of Sudlykow, *Degel Mahaneh Ephraim* (Jerusalem: Hadar, 1963), sec. *Yitro*, p.111.
22. *Sefer Ohel Elimelekh* (Jerusalem, 1968), para. 63, p.8b.
23. See *Shabbat* 21b.
24. This is also true of Passover. Some have explained the absence of mention of Moses in the Passover Haggadah as being related to the tradition's stress upon God's exclusive role in redemption, to the exclusion of human efforts or human agents. For example, the Passover Haggadah states, 'God took us out of Egypt not by an angel, not be a seraf, not by a messenger; rather the Holy One Himself'. A similar sentiment regarding the redemption of the people celebrated on Purim and Hanukkah is found in the *'al-ha-Nisim'* prayers recited on those festivals.
25. See the discussion of the meaning of Hanukkah offered by Judah Loew of Prague in his *Ner Mitzvah* (B'nai Brak, Israel: Yahadut, 1962); Byron L. Sherwin, '*Mai Hanukkah*: What is Hanukkah?', *CCAR Journal* 50:4 (Fall 2003): 19–28.
26. See the discussion in *Rosh ha-Shanah* 11a of when the final redemption will come and how it will occur in the same month as the liberation from Egypt. In the Sefardic *musaf-Kedushah* prayer, reference is made to God saying, 'I will redeem you in the end as in the beginning'. According to Saadya Gaon, a rational reason for expecting God's final redemption is because of the precedent set by the redemption from Egypt; see his *The Book of Beliefs and Opinions*, trans. S. Rosenblatt (New Haven, CT: Yale University Press, 1948), chap. 8, sec. 1.
27. *Berakhot* 57b.
28. Quoted in Will Herberg (ed.), *The Writings of Martin Buber* (New York: World, 1961), p.31.
29. On these themes, see the liturgy for *Rosh ha-Shanah* and Yom Kippur, as in the 'reader's repetition' of the *Amidah* prayer for *musaf*.
30. On the theosophical and theurgic motives as being dominant in Jewish mystical thought, Moshe Idel, *Kabbalah: New Perspectives* (New Haven: Yale University Press, 1988).
31. On the Sabbath in Jewish mysticism, see the thorough study by Elliot Ginsburg, *The Sabbath in Classical Kabbalah* (Albany: SUNY Press, 1989).
32. *Sefer ha-Bahir*, Reuven Margaliot (ed.) (Jerusalem: Mosad ha-Rav Kook, 1951), para. 181, p.79. See also *Zohar*, vol. 1, p.48b.
33. Isaiah Tishbi, *The Wisdom of the Zohar*,trans. David Goldstein, (Oxford: Oxford University Press, 1989), pp.1223–28, Ginsburg, *The Sabbath in Classical Kabbalah*, pp.69–74, 101–22.
34. Tishbi, *The Wisdom of the Zohar*, pp.1238–59 and sources noted there; Gershom Scholem, *On the Kabbalah and Its Symbolism* (New York: Schocken, 1965), pp.137–46.
35. See e.g., Mircea Eliade, *The Myth of Eternal Return* (Princeton: Princeton University Press, 1965), pp.23–27.
36. Scholem, *On the Kabbalah and Its Symbolism*, pp.151–52.
37. *Mekhilta de Rabbi Yishmael*, Jacob Lauterbach (ed.), (Philadelphia: Jewish Publication Society, 1933), sec. *Amalek*, 2, vol. 2, p.159.
38. On *Yom ha-Atzma'ut*, Shelomo Goren, *Torat ha-Moadim* (Tel Aviv: Zioni, 1964), pp.568–98. On *Yom ha-Atzma'ut* and *Yom Yerushalayim*, Charles S. Liebman and Eliezer Don-Yehiya, *Civil Religion in Israel* (Berkeley, CA: University of California Press, 1983), pp.153–55.
39. Liebman and Don-Yehiya, *Civil Religion in Israel*, p.16. Also see their extensive discussion and analysis of the reinterpretation of the Jewish liturgical year according to the civil religion of Israel.
40. Liebman and Don-Yehiya, *Civil Religion in Israel*, pp.52–53.
41. See e.g., Amos Elon, *The Israelis* (New York: Holt, Rinehart & Winston, 1971), p.206; Liebman and Don-Yehiya, *Civil Religion in Israel*, pp.151–53.
42. On the problematics of the date for *Yom ha-Shoah*, Abraham P. Bloch, *The Biblical and Historical Background of the Jewish Holy Days* (New York: Ktav, 1978), pp.253–58. Bloch rec-

ommends *Lag Ba'Omer*, the traditional festival of rejoicing because of a respite from catastrophe, as a proper day for *Yom ha-Shoah* as that coincides with the anniversary of Hitler's death. On Treblinka and *Tisha B'Av*, see Nora Levin, *The Holocaust* (New York: Schocken, 1973), p.319. In 1942 *Tisha B'Av* corresponded to July 23.

43. For an extensive presentation of the civil religion of American Jews, see Jonathan S. Woocher, *Sacred Survival: The Civil Religion of American Jews* (Bloomington, Ind.: Indiana University Press, 1986), esp. pp.131–57.
44. The 'back to nature' theme in Zionist ideology is too complex for discussion here. The 'return to the Bible' must be understood as a nationalistic trend, and not a religious one. Indeed, it articulates a rejection of Talmudic and medieval rabbinic authority, often identified by Zionist ideologists with the 'abnormal' diasporan Jewish experience.
45. *Highlights of the Council of Jewish Federations 1990 National Jewish Population Study* (New York: Council of Jewish Federations, 1991), p.28: 'Further analysis shows that less than 5 percent of all respondents consider being Jewish solely in terms of being a member of a religious group, whereas 90 percent define being Jewish as being a member of a cultural or ethnic group'.
46. On the discontinuity of Jewish memory in the modern period and the problems it poses, see the insightful work by Yosef Hayim Yerushalmi, *Zakhor: Jewish History and Jewish Memory* (Seattle: University of Washington Press, 1982). On p.93, Yerushalmi writes, 'Only in the modern era do we really find, for the first time, a Jewish historiography divorced from Jewish collective memory and, in crucial respects, thoroughly at odds with it'.
47. Abraham Joshua Heschel, *The Earth is the Lord's* (New York: Schumann, 1950), p.107.

CHAPTER NINE

Toward a Just and Compassionate Society

The Talmud tells that a certain Rabbi Joseph once became ill and he slipped into a coma. His father, Rabbi Joshua ben Levi, remained by his bedside praying for his recovery. Fortunately, Rabbi Joseph recovered. When he awoke from his coma, his father asked him: 'What did you see as you hovered between this world and the next world?'

Said Rabbi Joseph, 'I saw a world turned upside down. I saw a topsy-turvy world'.

Rabbi Joshua listened, thought for a while, and said, 'You saw a clear vision of how things really are. You saw the world as it is'.[1]

The topsy-turvy world seen by Rabbi Joseph is our world. As we move into the third millennium, there are many predictions of imminent catastrophe – ecological, military, medical, nuclear, political, social, economic, as well as terrorist attacks. We are searching for balance while living through an earthquake. The challenge before us is to apply our tradition to our condition, inherited wisdom to contemporary problems.

Judaism begins with Abraham's discovery that there is one God who created the world. The Talmudic rabbis asked: How did Abraham make this discovery? Their answer is in the form of a parable: 'Abraham may be compared to a man who was traveling from place to place when suddenly he saw a palace in flames. "Is it possible that there is no master who cares for this palace?" the man wondered. Then the master of the palace appeared and said, "I am the master of this palace."'[2]

The rabbis explained the parable this way: Abraham is every person. The palace is the world. The world is aflame with war, hatred and evil. And, God is the master of the palace. Later commentators amplified the meaning of the parable. The world is aflame. The master of the world, God's Presence in the world – called *Shekhinah* by the Talmudic rabbis and the Jewish mystics – is trapped in the palace. What is the task of the person who sees the palace on fire? What is our task? To enter the flaming palace, to save the master of the palace, to prevent the palace from being destroyed, and to labour to restore it. In this interpretation of the parable we can detect a number of vital teachings of classical Jewish theology that relate inherited traditions to contemporary conditions:

1. Our world is in danger, aflame with violence, injustice and evil.
2. Despite its fragile and endangered condition, our world has a master, a Lord.
3. The palace's being aflame offers a poignant challenge to religious faith, that is, to the claim that the palace has a master. The relevance of religious faith to our situation relates to how we deal with the burning palace.
4. We are obliged to fight the fires of cruelty and injustice that threaten the palace. Our obligation is to labor to save and to rebuild our world.
5. Our task is to redeem God's Presence in our world – to make our world an appropriate place for God's Presence to dwell, to allow God to feel at home in the world, to work in partnership with God towards a world where justice and compassion are not orphans.

That human history is God's nightmare, that the world is aflame with strife, has been a perennial observation of Jewish tradition, beginning with the Scriptures. The words of Job (9:24) echo throughout Jewish history and tradition: 'The earth is given into the hands of the wicked'.

It is a premise of Jewish theology, confirmed by the experience of the Jewish people in history, that ours is an unredeemed world. Shortly after the Holocaust, Martin Buber wrote, 'we [Jews] demonstrate with the bloody body of our people the unredeemedness of the world'.[3] Jewish theology teaches that ours is not a redeemed *messianic* world, but one that is unredeemed and *messy*. The human task is to clean up the world, to move history toward redemption, to fight the fire that threatens to engulf us, to work for justice and compassion, and against cruelty and injustice.

According to the Jewish mystics, there is the realm of the good and the holy. There is also the realm of wickedness and evil. Yet, there is also a third realm which is pervasive in our world. This is the realm of the intermingling of good and evil, of evil within good. While the task of fighting evil is great, the task of separating the evil from the good without destroying the good is even more difficult. More frustrating than the fact that evil is real and powerful is the fact that evil thrives so well disguised as the good. Redemption is therefore contingent upon the separation of good and evil, and not only upon the defeat of evil and the demonic.[4]

Even our best social, religious, educational and political institutions represent the commingling of good and evil. The individual person, even the righteous person, does evil and commits sins. 'For there is not a *righteous* person upon this earth that does good and sins not' (Eccles. 7:20). Mendel of Kotzk explained the verse in Leviticus (7:1), 'This is the law of the guilt offering; it is most holy', to mean: 'Where is guilt to be found? In the most holy'.[5] The problem, then, is not only how to contend with evil, how to do good, but also how to root out evil from the good – in our society, our institutions and in our own selves – without destroying the good that has given evil and sin a home.

Recognizing that our world is aflame, that it is torn by hatred and strife, that it is unredeemed, means being aware that messianic redemption is a future hope rather than a current historical condition. Jewish teachings caution against confusing the eschatological with the historical, messianic times with messy times, the utopian with the contemporary. The danger of eschatological thinking is the danger of producing eschatological results. Throughout Jewish religious literature, there are admonitions against 'hastening the end', against confusing historical times with messianic times.[6]

Though Kierkegaard asked us to take a 'leap of faith', it is prudent to look before we leap. Rushing ahead toward utopia can only lead to ultimate despair and eventual inaction. If we believe utopia is around the corner, we will become inactive, thereby allowing evil to succeed. If we expect too much, our eventual disappointment may lead us into abject despondency and despair. Scripture speaks about the pursuit of justice – 'justice, justice shall you pursue' (Deut. 16:20); the Declaration of Independence speaks of 'the pursuit of happiness'. Neither speaks about their attainment – only their pursuit. There is a danger when reach exceeds grasp. Our goal is to improve, not to perfect society. Perfecting society exceeds our grasp. The perfect society comes through divine grace, not human action.

Both Hebrew Scripture and the Talmudic rabbis saw human experience as a failed experiment of God. Human history demonstrated that God initially had been too utopian, too optimistic, too hopeful about the future of humankind. Though containing many stories, the Hebrew Scriptures may be read as two stories. The first is the story of God's hopes and expectations for humanity, and humanity's frustration and betrayal of those expectations. The second is the story of God's search for the righteous person, for the person who 'does justice and loves mercy' (Micah 6:8).

Does Scripture ever tell us that God saw that human righteousness was great on the earth and that God was glad to have created human beings? Rather, Scripture tells us that, 'The Lord saw how great was human wickedness on earth and how every plan devised by man's mind was nothing but evil all the time. And the Lord regretted having created human beings, and God's heart was saddened' (Gen. 6:5–6, cf. 8:21). As the old limerick puts it:

> God's plan had a hopeful beginning
> Then man spoiled his chances by sinning.
> We know that the story
> Will end with God's glory
> But right now, the other side's winning.

The palace is aflame; nonetheless, it does have a master. God is the master of the palace, of the world. God is the ultimate creator, the ultimate artist. But, like every artist, God learns to accept that there always is a gap between what an artist expects a work to be and what it actually turns out to be. Isaac Bashevis Singer wrote, 'every artist, every creator, painfully experiences the chasm between his inner vision and its ultimate expression'. God, claims Singer, is no different. Singer continued: 'God was for me an eternal *belle lettrist*. His main attribute was creativity … I quoted to myself that passage from the midrash that says God created and destroyed many worlds before He created this one. Like my brother and myself, God threw his unsuccessful works into the wastepaper basket. The flood, the destruction of Sodom, the wanderings of the Jews in the desert, the wars of Joshua, these were all episodes in a divine novel, full of surprise and adventure'.[7]

Singer's view that God's initial hopes must be modified, that the divine plan for creation must be revised in light of how the world God created turned out to be, is found in many classical Jewish sources. For example, according to a rabbinic tradition, the revelation at Sinai was supposed to initiate the redemption of the world. But, it does not. As Moses receives the Torah, the people build the Golden Calf. God's plan is once more frustrated. God's hopes are once more betrayed. Redemption does not come. The Talmudic rabbis compare the people's worshipping of the Golden Calf at the time and place of the making of the covenant at Sinai to a bride betraying her groom in the honeymoon bed.[8]

Moses descends from the mountain carrying the two tablets described by Scripture as written with 'the finger of God' (Exod. 31:18). According to a rabbinic tradition, the entire Torah was written on those tablets.[9] Moses sees the people worshipping the idol and he smashes the tablets. Later on, we read (Exod. 34:4): 'Moses carved two stone tablets, like the first'. As a Midrash comments on this verse, 'God said to Moses: It was I who wrote the first tablets, as it says – written with the finger of God. But now *you* write the second tablets and I will assist you'.[10]

Rabbinic commentators and Jewish mystics reflected upon this story. They asked: Why was the first set of tablets written by God while the second set was written by Moses? Are the two sets different? Why did Moses break the first set? The following is one line of interpretation offered to answer these questions. The first set of tablets, written by God, was completely spiritual. It represented a perfect Torah for a perfect and redeemed world. It represented the essential Torah – the Torah as it really is; the Torah whose abode is in heaven, the spiritual realm. In this view, Moses did not break the tablets out of anger, but he broke them from his realization, after seeing the people worshipping the Golden Calf, that redemption had not come, that the world remained sinful, corrupt and unredeemed. God realized that the perfect Torah, the spiritual Torah, the Torah written by 'the hand of God', had no place in such a world. It could not operate in the world as it is. Moses, therefore, broke the first set of tablets.

Later on, Moses writes a second set. The first set is written by God; the second by a human being. The first Torah is completely spiritual for a redeemed world. The second is a remolded Torah, shaped for an unredeemed world. In this view, God compromises the divine plan for the world, the Torah, to allow it to speak to an imperfect world. The completely spiritual Torah is meant for a world of peace, devoid of violence, injustice and corruption, for a redeemed world governed by justice and compassion. The actual Torah that we have deals with violence, war, murder, crime, deception and sin, which are features of human existence in our world. The text of the Torah that we have does not address a perfect world, a utopian world. It deals with the ugly side of human nature and experience. It does not demand perfection. It carries God's word, God's will, God's commandments for a messy world, not for a messianic world. As the Talmud reminds us, the Torah is given to human beings and not to angels.[11] In our world of falsehood, deception and sin, the Torah of absolute truth, perfection and spirituality could not endure, nor could it be endured by the world. As the *Zohar* says, 'The world could not endure the Torah if she had not garbed herself in the garments of this world'.[12]

Gershom Scholem summarized this Kabbalistic teaching as follows:

> The first tablets contained a revelation in keeping with the original state of man [before Adam sinned] ... This was the truly spiritual Torah, bestowed upon a world in which Revelation and Redemption coincided, in which everything was holy and there was no need to hold the powers...[of evil] in check ... .But the utopian moment soon vanished. When the first tablets were broken, 'the letters engraved on them flew away', that is, the purely spiritual element receded ... On the second tablets the Torah appears in a historical garment ... A hard shell is placed around the spiritual Torah, indispensable in a world governed by the powers of evil.[13]

The Jewish mystics taught that the Torah is in exile in our world, and is alienated from its completely spiritual nature.[14] Indeed, everything in our world is in a state of exile, of alienation. This includes not only the Torah and the human condition, but also the

Shekhinah. For the Jewish mystics, the path towards redemption begins with the realization of the unredeemed state of the world, with the realization that human history is out of step with God's dreams, that human history is a divine disappointment, that God's hopes for a redeemed world have been sabotaged by undesirable human deeds. The spiritual quest begins with the awareness that existence in history means existence in exile. To think otherwise must be viewed as an act of non-awareness – even worse, as an act of self-deception. As Mendel of Kotzk said, it is bad enough to be in exile, but it is even worse to be in exile and not to be aware of it.

God's Presence is in exile in our world. But God both transcends the world and is present in it. God is both transcendent and immanent. From God's transcendent attributes, divine grace flows into the world. God's grace can move the world, its inhabitants and the Shekhinah, closer to redemption. However, according to the Jewish mystics, the necessary catalyst for stimulating the flow of transcendent divine grace is the human performance of sacred deeds. In this regard, commenting on the verse in Psalms (121:5), 'The Lord is your shadow', Levi Yitzhak of Berditchev said, 'Just as a person's shadow does whatever a person does, so does God, as it were, do whatever a person does. Consequently, a person should perform sacred and good deeds such as showing compassion to those in need, so that God will likewise bestow divine goodness upon the world's creatures'.[15]

This idea, central to Jewish mysticism, is that human deeds not only influence God, but they also influence God's relationship to us. There is a flow upward of our activities and their effects upon God. However, there is also a perpetual downward flow of divine blessing and grace from God toward us that is affected by our activities. When the flow upward is characterized by human acts of goodness, virtue and unification, it affects the downward flow in a good and positive way. But, when the flow upward of human deeds is characterized by sinful and undesirable acts, it affects the downward flow in a negative way. In this view, the nature and quality of divine grace is, in a very direct way, related to the nature and quality of human deeds.

Though unredeemed, the world is yet redeemable. There is a partnership between God and human beings, a partnership with its foundations in an interdependent divine–human covenant. Both divine grace and human deeds are necessary in order to achieve the goal God and we both desire – the redemption of the world. Human beings are not passive bystanders in the drama of messianic redemption, but active protagonists. As our fate lies in God's hands, so the destiny of God's world, God's creatures and the divine presence in our world, lays in each of our hands. We need God and God needs us to accomplish the task of redemption. A rabbinic midrash comments on the verse in Psalms: 'My heart shall rejoice in Your [God's] salvation' (Ps. 13:6). 'Rabbi Abbahu taught: This is one of those difficult verses that declare that the salvation of God depends upon the salvation of God's people. Note that it is not written, "My heart shall rejoice in my salvation," but in *Your* salvation, by which the verse means: Your salvation, that is, God's salvation, depends upon our salvation'.[16]

According to this paradox, the Almighty God has chosen us out of love to help realize the divine purpose for the world. Our relationship to God is not one of passive compliance but of active assistance. God's Presence in our world, God's power in our world, paradoxically becomes linked to our attitudes and to our deeds. The theological boldness of this idea is already expressed by the Talmudic rabbis.

Commenting on the verse in Isaiah (43:12) 'You are My witnesses says God', a second-century rabbi said, 'When you are My witnesses, I am God. But, when you are not My witnesses, it is as if I am not God'.[17] Commenting on the verse in Psalms 'To God we give strength' (60:14), a rabbinic text says, 'When the people of Israel perform God's will, they add strength to God. But, when they do not perform God's will, they – as it were, weaken the great power of God'.[18] Following this tradition of the Talmudic rabbis, the medieval Jewish mystics, and the Hasidic masters, Jews perceived God as a neighbour in distress, as a relative in need of our help, our love.[19] They called God *'Gottenu'* – our little God, *'Tattenu'* – our little Father.

The road map toward redemption begins with empathy for the condition of the Shekhinah, the presence of God in our exiled world. Love of God is the catalyst for love of human beings. The Talmudic rabbis translate the well-known verse in Leviticus (19:18), 'You should love your neighbour as yourself; I am the Lord your God' as 'You should love your neighbour as yourself *because* I am the Lord your God'.[20] Love of human beings without love of God is a conclusion without a premise. Love of God without love of humanity is a premise without a conclusion.

The premise of *imitatio Dei* is *imago Dei*. Of all God's attributes, the ones we are most strongly enjoined to imitate are love, mercy, justice, righteousness, compassion, holiness and truth.[21] The Talmudic rabbis admonish us to practise *imitatio Dei:* 'Be like unto God; just as God is merciful and gracious, so be you merciful and gracious'.[22] But attitude alone is not sufficient. Specific deeds are also required. Commenting on the verse in Deuteronomy (13:5), 'After the Lord your God shall you walk', Rabbi Hama bar Hanina said: 'How can a man walk after God? Is God not a consuming fire? What is meant is that man should walk after God's attributes. Just as God clothes the naked, attends the sick, comforts the mourners, and buries the dead, do you likewise'.[23] It is significant and instructive that other attributes of God such as anger, jealousy and vengeance are specifically *excluded* by the rabbis as attributes of God that we should not imitate.

Perhaps surprisingly, the Talmud describes prayer as an attribute of God that we should emulate. According to a Talmudic interpretation of a verse in Isaiah (56:7), God prays. But, to whom does God pray? – to Himself. And, asks the Talmud, 'What is God's prayer?' God's prayer is: 'May it be My will that My mercy may suppress My anger, and that My mercy shall prevail over My other attributes, so that I may deal with My children in the attribute of mercy, and, on their behalf, restrain My attribute of strict justice'.[24]

In this text, we encounter three important ideas. The first relates to the role of polarity in Jewish theology. The second relates to the effect of human deeds upon God.[25] The third bears on the relationship of justice and compassion, justice and mercy, and justice and love, which are the critical components of the life and the society toward which we aspire. Jewish thought perceives reality as being characterized by polarity. In the words of Judah Loew of Prague, 'Everything that exists in the world is either of a certain essence or its opposite'.[26] According to one medieval text, 'God made each thing and its opposite ... All things cleave to one another, the pure and the impure. There is no purity except through impurity'.[27] For there to be up there must be down, for black there must be white, for good to be perceived there must also be evil, for repentance to be required sin must be present, for there to be mercy there must be justice. The major concepts of Jewish theology are not expressed in definitions that together comprise a systematic theology, but as descriptions of complementary polar opposites.

Philosophy offers definitions. Classical Jewish thought offers descriptions. These descriptions are offered not *de fine* – to define, to limit, but to present an entity or an idea in its fullness, in its totality. These descriptions are offered as pairs of complementary polar opposites, for example that God is both transcendent and immanent, human nature simultaneously embraces 'the image of God' (Gen. 1:26) and 'dust and ashes' (Gen. 18:27, Job 42:6), religion embraces God's revelation and human worship.

In Plato's dialogues, the primary agenda is the search for a definition, for example, of 'justice', of human nature. In Hebrew Scripture, God calls the people of Israel to be a people of witnesses to God (Isa. 43:10), not a committee of definers of God. The prophet Micah (6:8) requires the people not to *define* justice and mercy, but to *enact* justice and to love mercy. The prophet Amos does not define justice but he nonetheless admonishes those who do not practise justice. Justice and mercy are complementary polar opposites. They complement one another, temper one another, balance one against the other. According to a Midrash, God first created a world only with justice, but a world only with justice could not operate. So, God destroyed it. Then God created a world only with mercy, but with the same result. Only when God combined the two in our world, could the world endure.[28] In this regard, the *Zohar* states,

> When God came to create the world, light and darkness were wrapped in one another … So, too, good issues from evil and compassion issues from justice, and all are intertwined, the good impulse and the evil impulse, white and black – all depend upon one another … and when the world is judged [by God], it is judged with justice mingled with compassion; otherwise, the world could not exist for even an instant.[29]

Justice and mercy are attributes of God.[30] Without justice, evil would have license to run rampant. Without mercy, retribution for misdeeds would destroy the world. When divine justice is left unchecked, the problem of theodicy becomes inevitable. God's prayer, mentioned above, demonstrates that God is aware of the danger to creatures should the divine attribute of justice remain unrestrained. God's attribute of mercy must always remain somewhat dominant over the attribute of justice.[31]

In the rabbinic and Kabbalistic view, human deeds are the necessary catalyst for stimulating the divine flow of justice and compassion in the world. For example, a verse in Deuteronomy (13:18) states, 'God will show you mercy and will have compassion on you'. The Talmud interprets this verse to mean that God is compassionate to a person who is compassionate to others; to those who are not compassionate to others, compassion is not shown.[32] Furthermore, a verse in Isaiah (5:16) states that 'The Lord of Hosts is exalted through justice'. A Midrash interprets this to mean that God is exalted through our doing justice. The text reads, 'Because you exalt me through justice, I will act with righteousness and cause My holiness to dwell among you. And if you practise justice and righteousness, I will redeem you with a complete redemption'.[33]

In the human realm, there also must be a polarity of justice and mercy, law and love.[34] Each person, each society, must try to have the wisdom to know when to keep them in balance, as well as when one should take precedence over the other. For example, parents or teachers who show only compassion toward their children or students will leave them undisciplined, bereft of intellectual and moral guidance. One who is too compassionate toward the wicked will give them licence to pursue their evil deeds. A judge who is too compassionate can no longer offer impartial justice.[35] Though cruelty is considered among the worst moral vices (Jer. 6:23), there are nonetheless times when even cruelty, the opposite of compassion, is necessary. As a Midrash puts it, 'A person who is merciful when cruelty is needed, will end up becoming cruel when mercy is needed'.[36]

In Greek thought, justice is largely viewed as being retributive and distributive, as giving people their due.[37] In Jewish thought, justice is largely viewed as being substantive. Justice is not only something one should *do*, but something one should *be*.[38] A person should strive to *be* just. The just person is the foundation for the just society. But, the goal of justice is not only that all should get what is coming to them. The more important goal is the formation of a just society, the enhancement of social life. Society, however, is always in formation. The completely just society or the completely compassionate society are not features of historical times, but only of messianic times. Indeed, there is a tradition that in messianic times, the distinction between justice and mercy will be eliminated. In historical times, justice and mercy both conflict and coexist. But, in messianic times, they will become identical.[39]

A society without justice leads to moral anarchy and destruction. A society where justice is perverted is endangered. Justice tends to follow the rule of law, the rule of reason. Compassion tends to follow the rule of the heart. But, one not only needs to know when to temper law and justice with compassion, one also needs to know when to go above the limits of the law, beyond the strict dictates of justice, to do what is right. This is the role of righteousness which is lodged between justice and compassion. Righteousness requires going beyond the law when doing what is right demands it. As Nahmanides wrote, commenting on Leviticus 19:2, 'It is possible to be a moral scoundrel within the strict limits of the law'.

According to the Hebrew prophets and the Talmudic rabbis, when righteousness is not part of the social fabric, a society's very stability is endangered.[40] Yet complete righteousness is impossible to attain. 'There is no righteous person who does not sin', says Scripture.[41] Until messianic redemption, there is no society that can claim to be completely righteous, compassionate and just. But, while complete justice, compassion and righteousness elude our grasp, we must strive to be just, compassionate and righteous. The path toward such a society is by each individual practising justice, righteousness and compassion. The way toward a just, righteous and compassionate society must include three kinds of action: fighting against wickedness and injustice that already exist; trying to prevent additional wickedness and injustice from occurring (as with health care, preventative measures can allay the later need to deal with pathological phenomena); trying to improve the moral and spiritual quality of society by infusing the world with appropriate measures of justice, righteousness and compassion. It is not a question of either/or, a just and compassionate society or one that is its opposite; rather, social and moral life exist on a spectrum. At one end is absolute wickedness – the completely corrupt society; at the other is the messianic world. In history, we are always somewhere between these two poles, these two extremes. Our task is to try to prevent society from moving toward the pole of wickedness and to enable it to move closer toward the pole of messianic redemption.

What can people of religious faith do to move towards a just, righteous, and compassionate society?

1. They can try to act justly, righteously and with compassion. The starting point for building such a society is with the self. People of faith must set the standard for moral behaviour. But this has not always been a feature of religious life in our century. Instead of ecumenical fraternity, our times have witnessed and continue to witness ecumenical genocide, ecumenical nightmares instead of ecumenical harmony.

   Religions cannot expect to be credible in their opposition to strife unless they first eliminate triumphalism, strife, and injustice within and among themselves. Either we are ***all*** children of God or none of us are children of God. As Malachi said (2:10): 'Have we not all one Father? Has not one God created us? Why do we deal treacherously every one against his brother?'

   Commenting on the description of human beings as children of God, Matthew Arnold wrote, 'Children of God – it is an immense pretension – and how are we to justify it? By the works we do and by the words we speak'. Or, as Aaron of Karlin put it, 'What is the greatest sin a person can commit?: To forget that he is a prince or princess – a child of God, the King'.

   Job reminds us (31:15), 'Did not God who made me in the womb make him? Did not One God fashion us in the womb?' The Hebrew word for womb is ***rehem***. It is etymologically linked to the Hebrew word for compassion – ***rahamim***. Compassion is our link to one another and our link to God whom the Talmudic rabbis called *Rahmana* – the Compassionate One.
2. Rather than strive with one another, people of faith should join together to fight common enemies, while following the advice of the Talmudic rabbis to despise and to destroy the sin and not the sinner.[42] The greatest threats come from ideologies that deny human dignity and integrity, that teach cynicism and nihilism.
3. Despite adversity, the person of faith must be an optimist – against his better judgment. This means affirming that there is meaning despite absurdity, hope despite adversity, redemption

awaiting us at the twilight of history. But this also means that optimism and idealism must neither be utopian nor naïve. As Reinhold Niebuhr said, 'If democratic nations fail, their failure must be partly attributed to the faulty strategy of idealists who have too many illusions when they face realists who have too little conscience'.[43]

People of faith must learn how to employ love *and* law, justice *and* mercy, compassion and sometimes even cruelty. In the battle against evil, love and compassion are not adequate weapons. Ours, we must not forget, is a messy world. The messianic age will be an age of justice, righteousness, compassion and peace. But, meanwhile, there is war, injustice and corruption. As long as our world remains a messy rather than a messianic, an unredeemed rather than a redeemed world, there are no facile solutions to complex social problems. We must accept the fact that no social order is completely perfectible, that the best we do can never be enough.

4. Human beings can work to make the world worthy of redemption, but they cannot redeem the world. They can accelerate redemption; they can increase justice and compassion, but they cannot initiate a Messianic Age. As Abraham Heschel wrote, 'In messianic times evil will be conquered by the God who is one, but in historical times, evils must be conquered one by one'.[44] The human task is not to bring the Messiah, but to bring about the realization of holiness in history. The human task is to work in partnership with God in the fight against evil, separating the evil from the good, saving the palace from destruction, moving society from injustice toward justice, from cruelty to compassion, from corruption to holiness. The human goal is to correlate our reality with the statement God made when the world was created: 'And God saw that it was good' (Gen. 1:31).
5. For people of faith, social action must be grounded in authentic theological foundations. Theological scholars must find ways of relating the wisdom of the past to the perplexities of the present. Religious ethics is a form of applied theology. Theologians, scholars and clergy cannot remain cloistered in academies, churches and synagogues insulated from the problems that afflict our society. They must not only think actively but act actively as well. As a Midrash puts it, 'If a person in need comes to a scholar to help

obtain justice, and he responds: I am occupied with my studies, I have no time, God in reply proclaims to such a scholar: I consider you responsible for the chaos of society'.[45] Prerogatives for social action cannot be surrendered to politicians. According to Mendel of Kotzk, the challenge to people of faith is to be mixed up with the sometimes dirty business of the world and yet to be able to have clean hands.

6. As we move into the new century, the new millennium, the ominous words of André Malraux resonate, 'The third millennium must be a spiritual millennium or there will be no third millennium'.

In a world in search of spiritual moorings, religious tradition can offer a wealth of wisdom, experience and moral direction. People of faith are the custodians of those values which are the basis of all social justice and order. Ultimately, human dignity, human integrity, and the intrinsic sanctity of human life are theological axioms that rest upon the assumptions that there is a God and that we are created in the image of God. People of faith are the custodians of those ideas and values that are the ingredients for a life of moral and spiritual integrity. Their task is to keep those ideas and values alive, to cherish and to practise them, and to convey them to a world whose very survival depends upon them. Finally, people of faith must realize that their judgments are partial, their achievements limited, their grasp of truth remains flawed, their access to God's will is imperfect. The best one can do, in the words of Abraham Lincoln, is to act 'with malice toward none, with charity for all, and with firmness in the right as God gives us to see the right, let us strive to finish the work we are in'.

NOTES

1. *Pesahim* 50a.
2. *Genesis Rabbah* 39:1. The text is ambiguous. The Hebrew word *doleket* may mean 'illuminated' or 'aflame'. Many commentators, including David Luria and Zev Einhorn took it to mean 'aflame'. Rashi took it to mean 'illuminated'. The Hasidic master, Mendel of Kotzk, taught that the castle being aflame is the greatest challenge to religious faith. See Abraham Heschel, *Kotzk* [Yiddish] (Tel Aviv: Ha-Menorah, 1973), vol. 2, pp.603–5.
3. Quoted by Ernst Simon, 'Martin Buber: His Way Between Thought and Deed', *Jewish Frontier* (February 1948): 26.
4. See the discussion and sources cited in Abraham Heschel, 'Confusion of Good and Evil', in *The Insecurity of Freedom* (New York: Farrar, Straus and Giroux, 1966), pp.127–50.
5. Abraham Heschel, *A Passion for Truth* (New York: Farrar, Straus and Giroux, 1973), p.40.

6. Moses Maimonides, *Epistle to Yemen*.
7. Isaac Bashevis Singer, *Gifts* (Philadelphia: Jewish Publication Society, 1985), p.11. Singer undoubtedly refers to the Midrash in *Genesis Rabbah* 3:7, 9:2 and parallels. See also chap. 4 above.
8. *Shabbat* 88b.
9. Abraham J. Heschel, *Torah min ha-Shamayim*, vol. 2 (London: Soncino, 1965), pp.348–50.
10. *Exodus Rabbah* 47:2.
11. *Sabbath* 89a.
12. *Zohar* (Vina: Romm, 1882), vol. 3, p.152a.
13. Gershom Scholem, 'The Meaning of the Torah in Jewish Mysticism', in *On the Kabbalah and Its Symbolism* (New York: Schocken, 1965), pp.69–70.
14. Abraham Heschel, *God in Search of Man* (Philadelphia: Jewish Publication Society, 1955), pp.270–71.
15. Levi Yitzhak of Berditchev, *Kedushat Levi* (Brooklyn: Derbaremdiger, 1996), sec. *Nasso'* pp.315–16.
16. *Midrash on Psalms*, S. Buber (ed.) (Vilna: Romm, 1891), 13:4, p.56a.
17. *Sifre–Devarim* [*Sifre on Deuteronomy*], Louis Finkelstein (ed.) (Berlin: Jüdischer Kulterband in Deutschland Abteilung Verlag, 1939), para. 346, pp.403–4.
18. *Pesikta de-Rav Kahana*, S. Buber, ed. (Lyck, n.p.,1868), chap.26, p.166b.
19. The comparison of God to a relative or kinsman is stressed by Moses Cordevero in the first chapter of his *Tomer Devorah*.
20. *Avot d'Rabbi Natan*, Solomon Schechter (ed.) (2nd ed, New York: Feldheim, 1967), chap.16, end.
21. On *imitatio Dei* in Jewish thought, David S. Shapiro, 'The Doctrine of the Image of God and *Imitatio Dei*', *Judaism* 12:1 (Winter 1963): 57–78.
22. *Mekhilta de Rabbi Yishmael* (Hayyim Horovitz and Israel Rabin (eds) (Jerusalem: Wahrmann, 1960), on Exodus 15:2.
23. *Sota* 14a.
24 *Berakhot* 7a.
25 Moshe Idel, *Kabbalah: New Perspectives* (New Haven: Yale University Press, 1988), pp.164–65.
26 Judah Loew, *Hiddushei Aggadot*, vol. 2 (New York: Judaica Press, 1969), p.89; Heschel, *God in Search of Man*, pp.336–48.
27. *Midrash Temurah;* see *Sefer Yetzirah* (Jerusalem: Levin-Epstein, 1965), sec. 6:6.
28. *Genesis Rabbah* 12:15.
29. *Zohar* vol. 3, p.80a.
30. On God's attributes of justice and mercy, Abraham J. Heschel, *The Prophets* (Philadelphia: Jewish Publication Society, 1962), pp.195–221; 'Justice' in *Encyclopedia Judaica;* Kaufmann Kohler, *Jewish Theology* (1918; New York: Ktav, 1968), pp.118–34; Ephraim E. Urbach, *The Sages*, trans. Israel Abrahams (Cambridge, MA: Harvard University Press, 1987), pp.448–61.
31. This is a basic theme of the High Holiday liturgy and a fundamental teaching of Jewish mysticism that relates to the relationship between the *sefirot* of *hesed* and *din*. See *Pesikta Rabbati*, Meir Friedmann (ed.), (2nd. Ed., Tel Aviv: n.p., 1963), 40:2, on the need for a balance between divine justice and divine mercy.
32. *Sabbath* 151b.
33. *Deuteronomy Rabbah* 5:7.
34. On law and love, see chap. 6 above..
35. *Orhot Zaddikim*, trans. Seymour J. Cohen, (New York: Feldheim, 1960), sec. *Sha'ar ha-Ahzariut* On the virtue of compassion, Louis Jacobs, *Jewish Values* (London: Vallentine, Mitchell, 1960), pp.135–45. On the practice of justice and compassion, Samuel S. Cohon, *Judaism: A Way of Life* (New York: Union of American Hebrew Congregations, 1948), pp.183–226.
36. *Ecclesiastes Rabbah* 7:15, 1.
37. Plato, *Republic* I, 332.
38. 'Justice' in *Encyclopedia Judaica*.
39. This idea, found in earlier sources, is stressed in the moral philosophy of Hermann Cohen.
40. Generally speaking, I am identifying 'justice' with the Hebrew words *mishpat* and *din*, *hesed* with 'mercy'; *rahmanut* with 'compassion'; *zedek* with 'righteousness'. See the article on

'Righteousness' in *Encyclopedia Judaica* for sources and discussion. A poignant example of righteousness as doing right despite the strict interpretation of the law is in the Talmudic story of the wine porters in *Baba Metzia* 83a. For the idea that the absence or perversion of justice leads to the destruction of society, see *Exodus Rabbah* 30:19. For the idea that too strict and literal an interpretation of law leads to destruction, see *Gittin* 56a.

41. Eccles. 7:20, Ps. 143:2, Job 4:17, 15:14.
42. *Berakhot* 10a.
43. For this and many other insights contained in these pages, I am grateful to my teacher, the late Rabbi Seymour Siegel. See his 'Religion and Social Action', *Proceedings of the Rabbinical Assembly* (1961).
44. Heschel, *God in Search of Man*, p.377.
45. *Exodus Rabbah* 30:10.

Inward Journeys

'Why did God create human beings with *two* eyes, rather than with one or three of four?', a disciple once asked his master, Rabbi Mendel of Kotzk.

'Because human beings need no more and no less than two eyes', answered the master. 'They need one eye for looking outward, at the world. And, they need a second eye for peering inward, into the self'.

In the biblical text, God's first words to Abraham are '*Lekh lekha*' meaning 'you go out' (Gen. 12:1). This is one of the two parts of the polarity that the spiritual life embraces – going outside the self, transcending the self to encounter the world. The second part of the polarity relates to the inward journey. According to a Hasidic master, this dimension of the spiritual journey is also indicated by the words '*Lekh lekha*', which can be translated as 'go into yourself', travel inward. Jewish spirituality revolves around this polarity of the inward and the outward, the journey out to the world and the journey in to the self. One without the other is incomplete.

The spiritual pilgrim, like Abraham, is no voyeur on a tour of the world, but an exile in search of a spiritual homeland, an ephemeral subject in search of an elusive predicate. The spiritual pilgrim is a person who strives for self-transcendence rather than social approval. For such an individual, life is a continuous adventure in awareness, a perennial pilgrimage in perception. The spiritual seeker inhales wonder and exhales awe.

According to rabbinic legends, Abraham's quest began with an encounter with nature. His great innovation was the discovery that nature is not divine, but is rather a visa to encountering the divine. Abraham detected that to worship the world is idolatry, to consider nature as divine is like considering a book as having no author. For Abraham, the universe is a book written by God. Through studying the oeuvre, one can move closer to its Author. Commenting on the verse in Psalms, 'I look at the heavens, the work of God's fingers' (Ps. 8:4), Rabbi Nahman of Bratzlav told this parable:

Once, a prince lived far away from his father, the king. Each day he longed for his father's presence. One day, he received a letter from his father, and he was overjoyed and treasured the letter. Yet, the joy the letter gave him only increased his longing even more. He would sit and cry, 'Oh, if I could see my father and touch his hand. Merciful father, how would I love to touch and kiss your little finger'. And while he was crying, feeling the longing for the touch of his father, a thought came into his mind. 'Do I not have my father's letter, written in his own hand? And, is not the handwriting of the king comparable to his hand?' And, suddenly, a great joy burst forth in the heart of the prince.

In the encounter with creation, the story of 'Eyes' and 'No-Eyes' is the story of the spiritually enriched, and the spiritually deprived. 'Eyes' and 'No-Eyes' find themselves on a path in the midst of a dense forest. 'No-Eyes' feels obliged to traverse the path with dispatch. The goal is to arrive at the destination as quickly, as efficiently, and as comfortably as possible. Trudging along, 'No-Eyes' ignores the mystery and the marvels of the forest. 'No-Eyes' remains oblivious to the beams of sunlight that dance upon the leaves, to the gentle caress of the breeze upon his face, to the symphony of the animals that scamper in the brush, and to the manifold panorama of colour and hue that envelops the traveller. When 'No-Eyes' stops to look at a plant or at an animal, it is only to recall its name, merely to remember to which botanical species or zoological category it has been assigned. For 'No-Eyes', nature is a potential enemy to be dissected, mastered and controlled. Calculating what to do upon reaching the clearing of the forest, 'No-Eyes' remains oblivious to the pregnant drama of the moment.

'Eyes' walks along the same path. For 'Eyes', each step, each instant, is replete with wonder. Each tree is an unmasked miracle in disguise. Each moment is a marvel bursting with beauty. 'Eyes' hears the birds and sees the sunbeams calling out their salutations. The very journey is a joy. The grandeur of nature is inebriating. For 'Eyes', each instant is a destination, each glimpse a revelation, each breath a precious gift; each step opens a door to awe. For 'Eyes', each glance testifies to the Artist who created it all. Each murmur betrays the presence of the Composer of the symphony of life.

At the end of the path, 'Eyes' and 'No-Eyes', meet. 'No-Eyes', when told of 'Eyes'' adventures, refuses to believe they both had traversed the identical path. 'No-Eyes' fancies 'Eyes' as a hallucinatory dreamer. But, 'Eyes', who represents the spiritual pilgrim, would rather be perpetually entranced by the ineffable splendour of creation than rush through life like a window-shopping tourist in search of a bargain. No celibate where the world is concerned, the proclivity of the spiritual seeker is toward a romance with creation. For the spiritual seeker, the sensual can be a prelude to the spiritual. Marvelling in creation is foreplay for sacred intercourse with the Creator. The natural world is a garment that conceals the supernatural dimension of existence. The spiritual seeker desires to divest the world of its outer garment so as to enter into intimacy with the divine concealed beneath it.

In the midst of gently exchanging a series of shared caresses with creation, the spiritual seeker discovers that just to be is a blessing that has been bestowed by the Source of all blessings. Existence becomes co-existence with the remarkably diverse expressions of divine creativity that comprise the fellowship of creation. In the moment of deepest intimacy with creation, spiritual elation borders on revelation.

God is the ultimate creator, the ultimate artist. As a being created in the image of God, as the most superlative art work of the divine imagination, as the partner of God in the work of creation, the challenge is to complete God's unfinished artistic masterpieces – the world, and the self. Like the world, each of us is an unfinished masterpiece of God. Like a master artist, God leaves completion of what had been initiated by the master to the apprentice. Each of us is an artistic apprentice of God. The goal of the spiritual life is the creation of each of our lives as an art form, as a work of art of which both the Creator and the apprentice co-creator can be proud.

In creating life as a work of art, each of us is an initiate serving a perpetual novitiate. There are always concealed possibilities encoded in each of our souls waiting to be revealed, to be decoded. During a single life, the soul may transmigrate many times. Only with death is the definitive edition of each life complete. Until then, there are always new melodies to compose, new songs to sing, new pages of the novel that is each of our lives yet to be authored.

It is told that once a disciple of Levi Yitzhak of Berditchev asked his master, 'Why does each tractate of the Talmud begin with page number two, rather than with page number one?'

'To teach us', replied Levi Yitzhak, 'that no matter how much we know, we must always remember that we are still beginning, that we have not yet even gotten to the first page'.

The Jewish New Year, Rosh Hashanah, begins in the seventh month of the Hebrew calendar and not – as one might expect – in the first month. One of the commentators observes that the reason is to teach us that a person can begin anew at any time, and not only in the beginning. The quest to create life as an art form may still begin in mid-life, or even toward life's end. As the Hasidic masters taught, it is never too late and never too early to remove the rust that corrodes one's soul.

The soul is a seed implanted within each of us. Each person is like a tree that may choose whether or when to bring forth its own fruit. At life's end, one may return a diminished form of what was received, or more than was received at life's beginning. Each individual has the choice to corrode or to create, to pollute or to improve, what initially had been granted.

For Jewish spirituality, human existence is too precarious, life too fragile, and time too precious, not to be taken with the utmost seriousness. Commenting on the verse in Ecclesiastes (9:8), 'Let your garments always be white; let not oil be lacking on your head', Rabbi Israel of Rhyzen commented, 'A person should view himself or herself as being dressed in white silken garments with a pitcher of oil on his or her head, walking a tightrope over an abyss. A single wrong small step and the garments become stained. A single irretrievable step and the person falls into the abyss below'.

For Jewish spirituality, sacred deeds are the seeds toward creating life as a work of art. The sacred deed is faith in the form of action. The sacred act is not primarily viewed as a way of providing oneself a portion in the World-to-Come, but as a way of providing God with a presence in *this* world. Performance of the sacred deed is a way to bear witness to the Creator. Commenting on the verse in Isaiah (43:12), 'You are my witnesses says God', a Talmudic rabbi said: 'If you are My witnesses, then I am God. But, when you are not My witnesses, it is as if I am not God'.

The spiritual quest is a perpetual adventure of hide-and-seek, rather than a game of 'trivial pursuit'. The spiritual pilgrim is a person in search of the divine masked by creation.

It is told that the grandson of Rabbi Barukh of Miedzyborz was once playing hide-and-seek with a friend. The boy stayed in his hiding place assuming that his friend would come and look for him. After waiting a long time, it was clear that his friend had decided not to try to find him. The boy ran into the study of his grandfather complaining about how his hiding had been in vain. Upon hearing the story, Rabbi Barukh began to cry. 'Why are you crying, grandfather?', asked the boy. 'Because', said Rabbi Barukh, 'God, too, says "I hide. Will no one come to search for Me?"'

For the spiritually developed individual, there is but one entity that is surely no illusion, ephemeral fancy, passing fad, or public - relations stunt – and that is God. God is the anchor for each individual's spiritual quest as he or she attempts to navigate the currents of absurdity, the whirlpools of trauma, and the shifting winds of historical change. God is the meaning beyond absurdity, the source of truth beyond deceptions, ultimacy beyond the transient. As God may be found hiding behind the disguise of creation, God may also be found absconded within the self. In this view, the search for spiritual self-awareness, the inner journey, is simultaneously a quest for encounter with the divine.

Beginning in the sixteenth-century, Jewish mystics began to describe the individual soul as 'a part of God from above' (Job 31:2). In this view, each individual is an incarnation of God; each person carries an element of divinity within. From this perspective, the quest for self-knowledge and the quest for encounter with the divine begin not only with a journey into the world, but also with a journey inward, into the self. Without self-encounter, there is no self with whom to seek that which is beyond the self. Self-awareness is a path which, if properly traversed, can lead to the innermost chambers of the palace of God. Self-awareness is a critical step in the creation of life as art form. A person who encounters the world, a person who embarks upon the outward journey but who fails to encounter the self and the divine within the self, who does not also embark on the inward journey, becomes a conclusion without a premise, a contradiction, a spiritual fallacy.

Through the performance of sacred deeds that shape life as an art form, the individual human being can offer the divine a home within the self. Each person may extend an invitation to the divine to become incarnated within his or her own self. In this regard, the *Zohar*, the central work of the Jewish mystics, states: 'Happy is the person who lets God dwell in every single organ of his or her body, making a place for the divine to dwell there ... so that no organ is devoid of God'.

For Christianity, God became incarnate in one person. But for the Jewish mystics, the divine may become incarnated in *each* human person. For the Jewish mystics, each human being,through the performance of sacred deeds, can incarnate the divine within themselves.

In a similar vein, Mendel of Kotzk commented on a verse in Deuteronomy (6:6): 'These words shall be upon your heart'. 'Why', he asked, 'does the verse describe the word of God as being *upon* the heart, *on* the heart, rather than *in* the heart? Because', he said, 'the word of God lies *upon* the heart, waiting for the heart to open so that the word of God may enter the human heart. God dwells where the human being lets the divine enter'.

Each person is an envelope bearing a divine message, a divine presence. The spiritual challenge to each person is to convey and to bear witness to this message by the way in which we live. By realizing the presence of God implanted within each person, we can bring about not only the realization of our own individual spiritual selves, but also the augmentation of the Source of all selves. The danger, however, is that we may become messengers who either lose or forget the message.

According to Jewish spirituality, there are four converging paths to the creation of life as an art form, four roads to spiritual self-development, four paths that can lead to the divine: the world, the self, the sacred deed, and the sacred word. The sacred word is a road and a rope with each of us at one end and God at the other end.

Just as a person can encounter the Author of the book which is the world through the *work* the Author has composed, so can one encounter the author of the *word* – the author of the Torah – through study of the letters and the words that comprise it. The sacred word can be a rendezvous of the human and the divine. Commenting on the verse in Exodus (25:8): 'They shall make Me [God] a sanctuary so that I can dwell among them', Rabbi Moses Hayyim Ephraim of Sudlykow said, 'This verse means that each of us must create a sanctuary within ourselves for God to dwell. But how can we make it so that God dwells within us? The way is through the Torah which is God's Name. Since the Torah is God's Name, it is identical with God'.

According to the Gospel of John (1:1), 'In the beginning there was the word and the word was with God, and the word was God'. However, according to the Jewish mystics, it is the opposite. In the beginning there was God, and God becomes the word. God infused the divine Name, the divine presence, into the letters and the words of the text of the Torah. By entering the word, we encounter the divine. The quest for God, for truth, for self-knowledge, for instruction in creating life as a work of art, begins with the Torah, with the word of God, with meeting God in the word *of* God, the word that *is* God, the word where the divine presence dwells.

In Hebrew, the word for letter is *teivah*. But *teivah* is also the word for 'ark'. The Ba'al Shem Tov interpreted God's command to Noah as a command to each person: 'Enter the *teivah*; enter the letter'. By entering the holy letter, through study of the sacred text, through praying the sacred word, one enters the word; there one can have a rendezvous with God.

By encounter with the world, a person can become God's partner in the work of creation. By entering the word, an individual can become God's partner in the work of revelation. One can become a co-author of the Torah, a co-creator of the sacred text. As Moses Hayyim Ephraim of wrote: 'Until the sages interpreted it, the Torah was not considered complete, but only half-finished. It is the rabbinic sages through their interpretations that make the Torah whole'.

Just as in the spiritual quest, one is always beginning, so in the understanding of the words of the Torah, no one but God has the final word. The liturgical blessing over the reading of the Torah describes God as the One 'who *gives* the Torah', that is to say, the Torah is perpetually being given, always being revealed, continuously being understood.

As the quest for self-knowledge is perpetually continuous, the quest for the knowledge of the Torah is always ongoing. The quest for truth is never-ending. Indeed, the truth is that *the* Truth cannot be fully known in our world of falsehoods, veils, lies and illusions. As the Jewish philosopher Franz Rosenzweig put it, 'Truth is a noun only for God; for human beings the truth must remain a tenuous adjective'.

For the Jewish mystics, since truth is a spiritual reality, it can only be truly known in a completely spiritual realm, which our world, alas, is not. We only can know partial truths, truths tainted with falsehood, compromised truths, what Martin Buber termed 'moment truths'.

The spiritually adept person is one who is aware that our most dearly affirmed convictions may only be deceptions travelling incognito, that our supposed intellectual sureties may simply be grand illusions, that what we tend to equate with reality may merely be an illusion in the mind of God, that human history may only be a bad dream from which God will one day awaken. For the spiritual pilgrim, scepticism should not be an invitation to despair, but an antidote against intellectual vulgarity and arrogance. Doubt is not a catalyst for hopelessness or an invitation to cynicism, but a weapon in the constant battle against self-delusion. In the spiritual quest, hypocrisy is a greater danger than heresy, self-delusion a more urgent fear than failure. When asked, 'Who is a *Hasid*? Who is pious?', Rabbi Bunam of Przysucha replied, 'A *Hasid* is one who does more than the law requires. The law demands that one not deceive one's own neighbour. A *Hasid* is one who goes above the letter of the law. A *Hasid* is one who endeavours not to deceive his or her own self'. But, even worse than self-deception, is deceiving the self and remaining oblivious to it. As Rabbi Mendel of Kotzk put it, 'It is bad enough to be in a state of exile, of alienation. But, it is even worse to be in a state of exile and not even know it'.

At the heart of the spiritual journey is the promise of self-transformation. Various spiritual disciplines offer road maps as to how such self-transformations can be achieved. The Jewish mystics perceived the spiritual quest as an encounter with one's own self-realized spiritually developed self. Once this encounter with the vision of one's self-realized self had been achieved during an intensified mystical experience, the subsequent task became to effect the transformation of the self from who and where one is, to where one can be and to whom one can become. The goal is to find oneself by losing oneself in God. In this view, once a person succeeds in envisioning his or her spiritually realized self, he or she can then embark upon the task of revisioning his or her spiritual profile; a person can focus on how to make the transformation from who one is to whom one can and should become.

For the Jewish mystics, the performance of sacred deeds and the study of sacred texts are critical components in this process of self-realization. In discussing this process, the Jewish mystics refer to two similar Hebrew words: *zel* and *zelem*. *Zel* means 'shadow'; *zelem* refers to the 'image of God', to the individuating principle that defines who each of us can become. In other words, a person may choose to remain a *zel*, a shadow of one's potential spiritual self; or, an individual can opt, through spiritual development, to realize one's potential as *zelem*, as 'the image of God', as one's realized spiritual self.

In the final analysis, the spiritual journey is a challenge to become who each of us can be. For Jewish spirituality, the spiritual journey is not an attempt to escape the world but to transform it, not to obliterate the self but to fulfil it.

Of Rabbi Zusya of Hanipol, it is told that when he was on his deathbed, he began to cry. His disciples asked, 'Why do you cry, master? Are you afraid that when you arrive before the heavenly tribunal, they will ask you: Why were you not like Isaiah, or like Rabbi Akiva, or like Maimonides? Why were you not like the great prophets, sages and scholars of times past?'

Zusya said, 'No. That is not what I'm afraid of, for I am not a prophet, a sage, nor a scholar'.

'Then, master, why are you crying?', his disciples asked again. 'What do you fear they will ask you when you appear in the next world before the Heavenly Court'.

And Zusya said, 'I am afraid they will ask me: Zusya, why weren't you Zusya? Why did you permit yourself to be deluded? Why did you not become all you could have become during life? If I am asked these questions, then I shall truly be lost'.

There is an old Jewish tradition related to Rosh Hashanah that God records each person's deeds in a book. Upon the death of each individual, he or she is presented with the book of his or her own life. In this view, through his or her deeds, each person composes a novel that represents his or her own life. At life's end, the last words are written. The definitive edition is completed. At that point, the volume becomes the provenance of the critics. The question each person must therefore face as he or she goes through life is: What will the reviewers say about the book, about the story of my life, about the quality of the work of art that is my life?

PART II
JEWISH AND CHRISTIAN THEOLOGY

CHAPTER ELEVEN

Toward a Jewish Theology of Christianity

In 1985, at an event in Rome celebrating the twentieth anniversary of *Nostra Aetate*, Vatican II's historic statement on the relationship of the Catholic Church to non-Christian religions, John Paul II said,

> In our days one can sometimes have the sad impression of an absence of God and his will from the private and public lives of men and women. When we reflect on such a situation and its tragic consequences for mankind, deprived of its roots in God and therefore of its basic moral orientation, one can only be grateful to the Lord because we believe in him, as Jews and Christians, and we both can say in the words of Deuteronomy [6:4], 'Hear O Israel, the Lord our God is one God'.[1]

John Paul II suggested that Jews and Christians can affirm their belief in God, express their gratitude for the gift of faith in God, articulate the conviction that God is the source of their moral norms, and worship God, by reciting this verse from Deuteronomy that Jews usually translate as 'Hear, O Israel! The Lord is our God, the Lord is one' or 'Hear, O Israel! The Lord is our God, the Lord alone'.[2] Yet when Jews and Christians recite this verse from Deuteronomy, do they take it to mean the same thing? Are they affirming belief in the same God? Are they praying to the same God? How do their doctrinal differences affect how Jews and Christians respond to these questions and to how they implement theological dialogue?

Christians have often understood the three references to God in this verse (the Lord, our God, the Lord) as referring to the Trinity. On the other hand, medieval Jewish commentators took it as an affirmation not only of the one God, but also of the exclusive election of the people of Israel by God. They interpreted the phrase,

'Hear O Israel' to mean that this verse is addressed exclusively to the people of Israel.[3] Commentators like Yosef Bekhor Shor claimed that the daily recitation by Jews of this verse is meant to be a polemic against the Trinitarian view that he and others considered false, heretical, polytheistic and idolatrous.[4] Indeed, at various junctures in Jewish history, especially during the Middle Ages, Jewish martyrs would recite this verse when choosing to surrender their lives rather than accept forced conversion to Christianity. That Jews did so indicates that they considered Christianity to be an idolatrous and polytheistic religion that believes in and worships other gods than the true God.[5] For these medieval Jews, Christians neither believe in nor worship the same God as Jews.

Midrashic literature anticipated the interpretations of the medieval Jewish biblical exegetes on this verse. For example, the Midrashic collection *Sifrei on Deuteronomy*, interprets the phrase 'our God' as referring to the God of Israel and the term 'the Lord is one' as referring to the God of other peoples. But, says *Sifrei*, now, in pre-messianic times, only the people of Israel believe in and worship the true God, the only God, the God who is one. Others do not. Only in the messianic age yet to come will non-Jews come to acknowledge the true and only God. The phrase 'the Lord is our God', the God of Israel, refers to this world (*olam ha-zeh*), the pre-messianic world, while 'the Lord is one' refers to the messianic world (*olam ha-ba*). Until the messianic age arrives, God is not really one – not because oneness is not God's nature, but because until then, humanity will not recognize God as being truly one. As a proof text, this passage quotes the verse in Zechariah (14:9): 'On that day the Lord shall be one and his name one'. For *Sifrei*, in our times only Jews believe in and worship the true God; others do not.[6]

The claim that this verse from Deuteronomy is addressed exclusively to Jews, and that it establishes that God considers Israel uniquely and exclusively chosen by God, is clearly stated by the Talmudic rabbis. As God is one, unique, so is Israel unique, in that Israel is God's exclusively chosen people (see 1 Chron. 17:21 as cited by this Talmudic passage). From this perspective, only the people of Israel believe in, worship, and have been exclusively chosen by God.[7] Even today, in some synagogues, an ancient version of the *Aleinu* prayer is recited in which this view is articulated. The text reads, 'our lot is not like that of their masses. For they bow to something vain and employ and pray to a god who cannot save, but we bow to the King of kings'.[8] Like *Sifrei*, the *Aleinu* prayer quotes the aforementioned verse from Zechariah and looks forward to a messianic age in which all peoples will worship God while contrasting that age with their own in which only the people of Israel affirms the true God.

Christian–Jewish relations were not a *creatio ex nihilo*. They are rooted in a long history of bitter social tensions, deep hostilities and combative theological disputations. For most of this history, Christianity was viewed by Jewish scholars as being a polytheistic, idolatrous faith and not a monotheistic religion. Christians were considered dangerous, demonic, impure.[9] At the same time, the Jew was viewed by the Christians as demonic, anti-Christ, criminal, blasphemous, heretical and either blind or stubbornly recalcitrant to Christian truth. The Jew was neither considered to believe in or to worship the true God. Rather, the Jew was considered to be an agent, an ally and a worshipper of Satan. The Jew was accursed for having committed the sin of deicide. He was accused of having perverted both the text and the meaning of Scripture. He was considered to be physically and metaphysically different from, and inferior to, Christians.[10] Thus, in the medieval Christian view, the Jew neither believed in nor worshipped the same God as the Christian. Christian teachings about Jews and Judaism largely embraced what Jules Isaac called 'the teaching of contempt', which often led to what Fr. Edward Flannery in his now classic book, called 'the anguish of the Jews'.[11] In other words, medieval Jewish views of Christianity and Christians and medieval Christian views of Jews and Judaism were a mirror image of one another. The primary difference was that Christians possessed the power to implement their attitudes and views.

As many of these theological and social views of the past need to be revised, so do many of the apologetic views of more recent years. One such view coalesces around the claim of a 'Judeo-Christian' tradition. The affirmation of a Judeo-Christian tradition perpetuates the illusion that Judaism and Christianity basically embrace the same beliefs, doctrines, ethical categories and sacred texts. But this is not the case.[12] Jewish and Christian beliefs and doctrines differ in many essential ways. The principles and categories of ethics and the manner and methods in which they are applied are different.

Different texts are considered to be canonical and authoritative. The texts that are shared (for example, Hebrew Scripture) bear different interpretive overlays that in effect transform them into different texts, depending on the perspective of the reader. If we assume that texts are what they mean more than what they say, then even the shared texts differ.

How can the often tragic past history of Catholic–Jewish relations be overcome without sliding into apologetics? How can the unfortunate and undesirable traditions of the past be confronted and transcended? In this regard, it is important for Jews to acknowledge that the Roman Catholic Church, especially since Vatican II, has made enormous and courageous strides in positively restating its theological and social teachings about Jews and Judaism. These include teachings related to such critical issues such as: supersession, displacement, mission to the Jews, the deicide claim, the perpetuation of the covenant between God and the people of Israel, anti-Semitism and the State of Israel. As I have discussed elsewhere, the Holy See's Commission on Religious Relations with the Jews since its inception, the statements and deeds of John Paul II throughout his pontificate, along with the words of various national episcopates, individual theologians, scholars and prelates, have produced a new though unquestionably authentic Catholic theology of Jews and Judaism.[13] This Catholic theology of Jews and Judaism has reduced what once seemed to be insurmountable barriers to fraternal dialogue. It has made dialogue both possible and desirable. By affirming 'common meeting in the presence of God', the Church acknowledges that Jews and Catholic Christians affirm and pray to the same God, and therefore encourages that 'from now on, real dialogue must be established'.[14]

Despite the legion efforts made by the Catholic Church to remove theological and social barriers to 'real dialogue' and to forcefully encourage such dialogue, one must candidly admit that, regretably the Jewish community has not reciprocated in kind. It has not evaluated, reconsidered or restated many of its medieval – and, I would add, undesirable – attitudes toward Christianity and Christians. So, unfortunately, for many Jews today, the medieval attitudes of enmity, suspicion, stereotyping and bitter polemics still obtain. The Church is still often seen as an adversary and not as a friend. Unfortunately, many Jews today generally remain unaware of the considerable strides toward reconciliation taken by the Church in recent decades. For such individuals, it is as if nothing has changed in Catholic teachings regarding Jews and Judaism since the Middle Ages. As Cardinal Edward Cassidy put it, while serving as President of the Holy See's Commission on Religious Relations with the Jews, 'I am truly amazed at times to read Catholic teaching and doctrine explained in Jewish publications in such a way that no Catholic would recognize them as part of his or her faith'.[15]

A careful reading of post-Vatican II Church teachings on the Jews and Judaism, although they overturn earlier long-standing pervasive views, are represented as being continuous with traditional Catholic teachings. In other words, past Catholic teachings have been revised without threatening either the continuity or the authenticity of the Church's views on Jews and Judaism. On the other hand, the – as of yet – largely unmet challenge to Jewish theologians is to similarly reconstruct and to revise attitudes and views towards Christians and Christianity. In what now follows, I hope to make a contribution toward meeting that challenge. Utilizing classical and authoritative Jewish religious sources, I shall now propose a reformulated Jewish theology of Christianity, especially insofar as Christian teachings about God, Jesus, the Trinity and Incarnation are concerned. I begin this investigation by reviewing a curious responsum, an example of Jewish case law, that considers the question of whether it is permissible for a believing Jew to contribute funds toward the building of a church. This responsum was composed in 1891 by Marcus Horowitz, rabbi of the Orthodox Jewish community of Frankfurt.

In this responsum, Horowitz cites the views of past (mostly medieval) Jewish authorities who discuss the status of Christianity according to Jewish law, particularly those who reject the typically medieval Jewish premise that Christianity is a form of polytheism and idolatry. Consequently, he rules that it is not only permitted for Jews to contribute funds to build a church, but that it is also a *mitzvah* and a 'sanctification of God's Name'. 'We all acknowledge', writes Horowitz, 'that whoever is not a Jew can become of the saints and great men of the world and admitted to the World-to-Come, if he keeps the Noachian laws given to all humankind'.[16]

Horowitz's responsum is significant in a number of ways. First, it indicates that the views of earlier Jewish scholars who considered

Christianity as theologically illegitimate and untenable, an idolatrous and polytheistic religion, are neither definitive nor ultimately authoritative. Second, Horowitz demonstrates that there are adequate precedents for considering Christianity to be theologically respectable and viable, at least for Christians. Third, in citing the Talmudic notion of the covenant of the descendents of Noah, he provides a Halakhic framework for dealing with non-Jewish monotheists. According to the Talmud, the Noahide covenant requires monotheistic belief. By considering believing Christians as adherents to the Noachian covenant, Horowitz therefore claims that Christians are monotheists. They therefore believe in and pray to the same God as Jews and other monotheists.[17]

Anticipating certain more recent advocates of a 'dual covenant' theory, espoused by Franz Rosenzweig and others, Horowitz implies that there are two co-existing covenants: the covenant between God and Israel, and the covenant between God and 'the descendants of Noah', the rest of humankind.[18] Those non-Jews who obey the commandments of the Noahide covenant, especially the commandment to affirm the one God, are monotheists who affirm and worship the same God as the people of Israel, albeit in a different manner. For Horowitz, therefore, believing Christians are monotheists, and are covenanted through the Noahide laws. Though Horowitz's view represents a dramatic advance over earlier views, his approach does not go far enough in that it does not recognize the validity of Christianity per se. Nor does it explicitly deal with specific Christian theological claims about God. It merely lumps Christians together with other Noachians.

Monotheism rests upon the presupposition that there is only one God, and that, as the *Shema* (Deut. 6:4) puts it, 'God is one'. According to Maimonides, to say God is 'one' means that God is unique, *sui generis*, one of a kind.[19] As modern logicians might put it: God is a member of a class of beings of which God is the only member. From the monotheistic premise that there is but one God, it follows that all monotheists believe in and worship the same God. Since Judaism, Christianity and Islam – the Abrahamic faiths – are all monotheistic faiths, it would follow that their faithful adherents all believe in and worship the same God. How, then, can we account for the fact that the beliefs articulated by these faiths and the ways employed by them to worship this same God, differ, sometimes substantially? This question is particularly relevant insofar as Judaism and Catholic Christianity are concerned, given the theological disputations on fundamental issues of faith, liturgical language and biblical hermeneutics that historically have placed them in conflict. An excursion into a few classical Jewish sources regarding the nature of God may provide some insights to these problems.

God

In his erudite and voluminous writings, the sixteenth-century Jewish mystic, theologian, Halakhist, commentator and communal leader, Judah Loew of Prague, employs a phrase that proves helpful to our inquiry. That phrase in Hebrew is: *ha-kol hu mi-tzad ha-mekabeil*, 'everything is from the side of the recipient'. However, vocalized another way, this could also be read, *ha-kol hu mi-tzad ha-mekubal*, 'everything is from the perspective of the mystic'. The context in which Loew utilizes this term is his discussion of the nature of God.[20] Both readings are pertinent to our discussion.

According to Judah Loew, we know nothing and can know nothing about the nature or essence of God. It would be a presumption for human beings to claim knowledge of God's essence.[21] Loew's predecessors in the history of Jewish thought already had established this claim.[22] When Loew says, 'everything is from the side of the recipient' insofar as God is concerned, he means that though we do not know God's essence or nature, what we have, all we have, are our perceptions, experiences and traditions about God. These do not have God as God really may be, as their referents. Rather, all of our thinking, speaking and theologizing about God, have our own perceptions, experiences and traditions as their referents. Therefore, our predication of divine attributes does not necessarily have God as its referent but rather has the word 'God' and our own perceptions of God as its referent.

If we concur with Loew's view that the nature and essence of God are unknowable and that our theologies represent human apprehensions of the divine, then we may say that neither Judaism nor Christianity knows the essence or nature of God. All we have are our own apprehensions, experiences and traditions. The God in whom we believe and whom we worship is the same, but our conceptions of God differ. But are they valid? I shall discuss this question below.

In his writings, Loew makes reference to his eclectic contemporary,

Eliezer Ashkenazi, a rabbi as well as a physician, originally from the Middle East who ended up in Poland. Ashkenazi composed most of his magnum opus, *Ma'aseh Ha-Shem, The Works of God*, in Gneizno, the primatial seat of Poland. This work contains a remarkable statement, given its time and place, about religious diversity.[23] In his commentary on the biblical story of the Tower of Babel, Ashkenazi reiterates the views of earlier commentators that the people who built the Tower were not only, as the Bible says, 'of one language', but also of one religion. God therefore intervened in this situation. For Ashkenazi, anticipating Heschel's statement that 'religious pluralism is the will of God', the existence of a single religion precludes free intellectual, theological investigation.[24] Ashkenazi further states that only with this divine intervention at the Tower could it become possible for Abraham to engage in the theological investigations, that according to rabbinic legend, led Abraham to establish monotheistic belief, and the Abrahamic faiths.[25] For Ashkenazi, religious diversity is a precondition for free theological investigation. Further, as Heschel puts it, also when reflecting on the biblical story of the Tower of Babel, '[people] all over the world, though they confess different conceptions of God, are really worshipping one God … Religions, true to their own convictions, disagree profoundly and are in opposition to one another on matters of doctrine … [But] the voice of God reaches the spirit of man in a variety of ways, in a multiplicity of languages. One truth comes to expression in many ways of understanding'.[26] Yet how can specific doctrinal differences be dealt with? Specifically, how can Judaism relate to Christology, Jesus, the Trinity, Incarnation?

Christology

With regard to Christology, let us consider a remarkable statement by the fifteenth-century Italian rabbi, Abraham Farisol. He wrote,

> Let us assume that their Christ is a Messiah for them and we [Jews] shall neither deny nor affirm that which befell their Messiah. For to my mind, it is distinctly feasible that they be justified in designating him as their rightful redeemer. For they have declared – and it is in fact true – that since he came and imparted his doctrines, they have been redeemed and cleansed of the pollution of idol worship.[27]

Farisol makes a number of critical observations here. One is that Christians' belief in Jesus as the Messiah, rather than leading them to incorrect belief, actually liberated them from idolatry and brought them to monotheistic faith. Unlike many of his contemporary Jewish scholars, Farisol does not consider Christianity as having introduced a new form of idolatry into the world, but rather as having introduced a new form of monotheism into the world for the non-Jews. The second claim that Farisol makes is that while Christian doctrinal belief is not true for Jews, within the framework of monotheism it is nonetheless valid for Christians. Indeed, without Christology, those who are now Christians would have remained polytheists and idolators. In other words, religious diversity is both desirable and acceptable. Furthermore, religious truth need not be absolute nor universal to retain its truth value. Within the context of monotheistic faith, more than one religion may be valid. Everything is from the perspective of the tradition and the experience of its recipients. Jewish theology is valid and true for Jews. Christology is valid and true for Christians, but not for Jews or Judaism. For Judaism, Christology is superfluous.

This view negotiates a position between the rigidity of absolutism and triumphalism, and the potential chaos and anarchy of relativism. It claims that monotheistic religions are true, but that non-monotheistic religions are not true. For Jews, this means that Judaism is true and is binding exclusively upon Jews. Indeed, the notion of Jewish election, often denigrated by non-Jews, actually can serve as a foundation for accepting the validity of other faiths, especially when one considers that the concomitant of chosenness is a formidable restraint on the missionary impulse. This also means that, for Jews, other monotheistic religions such as Christianity and Islam have their own integrity, authenticity and validity. Indeed, for Judah Ha-Levi and Maimonides, other monotheistic faiths have a distinct mission in conveying monotheistic faith and ethical principles to the peoples of the world. In this way, they are *preparatio messianica*, preparing the world for the day when all peoples will believe in and worship the one God.[28]

The critical issue here is the presumption of a belief in monotheism and the unity and oneness of God. According to some, this also entails the doctrine of *creatio ex nihilo*, that the world was created by God from nothing. For example, a seventeenth-century Lithuanian

Talmudist, Rabbi Moses Rivkes, contends that members of a faith community, for example, Christians, who affirm these doctrines, cannot be considered as idolators, and must be considered as sharing the essentials of monotheistic faith: in that sense, their faith has truth and validity.[29] Put another way, as long as non-Jews affirm monotheism, their particular theological doctrines pose no problem for Judaism. Within the context of their own traditions and theology, Christianity is true for Christians. That Rivkes' statement is part of an important commentary on an authoritative legal code gives his view not only theological but also legal status.

Trinity

As we have seen, the Trinity was considered an heretical and polytheistic idea by most medieval Jewish scholars, especially philosophers. However, with the decline of medieval Jewish philosophy and the emergence of certain Jewish mystical ideas, the Trinity became a largely passé issue in Jewish writings on Christianity.[30] Indeed, there seems to be a linkage between the emergence of Kabbalah and the decline of Jewish polemical concern with the Trinity. Here we can evoke Judah Loew's statement that 'everything is from the perspective of the mystic'.

Maimonides had produced a philosophically elegant way of speaking about God even when we know nothing of God's essence. In an attempt to protect God's perfection (perfection understood in Aristotelean terms), Maimonides claims that God cannot have any relationship with God's own creatures, including human beings, because a relationship between a perfect being (God) and an imperfect being (humans) would compromise and corrupt God's perfection. As St Thomas Aquinas already pointed out, this view is untenable.[31] After all, religion is grounded in the divine–human relationship. Maimonides' view may be philosophically convincing but it is theologically counterproductive. As Judah Loew notes, without the divine–human relationship, what is religion? How could there be creation, revelation, prayer or redemption, unless there is a relationship between God and God's creatures, especially human beings?

Like earlier Jewish mystics, Loew distinguishes between God in essence (*En Sof*) and God in manifestation (*sefirot*), the *Deus absconditus* and the *Deus revelatus*: God as fire and as flame; God as God is, and, God as God is manifest to and perceived by us.

According to the Jewish mystics, there are ten emanations or manifestations of the divine called *sefirot* (sing.: *sefirah*). Jewish philosophical opponents to Jewish mysticism claimed that whereas Christians ascribed three ways in which God manifests himself, the Kabbalists ascribed ten such ways. In his commentary to Deuteronomy 6:4, noted above, Bahye ben Asher feels obliged to try to distinguish the Kabbalistic idea of the *sefirot* from the doctrine of the Trinity; yet both maintain that the Godhead is manifest in a number of ways.[32] It may well be that Kabbalistic teachings about the *sefirot* made Jewish opposition to the Trinity less plausible. The Trinity was now apparently considered to be an idea that did not compromise monotheism, though it was an idea that could not become a feature of any authentic theology of Judaism.

By the time we arrive in the eighteenth century, we find even such a conservative Halakhist as Rabbi Jacob Emden referring to Christians as 'holy brothers' and as members of a 'holy community of God'. Emden unequivocally considers Christians to be monotheists whom he asks to be true to their religion, especially its moral principles which, in his view, should hopefully lead them to love Jews as well as others. Though Emden required a more rigorous monotheism of Jews than he did of Christians, he did not consider the Trinity as compromising monotheistic belief among Christians.[33]

The Kabbalistic teachings about the *sefirot* often bestow 'gender' designations on them. In this view, the aspect of the divinity most proximate and accessible to us is the tenth emanation or *sefirah*, known as *Malkhut* or Shekhinah, which is considered to be a 'feminine' aspect of the divine. Recent scholarship has argued that the formulation of the idea of the Shekhinah in Jewish mysticism was influenced by a variety of Christian theological traditions about Mary.[34] Here we see in Jewish mystical literature, a literature that emphasized Jewish theological and national exclusivity, that we nonetheless encounter a profound Christian theological influence.[35] Here, we have an example of the influence of Christian theology on a significant Jewish view of the Godhead. Such examples demonstrate the interpenetration of Jewish and Christian theologies of God and demonstrate that, not only did Judaism theologically influence Christianity, but that Christian theology also influenced Jewish theology.

From the eighteenth century, an expression began to be used by

Jewish mystics and later by Hasidic leaders that seemed to represent a distinctly Jewish 'trinitarian' view. The expression is 'God, the Torah and Israel are one'.[36] In this view, three of the divine emanations or *sefirot* are united, one. But, Torah and Israel are not only identified with individual *sefirot*, that is, *Tiferet* and Shekhinah, but also with their earthly 'garments'. In this view, the text of the Torah that we have is a terrestrial manifestation of the divine Torah that is part of the Godhead.

Just as Jesus is part of the Godhead according to Christianity, the Torah is part of the Godhead according to the Jewish mystics. Just as Jesus manifests himself in physical form, so does the Torah. As the fourteenth-century Jewish mystic, Menahem Recanati, puts it, 'God is incomplete without the Torah. The Torah is not something outside God and God is not outside the Torah. Consequently, the mystic stated that God is the Torah'.[37] Or, as the *Zohar* bluntly puts it, 'The Torah is no other than the Holy One, blessed be He'.[38] Similarly, as will be discussed further below, the people of Israel is identified with the Shekhinah and each Jewish person is considered to be a limb of the body of the Shekhinah. It is interesting that toward the beginning of the twentieth century, Solomon Schechter already noted that the symbolism of a dove was commonly used by the rabbis to indicate both the Congregation of Israel (*Kenesset Yisrael*) and the Holy Spirit. Schechter suggests this to be the origin for the Christian symbolism of the dove for the third person of the Trinity.[39]

Incarnation

As the doctrine of the Trinity became increasingly irrelevant to the Jewish recognition of Christianity as a monotheistic faith, so did the doctrine of the Incarnation which had been a major issue in Jewish–Christian medieval philosophical disputation. As time progressed, it too came to be viewed as part of how the Christian tradition perceives the one God. However, another reason for the relenting of Jewish disputation regarding the Incarnation may be due to the presence of similar ideas found in the Jewish mystical tradition.

Throughout the history of Judaism a sharp dividing line between the divine and the human was established. In early Israelite religion this was done to distinguish its teachings from those of the religions of the ancient Near East that made no real distinction between the 'stuff' of which the gods, nature and humans are made. Later on, this sharp division between the divine and the human was partially made as a contribution to a polemic against the Christian idea of the Incarnation. However, in the Jewish mystical tradition, particularly, beginning with the sixteenth century, this Jewish distinction between the divine and the human begins to diminish. For example, following a Midrashic tradition, Judah Loew translated the beginning of Psalm 90 as follows. '*U-Moshe ish-ha-elohim*' ('And Moses was the man of God') as 'And Moses was the man-God', that is, Moses was both divine and human.[40] Elsewhere Loew writes, 'Within the human being dwells the soul which is a spark of God'.[41] As is well known, Scripture describes God as a fire (Deut. 4:24). In Loew's view, the human soul is a spark of this fire, a part of the divine. Not only is Moses part human and part divine, but so for Loew is every Jewish person.

While Loew uses figurative language to describe the human soul as a part of God, later sources become more explicit. For example, commenting on the verse in Deuteronomy (32:9), 'For the portion [Hebrew: *helek*, literally 'part'] of the Lord is His people', the sixteenth-century mystic, Rabbi Elijah de Vidas writes, 'The soul of each member of the people of Israel is an actual part of God'.[42] Probably influenced by de Vidas, and Loew, Rabbi Shabbatai Sheftel Horowitz comments on the same verse in Deuteronomy and writes, 'It is known that the souls of the people of Israel are "part of God from above"' [*helek elohah mi'maal*; see Job 31:2 for the origin of this phrase]. And this leads Horowitz to a novel translation and understanding of the *Shema* as: 'Hear! Israel and the Lord our God are One ... Israel is united with God in the upper worlds'.[43] In other words, the line between the divine and the human has been removed. In this view, not only one person, Moses, is essentially divine, but all persons. How then, could Judaism consider the doctrine of the Incarnation as problematic when such prominent spokespersons of its mystical tradition took a view which is not that dissimilar? In this view, not one person is essentially divine, but each Jewish person is.

In early east European Hasidic literature, a phrase begins to appear with increasing frequency: 'Each member of the people of Israel is a limb [of the body] of the Shekhinah'.[44] In other words, each Jew is a limb of the *Corpus Domini*.[45] Here we encounter an interesting development. In the theology of perhaps the most theologically insulated Jewish community imaginable, east European Hasidic Jewry, we encounter two ideas apparently influenced by Christian theology: first the Jewish mystical idea of the Shekhinah, and, second the idea of each member of the faith-community as a limb of the *Corpus Domini*, the body of God.[46]

In the Christian view, rooted in the New Testament, each Christian is a limb of the body of Christ, the *Corpus Christi*, the *Corpus Domini*. In Jewish mystical and Hasidic tradition, each Jew is a limb in the body of the Shekhinah, the body of God. The *Zohar* – the central work of the Kabbalists that appears in late thirteenth-century Spain, apparently served as a conduit for a Christian theological idea, rooted in the New Testament, to penetrate medieval Jewish theology, and to be developed further during the early modern period.[47] Before moving to a summary and conclusion, some observations about Jesus now follow.

Jesus

Most classical Jewish theological teachings express a negative view of Jesus. Though the twentieth-century Jewish philosopher, Martin Buber, called Jesus his 'brother',[48] much of classical Jewish theological teaching considered Jesus as an 'other' (*otoh ha-ish*; literally, a derogatory term for 'that man'), an apostate who subverted the teachings of Judaism, a Jew whose teachings were utilized by his followers as a justification for the persecution of the Jewish people in many lands over many centuries, and as the paradigmatic false Messiah. Jews, in effect, excommunicated Jesus from the Jewish faith and from the Jewish people.[49] On the other hand, almost every Christian nation has tried to expropriate Jesus from his own people – the Jews.

It is now time for Christians to accept Jesus as a Jew. It is also time for Jews to reclaim him as a legitimate and honoured member of the Jewish people – as a brother.[50] In this regard, the sainted Rabbi Leo Baeck, the most important Jewish leader in Nazi Germany, who survived the Holocaust, wrote, that in beholding Jesus,

> we behold a man who is Jewish in every feature and trait of his character, manifesting in every particular what is pure and good in Judaism. This man could have developed as he came

> to be only on the soil of Judaism, and only on this soil, too, could he find disciples and followers as they were. Here alone, in this Jewish sphere, in this Jewish atmosphere ... could this man live his life and meet his death – a Jew among Jews.[51]

Recent Jewish and Christian scholarship of the New Testament and of Judaism in the first century demonstrates that Jesus was much more a part of, than apart from, Jewish life and thought in his time and place than had been previously assumed. Jesus lived, taught and died as a Jew. Indeed, one cannot fully understand the life and teachings of Jesus when separated from the Jewish context from which they derive. This realization has led some contemporary scholars to maintain that it is precisely because earlier Jews and Christians failed to appreciate Jesus' rootedness in the Judaism of his time and place that led them to believe that Jesus' teachings are anti-Semitic or anti-Judaism. For these scholars, an appreciation of the Jewish nature of Jesus' life and teachings can serve as the basis for a more sympathetic view of Judaism by Christians and for a more sympathetic view of Jesus by Jews. For both Christians and Jews, understanding Jesus as a Jew can serve as the basis for removing barriers between Christians and Jews, and for establishing a foundation for fraternal dialogue. It may be observed, however, that the recovery of Jesus' 'Jewishness' poses new problems for the formulation of contemporary Christologies. However, that concern is beyond the scope of this essay. The concern here is with the meaning Jesus may have for Jews today. In that regard, the recovery of the Jewishness of Jesus may offer more of an opportunity than a problem for Jewish theologians than it does for Christian theologians.

Traditionally, Judaism considers Jesus as a *false* messiah, whether the claim that he was the Messiah was made by him or only by his followers. But Jesus was not only a false messiah for Jews, he is also considered to be a *failed* messiah because he did not attain his ultimate goal.[52] To be a failure, however, is not unusual among those with elevated goals. In a sense, the Hebrew prophets were failures because they did not achieve their ultimate goals of convincing the people to repent and to obey God's will. Moses was a failure because he did not enter the promised land, and he did not guide the people into the land. Even God failed, for according to Jewish tradition, the Kingdom of God on earth was supposed to begin with the revelation of the Torah at Sinai. But, the people built the Golden Calf and God's expectation was not realized. Indeed, God failed so badly in creating the human race that God had to erase it with a flood and start again, like an artist who makes a mistake and must erase it, accept failure, and begin again. Indeed, the greatest individuals are always failures because their goals are so exalted. Not all failures are great people, but – in a sense – all great people are failures. Precisely because their goals exceed their abilities, they are able to accomplish more than reasonably can be expected. In his study of 'Biblical Leadership', Martin Buber observed:

> The Bible knows nothing of the intrinsic value of success. On the contrary, when it announces a successful deed, it is duty-bound to announce in complete detail the failure involved in the success. When we consider the history of Moses, we see how failure is mingled in the one great successful action ... True, Moses brought the people out of Egypt; but each stage in this leadership is a failure ... and yet his work survives also in a hope which is beyond all these failures ... This glorification of failure culminates in a long line of prophets whose existence is failure through and through. They live in failure; it is for them to fight and not to conquer. This is the fundamental experience of biblical leadership ...[53]

Jesus was a failure because he did not bring about the final and complete redemption of the world. If he had completely succeeded, a *parousia*, a second coming, would not have become necessary. Summarizing earlier Jewish traditions regarding failed messiahs, Maimonides wrote: 'If he does not meet with full success, or is slain, it is obvious that he is not the [final] messiah promised in the Torah. He is to be regarded like all the other wholehearted and worthy kings of the House of David who died and whom God raised up to test the multitudes'.[54]

For Christians, Jesus was *not* a failed messiah because he brought complete spiritual redemption. Jews do not accept this claim. But, even were Jews to accept it, Jesus would still not have been a successful messiah. According to Jewish theology, messianic redemption is not limited to the spiritual realm. The dominant motif in Jewish messianism is that messianic redemption occurs in time and space, in history, in the socio-political realm. To be complete, messianic redemption must take place in the physical as well as the spiritual realm. For Judaism, the physical and the spiritual are interrelated, interlocked. The Jews could not accept Jesus as the Jewish messiah because he did not bring the type of redemption anticipated by Jewish teachings about the messianic age.[55] For example, Jewish messianism anticipated a messianic era that would fulfil the prophetic dream of a world without war, of a world at peace, of a world where 'nation shall not lift up sword against nation, nor shall anyone experience war anymore' (Isa.2:4), a world ruled by justice and compassion, a world devoid of prejudice and physical oppression. As Martin Buber wrote shortly after the Holocaust, 'we [Jews] demonstrate with the bloody body of our people the unredeemedness of the world'.[56] Until peace, justice and compassion reign, Jews will continue to view God's Kingdom as *yet to come*. Jews will continue to view our world as pre-messianic, as unredeemed. However, while our world cannot be viewed by Jews as a redeemed world, and while Jesus cannot be viewed by Jews as *the* ultimate and final Jewish messiah, my radical suggestion is that he may be considered as *a* Jewish messiah, as a *failed* Jewish messiah, as being a part *of* rather than being apart *from* the life of his people and their messianic hope.

Jewish theological literature speaks of a failed messiah. In most texts, he is named Messiah son of Joseph (or Messiah son of Ephraim). He is a preliminary messiah, coming in anticipation of and paving the way for the final messiah, the Messiah son of David. He is a messiah who dies to prepare the way, to provide the opportunity for the final redemption to take place.[57] According to some Jewish historians, the idea of the Messiah son of Joseph was developed by the students of Rabbi Akiva to justify their master's claim that Bar Cochba, who led a revolt of Jews against Romans, was the messiah. When Bar Cochba was defeated and killed, it was clear that Akiva was wrong; he was not the final messiah. Wars still occurred; political oppression continued. As was noted before, Jews could not accept as a final messiah anyone who did not bring an end to war and oppression. So, Akiva's students concluded that their teacher could not be wrong, therefore, Bar Cochba was a messiah, but not the final messiah. He was the penultimate Messiah son of Joseph, not the final Messiah son of David.[58]

According to other Jewish historians, the idea of Messiah son of Joseph was developed as an attempt to give Jesus a place within Jewish messianic theology. In this view, the idea of the Messiah son of Joseph was developed to try to convince those Jews in the first few centuries who believed in the messiahship of Jesus that he was indeed *a* messiah, though not *the* final Jewish messiah. This attempt, it was hoped, would prevent a separation of such Jews from the Jewish community. Those who hold this view argue further that the claim that Jesus descended from David and was the Davidic messiah was ascribed to Jesus by the gospels long after his death, and without any basis. In fact, they claim, Jesus was the son of Mary and Joseph; hence, the name Messiah son of Joseph.[59]

According to one Jewish tradition, a Messiah son of Joseph comes in each generation to pave the way for the final redemption.[60] If the generation is unworthy, he is not followed by the Messiah son of David. If the generation is worthy, the Messiah son of David comes.[61] According to Jewish tradition, the Messiah son of David has not yet come. Yet, a number of Messiahs son of Joseph may already have come. Jesus may be considered *a* Jewish messiah, *a* Messiah son of Joseph. This would give Jesus a place within Jewish theological discourse and would end the centuries-long tradition of his virtual excommunication from the faith community of which he was a part. Further, it should provide him not only with a role in Jewish theology, but with some *messianic* role within Jewish theology.

Already in the Middle Ages, Jewish theological texts mention Jesus in the context of discussions regarding the Messiah son of Joseph. Though most of these texts do not accept Jesus as a Messiah son of Joseph, that is., as a Jewish messiah, this may be because they were reacting to Christian persecution of Jews at that time. However, perhaps today, we can affirm an identification of Jesus with a Messiah son of Joseph. One may further assume that it would not have been necessary for medieval Jewish thinkers to reject this identification of Jesus with a Messiah son of Joseph, unless such an idea already had been proposed within Jewish circles.

Identification between Jesus and a Messiah son of Joseph is alluded to in the writings of the thirteenth-century Spanish Jewish mystic, Abraham Abulafia.[62] It is explicitly stated in the writings of the sixteenth-century Jewish statesman and commentator, Don Isaac Abravanel, who considered the tradition about the Messiah son of Joseph to have been the source that influenced the formulation of the 'historical Jesus'. In Abravanel's view, the earliest Christians accepted the idea of the Messiah son of Joseph but changed his name to Jesus.[63] Furthermore, as is well known, Christian tradition often identifies and compares Jesus with the prophet Jonah (for example, Matthew 12:40, Luke 11:30). In Jewish mystical texts, including some of those composed in seventeenth-century Poland, Jonah is identified and compared to the Messiah son of Joseph, with clear references to the further identification of Jesus with a particular portrayal of the the Messiah son of Joseph.[64]

The final messiah, Messiah son of David, is often compared by Jewish texts to the seventh day of the week, the Sabbath, because the messianic era is described as the Sabbatical age that comes at the end of human history. The day before the Sabbath is 'the sixth day', in Hebrew, *Yom ha-Shishi*. In Hebrew, each letter is also a number. The Jewish mystical tradition put great value in numerology, the numerical value of Hebrew words. The numerical value of *Yom ha-shishi* is 671. The numerical value of *Yeshu ha-Notzri*, Jesus of Nazareth, is also 671.[65] Here is a numerological description of Jesus as *preparatio messianica*.

Though the view of Jesus presented here may have been anticipated by classical Jewish literature, it is virtually unprecedented within Jewish theological discourse. It goes far beyond whatever has been suggested until now. It offers Jesus and Christianity not only a place, but a messianic role within Jewish theology. Jews will undoubtedly find it much too bold. Christians may consider it not far enough a leap.

It was Martin Buber, the first Jewish thinker to refer to Jesus as 'brother', who foresaw the time when, in Buber's words,

> the Jewish community, in the course of its renaissance, will recognize Jesus; and not merely as a great figure in its religious history, but also in the organic context of a messianic development extending over millennia, whose final goal is the redemption of Israel and the world. But I believe equally firmly that we will never recognize Jesus as the Messiah Come, for this would contradict the deepest meaning of our Messianic passion.[66]

Implications

What are the implications of the preceding for the future of Jewish–Christian relations in general and Catholic–Jewish dialogue in particular?

1. This essay began by quoting John Paul II's observation that faith is especially important at a time when many people live without faith in God. In such times, it is important for faiths to come together in fraternal dialogue rather than to perpetuate past enmities, hostilities and disputations. The project of interfaith relations is therefore an important and desirable enterprise. In a similar vein, Abraham Joshua Heschel said that 'The first and most important premise of interfaith is faith … However, at a time of paucity of faith, interfaith may become a substitute for faith, suppressing authenticity for the sake of compromise'. As Heschel further said, '[Interfaith] is not an enterprise for those who are half learned or spiritually immature. If it is not to lead to the confusion of the many, it must remain the prerogative of the few'.[67] This is especially true insofar as theological dialogue is concerned. Similarly, John Paul II said that the 'work [of Catholic–Jewish dialogue] that is of poor quality and lacking precision would be extremely detrimental to this field'.[68] This means that real, competent and authentic Catholic–Jewish theological dialogue is ultimately the provenance of theologians and scholars. The essence of the dialogue must be theological. As Cardinal Cassidy put it, 'We are not two humanitarian societies; far less are we two debating clubs. We are two faith-communities, and as such we are being called to respond to a common dialogue'.[69] Regretably, this has largely not been the case insofar as Jewish representatives in dialogue have been concerned. More often than not, lay representatives of secular Jewish communal and advocacy organizations have served as spokespersons for Judaism, often focusing only on a Jewish communal agenda, rather than a theological agenda. This has cast interfaith dialogue as an exercise in either social action or apologetics, rather than in authentic inter-faith dialogue. As Heschel has stated, 'God is of no importance, unless He is of supreme importance'.[70] What then, is more important for us to discuss together than God? How can

there be real interfaith dialogue without a discussion of God?

2. Though the participant in interfaith dialogue must recognize past hostilities and obstacles to dialogue, he or she must also be committed to try to overcome them while still remaining faithful to the authenticity, integrity and the continuity of their respective faith traditions. Since Vatican II, the Church has accomplished this by developing a new Catholic theology of Judaism. The Jewish community remains at a nascent stage of a parallel and reciprocal enterprise. However, as the preceding has hopefully demonstrated, Judaism can maintain its theological integrity while replacing negative views characteristic of the Middle Ages with a positive attitude toward Christianity and Christians. Such views can rest on authoritative classical Jewish texts and precedents.
3. Both theologically and Halakhically, Judaism can affirm Christianity as a theologically valid monotheistic religion. This means that faithful Jews can acknowledge that Christians and Jews believe in and worship the same God.
4. Though Judaism cannot consider Christian doctrines as being true for Jews, it can acknowledge them, as being valid for Christians. In this view, Christian doctrines such as Christology, Trinity and Incarnation no longer need be considered impediments for Jews recognizing Christianity as a valid and legitimate monotheistic faith. Neither should the doctrines of the election of the people of Israel or the Jewish refusal to accept Jesus as the Christ be an impediment to the Christian recognition of the theological validity of Judaism for Jews.
5. Demonstrations of the interpenetration of Jewish and Christian theological ideas by recent scholarship and studies of similarities in Jewish mystical teachings to ideas such as the Trinity and the Incarnation indicate that the gulf between Jewish and Christian doctrines of God may not be as radical as had once been assumed.[71] Though such doctrinal differences remain, they should not be considered as impediments to interreligious dialogue or to affirming that Jews and Christians believe in and worship the same God.
6. If Jews and Christians can agree that 'everything is from the perspective of the recipient', then they must admit that neither

> has access either to absolute truth or is privy to knowing the essential nature of God. As Franz Rosenzweig once put it, 'Truth is a noun only to God. To humans it is but an adjective'. And, as Heschel says, 'Human faith is never final, never an arrival, but an endlesss pilgrimage, a being on the way … No word is God's last word, no word is God's ultimate word'.[72]

All that Jews and Christians possess is their experiences of God, their traditions about God, and the word of God. But, the word of God that they have speaks in human language and is limited by the conditions of our world and our moment in history. Conceptions of God may be different, but the God whom Jews and Christians love, pray to and believe in, is the same. God will outlast us and our doctrines.

I conclude with the words of Abraham Heschel:

> What, then, is the purpose of interreligious cooperation? It is neither to flatter nor to refute one another, but to help one another; to share insight and learning, to cooperate in academic ventures on the highest scholarly level and, what is even more important, to search in the wilderness for wellsprings of devotion, for treasures of stillness, for the power of love and care for man … to keep alive the divine sparks in our souls, to nurture openness to the spirit of the Psalms, reverence for the words of the prophets, and faithfulness to the Living God.[73]

NOTES

1. John Paul II, *Spiritual Pilgrimage: Texts on Jews and Judaism 1979–1995*, Eugene J. Fisher and Leon Klenicki (eds) (New York: Crossroad, 1995), p.53.
2. See the English translation in *The Torah* (Philadelphia: Jewish Publication Society, 1962), Deut. 6:4. The translation 'the Lord alone' is based on medieval commentaries such as that of Samuel ben Meir (Rashbam); see his *Commentary on the Torah* [Hebrew] (New York: Ohm, 1949) to Deut. 6:4, p.206. See also Abraham J. Heschel, *Man in Not Alone* (Philadelphia: Jewish Publication Society, 1951), pp.114–119.
3. Bahye ben Asher, *Commentary on the Torah*, vol. 3 [Hebrew] (Jerusalem: Mosad ha-Rav Kook, 1968), pp.274–78, on Deut. 6:4. See also *Berakhot* 6a.
4. Joseph Bekhor Shor, *Commentary on the Torah* [Hebrew] (Jerusalem: Slavuta, 1959), vol. 3, pp.13–14 on Deut. 6:4. Similarly, the Jewish polemical treatise *Nitzahon Vetus*, trans. and ed. by David Berger in his *The Jewish–Christian Debate in the High Middle Ages* (Philadelphia: Jewish Publication Society, 1979), p.78; Daniel Lasker, *Jewish Philosophical Polemics Against Christianity in the Middle Ages* (New York: Ktav, 1977). Note e.g., Saadia Gaon, *The Book of Beliefs and Opinions*, trans. S. Rosenblatt (New Haven: Yale University Press, 1948), Treatise 2, chap.5, p.103; Moses Maimonides, *Guide of the Perplexed*, trans. S. Pines (Chicago: University of Chicago Press, 1963), Book 1, chap. 50, p.111.
5. Based on *Sanhedrin* 74a. See Jacob Katz, *Exclusiveness and Tolerance* (New York: Schocken, 1962), pp.82–105.
6. *Sifrei–Devarim* [*Sifre on Deuteronomy*], Louis Finkelstein (ed.) (Berlin: Judischer Kulturband

in Deutschland Abteilung Verlag, 1939), chap. 31, p.54, on Deut. 6:4. See also Rashi on Deut. 6:4 quoting the *Sifre*.

7. *Berakhot* 7a.
8. Ismar Elbogen, *Jewish Liturgy*, trans. R. Scheindlin (Philadelphia: Jewish Publication Society, 1993), p.71.
9. A notable pre-modern exception is the fourteenth-century talmudic commentator, Menahem ha-Meiri. Both Halakhically and theologically, he took a positive view of Christianity and emphatically considered it to be a monotheistic faith. Unfortunately, his little-known views had sparse impact on Jewish thought until they were 'rediscovered' in modern times. See Katz, *Exclusiveness and Tolerance*, pp.114–128.
10. Joshua Trachtenberg, *The Devil and the Jews* (New Haven: Yale University Press, 1943); Rosemary Ruether, *Faith and Fratricide* (New York: Crossroad, 1974) on the *Adversos Judaeos* tradition in the Church Fathers, and Salo W. Baron, *A Social and Religious History of the Jews* (New York: Columbia University Press, 1967), vol. 11, pp.122–191.
11. Jules Isaac, *The Teaching of Contempt* (New York: Holt, Rinehart and Winston, 1964). This work had a profound impact on John XXIII. Edward Flannery, *The Anguish of the Jews* (New York: MacMillan, 1965).
12. Arthur A. Cohen, *The Myth of the Judeo-Christian Tradition* (New York: Schocken, 1971).
13. Byron L. Sherwin, 'John Paul II's Catholic Theology of Judaism', in Byron L. Sherwin and Harold Kasimow (eds), *John Paul II and Interreligious Dialogue* (Maryknoll, N.Y.: Orbis Books, 1999), pp.139–166, and chap. 12 below; John Paul II, *Spiritual Pilgrimage*; Joseph Cardinal Bernardin, *A Blessing to One Another* (Chicago: LTP, 1996).
14. See the December 1974 Commission for Religious Relations with the Jews' 'Guidelines and Suggestions for Implementing the Concilar Declaration *Nostra Aetate*'.
15. Cardinal Edward I. Cassidy, 'The Next Issues in Jewish–Catholic Relations', *Origins* 26:41 (April 3, 1997): 669.
16. Marcus Horowitz, *Mateh Levi*, Part II (Frankfurt, 1932), sec. '*Yoreh De'ah*', no. 28. See discussion of this text in Louis Jacobs, *Theology in the Responsa* (London: Routledge and Kegan Paul, 1975), p.281. As a responsum, Horowitz's view has some legal authority.
17. On the development of the Noachian laws and their implications for Jewish–Christian dialogue, see David Novak, *Jewish–Christian Dialogue* (New York: Oxford University Press, 1989), pp.26–41.
18. On single covenant and dual covenant theories in contemporary Christian theology, see Michael B. McGarry, *Christology After Auschwitz* (New York: Paulist Press, 1977), pp.72–96; Maurice Bowler, 'Rosenzweig on Judaism and Christianity – The Two Covenant Theory', *Judaism* 22:4 (Fall 1973): 475–481.
19. Moses Maimonides, *Guide of the Perplexed*, Book 1, chap. 55, p.128. See also Alexander Altmann, 'The Divine Attributes', *Judaism* 15:1 (Winter 1966): 41–60, and the many related studies of Maimonides' predication of divine attributes by Harry Wolfson.
20. Judah Loew, *Be'er ha-Golah* (New York: Judaica Press, 1969), chap.4, p.64. On Loew's discussion of God, see Byron L. Sherwin, *Mystical Theology and Social Dissent* (Oxford: Oxford University Press, 1982), pp.56–69.
21. Judah Loew, *Hiddushei Aggadot* (New York: Judaica, 1969), vol. 2 p.87 on *Sota* 48b.
22. Alexander Altmann, 'The Divine Attributes', *Judaism* 15:1 (Winter 1966): 41–60.
23. Eliezer Ashkenazi, *Sefer Ma'aseh ha-Shem* (Venice, 1583), sec. *Ma'aseh Bereshit*, chap.31.
24. Abraham J. Heschel, *Moral Grandeur and Spiritual Audacity* (New York: Farrar, Straus, Giroux, 1996), pp.272, 244.
25. Louis Ginzberg, *The Legends of the Jews* (Philadelphia: Jewish Publication Society, 1968), vol. 1, pp.209–15 and sources noted there.
26. Heschel, *Moral Grandeur*, p.245.
27. Quoted from manuscripts of Abraham Farissol's *Magen Avraham* in Samuel Lowinger, '*Recherches sur l'oeuvre apologetique d'Abraham Farissol*', *Revue des Etudes Juives*, vol. 5 N.S. (1940): 38.
28. Heschel, *Moral Grandeur*, pp.248–49 and sources noted there.
29. Moses Rivkes, *Be'er ha-Golah*, commentary on Joseph Karo, *Shulhan Arukh* (Vilna: Romm, 1911), sec. *Hoshen Mishpat*, para. 425.
30. This suggestion is made by Novak, *Jewish–Christian Dialogue*, p.51.
31. Harry Wolfson, 'St. Thomas on Divine Attributes', *Mélanges Offerts a Etienne Gilson* (English section) (Toronto: Pontifical Institute, 1959).

32. Bahye ben Asher on Deut. 6:4, pp.276–277. See also Isaac ben Sheshet Parfat's statement that 'Once I heard one of those involved in philosophy speak contemptuously of the kabbalists saying: the idolators believe in the Trinity and the kabbalists believe in a tenfold God', quoted in Novak, *Jewish–Christian Dialogue*, p.50.
33. On Emden's views of Christianity, see Blu Greenberg, 'Rabbi Jacob Emden: The Views of an Enlightened Traditionalist on Christianity', *Judaism* 27:3 (Summer 1978): 351–363, and sources noted there.
34. Arthur Green, 'Shekhinah, The Virgin Mary, and the Song of Songs', *AJS Review* 26:1(April 2002):1–52; Peter Schaefer, 'Daughter, Sister, Bride and Mother', *Journal of the American Academy of Religion*', 68 (2000): 221–242.
35. After reviewing similarities between the Trinity and various Jewish mystical ideas, Yehudah Liebes in his *Studies in the Zohar* (Albany: SUNY Press, 1993), p.161, concludes that 'the spiritual affinity between the two religions was among the causes for the animosity between them'.
36. As Heschel demonstrates, this term is not found in the *Zohar* as is often claimed, but was first used in the eighteenth-century by Rabbi Moses Hayyim Luzzatto in his *Adir ba-Marom*. It became popular in Hasidism. See Heschel, 'God, Torah and Israel', trans. Byron L. Sherwin in Heschel's *Moral Grandeur*, pp.191–208.
37. Heschel, *Moral Grandeur*, p.199. See also Moshe Idel, *Absorbing Perfections* (New Haven: Yale University Press, 2002), pp.69–70. It is beyond the scope of this essay to discuss the many similarities of the role played by the Torah in Judaism and by Jesus in Christianity. On other trinitarian views in Judaism, see Joseph Kaspi who agreed that the Trinity was not intrinsically incorrect and that the Torah taught a trinitarian doctrine of God as father, with the agent intellect (son) and the Holy Spirit proceeding from Him. See Lasker, *Jewish Philosophical Polemics*, p.215, n. 270. It is also well known that Christian Kabbalists attributed the roots of the Trinity to the teachings of the Jewish mystical tradition.
38. *Zohar* (Vilna: Romm, 1882), vol. 2 , p.60a.
39. Solomon Schechter, 'On the Study of the Talmud', in *Studies in Judaism* (New York: Meridian, 1958), pp.60–61.
40. *Midrash on Psalms* [Hebrew], S. Buber (ed.) (Vilna: Romm, 1891), 90:5, p.388. Judah Loew, *Tiferet Yisrael* (New York: Judaica Press, 1969), chap. 21, pp.67–68. See Sherwin, *Mystical Theology*, p.81.
41. Judah Loew, *Nezah Yisrael* (New York: Judaica Press, 1969), chap. 51, p.195. See Sherwin, *Mystical Theology*, p.137.
42. Elijah de Vidas, *Reshit Hokhmah* (Tel Aviv: Esther Press, n.d.), '*Sha'ar ha-Ahavah*', chap. 3, secs. 5, 7.
43. Horowitz, *Nishmat Shabbtai Halevi* (Prague: n.p., 1616), chap. 7; Louis Jacobs, 'The Divine Spark in Man in Jewish Sources', in R. Loewe (ed.), *Studies in Rationalism, Judaism and Universalism* (London: Routledge and Kegal Paul, 1966).
44. Menahem Nahum of Chernobyl, *Sefer Ma'or Einayim* (Jerusalem: Ma'or Einayim, 1966), sec. *Kedoshim*, p.142; Moses Hayyim Ephraim of Sudlykow, *Degel Mahaneh Ephraim* (Jerusalem: Hadar, 1963), sec. *Kedoshim*, p.178.
45. Ironically, this view that obviates the problem of the Incarnation for Jewish theology is probably an anti-Christian polemic, since the claim that one Jew, Jesus, is essentially divine is not unique to him; rather all Jews are essentially divine. See Byron L. Sherwin, '*Corpus Domini*: Traces of the New Testament in East European Hasidism?', *The Heythrop Journal* 35:3 (July 1994): 274.
46. Sherwin, '*Corpus Domini*', pp.267–280.
47. Ephesians 5:30; Romans 12:4–5, 1 Corinthians 12:26, 27; Augustine, *Sermons*, nos. 268, 267 in *Opera Omnia,* Migne, *Patrologia Latina*, vol. 8; articles in *The New Catholic Encyclopedia* (New York, 1967), 'Membership in the Church', 'Mystical Body of Christ', 'Incorporation in Christ'; the 1943 encyclical of Pius XII, *Mystici Corporis Christi*; Avery Dulles, *Church Membership as a Catholic and Ecumenical Problem* (Milwaukee: Marquette University Press, 1974).
48. Martin Buber's description of Jesus as 'my great brother', is found in the 'Forward' to his study of the relationship of Judaism and Christianity, *Two Types of Faith*, written in 1948. Probably the most positive view of Jesus and of Christianity among classical Jewish thinkers is found in the writings of the eighteenth-century German rabbi, Jacob Emden. See Harvey Falk, 'Jacob Emden's Views of Christianity', *Journal of Ecumenical Studies* 19 (Winter 1982): 105–11.
49. For a succinct summary of positive views of Christianity and Jesus by Jewish scholars since

the 1950s, see John T. Pawlikowski, ***What Are They Saying about Christian–Jewish Relations?*** (New York: Paulist Press, 1980), chaps. 3 and 4. An article on Jesus by Kaufmann Kohler in the early twentieth-century ***Jewish Encyclopedia*** states that 'In many ways his [Jesus'] attitude was specifically Jewish, even in directions which are considered signs of Jewish narrowness'. More recently, the writings of Jewish scholars such as Geza Vermes, David Flusser, Ellis Rivkind, Alan Segal, and others have taken a more positive view of Jesus as a Jew. See essays in James Charlesworth (ed.), ***Jesus' Jewishness*** (New York: Crossroad, 1991). Compare David Schwartz, 'Is there a Jewish Reclamation of Jesus?', ***Journal of Ecumenical Studies*** 24:1 (Winter 1987): 104–109.

50. The recovery of the Jewishness of Jesus may pose a problem for the formulation of contemporary Christologies by Christian theologians. See Phillip L. Culberston, 'What is Left to Believe in Jesus after the Scholars Have Done with Him?', ***Journal of Ecumenical Studies*** 28:1 (Winter 1991): 1–17. On Christology and Judaism, see a fine summary of recent scholarship in John T. Pawlikowski, 'New Trends in Catholic Religious Thought', in Eugene Fisher et al. (eds), ***Twenty Years of Jewish–Catholic Relations*** (New York: Paulist Press, 1986). See also, Allan R. Brockway, 'Learning Christology Through Dialogue with Jews', ***Journal of Ecumenical Studies*** 25:3 (Summer 1988): 347–48; Eugene Borowitz, ***Contemporary Christologies: A Jewish Response*** (New York: Paulist Press, 1980).
51. Leo Baeck, ***Judaism and Christianity*** (Philadelphia: Jewish Publication Society, 1958), p.101.
52. The idea of Jesus as a failed rather than a false messiah has already been suggested by Irving Greenberg, 'The Relationship of Judaism and Christianity: Toward a New Organic Model', in Eugene J. Fisher (ed.), ***Twenty Years of Jewish–Catholic Relations***, pp.197–203. See also Irving Greenberg, ***For the Sake of Heaven and Earth*** (Philadelphia: Jewish Publication Society, 2004), pp.31–48, where Greenberg reflects on this position and the accusations of 'heresy' it evoked from the Orthodox rabbinate against him. See especially, p.48, no. 5, where he distinguishes his view from mine.
53. Martin Buber, 'Biblical Leadership', chap. in his ***Israel and the World*** (New York: Schocken Books, 1963), pp.125–26.
54. Moses Maimonides, ***Mishneh Torah – Book of Judges***, sec. 'Laws of Kings and Wars', 11:4 in uncensored editions.
55. Joseph Klausner, 'The Jewish and Christian Messiah', in ***The Messianic Idea in Israel*** (New York: Macmillan, 1955), pp.519–33.
56. Quoted in Ernst Simon, 'Martin Buber: His Way Between Thought and Deed', ***Jewish Frontier*** (February 1948): 26.
57. For sources about the Messiah son of Joseph, see ***Sukkah*** 52a. The classical text in Midrashic literature is ***Pesikta Rabbati***, chaps. 36, 37. In this text, one finds the idea of the messiah as a suffering messiah. This idea of a suffering messiah is, in my view, native to Jewish messianism. The idea of Messiah son of Joseph was developed in Midrashim of the gaonic period; see those collected by Yehudah Even Shmuel Kaufmann, ***Midreshei Geulah*** (Jerusalem: Masada, 1954), especially pp.90–112, 133–142, 318–23. See the discussion and sources collected in Klausner, ***The Messianic Idea***, pp.483–502. An attempt to demonstrate the significance of the idea of Messiah son of Joseph for Christianity is found in Richard von der Alm, ***Die Urtheile heidnischer und jüdischer Schriftsteller der vier ersten christlichen Jahrhunderte uber Jesus und die ersten Christen*** (1864).
58. For Bar Cochba as a messiah, see e.g., ***Lamentations Rabbah*** II, 2, no. 4. Akiva's colleagues said, 'Akiva, grass will grow on your cheeks if Bar Cochba is the messiah'. The idea that the Messiah son of Joseph was developed by Akiva's students was the theory of Joseph Klausner. It may be also noted that Rabbi Akiva died a martryr's death and that his father's name was Joseph. On Jewish and Christian perceptions of the alleged messiahship of Bar Cochba, see Adele Reinhartz, 'Rabbinic Perceptions of Simeon Bar Cosiba', ***Journal for the Study of Judaism*** 20:2 (December 1989): 171–195.
59. A good summary of the views of various scholars regarding the origin of the idea of the Messiah son of Joseph may be found in Joseph Heinemann, 'The Messiah of Ephraim', ***Harvard Theological Review*** 68 (1975): 1–15. See also Charles C. Torrey, 'The Messiah son of Ephraim', ***Journal of Biblical Literature*** 3 (1947): 253–77. Though most texts regarding the Messiah son of Joseph post-date the rise of Christianity (some substantially), Torrey claims that the 'doctrine antedated the Christian era by several centuries'. I agree that the idea pre-dated Christianity and is intrinsic to Jewish messianism rather than being an 'aber-

ration' as Moore suggested; see George Foot More, *Judaism in the First Centuries of the Christian Era* (Cambridge: Harvard University Press, 1927), vol. 2, p.370.

60. For example, in the sixteenth century, Isaac Luria was considered as Messiah son of Joseph for his time; see Meir Benayahu (ed.), *Sefer Toledot ha-Ari* (Jerusalem: Hebrew University Press, 1967), p.199 and p.258 where Luria is described as dying for the sins of others.
61. Hayyim Vital, *Sefer Pri Etz Hayyim* (Koretz, 1784), sec. *Sha'ar ha-Amidah*, chap.19, p.52b (note also the reference there to Luria as the Messiah son of Joseph).
62. See the discussion in Moshe Idel, 'Abraham Abulafia on the Jewish Messiah and Jesus', in *Studies in Ecstatic Kabbalah* (Albany: SUNY Press, 1988), pp.53–55, 59, 60, and sources noted there.
63. Don Isaac Abravanel, *Mashmia Yeshuot* (Amsterdam, 1644), p.13; *Ma'ayenei ha-Yeshua* (1607), pp.45, 74; Idel, *Studies in Ecstatic Kabbalah*, p.60; Joseph Saracheck, *The Doctrine of the Messiah in Medieval Jewish Literature* (New York: Hermon Press, 1968), p.263. The death of the Messiah son of Joseph is mentioned in the Talmud; see *Sukkah* 52a. Besides the identification of Jesus with the Messiah son of Joseph in Abulafia and Abravanel, we also find such an identification in Flavio Mithridates; see Chaim Wirzubski (ed.), *Sermo de Passione Domini* (Jerusalem: Israel Academy of Sciences and Humanities, 1963), p.121, n. 4. On this idea in the Sabbatean theologian Cardozo, see the manuscript published by Gershom Scholem in his Hebrew work, *Texts Concerning the History of Sabbatianism and its Metamorphosis* (Jerusalem: Mosad Bialik, 1974), p.289, 'The first messiah ... is Jesus of Nazareth who corresponds to the Messiah son of Ephraim'. As was noted above, Messiah son of Ephraim is another name for Messiah son of Joseph.
64. See Yehudah Liebes' Hebrew essay, 'Jonah as Messiah ben Joseph', chap. in Joseph Dan and Joseph Hacker (eds), *Studies in Jewish Mysticism, Philosophy and Ethical Literature* (Jerusalem: Hebrew University Press, 1986), pp.269–315. As might be expected, the particular portrait of Messiah son of Joseph with which Jesus is identified is not a very positive one, as in the writings of the seventeenth-century Jewish mystic, Samson Ostropoler, who died a martyr's death in 1648.
65. This numerology is noted by Idel, *Studies in Ecstatic Kabbalah*, p.59, referring to Abulafia. On Abulafia's identification of Jesus with the sixth-day, see Idel, *Studies in Ecstatic Kabbalah*, p.51, quoting from MS, New York, JTS, 843, p.80. Note that this numerology assumes a *haser*, spelling, that is, without the letter *vov* in *ha-notzri*. It is interesting that a number of medieval Jewish thinkers described Jesus and his disciples as Jewish mystics, that is, Kabbalists. See the text of a fourteenth-century Spanish-Jewish work quoted by Gershom Scholem in his essay, *'Zur Geschischte Der Anfange Der Christlichen Kabbalah'*, in *Essays Presented to Leo Baeck* (London: East and West Library, 1954), p.177, n. 2. This idea was popular among Christian Kabbalists of the Renaissance period, for example, Pico del la Mirandola.
66. Cited in Maurice S. Friedman, *Martin Buber: The Life of Dialogue* (New York: Harper, 1955), p.279.
67. Heschel, *Moral Grandeur*, p.241.
68. John Paul II, *Spiritual Pilgrimage*, p.19.
69. Cassidy, 'The Next Issues in Jewish–Catholic-Relations', p.669.
70. Heschel, *Man is Not Alone*, p.92.
71. On the interpenetration of theological ideas, see sources already noted, and, Yehuda Leibes, *Studies in the Zohar*, chap. 3; Yitzhak Baer, *A History of the Jews in Christian Spain*, trans. L. Schoffman (Philadelphia: Jewish Publication Society, 1966), vol. 1, pp.268–77; Michael Meyer, 'Christian Influences on Early German Reform Judaism', in Charles Berlin (ed.), *Studies in Jewish Bibliography, History and Literature in Honor of Edward Kiev* (New York: Ktav, 1971), pp.289–303.
72. Heschel, *Moral Grandeur*, p.245.
73. Ibid., pp.249–250.

John Paul II's Catholic Theology of Judaism

Relationships among religions are shaped by specific epistemological postures:

1. A religion may be either true or false. 'Since my religion represents absolute truth, your religion must be false'. This is the dominant position of medieval scholastic philosophical theology.
2. Truth is relative. There is no absolute truth. 'My religion is true for me; your religion is true for you'. Though all religions may contain truth, none has the monopoly on truth.This is a typically modern position that enables the posture of religious pluralism.
3. Absolute truth may exist, but it is beyond the ken of human comprehension. 'The truth is a noun only for God, for humans however it is an adjective' (Franz Rosenzweig). Religions contain truth. However, some contain more truth than others. 'My religion contains more truth than yours'.
4. There are truths and there is falsehood. Some religions contain truth, but others are false. 'My religion contains truth while your religion may contain truth or it may be false'.
5. There is absolute truth, relative or incomplete truth, and there is falsehood. 'My religion is true; your religion may either contain truth or it may be false'. This position affirms the possibility of religious plurality, but not the posture of religious pluralism.

Nostra Aetate, the primary document of the Second Vatican Council that deals with the relationship of the Roman Catholic Church towards non-Christian religions (adapted October 27, 1965), moved the Church from its historical rootedness in the first attitude (number 1) to a new position characterized by the final, fifth attitude.[1] While this more recent position is one that acknowledges the legitimacy of religious *plurality*, it is not one that affirms religious *pluralism*. For *Nostra Aetate*, truth is contained in some other religions, while still others rest upon false and unenlightened doctrines. The truth is embodied in the Catholic faith. Other religions contain truth only insofar as they reflect the truth of Catholic doctrine. Catholic truth serves as the ultimate arbiter of whether other religions contain truth. With regard to non-Christian religions, *Nostra Aetate* states (para. 2): 'The Catholic Church rejects nothing of what is true and holy in these religions. She has a high regard for the manner of life and conduct, the precepts and doctrines which, although differing in many ways from her own teaching, nevertheless often reflect a ray of that truth which enlightens all men. Yet she proclaims and is duty bound to proclaim without fail, Christ who is "the way, the truth and the life" (John 14:6)'.[2]

With specific regard to Judaism, the dominant doctrinal stance of the pre-Vatican II Catholic Church was that Catholicism is true while Judaism is false (attitude number 1). But since Christianity had emerged out of Judaism, this attitude toward Judaism differed from the Church's attitude toward other non-Christian faiths. According to this view, Judaism had *once* been true, as it was rooted in a covenant made by God with the people of Israel. However, the people of Israel rejected the covenant, as evidenced by their sinful behaviour. God sent Jesus to redeem them. They rejected Jesus and his teachings. They crucified Jesus, thereby committing the most heinous of sins – deicide. Consequently, God rejected the Jews and abrogated the covenant with them that was originally made with their ancestors. God held the Jews to be reviled and accursed because of their sins and punished them with perpetual wandering and degradation. Their only hope became accepting baptism, converting to Christianity, and embracing Christ, whom they had rejected. The Church, therefore, has a 'mission to the Jews' to convert them to Christianity, to bring them the 'good news', the Truth. Having rejected and nullified the 'Old' Covenant, and the 'old' people of the covenant, God established a 'new' covenant, a New Testament with the 'new Israel', now the 'people of God', the universal Church, the Catholic Church. In theological parlance, aspects of this position came to be known as the 'Displacement

Doctrine' and the 'Supersessionist Doctrine': Christianity supersedes Judaism and the 'new Israel' displaces the 'old Israel' as the covenanted people of God. The truth of the old covenant is similarly superseded and displaced by the new covenant. These doctrines served through the centuries as a theological foundation for Christian anti-Semitism, which, according to various historians, served as a contributing cause of the Holocaust.[3]

An example of the pre-Vatican II claim that Judaism had once been a true religion that had relinquished that status may be seen in the typical pre-Vatican II *Baltimore Catechism* (Question 391): 'Why did the Jewish religion, which up to the death of Christ had been the true religion, cease at that time to be the true religion? [Answer]: The Jewish religion ... was only a promise of the redemption and figure of the Christian religion, and when the redemption was accomplished and the Christian religion established by the death of Christ, the promise and the figure were no longer necessary'.

Nostra Aetate altered the former teachings of the Church regarding Judaism and the Jews, while deliberately offering the impression that the new teaching of the Church had always been the teaching of the Church. In very subtle terms, the 'Displacement Doctrine' was virtually expunged, while a revised version of the 'Supersessionist Doctrine' remained. *Nostra Aetate* rejects the 'Displacement Doctrine' by affirming that God's covenant with the people of Israel was not revoked because that covenant is irrevocable 'since God does not take back the gifts he bestowed or the choice he made'. Yet, a version of the supersessionist argument remains in the claim that, despite the fact that the covenant with the people of Israel remains in force, 'it is true that the Church is the new people of God'. Nonetheless, the idea of 'mission to the Jews', which had been a critical component of the 'Supersessionist Doctrine', is noticeably absent from the text of *Nostra Aetate*.[4] The integrity of Jews as Jews and of Judaism as a religion is affirmed. No longer is Judaism depicted as an obsolete religion. No longer are Jews primarily defined as potential Christians.

The 'Displacement Doctrine' is rooted in the claim that the Jews killed Jesus and that they are therefore accursed. *Nostra Aetate* rejects this claim by affirming that the Jews as a group are not responsible for the crucifixion and the death of Jesus: 'Neither all

Jews indiscriminately at that time, nor Jews today, can be charged with the crimes committed during his [Jesus'] passion'. Consequently, 'the Jews should not be spoken of as rejected or accursed, as if this followed from Holy Scripture'. Anti-Semitism is therefore now deplored: '[The Church] deplores all hatreds, persecutions, displays of anti-Semitism leveled at any time or from any source against the Jews'. Rather than enmity, 'mutual understanding and appreciation' of the 'common spiritual heritage' of Christians and Jews are now encouraged by the Church.

Nostra Aetate not only redefined the Church's attitude to non-Christian religions, but it also affirmed that the relationship between Judaism and Catholicism is uniquely different from that which the Church has with any other non-Christian religion. This affirmation was further expressed in Paul VI's establishment in 1974 of the Holy See's Commission for Religious Relations with the Jews, while all other non-Christian religions are dealt with through the Holy See's Council for Interreligious Dialogue.

Within a decade after *Nostra Aetate*, in December 1974, the Commission for Religious Relations with the Jews issued 'Guidelines and Suggestions for Implementing the Conciliar Declaration *Nostra Aetate* (para. 4)'.[5] Building upon *Nostra Aetate*, the 'Guidelines' both amplified and expanded the positions taken in the Vatican II document.

Nostra Aetate means 'in this age of ours'. By beginning with these words, the authors wanted to emphasize that the Church's reconsideration of its relationship with other religions takes place within the context of recent history and the present historical situation. This awareness is expanded in the 'Guidelines' by its opening statement which squarely places Jewish–Catholic dialogue within the context of the immediate post-Holocaust era. Though this document restates a condemnation of anti-Semitism, it fails, however, to acknowledge or to express contrition for beliefs or acts of Christian anti-Semitism. In a sense, this is surprising, since the initial impetus for *Nostra Aetate* (as well as for Vatican II) came from John XXIII, who was well aware of the social and historical impact of earlier anti-Jewish Church doctrine on anti-Semitic acts throughout the centuries.

Two factors clearly stimulated John XXIII to encourage the Church to alter its teachings about the Jews and Judaism. The first was the impact of his having read Jules Isaac's study of the history of Christian anti-Semitism, *The Teaching of Contempt*, in which the author demonstrated the irrefutable link between Church doctrine regarding the Jews and the centuries-long persecution of Jews by Christians with doctrinal sanction.[6] That Christian anti-Semitism was a contributing cause of the Holocaust was not lost on John XXIII. A second factor that informed John XXIII's intentions was his own activities as a member of the Vatican's diplomatic corps during World War II. Though he never publicly criticized either the sometimes pro-German attitudes and actions of his immediate predecessors, or their apparent apathy to the fate of European Jewry during the Holocaust, his own actions during that period – possibly in opposition to official Vatican policy – testify to his own legion attempts to save Jews during the Holocaust. We know, for example, that while serving in Bulgaria, he was instrumental in convincing the Bulgarian government – an ally of Nazi Germany, not to accede to German demands to round up and to deport Bulgarian Jews to the death-camps. While serving in Turkey, he personally helped save hundreds of Jewish children. At a diplomatic reception in Turkey, he was approached by the German ambassador, who asked if the Holy See could issue a statement condemning the atheistic Communists whom the Germans were then fighting. In blunt and undiplomatic language, he replied, 'What shall I tell them about the millions of Jews your countrymen are murdering in Germany and Poland?'[7] As will be discussed below, these issues of Christian anti-Semitism and Holocaust awareness became pivotal as Catholic–Jewish relations continued to develop during the pontificate of John Paul II.

A second issue stressed in the 'Guidelines' is the recognition of Judaism, not as a religion defined only in Christian theological categories, but as a religion with its own integrity, grounded in its own self-definition: 'Christians must therefore strive … to learn by what essential traits the Jews define themselves in light of their own religious experience … Dialogue demands respect for the other as he is; above all, respect for his faith and his religious convictions'. Here one finds an acknowledgement that Judaism is not an obsolete nor a fossilized religion, as Toynbee had claimed, but a living faith – another theme that will develop in subsequent Church teachings about relations with Judaism.

The link between the rejection of the 'Displacement Doctrine' and the recognition of the integrity of Judaism was further strengthened in the Holy See's 1985 document, 'Notes on the Correct Way to Present the Jews and Judaism in Preaching and Catechesis in the Roman Catholic Church'. Issued to mark the twentieth anniversary of *Nostra Aetate*, this document emphasizes the ongoing and contemporary vibrancy of Jewish faith. Unlike earlier teachings that described Judaism as being relegated to obsoletism after the destruction of the Second Jewish Commonwealth in the year 70 as a punishment for the sin of deicide, the new teaching proclaims (para. 25) that 'the history of Israel did not end in 70 … It continued, especially in numerous Diasporas which allowed Israel to carry to the whole world a witness … The permanence of Israel (while so many ancient people have disappeared without a trace) is a historical fact and a sign to be interpreted in God's design'.[8]

A third issue developed by the 'Guidelines' relates to 'mission to the Jews'. While affirming the missionary nature of Christianity, the 'Guidelines' express careful sensitivity to 'religious liberty' and to the 'offence' that missionary efforts directed at Jews causes members of the Jewish people. The 'Guidelines' are implicitly aware that many Jews remain suspicious that the Church's initiatives for dialogue might really have a hidden missionary agenda. As one Vatican document clearly puts it, one obstacle to interreligious dialogue is that 'the weight of history makes proclamation [of the Gospel] more difficult, as certain methods of evangelization in the past have sometimes aroused fear and suspicion on the part of followers of other religions'.[9]

A fourth issue developed by the 'Guidelines' is the need for the Church to examine various liturgical, canonical, catechetical, educational and other texts it utilizes and promulgates to help ensure that such texts conform to post-Vatican II teachings on Judaism and the Jewish people.

Beginning with his election to the papacy in 1978, John Paul II's teachings regarding the Church's relationship with Judaism and the Jewish people were primarily shaped by two factors: Vatican statements such as *Nostra Aetate* and the subsequent 'Guidelines', and the Pope's personal experiences in his native Poland. Indeed, probably no Bishop of Rome since St Peter lived in closer proximity to Jews than John Paul II.[10]

The Pope's native Poland had been a major spiritual and demographic centre of Jewish life for centuries. At the time of his birth in 1920, there were about 3.5 million Jews in Poland, representing about 10 per cent of the total population. In his town of Wadowice, the Jewish population was about 25 per cent. Despite the considerable escalation of anti-Semitism in interwar Poland, and despite the often openly anti-Semitic teachings of the Polish Church, the young Karol Wojtyla seemed remarkably immune to either social or doctrinal anti-Semitism.[11] He did not hear it from his local priest. His father (who raised him after his mother's death) had cordial relationships with local Jews. When one of the future pope's Jewish friends announced that she would be emigrating to Palestine because of the rise of Polish anti-Semitism in the 1930s, his father said to her, 'Not all Poles are anti-Semitic. You know I am not'. Reflecting upon this event almost half a century later, Karol's boyhood friend, Ginka Beer Riesenfeld, recalled that she said to Karol's father that 'very few Poles were like him'. She further remembered that the young Karol was even more upset during this exchange than was his father.[12]

In the building where the young Wojtyla lived and in the schools he attended, there were Jews who befriended him and whom he befriended. Foremost among them was Jerzy Kluger, the Pope's lifelong friend, whose father served as president of the Jewish community of Wadowice. After losing track of one another after World War II, they were reunited in Rome where Kluger went to live after the war. In Tad Szulc's biography of John Paul II, he writes, 'Clearly, the pope misses the contact with his childhood friends and Wadowice ... To chat informally in Polish [with Jerzy Kluger] about the past and mutual friends, and away from papal protocol, may be the most important form of mental relaxation for the overworked Wojtyla'.[13] Kluger was the first person received by the new pope in private audience after his election in 1978.[14]

In 1989, John Paul II asked Kluger to represent him in placing a commemorative plaque on the site of the synagogue in Wadowice that had been destroyed by the Nazis. The Pope wrote: 'I remember very clearly the Wadowice Synagogue, which was near to our High School. I have in front of my eyes the numerous worshippers, who during their Holidays passed on their way to pray there'.[15] From his courtyard, Karol Wojtyla would watch Jews enter the synagogue to celebrate the Jewish holy days. At least once, he attended religious services there on Yom Kippur, the Day of Atonement.[16] When the students in their high school played football, they would form a Jewish team and a Catholic team. Because the Jewish team was usually undermanned, the young Wojtyla would often play for them.[17]

In various addresses delivered throughout the world, John Paul II reflected upon his experiences in Poland of sharing both the joys and the tragedies of his Jewish countrymen. For example, in his first visit as Pope to the United States in October 1979, John Paul II reminded the Jewish community of New York, 'As one who in my homeland has shared the suffering of your brethren, I greet you with the word taken from the Hebrew language: *Shalom*!' Speaking about the Holocaust to Jewish leaders in Warsaw in 1987, he said, 'The Polish pope has a particular relationship with all this, because, along with you, he has in a certain sense lived all this here, in this land'. In his later address to the Jewish community in Poland in 1991, the Pope lamented that 'that which threatened you also threatened us. The threat to us was not fulfilled to the same extent as the threat to you ... You have the terrible sacrifice of destruction ... a sea of terrible suffering and of the wrongs endured should not divide, but unite us. The places of execution, and in many cases, the common graves, call for this unity'. Reflecting on his meeting with Jews in Poland, the Pope said, 'The Pope's meeting with Jews on Polish soil was very cordial because it called to mind and renewed the personal bonds formed at the time of his youth and the difficult years of the occupation'.[18] However, most telling is the Pope's reflection on Judaism and the Jewish people in his book *Crossing the Threshold of Hope*. Here, the direction for Catholic–Jewish relations set down in *Nostra Aetate* and the Pope's experiences in his native Poland converge to serve as a framework for his perspective on Judaism and on Catholic–Jewish relations. He wrote: 'The words of the Council's Declaration [*Nostra Aetate* para. 4] reflect the experience of many people, both Jews and Christians. They reflect *my personal experience* as well, from the very first years of my life in my hometown ... Both religious groups, Catholics and Jews, were united, I presume, by the awareness that they prayed to the same God. Despite their different languages, prayers in the church and in the synagogue were based to a considerable degree on the same texts'. Then says John Paul II:

> Then came the Second World War, with its concentration camps and systematic extermination. First and foremost, the sons and daughters of the Jewish nation were condemned for no other reason than that they were Jewish. Even if only indirectly, whoever lived in Poland at that time came into contact with this reality. Therefore, this was also a personal experience of mine, an experience I carry with me even today ... But a truly exceptional experience for me was certainly my *visit to the synagogue of Rome* ...During that memorable visit, I spoke of the Jews as our *elder brothers in the faith* [emphasis in the original]. These words were an expression both of the Council's teaching, and a profound conviction on the part of the Church. The Second Vatican Council did not dwell on this subject at length, but what it did affirm embraces an immense reality which is not only religious but also cultural ... Thus the way two great moments of divine election – the Old and the New Covenants – are drawing closer together.[19]

Because of the Pope's close personal associations with Jews during his formative years, and because of his painful empathetic awareness of the plight of Jews during the Holocaust, particularly in Poland, the improvement of Catholic–Jewish relations has emerged as one of the leading issues that had preoccupied John Paul II during his papacy.[20] In his many journeys, the 'travelling Pope' made a point of meeting with representatives of local Jewish communities wherever there was one, even if it was not large. He was the first Pontiff to visit a synagogue, in Rome in 1986.[21] In 1993, he personally interceded in the Auschwitz convent controversy – which had become a grating obstacle to the stability of Catholic–Jewish relations – by ordering the convent's nuns to relocate.[22] In April 1994, he hosted a concert at the Vatican in memory of the victims of the Holocaust, and later that year,[23] through his direct influence, the Holy See established full diplomatic relations with the State of Israel.[24]

The Vatican's establishment of diplomatic ties with Israel is a concrete and specific expression of the Church's rejection of the 'Displacement Doctrine'. By recognizing the Jewish state, the Holy See implicitly set aside the claim that the loss of Jewish political sovereignty in the Holy Land was a punishment for the sin of deicide. In concrete terms, it eliminated the earlier claim that the

Jews have been punished and are accursed with perpetual wandering and humiliation. With regard to the Vatican's official diplomatic recognition of Israel, as with so many issues related to Catholic–Jewish relations, John Paul II posits a continuity of Church policy rather than the initiation of a new Church policy. He offers the impression that such initiatives and innovations merely make explicit what have been long-standing implicit Church policy and doctrine.[25] For example, in *Crossing the Threshold of Hope*, he wrote, 'As for the recognition of the State of Israel, it is important to reaffirm that I myself never had any doubts in that regard'.[26] Furthermore, as early as 1980, the Pope clearly recognized a link between the Holocaust and the establishment of the State of Israel: 'The Jewish people, after tragic experiences connected with the extermination of so many sons and daughters, driven by the desire for security, set up the State of Israel'.[27]

When Karol Wojtyla was elected Pope at the comparatively young age of 58, the Catholic Church was in disarray. The Vatican was in fiscal and spiritual chaos. The long pontificate of Paul VI had ended with a plethora of proposed new policies and procedures that had come out of the Second Vatican Council. Conservatives in the Church aimed at stifling these proposed changes. Reformers wanted immediate and sometimes radical implementation. Moderates called for prudence and slow-going. Some characterized the immediate post-Vatican II period as a train that had no idea of which track to follow and where to go. John Paul I's election had promised stability and balance, but weeks after his assent to the papacy, the new pope suddenly died. Upon his election on 16 October 1978, John Paul II found the Church in a quandary. Could it, would it, should it fully implement the teachings of Vatican II? What do they mean in terms of actual implementation? What would the implications of such implementation be?[28]

It is beyond the scope of this essay to discuss John Paul II's handling of these challenges. However, of all the issues posed by Vatican II, particularly those that do not directly relate to the direct governance of the Church, John Paul II clearly paid inordinate attention to the issues regarding Catholic–Jewish relations as shaped by one paragraph in one document of the Second Vatican Council, that is, paragraph 4 of *Nostra Aetate*.

Both in itself, and in view of the many challenges that faced the

Pope throughout his pontificate, John Paul II's legion efforts in combating anti-Semitism and furthering Catholic–Jewish relations were nothing less than remarkable. Many representatives and leaders of the Jewish community have acknowledged, applauded and lauded John Paul II's efforts in improving Catholic–Jewish relations. However, the largely secular Jewish communal leadership tends to evaluate these achievements from the often myopic perspective of the Jewish communal agenda. What they fail to realize is that the Pope's teachings on Catholic–Jewish relations emerged out of a framework of faith, that is, out of a particular Catholic theological perspective. John Paul II's mission was to articulate Catholic doctrine to Catholics. His views on Judaism and the Jewish people, despite the influences of his personal experiences, represent a Catholic theology of Judaism that he desired to define and to convey to Catholics. Though his views on the Jewish people often dovetailed with Jewish communal interests, they must be understood primarily in theological terms. While the impetus for, and the direction of Catholic–Jewish relations during the papacy of John Paul II, may have been stimulated by his personal experiences, his theology of Judaism was shaped and defined by Catholic doctrinal teachings. His Catholic theology of Judaism may be viewed as an amplification of, and as a commentary on, *Nostra Aetate* and various subsequent Vatican documents and episcopal pronouncements.

When John Paul II ascended to the papacy, it became his challenge and his responsibility to guide a huge institution seeking direction, one which was fragmented and threatened by instability. The Pontiff clearly understood that the institution he led – rooted in long-standing ancient and medieval traditions, yet operating under a mandate for change – could only effectively implement change when it was integrated into the continuity of tradition. Change had to be interpreted, not as a break with the past, but as flowing out of the doctrinal teachings and the historical experiences of the past. Otherwise, change could bring a rupture of the continuity of the tradition and, consequently, could pose a further threat to an already fragile institutional structure. The American penchant for change for the sake of change finds little resonance in fundamentally European institutions such as the Holy See.

The teachings of *Nostra Aetate* regarding Judaism and the Jewish people proclaimed a doctrinal change of direction from the past.

However, these developments have often been treated by the Holy See and by John Paul II as if they represent doctrinal continuity with the past. The Pope often evoked a claim of theological continuity in his vigorous attempt to steer his Church from a position of condemnation of Judaism to one of reconciliation with Judaism. As the Pope has said, 'the relations between the Catholic Church and Judaism have been built on a new foundation which is in fact very old … a spiritual bond'.[29]

Paul VI made an unprecedented breakthrough in ecumenical relations by using such terms as 'fraternal' to refer to Orthodox and Protestant Christians.[30] John Paul II extended use of this terminology to Jews. Here, too, there is an attempt to initiate radical change under the guise of continuity. Classical Christianity used the biblical motif of Israel as the 'older brother' to fortify the 'Displacement Doctrine'. In Hebrew Scriptures, older brothers (for example, Esau) were displaced in favour of younger brothers (Jacob).[31] Historically, the Church (the younger brother) saw itself as displacing the Synagogue (the older brother), and as the rightful heir of the inheritance of the true faith. Now, John Paul II was reiterating the term 'older brother', but infusing it with a positive meaning, rather than using this image to illustrate the 'Displacement Doctrine'. Undoubtedly, he was influenced in this regard by the positive use of the term 'elder brother' when referring to the Jewish people, in the writings of the great Polish poet, Adam Mickiewicz.

Ironically, both the 'Displacement Doctrine' and its rejection underscore the unique relationship between Judaism and Christianity. Christianity developed out of Judaism. This is a relationship which Christianity has with no other religion. As John Paul II acknowledged on numerous occasions, 'With Judaism, therefore, we have a relationship which we do not have with any other religion'. But now, this relationship was no longer adversarial, but integral. 'The Jewish religion is not "extrinsic" to us, but in a certain way is "intrinsic" to our own religion'.[32]

In a way, John Paul II embraced a version of the 'dual covenant theory', formulated in the early twentieth century by the German-Jewish philosopher, Franz Rosenzweig.[33] While Rosenzweig used this approach to find a place for Christianity within Jewish theology, John Paul II seems to have utilized it in order to formulate a theology of Judaism within a Catholic framework. From his perspective, there is the Jewish covenant and the Christian covenant. The Jewish covenant (following the 1974 'Guidelines') was established by God and was shaped by the ways in which Jews define themselves, that is, by Jewish theological self-understanding. Judaism is no longer viewed by the Church as a religion that had become obsolete in the first century, but rather as a 'living heritage' rooted in the past and vibrantly alive in the present. It is with the living and contemporary Jewish people – heirs to an irrevocable and enduring covenant – that the Church enters into fraternal dialogue.[34]

The Christian covenant is now seen, not as replacing, but as continuing and amplifying the covenant made with Israel. Consequently, theological anti-Semitism, rather than being integral to Christian teachings, becomes anathema to it. However, from the Pope's theological perspective, rejection of the 'Displacement Doctrine' and its replacement with a recognition of the permanence of the covenant with Israel, leads not only to a recognition of the theological integrity of Judaism, but also to the integration of the covenant with the Jews into the process of Christian self-identity. Precisely because Christianity emerged from Judaism – because the original 'Jewish' covenant is understood to be an integral part of the Christian covenant, because Jesus and the apostles identified themselves as Jews, because of liturgical and other influences of Judaism upon Christianity – Christian identity has now become irrevocably and integrally related to an encounter with Judaism.[35] These themes were expressed by John Paul II in a number of ways on numerous occasions. Almost as a commentary on *Nostra Aetate*'s brief reference to 'the spiritual ties that link the people of the New Testament to the stock of Abraham', John Paul II substantially amplified the original meaning of this phrase. For example, rather than seeing Jesus as a barrier for Christians when encountering Judaism, he perceived Jesus as a conduit enabling Christians to encounter the traditions and the beliefs of Jesus' people: 'Whoever meets Jesus Christ meets Judaism'.[36] No longer is there a fissure between Judaism and Christianity, but rather a familial continuity, an organic relationship.[37]

Yet, despite his affirmation of the 'old' covenant, the Pope, as might be expected, saw the old covenant as a prelude and anticipation of the 'new', which is described as the fulfilment of the old, and in a real sense as surpassing and fulfilling, if not also superseding (though not displacing), the old.[38] The old covenant is the necessary premise of the new covenant, which is its inevitable fulfillment. Here we see an extension of *Nostra Aetate*'s rejection of the 'Displacement Doctrine', although accompanied by the perpetuation of a version of the 'Supersessionist Doctrine'. The Pope, however, seemed not to see an endemic tension between the claims of the two covenants, though he admitted that contradictions between them, especially on issues such as messianism and Christology, will be resolved in favour of Christian truth, in the eschatological future. Surely, when the Pope spoke of the one faith of humankind in the eschaton, he was referring to Catholic faith.[39] However, until the eschaton, during historical times, the two covenants coexist.

While the Christian covenant remains largely irrelevant for Jewish self-identity, the Jewish covenant takes on a pivotal role in Christian self-identity. This view of the organic development of Christianity out of Judaism, this claim of the extension of Christianity beyond Judaism, this virtual absorption and incorporation of aspects of Judaism into Christianity, was not considered by John Paul II to be inimical either to Judaism or to Catholic–Jewish dialogue. Rather, it is understood to be part of an internal dialogue *within* Christianity about the mystery of its own nature.[40]

On one level, John Paul II articulated and enacted a theological framework, directed both at Jews and at Catholics, for enabling Catholic–Jewish dialogue to proceed and to flourish. However, on another level, he formulated a Catholic theology of Judaism that was directed at Catholics in search of spiritual self-understanding and Catholic identity. Consequently, a review and analysis of John Paul II's teachings about Judaism and the Jews must be understood on both levels.

Removal of the 'Displacement Doctrine' serves as the theological foundation for the Church's repudiation of anti-Semitism and of the rejection of the claim that the Jews are collectively responsible for the death of Jesus.[41] John Paul II consistently rejected the deicide claim and vigorously condemned anti-Semitism throughout his pontificate.[42] Considering the gravity which the Catholic Church assigns to sin, it is especially significant that John Paul II has identified anti-Semitism as a specific sin.[43] Inextricably related to John Paul II's unequivocal and harsh condemnation of anti-Semitism was his personal and theological preoccupation with the Holocaust.

For John Paul II, the Holocaust was not an abstractly evil event. Rather, it is a historical experience that 'surpass[es] in horror anything that can be imagined'.[44] It is a tragedy that he witnessed as it unfolded in his native Poland. He saw the Jews of Poland, including the families of many of his friends, disappear before his very eyes. Throughout his writings and his speeches, the experience of the Jews during the years of World War II is a constant referent. Besides the citation above from *Crossing the Threshold of Hope*, the following examples may be cited. During his historic visit to the synagogue in Rome in 1986, John Paul II reiterated what had by then become a common theme in this thinking: 'I would like once more to express a word of abhorrence for the genocide decreed against the Jewish people during the last war, which led to the Holocaust of millions of innocent victims'.[45]

The Pope's reflections on the Holocaust, delivered in Poland, have a special poignancy. Until recent years, Poles focused primarily on their own suffering during the Nazi occupation, often ignoring or suppressing memories of the plight of Polish Jewry. When discussing the war years, Poles would treat the experience of Jews as a matter of a competitive martyrology, with themselves seen as the primary victims of the German occupation.[46] To the Pope's great credit, he always acknowledged that Jewish suffering during the Holocaust was unsurpassed by any group, even though this must have roused the ire of many of his fellow Poles. For example, while on pilgrimage to Auschwitz in 1979, he emphasized the plight of the Jewish victims who met their deaths there, despite the then current policy of the Polish Communist government not to do so. Referring to a Hebrew inscription at the site of the former death camp, the Pope said, 'This inscription awakens the memory of the people whose sons and daughters were intended for total extermination ... The very people who received from God the Commandment, "thou shalt not kill," itself experienced in a special measure what is meant by killing. It is not permissible for anyone to pass by this inscription with indifference'.[47] In an Apostolic Letter on the fiftieth anniversary of the outbreak of World War II, the Pope stated that 'the Jews of Poland, more than others, lived this immense suffering'.[48]

John Paul II consistently condemned anti-Semitism, linked that condemnation to his close personal awareness of the unique experience of the Jews during the Holocaust, and considered a confrontation with the Holocaust to be a critical item on the agenda of Catholic–Jewish dialogue: 'No dialogue between Christians and Jews can overlook the painful and terrible experience of the *Shoah*'.[49] Nonetheless, in his statements on the Holocaust, the Pope offers a historiography and theology of the Holocaust that is problematic, especially for Jews.

Though the Pope readily acknowledged the activity, complicity, and apathy of Christians with regard to the Holocaust; though he recognized the correlative guilt of such individuals; and, though he has called for their contrition, repentance, and reconciliation toward the Jewish people, John Paul II nonetheless apparently refused to acknowledge the role of Christian doctrinal anti-Semitism as a contributing cause of the Holocaust, and he did not explicitly confront the less than admirable behaviour of the Holy See during the Holocaust. In an address to the German ambassador to the Holy See, the Pope said, 'For Christians the heavy burden of guilt for the murder of the Jewish people must be an enduring call to repentance; thereby we can overcome every form of anti-Semitism and establish a new relationship with our kindred nation of the Old Covenant'.[50] Yet, in a 1988 address to the Jewish community of Vienna, the Pope said, 'It would be, of course, unjust and untrue to put the blame for those unspeakable crimes on Christianity'.[51]

It might be unreasonable to expect the Pope to condemn the Holy See for its behaviour during World War II, even though, as a Pole, he had much to condemn.[52] Rather, one might have expected the Pope simply to be silent with regard to the Church's behavior during the war years. Instead, we find John Paul II portraying Pius XI and Pius XII as active advocates for the Jews.[53] We find him exaggerating the degree of actual help given to Jews during the war years by local churches.[54]

The Pope circumvented all possible links between Christian anti-Semitism and the Holocaust. He similarly side-stepped the problematic historical issue of the behaviour of the Church during the war years. Instead, he tried to forge continuity between the supposedly pro-Jewish doctrines and actions of the Church before Vatican II and the truly pro-Jewish doctrines and actions of the Church during his own pontificate. This, then, gave the Pope an opening to identify what he considered to be the source of the ideology that engendered the Holocaust as well as many subsequent assaults against human life and dignity: *secular atheism*. Using the Holocaust as a paradigmatic and supreme example of dehumanization, the Pope identified secular humanism as the primary cause of the Holocaust and of other horrors in recent history. Speaking about the Holocaust, he observed that 'it is precisely an absence of faith in God … which can easily bring about such disasters'.[55] Speaking in Germany in 1987 about Nazism, John Paul II said, 'Let us pause … to reflect on the terrible consequences which can arise from a denial of God … [We must] remain alert for new forms of anti-Semitism, racism, and neo-pagan religious persecution'.[56] Similarly, in a 1987 letter to Archbishop May of St Louis, the Pope wrote, 'Reflection upon the *Shoah* shows us to what terrible consequences the lack of faith in God and a contempt for man created in his image can lead'.[57] John Paul II perceived the secularism that propelled Nazism to be a 'new paganism' aimed against both the Jews and against Christianity.[58] He depicted Marxism as such an ideology.[59] He linked this ideology with all the 'Auschwitzes of our time', including the practice of abortion.[60]

For John Paul II, one of the driving forces behind interreligious dialogue is the attempt to forge an interreligious alliance against a common enemy and challenge, that is, atheism, secularism and materialism, which he saw as being at the root of dehumanization and as inimical to human life, dignity and freedom. Though John Paul II never minimized the extent of Jewish suffering during the Holocaust, he nonetheless saw Holocaust awareness as a foundation for a universal moral theology and as a stimulus for a programme of social action.[61]

John Paul II always found great meaning and virtue in suffering. This view is consonant both with Catholic teaching and with a particularly Polish-Catholic proclivity for 'messianic' self-understanding.[62] It is not surprising, therefore, that the Pope applied such a theological attitude to his understanding of the Holocaust. In the catastrophe that befell the Jews, the Pope found multifaceted meaning. Such suffering, he contends, is simultaneously vicarious, purifying, pedagogic, and redemptive. It is a way in which Jews can bear witness to their 'irrevocable calling' by God. 'After all', said the Pope, quoting the Gospel of John (4:22), 'salvation is from the Jews'.[63] Addressing Jewish leaders in Warsaw in 1987, the Pope said:

> It was you who suffered this terrible sacrifice of extermination. One might say that you suffered it also on behalf of those who were in the purifying power of suffering. The more atrocious the suffering, the greater the purification. The more painful the experience, the greater the hope ... Because of this terrible experience, you have become a loud warning voice for all humanity, for all nations, all powers of this world, all systems and every person. More than anyone else, it is precisely you who have become this saving warning. I think that in this sense you continue your particular vocation.[64]

Echoing motifs usually reserved by Catholics for Christ and by Poles for Poland – the 'Christ of the Nations' – John Paul II described Jewish suffering during the Holocaust as having been vicarious suffering for humankind and therefore redemptive. Using the Christological motif of 'sacrifice', he stated: 'You bore this sacrifice for others who were also supposed to be destroyed'.[65] Elsewhere, he said that when confronting the horrors of the Holocaust, 'we hear the voice of Christ'.[66]

While affirming the irrevocable election of Israel by God, John Paul II saw suffering as an endemic component of that election, an election that the people of Israel, in his view, share with one of their sons – Jesus. 'This extraordinary people continues to bear signs of its divine election.... Israel has truly paid a high price for its election. Perhaps because of this, Israel has become more similar to the Son of man, who, according to the flesh, was also a son of Israel'.[67]

John Paul II's reflections on the Holocaust integrated not only past, but also recent Jewish experience into his Catholic theology of Judaism. He attempted to infuse meaning into horror. He wanted to elicit reconciliation between Jews and Catholics, especially between Jews and Poles, from an event that evoked hostility and mistrust between these two groups. His comparisons of Jewish suffering to the passion of Christ can only be seen as intending to further such reconciliation. Nonetheless, from a Jewish perspective, the Pope's understanding of the Holocaust is problematic.

Classical Jewish theology recognizes the virtue of martyrdom. Jewish commentaries to the biblical text describing the 'suffering servant' (Isa. 53) relate it to the people of Israel. However, post-Holocaust Jewish thought is strongly resistant to discerning redemptive meaning from the systematic murder of one third of the Jewish people, including over one million Jewish children. To ascribe meaning is to offer justification, to assign a reason for why so many had to suffer so many unspeakable horrors. To ascribe meaning to this catastrophe could readily lead to the view that what happened was inevitable, that the perpetrators were the agents of destiny or even of God. As Elie Wiesel has put it, 'Suffering does not lead to saintliness. I think suffering is evil. Man is not created in order to suffer. If this were so, then God could not be holy. God does not want man to suffer; man suffers against God. We believe that suffering is not the answer; suffering is only the question'.[68] Jews do not aspire to be 'the Christ of the nations'. It is told of a Hasidic master that during a time of persecution, he prayed to God, 'We've had enough of suffering. If to be Your chosen people means that we are chosen to suffer, then choose someone else'.

Particularly problematic for Jews was the Pope's beatification of Edith Stein, a Jewess who went to her death during the Holocaust as a baptized Jew, as a Catholic nun. In stating that her 'baptism was by no means a break with her Jewish heritage', John Paul II reiterated his Catholic theology of Judaism which, in effect, absorbs Judaism into the continuum that culminates in Christian faith.[69] The integrity of Judaism is affirmed, but the hope and even the expectation of the conversion of the Jews is also expressed. Though 'mission to the Jews' as an aggressive or coercive task is no longer considered viable, the hope for the baptism of Jews remains, and the lauding of those, such as Edith Stein, who have taken this road, continues. Indeed, most Jews would find offensive the Pope's statement that, 'On the strength of Christ's willingness to sacrifice himself for others she [Edith Stein] saw in her seeming impotence a way to render a final service to her people', like the biblical figure of Esther.[70] From the Pope's Catholic point of view, Edith Stein is a saint, a 'Catholic Jew' who found fulfilment in Jesus Christ and who died a sacrificial death like her adopted Saviour. But for Jews, Edith Stein was a Jewish apostate who abandoned the faith of her ancestors, who elected to receive that which Jewish martyrs throughout the centuries had perished rejecting. For many Jews, some of the teachings of the faith she accepted were a contributing cause of the event that claimed her life and the lives of millions of others of the faith she rejected. Those who took her life, and the lives of millions of others, were practising adherents of the faith she embraced.

To be sure, evangelization is central to the mission of the Church.[71] It would be unreasonable to expect the Church to renounce a doctrine so central to its mission in the world. However, under John Paul II, the Church revised its doctrine of evangelization from one of aggressive coercion to more benign forms in which the individual joins the Church through a free expression of conscience and conviction.[72] Long before Vatican II, John Paul II practised what he was later to preach. A variety of sources have confirmed, for example, that in 1949, in Poland, a woman came to the young Father Wojtyla asking him to baptize her adopted son. From questioning her, Wojtyla learned that the child was Jewish. His parents had given him into the safe keeping of the woman during the Nazi occupation. They had explicitly requested that the child remain a Jew and be sent to his mother's family after the war, should they not survive. The parents were both killed. Wojtyla refused to baptize the child, respecting the will of his parents. He told the foster mother to arrange for the child to go to America to be reunited with his family and with his faith. Despite the pain of separation from her adopted son, the woman complied.[73]

As has been noted, John Paul II's social agenda rested upon his understanding of Catholic moral theology and his fierce opposition to secularism. While he linked specific moral positions, such as his views of abortion, to his understanding of the Holocaust, this perspective is not largely shared by the representatives of most Jewish organizations with which the Church has been engaged dialogically. Here, one of the many incongruities in Catholic–Jewish dialogue as it is actually practised becomes evident. While the Pope found abortion, birth control, most forms of infertility treatment and many positions endorsed by feminists to be immoral, it is precisely these issues that most of the Jewish organizations involved in dialogue with the Church are advocating; for example, a pro-choice stance on abortion.

This incongruity deepens when one realizes that Catholic–Jewish dialogue in practice mostly obtains between the Church – a religious institution – and secular Jewish organizations that identify with the ideology the Pope depicted as the arch-enemy of religion: namely, secular humanism. On the Catholic side of the dialogue there is a hierarchical Church, grounded in theology, and usually represented in interfaith dialogue by theologians who are clerics, or at least by clergy. On the Jewish side, there is a plethora of Jewish voluntary agencies, usually secular in nature, being represented by managerial staff and lay leaders untutored in theology and often of a secular or even an antireligious bent. The Catholic 'language' of expression is theological. The Jewish 'language' is often liberal secularism. The Catholic framework for discussion is theological. The Jewish framework is primarily informed by the Jewish communal agenda. As Cardinal Edward Cassidy, the former President of the Holy See's Commission for Religious Dialogue with Judaism, put it, 'We are not two humanitarian societies; far less are we two debating clubs. We are two faith communities and as such we are being called to respond to a common challenge'.[74]

When Catholic–Jewish dialogue began in the United States, Catholics and Jews shared a social agenda. Both groups suffered social and economic discrimination and exclusion in Protestant America. As Catholics (primarily Irish and Italian) and Jews became integrated into the American fabric, as anti-Catholic and anti-Jewish discrimination abated, the social and political agendas of Catholic-Americans and Jewish-Americans diverged. Furthermore the 'official' position of the Church on human sexuality, abortion, euthanasia and other issues finds little resonance in the predominantly liberal and highly secularized Jewish communal structure. Outside of North America, especially in largely Catholic countries, Jewish communities find themselves often too small to participate effectively in dialogue with the Catholic Church. The questions of who is the Church's actual and most appropriate partner in religious dialogue with Judaism and how authentic theological dialogue can be maintained are often problematic.

The Church desires dialogue not simply with Jews, but with Judaism. As the name of the Holy See's Commission on *Religious* Relations with the Jews suggests, it seeks *religious*, theological dialogue between two 'faith communities', and not primarily social dialogue. It perceives social issues as being inextricably related to matters of faith and theology, and not simply as agenda items for inter-group relations. The Commission has called for a real 'theological dialogue', that is, a dialogue on theological issues by those on both sides competent to contribute. Perhaps the present incongruity in Catholic–Jewish theological dialogue is what the Pope had in mind when he warned that 'Work [of Catholic–Jewish dialogue] that is of poor quality or lacking in precision would be extremely detrimental to dialogue in this field'.[75]

The incongruity of religious dialogue between the Church and Jewish social advocacy groups has created a situation in which one side is speaking theological discourse while the other is speaking from the framework of a specific group's communal agenda. This is not a dialogue, but two monologues speaking different languages. Though theological concerns have been of paramount importance to the Church, and though the Church has recast its theology in terms of its relationship to Judaism, and though John Paul II formulated a Catholic theology of Judaism, there has been little reciprocity from the Jewish side. Little attention has been paid in the Jewish academic, religious, or communal arenas to recasting the often negative classical Jewish theological attitudes and views of Christianity.[76] Few efforts have been expended to revise negative popular Jewish stereotypes of Christianity and of Christians. Changes in how Jews are portrayed in the Catechism, liturgy and Catholic textbooks reflect the Church's new understanding of the Jews and of Judaism. Yet, such changes have not been reciprocated by the Jewish community in terms of how Catholics and Catholicism ought to be understood by Jews. Little has been done by the Jewish community to make Jews aware of post-Vatican II teachings about Jews and Judaism. As Cardinal Cassidy bluntly put it, 'I am truly amazed at times to read Catholic teaching and doctrine explained in Jewish publications in such a way that no Catholic would recognize them as part of his or her faith'.[77] He further expresses dismay at the widespread lack of Jewish interest in, and knowledge of, the evolution of Catholic self-understanding with regard to Judaism and the Jewish people.

The Church's strong affirmation of Hebrew Scriptures and of the Jewish identity of Jesus, Mary and the apostles has led to a veritable explosion of Catholic scholarship and education aimed at understanding and reclaiming aspects of Judaism at the time of Jesus and even some of the rituals of ancient and contemporary Judaism. The identity of Jesus as a Jew was embraced by the Pope and by Catholic doctrine. However, scant attention has been paid by the Jewish community to the identity of Jesus as a Jew. Few attempts have been made by Jewish scholars and theologians to rethink and to recast the largely negative portrait of Jesus and the apostles found in classical Jewish religious thought and in popular Jewish attitudes.

Under the influence of John Paul II, the Church developed a Catholic theology of Judaism that has been translated programmatically in a manner that has immeasurably improved Catholic–Jewish relations. As has been indicated above, this Catholic theology of Judaism is both promising and problematic from a Jewish perspective. For Catholic–Jewish relations to build on the substantial progress already achieved, and for the work of dialogue and reconciliation to proceed further, a new Jewish theology of Christianity is a desideratum, including a rethinking of Jewish attitudes toward Jesus and the apostles.

In various official documents, the Holy See has addressed most concerns of the Jewish communal agenda that relate to Catholic–Jewish relations. Anti-Semitism has been summarily condemned and defined as a sin against God. Holocaust awareness has heightened. Israel has been recognized by the Holy See, and full diplomatic relations have been achieved. Vatican recognition has triggered substantial positive effects for Israel diplomatically, politically and economically. As a result of Israel's recognition by the Holy See, formerly closed diplomatic channels and economic opportunities in Catholic countries have opened up.

The Church is now calling for 'a *theological* dialogue with Jewish representatives'. The major item on the agenda that will determine the future complexion of Catholic–Jewish dialogue is whether the Jewish community is prepared to enter into serious and authentic *theological* dialogue with the Church. The Church, especially under the leadership of John Paul II, has moved boldly and comparatively rapidly in recasting and reshaping its theology, policies and activities with regard to Judaism and the Jewish people. Whether reciprocity in the areas of theology, policy, liturgy, education and related programmes will take place within the Jewish community currently remains an unanswered question.[78] But, underlying the sacred work of Jewish–Catholic dialogue is both a prayer and a hope. In the words of John Paul II: 'As Christians and Jews, following the example of the faith of Abraham, we are called to be a blessing for the world. This is the common task awaiting us. It is therefore necessary for us, Christians and Jews, to first be a blessing to one another'.[79]

NOTES

1. The text of *Nostra Aetate* may be found in Francesco Gioia (ed.), *Interreligious Dialogue: Official Teachings of the Catholic Church,* 1963–1995 (Vatican: Pontifical Council for Interreligious Dialogue, 1997), pp.37–40. See John T. Pawlikowski, '*Nostra Aetate:* Its Impact on Catholic–Jewish Relations', *Thought* 67 (December 1991): 371–84.
2. See also, Gioia, *Interreligious Dialogue*, pp.239, 499, 547.
3. For good summaries of the 'Displacement Doctrine', see Franklin Littell, *The Crucifixion of the Jews* (New York: Harper and Row, 1975), pp.28–32; Rosemary R. Ruether, *Faith and Fratricide: The Theological Roots of Anti-Semitism* (New York: Seabury Press, 1974); Joseph Cardinal Bernardin, *A Blessing To Each Other* (Chicago: Liturgy Training Publications, 1996), pp.146–55.
4. The eminent Jewish theologian Abraham Joshua Heschel was deeply involved in negotiating the final draft of para. 4 of *Nostra Aetate*. In meetings with Cardinal Augustin Bea and with Paul VI he fought for the exclusion of any mention of 'mission to the Jews' in that document. When such a reference appeared in an early draft, he issued a strong rebuke, saying, 'I'd rather go to Auschwitz than give up my religion'. As Heschel said in an interview, 'I succeeded in persuading the Pope ... He personally crossed out a paragraph in which there was a reference to conversion or mission to the Jews. The Pope [Paul VI] himself. And the declaration published by the Ecumenical Council – if you study it carefully, you will notice the impact of my effort. There isn't the slightest reference to mission to the Jews'. See Abraham J. Heschel, *Moral Grandeur and Spiritual Audacity* (New York: Farrar, Straus and Giroux, 1996), p.405. On the revised attitude of the Catholic Church on 'mission to the Jews', see Eugene Fisher, 'Is There a Christian Mission to the Jews?', in Clark Williamson, ed., *A Mutual Witness* (St. Louis: Chalice Press, 1992), pp.15–33.
5. The 'Guidelines' were published on 1 December 1974, over the signature of Johannes Cardinal Willebrands, President of the Commission for Religious Relations with the Jews. The text of the 'Guidelines' is found in Eugene J. Fisher, *Seminary Education and Christian–Jewish Relations* (Washington, DC: National Catholic Educational Association, 1983), pp.81–6.
6. Jules Isaac, *The Teaching of Contempt* (New York: Holt, Rinehart and Winston, 1964).
7. Louis Michaels, *The Humor and Warmth of Pope John XXIII* (New York: Pocket Books, 1965), p.53. On John XXIII's help to Jews during the Holocaust, see Lawrence Elliott, *I Will Be Called John* (New York: Berkley, 1973), pp.159–65.
8. Bernardin, *A Blessing to Each Other*, pp.151–52.
9. Gioia, *Intereligious Dialogue*, p.635.
10. Carl Bernstein and Marco Politi, *His Holiness: John Paul II and the Hidden History of Our Time* (New York: Doubleday, 1996), p.30.
11. On attitudes of the Polish Church toward the Jews in the immediate years before World War II, see Ronald Modras, *The Catholic Church and Antisemitism, Poland 1933–1939* (Chur, Switzerland: Harwood Academic Publishers, 1994). On Polish–Jewish relations between the world wars, see Yisrael Gutman, Ezra Mendelsohn, Jehuda Reinharz and Chone Shmeruk (eds), *The Jews of Poland Between Two World Wars* (Hanover, N.H.: University Press of New England, 1989). On attitudes of the Polish Church immediately after the war, see Aryeh Josef Kochavi, 'The Catholic Church and Antisemitism in Poland Following World War II as Reflected in British Diplomatic Documents', *Gal-Ed* (1989): 116–28.
12. Bernstein, *His Holiness*, p.44.
13. Tad Szulc, *Pope John Paul II: The Biography* (New York: Pocket Books, 1995), pp.74–75. On John Paul II and Kluger, see also relevant references in Bernstein and in Gian Franco Svidercoschi, *Letter to a Jewish Friend* (New York: Crossroad, 1994).
14. Szulc, *John Paul II*, p.305.
15. Svidercoschi, *Letter to a Jewish Friend*, p.93.
16. Bernstein, *His Holiness*, p.31.
17. Ibid., p.32; Szulc, *John Paul II*, p.66.
18. Most of John Paul II's statements regarding Judaism and the Jewish people – many delivered at meetings with representatives of various Jewish communities throughout the world – have been collected in Eugene J. Fisher and Leon Klenicki (eds), *John Paul II: Spiritual Pilgrimage – Texts on Jews and Judaism, 1979–1995* (New York: Crossroad, 1995). For citations noted here, see pp.8, 99, 151, 153–4.

19. John Paul II, *Crossing the Threshold of Hope* (New York: Knopf, 1994), pp.98–100.
20. James Carroll, 'The Silence', *New Yorker*, 7 April 1997, p.66.
21. Fisher, *Spiritual Pilgrimage*, pp.60–73; Bernstein, *His Holiness*, pp.443–44.
22. Fisher, *Spiritual Pilgrimage*, pp.167–69. On the 'Convent Controversy', see Wladyslaw T. Bartoszewski, *The Convent at Auschwitz* (New York: George Braziller, 1990); Carol Rittner and John K. Roth (eds), *Memory Offended: The Auschwitz Convent Controversy* (New York: Praeger, 1991).
23. John Paul II, *Crossing the Threshold*, pp.188–91; Szulc, *Pope John Paul II*, pp.494–96.
24. John Paul II, *Crossing the Threshold*, pp.191–99, 203–8; Szulc, *Pope John Paul II*, pp.489–93.
25. Fisher, *Spiritual Pilgrimage*, pp.36, 46, 187.
26. John Paul II, *Crossing the Threshold*, p.100.
27. Fisher, *Spiritual Pilgrimage*, p.12.
28. On the situation of the Church at the time of John Paul II's election, see Szulc, *Pope John Paul II* pp.338–59; Bernstein, *His Holiness*, pp.96–8, 155–60.
29. Fisher, *Spiritual Pilgrimage*, p.89.
30. Ibid., p.xxii. John XXIII in his first meeting with Jewish representatives as Pope introduced himself as 'Joseph, your brother' (Gen. 45:4).
31. The story of Cain and Abel is also relevant here. Earlier Church teachings compared the Jews to the fratricidal Cain, and Jesus and the Church to Abel. The 'Displacement Doctrine' placed the 'mark of Cain', and his punishment of eternal wandering upon the Jews. See Ruether, *Faith and Fratricide*, pp.133–34.
32. Fisher, *Spiritual Pilgrimage*, p.63. See also the *Catechism of the Catholic Church* (Mahwah, N.J.: Paulist Press, 1994), issued during the pontificate of John Paul II and endorsed by him, para. 839, p.233, 'The Jewish faith, unlike other non-Christian religions, is already a response to God's revelation in the Old Covenant'. Note John Borelli, 'The Catechism and Interreligious Dialogue: The Jews and World Religions', in Bernard L. Marthaler (ed.), *Introducing the Catechism of the Catholic Church* (New York: Paulist Press, 1994), pp.72–87.
33. Franz Rosenzweig, *The Star of Redemption*, trans. William H. Hallo (New York: Holt, Rinehart and Winston, 1970), pp.298–380. See also Maurice Bowler, 'Rosenzweig on Judaism and Christianity: The Two Covenant Approach', *Judaism* 22 (1973): 475–82; Michael B. McGarry, *Christology After Auschwitz* (New York: Paulist Press, 1977), especially pp.73–93 on dual covenant theory. Note that McGarry's book was published before the pontificate of John Paul II.
34. Fisher, *Spiritual Pilgrimage*, p.15.
35. Ibid., p.18.
36. Ibid., p.14.
37. While John Paul II uses a 'fraternal' model for the Jewish–Christian relationship, he also tends to depict Christianity as the 'daughter' religion of Judaism. He describes the relationship as a 'real parentage'. See Fisher, *Spiritual Pilgrimage*, p.56; as an 'organic' relationship, see p.74. In recent years, it has become popular to depict the relationship of Judaism and Christianity as one of siblings, whereas before Christianity was depicted as a 'daughter' religion of Judaism. The image one uses has direct implications for interreligious dialogue.
38. Fisher, *Spiritual Pilgrimage*, pp.174–75. See also *Catechism of the Catholic Church*, paras. 65, 66, pp.22–23; para. 840, p.233; para. 1093, p.284.
39. John Paul II, *Crossing the Threshold*, p.100; Fisher, *Spiritual Pilgrimage*, p.74.
40. Fisher, *Spritual Pilgrimage*, p.15.
41. The removal of collective Jewish responsibility for the death of Jesus is restated by John Paul II and is linked by him to the rejection of any theological justification for anti-Semitism; see Fisher, *Spiritual Pilgrimage*, p.63. The *Catechism of the Catholic Church* (paras. 595–98, pp.153–54) amplifies further upon this theme and states (para. 598), 'Taking into account the fact that our sins affect Christ himself, the Church does not hesitate to impute to Christians the gravest responsibility for the torments inflicted upon Jesus, a responsibility with which they have all too often burdened the Jews alone. We must regard as guilty all those who continue to relapse into their sins ... And it can be seen that our crime in this case is greater in us than in the Jews'. Para. 599 states further, 'Jesus' violent death...is part of the mystery of God's plan'.
42. Fisher, *Spiritual Pilgrimage*, pp.62, 128, 139. On his renunciation of the deicide claim, see p.124.
43. See John Paul II, 'The Sinfulness of Anti-Semitism', *Origins* 23:13 (September 5, 1991). See

Fisher, *Spiritual Pilgrimage*, pp.140, 158 and John Paul II, *Crossing the Threshold*, p.97.

44. Fisher, *Spiritual Pilgrimage*, p.131.
45. Fisher, *Spiritual Pilgrimage*, p.62; see John Paul II's poetic and moving 'lamentation' at Mauthausen Concentration Camp, pp.116–18.
46. Ibid., p.151. Note Yisrael Gutman and Shmuel Krakowski, *Unequal Victims: Poles and Jews During World War Two* (New York: Holocaust Library, 1986); Michael C. Steinlauf, *Bondage to the Dead: Poland and the Memory of the Holocaust* (Syracuse, N.Y.: Syracuse University Press, 1997); Antony Polonsky, 'Polish–Jewish Relations and the Holocaust', *Polin* 4 (1989): 226–42; Andrej Bryk, 'Polish Society Today and the Memory of the Holocaust', *Gal-Ed* (1991): 107–29.
47. See Fisher, *Spiritual Pilgrimage*, pp.6, 62.
48. Ibid., p.131.
49. Ibid., p.142.
50. Ibid., p.139.
51. Ibid., p.120. See also p.152.
52. On Pius XII's apparent apathy to the plight of Poles and Jews in Nazi-occupied Poland, see Carlo Falconi, *The Silence of Pius XII* (Boston: Little, Brown and Co., 1965).
53. On Pius XI and Pius XII's alleged pro-Jewish postures, see *Pilgrimage*, pp.5, 32, 107. For a historically documented study that offers a very different view, condemning the often pro-German attitudes and actions of Pius XI and Pius XII, see Guenter Lewy, *The Catholic Church and Nazi Germany* (New York: McGraw Hill, 1964).
54. On the aid given Jews by local churches see Fisher, *Spiritual Pilgrimage*, pp.14, 62, 107, 203.
55. Ibid., p.52, p.21.
56. Ibid., p.91.
57. Ibid., pp.101, 149.
58. Ibid., pp.131–32.
59. Ibid., p.101.
60. Ibid., pp.209, 150, 123. See Bernstein, *His Holiness*, p.518: 'He would fight tooth and nail against "a new massacre, a true slaughter of the innocents, a new Holocaust." The Holocaust was precisely the image that came to his mind every time he heard the word *abortion*'.
61. Fisher, *Spiritual Pilgrimage*, pp.127, 180.
62. Szulc, *Pope John Paul II*, pp.7, 22–25, 118, 383. See Waldemar Chrostowski, 'The Suffering, Chosenness and Mission of the Polish Nation', *Occasional Papers on Religion in Eastern Europe* 11:4 (August 1991): 1–14.
63. Fisher, *Spiritual Pilgrimage*, pp.98–99.
64. Ibid., p.99. See also, pp.126–7.
65. Ibid., p.151. The direct reference here is to the Poles. It could not be lost on his Polish listeners that here the Pope depicts Jews rather than Poles as 'the Christ of the nations'.
66. Fisher, *Spiritual Pilgrimage*, p.98.
67. John Paul II, *Crossing the Threshold*, p.99.
68. Harry J. Cargas, *In Conversation with Elie Wiesel* (New York: Paulist Press, 1976), p.19.
69. Fisher, *Spiritual Pilgrimage*, p.95.
70. Ibid., p.93.
71. See Gioia, *Interreligious Dialogue*, p.407, 'The Church is missionary by her very nature'. See also *Catechism of the Catholic Church*, paras. 849–56, pp.225–26. Note how post-Vatican II documents deal with the claim 'Outside the Church there is no salvation'. In view of the Church's commitment to interreligious dialogue, see *Catechism of the Catholic Church*, paras. 846–48, pp.244–45, and Gioia, *Interreligious Dialogue*, p.547.
72. Gioia, *Interreligious Dialogue*, p.577. Here the Curia bluntly states that conversion must be a freely chosen act, but that 'In the context of dialogue between believers of various faiths, one cannot avoid reflecting on the spiritual process of conversion'.
73. Szulc, *Pope John Paul II*, p.173. For a more complete account, see Yaffa Eliach, *Hasidic Tales of the Holocaust* (New York: Oxford University Press, 1982), pp.142–7.
74 Cardinal Edward I. Cassidy, 'The Next Issues in Jewish–Catholic Relations', *Origins* 26:41 (3 April 1997): 668.
75 Fisher, *Spiritual Pilgrimage*, p.19.
76. A few Jewish theologians have attempted to formulate a Jewish theology of Christianity. See David Novak, *Jewish–Christian Dialogue: A Jewish Justification* (New York: Oxford University Press, 1989). For a new Jewish theological understanding of Jesus, see Byron L.

Sherwin, '"Who Do You Say That I Am?" – A New Jewish View of Jesus', *Journal of Ecumenical Studies* 31:3/4 (1994): 255–69. See also chap. 11 above.

77. Cassidy, 'The Next Issues', p.669.
78. Because of the nature of the Church, it is doubtful that the momentum toward stabilizing and improving Catholic–Jewish relations, as affirmed in Church documents and as stated during the 'magisterium' of John Paul II, will be stifled in the future. His successor, Benedict XVI, has indicated that he will sustain these relations; however, whether he will pursue these dialogic relations with the vigour of John Paul II remains to be seen.
79. Fisher, *Spiritual Pilgrimage*, p.169.

CHAPTER THIRTEEN

Original Sin in the Passover Haggadah?

Though most Jews may not be conversant with the intricacies of the laws of Passover observance, they are, however, familiar with the refrain '*dayyenu*' from the Passover Haggadah. Throughout the Passover seder, questions are posed and answered, both in the liturgy and in social conversation. '*Dayyenu*', however, seems to pose no questions. The text seems clear, simple and forthright. Nonetheless, in twelfth-century France, Rabbi Abraham ben David of Posquieres, known by the acronym 'Ravad', wrote an unusual responsum in which he questions the meaning of a particular section of the '*Dayyenu*'.[1] Ravad was a leading Talmudist of the late twelfth century. As is evident from his many and diverse works, Ravad had mystical leanings, and eschewed philosophical speculation. Ravad's best-known work is, arguably, his collection of glosses on Maimonides' *Mishneh Torah*. As a communal rabbi and as a leading Halakhic authority, Ravad wrote responsa and offered legal opinions on a wide range of issues.[2]

The particular responsum (pl., responsa; a decision in Jewish case law) in which Ravad deals with a section of '*Dayyenu*' is unusual for at least three reasons. One reason is that the text, though included in the collection of his responsa and legal decisions, is neither a responsum, nor a legal decision. A responsum is usually a response to a legal question put forth by a questioner, such as a litigant or another rabbi asking the advice of a more prominent Halakhic authority than himself. Here, however, there is no external questioner. Indeed, the questioner here seems to be Ravad himself. Second, a responsum is a legal document, usually dealing with an issue of 'case law', a specific situation that comes before a legal decisor (a *poseik*). Here, as we shall see, the subject of this text is not of an Halakhic nature, but is rather of theological import. In a responsum such as this, that deals with a liturgical text, we might expect a Halakhic question to be raised such as: Is reciting the particular section of '*Dayyenu*' under discussion required (*hovah*), forbidden (*assur*), or permitted (*reshut*)? Yet no such question is posed here. A third unusual feature of this responsum is that it is unusually terse, consisting of only twenty-nine words, whereas Ravad's responsa are usually characterized by a depth and breadth of erudition, discussion and analysis.

The responsum under discussion reads as follows: '"If He [God] had brought us before Mount Sinai" – for it brought benefit to Israel, as it is said, "The contaminating lust of the nations ceased for Israel who stood at Mount Sinai; but for those who did not stand at Mount Sinai, their contaminating lust did not cease." And, thus [the passage from the] Haggadah is explained'.

The section of the Haggadah text that is explained here is a section of the '*Dayyenu*', partially quoted at the beginning of the responsum: 'If He [God] had brought us before Mount Sinai, but had not given us the Torah, it would have been sufficient for us'. Ravad questions the assumption here. If a major purpose of the Exodus was to bring the people of Israel out of Egypt in order to receive the Torah at Mount Sinai, how would it have been sufficient if God had merely led them to stand near the mountain, but had not then given them the Torah? Is there any intrinsic value or 'benefit' (*hana'ah*) – to use the Rabad's term, in the fact that the people simply stood at the foot of the mountain?

Ravad replies to these questions and explains how the people's standing at Sinai brought them a 'benefit', by referring to a passage that appears three times (with variants) in the Babylonian Talmud. That passage is as follows: 'Why are Gentiles contaminated with lust? [Rabbi Jonathan said,] Because they did not stand at Mount Sinai. For when the serpent came upon Eve he injected a contaminating lust into her. [However,] the Israelites who stood at Mount Sinai, their contaminating lust departed. The Gentiles, who did not stand at Mount Sinai, their contaminating lust did not depart'.[3]

According to this text, the 'benefit' achieved by the Israelites was the removal of the lustful nature that human beings inherited from Eve. That lustful nature is what leads human beings to commit deeds such as immodest sexual behaviour, adultery and bestiality. Though the people of Israel were freed of this sexual proclivity simply by standing at Sinai, the Gentiles – who did not stand at Sinai, retained it. For example, one variant of the Talmudic text noted above is immediately preceded by this observation: 'Gentiles [sexually] prefer the cattle of the Israelites to their own wives'.[4]

The contaminating lust (*zihum*) referred to in this Talmudic text and quoted in Ravad's responsum is based upon a particular rabbinic interpretation of the biblical story of the first sin in the Garden of Eden (Gen. 3:25–4:1). In this reading of the biblical narrative, Eve is not simply the temptress who seduces Adam into eating the forbidden fruit. Nor is she only seduced into eating the forbidden fruit by the shrewd serpent. In this reading, Eve is also seduced by the serpent into having sexual relations with him, thereby committing adultery. During that act, the serpent contaminates Eve with his ejaculate. That substance contaminates not only Eve, but also all of her descendants with the lust of the serpent. In this view, the source of the lust removed at Sinai is the contaminating substance that the serpent injected into Eve. Not coincidentally, the serpent is identified by the rabbis with the evil inclination (*yetzer ha-ra*). The evil inclination is further identified with the Satan and the Angel of Death.[5] In other words, the inclination to sin and the presence of death enter into human experience with the sin of Eve.

According to a tradition preserved in the Midrashic collection *Pirke de Rabbi Eliezer*, the serpent was but a tool of Sammael, that is, the Satan: 'All the deeds which it [the serpent] did, and all the words it spoke, it did not do or speak, except by the intention of Sammael'.[6] The text further tells us: '[Sammael] riding on the serpent came to her [Eve], and she conceived. Afterwards, Adam came to her and she conceived Abel, as it is said, "Adam knew his wife" (Gen. 4:1). What is the meaning of "knew"? [Adam knew] that she had conceived. And she saw his [Cain's] likeness that it was not of the earthly beings, and she prophesied and said, "I have begotten a man with the Lord" (Gen. 4:1)'.[7]

According to this Midrashic tradition, Eve was seduced into eating the forbidden fruit by Sammael's agent, the serpent. She then had intercourse with Sammael. Fearing that she would be punished with death for her sins, and that Adam would then marry another, Eve tricked Adam into eating the forbidden fruit. He ate it without being aware that the fruit she gave him was the forbidden fruit. As the serpent tricks Eve, so Eve tricks Adam. In this view, Adam sinned unknowingly. Later, when Adam realized that Eve was pregnant, he understood that the child was not his, but Sammael's. The Midrash interprets the phrase, 'Adam knew his wife and she conceived', to mean that Adam knew that his wife had conceived with Sammael. The child of that union was Cain. Since Sammuel was an angel, a supernatural being, the child, Cain had angelic or divine features. Later, Eve conceives a second child from Adam, Abel. According to these traditions, Eve, and not Adam, is primarily responsible for the entrance of sin and death into human experience. As Ben Sira puts it (25:24): 'Sin began with a woman, and because of her, we all die'. Similarly, according to a Midrash, after the sin, God 'showed her how many generations she had destroyed'.[8]

The Talmudic rabbis claimed that Eve's seducing Adam to eat of the forbidden fruit brought death into the world.[9] Because of her actions, both she and Adam were punished with mortality. Until then, they were presumed to be immortals. However, the Talmudic rabbis did not unanimously accept the view that the descendants of Adam and Eve were doomed to die because of the sin of the first couple.[10] In their view, human sin comes about by individual choice and not by inherited human nature. For many of the rabbis, each person dies as a punishment for his or her own sin and not because of the sin of the first couple. As the prophet Ezekiel said, 'The person who sins, he shall die' (Ezek.18:20). Indeed, that the rabbis identify four specific biblical figures who died 'because of the serpent' indicates that they believed that all other individuals die because of their own sins.[11] Death may have come into the world because of the first sin, but each individual's death occurs because of that individual's sins. As the *Zohar*, echoing earlier rabbinic statements, puts it:

> As a person is in his last hour, Adam comes before him and asks him why he is departing from the world. The man says: Woe unto you that I must die because of you. Adam answers: My child, one commandment did I break and was punished for it, but see how many of the commandments of your Master, both positive and negative that you have transgressed ... Rabbi Yesa said: Adam comes before every person the moment he or she is about to leave this life, in order to declare that he or she

> is dying not because of Adam's sin, but on account of his or her own sins, as the sages say, 'There is no death without sin'.[12]

The statement of the sages cited by the *Zohar* here is that of Rabbi Ammi: 'There is no death without sin'. The example given here is Adam: Adam died because he sinned. However, the nexus between sin and death is not universally accepted by the rabbis. The Talmudic text counters with the view of Rabbi Simeon ben Eleazar that 'there *is* death without sin and suffering without iniquity', as in the case of Moses.[13] The claim that there is a causal relationship between sin and death is debated by the rabbis. So is the claim that because of the first couple's sin, people continue to die today. However, none of the rabbis disputes the claim that death entered the world because of the first sin in the Garden of Eden.

Neither do the rabbis deny that the disposition of humankind was negatively affected by the first sin.[14] For example, the Talmudic rabbis describe how Adam's stature was diminished and how his original abilities deteriorated as a consequence of the first sin. All of his descendants share his diminished stature, qualities and abilities.[15] Adam and Eve are expelled from Eden, and access to Eden is denied to their descendants in this world. Eve's punishments, which includes the pain of childbirth, and that the rabbis take to include the pain of menstruation, are shared by all subsequent generations of women.[16] It would seem, therefore, that the Talmudic rabbis had some notion of 'original sin', that the first human sin had a negative impact on the future of humankind. Indeed, various expressions of an idea of original sin are found both in Talmudic literature as well as in medieval Jewish philosophical and mystical literature.[17] To claim that there is no notion of original sin would be to say that humankind remained unaffected by the results of the punishments that Adam and Eve received for having committed the first sin.

The text cited from the Talmud that concerns Ravad would seem to express a rabbinic formulation of the idea of original sin. The human proclivity toward illicit lust is described by this text as having been the direct result of Eve's sinning with the serpent. The substance that the serpent injected into Eve is described as having affected the nature and the behaviour of her descendants. It may be readily assumed that Ravad was at least vaguely aware of the Christian doctrine of original sin as it had developed by his own time. In medieval Jewish polemical literature, the refutation of the Christian doctrine of original sin became a major enterprise.[18] Already in Ravad's times, Joseph Kimhi addressed the subject in his *Sefer ha-Brit*.[19] As the doctrine of original sin was perceived by Jewish writers to be a foundational doctrine upon which all of Christian faith was based, it received increasing attention from Jewish polemicists.[20]

Though the doctrine of original sin varies throughout the history of Christianity, there are a number of features that characterize its formulation, especially during the Middle Ages. Most significant among them is the claim that the presence of original sin is what made the incarnation necessary, and what required Jesus' death as an atonement. In this view, only faith in Jesus as God-incarnate, as Messiah, and as the 'perfect sacrifice' to atone for the original human sin, can grant divine grace and atonement. Those who do not accept Jesus remain tainted by original sin and are devoid of divine grace. Furthermore, the Christian doctrine of original sin teaches that all human souls, including those of the righteous, were tainted by original sin and are subject to punishment because of it. Not only is the body infected with sinfulness and lust, and hence is predestined to sin, but the soul as well. In this view, all human creatures are immediately afflicted with original sin upon entering the world. The source of this original sin is claimed to be the sin of the first couple in the Garden of Eden. For Paul, just as one man's (Adam's) actions introduced the taint of original sin into the world, so one man's actions (Jesus') remove it (Romans 5:12–21).[21]

As was noted above, Talmudic and medieval rabbis readily admitted that certain effects of the first sin by the first human couple were transmitted to their descendants. However, they categorically denied certain central features of the Christian doctrine of original sin. For example, Jews rejected the claim that Adam's sin generated a permanent corruption of the souls of all human beings. Jews further rejected the need for a divine incarnation to atone for original sin. For Jews, observance of the commandments of the Torah and repentance served as adequate remedies for sinfulness.[22] This view may be a counterclaim against the Pauline teaching that, precisely because the Torah, observance of the commandments and individual repentance are ineffective in removing original sin, the incarnation and death of Jesus became necessary.[23]

Throughout the Middle Ages, Jewish thinkers polemicized against the Christian doctrine of original sin, usually on the basis of Scripture and logic. For example, one scripturally based argument of the Jewish polemicists was that the Christian doctrine contradicted Ezekiel's maxim: 'The person who sins, he shall die' (Ezek. 18:20). From this perspective, punishment for sin cannot be transferred from one person to another or from one generation to another. One popular argument from logic, for example, maintained that considering others, especially the righteous, as bearing the taint of the sin of Adam and Eve, would contradict the theological presupposition that God is just. A just God would not punish one person, especially a righteous person, for the sins of another.[24]

As was noted above, some medieval Jewish thinkers embraced a particularly Jewish version of the idea of original sin. Simultaneously, however, others disputed the Christian doctrine of original sin. In the case of Ravad, we encounter what appears to be a novel approach to the problem of original sin in classical Jewish literature. Ravad located the foundation for his approach in the Talmudic text cited in his responsum that has been discussed above.

For Ravad, Judaism affirms a concept of original sin; human beings are tainted by the poisonous lust that the serpent injected into Eve, as is reported by the Talmud. However, according to this Talmudic text, the taint of the original sin was removed for members of the people of Israel at Sinai. Future generations of the people of Israel have been freed from this taint precisely because their forbears stood at Mount Sinai. However, the text further tells us that the taint of original sin was not removed from those whose ancestors did not stand at Mount Sinai. In other words, Ravad takes an approach to disputing the Christian doctrine of original sin that seems not to have been employed by any other Jewish writer on the subject.

Ravad turns the Christian argument on its head. He does not try to refute original sin, but rather uses it to articulate a polemic against the Christian claim about the implications of original sin. The classical Christian claim is that those who accept Jesus as the Christ and incarnated God are free from the taint of original sin, but others – particularly the Jews – who have not accepted Jesus, are not free from this taint. In Ravad's times, a central element of the Christian notion of original sin was Augustine's teaching that carnal lust was part of the punishment for the sins of the first couple that was passed down to their descendants.[25] Against this, Ravad implicitly argued that the opposite is really the case; namely, the Jews are free of the taint of original sin, especially the proclivity for carnal lust, because their ancestors stood at Sinai. The Gentiles, especially the Christians, whose ancestors were not present there, still continue to bear the taint of original sin. Though the Jews have been cleansed of the effects of the poisonous lust of the serpent, the Christians have not. God's bringing the Jews to stand at Sinai is an act of divine grace connected to the people of Israel's future receipt of the Torah. The Christians, however, who neither stood at Sinai nor received the Torah, remain tainted by the original sin and retain carnal lust. Consequently, the Christians, with or without Jesus, have not yet attained a state of grace; the Jews have.

For Ravad, the intrinsic 'benefit' of Israel's standing at Sinai was that they and their descendants were liberated from the taint of original sin. The Gentiles, however, continue to bear the taint of original sin. In other words, rather than using Scripture or logic to dispute the Christian doctrine of original sin as most medieval Jewish polemicists do, Ravad uses a Jewish version of the notion of original sin to offer a powerful polemic against the Christian doctrine of original sin. In so doing, he explains an enigmatic statement in the '*Dayyenu*': 'If He [God] had brought us near to Mount Sinai, but had not given us the Torah, it would have been sufficient for us'.

NOTES

1. Abraham ben David, *Teshuvot u-Fesakim* (Jerusalem: Mosad ha-Rav Kook, 1964), no. 11, p.55; Louis Jacobs, *Theology in the Responsa* (London: Routledge and Kegan Paul, 1975), pp.49–50.
2. On Abraham ben David of Posquieres, see the informative work by Isadore Twersky, *Rabad of Posquieres* (Cambridge, Mass.: Harvard University Press, 1962).
3. *Shabbat* 145b–146a; see also *Yebamot* 103b, *Avodah Zarah* 22b.
4. *Avodah Zara* 22b; see also *Gittin* 38a.
5. *Baba Batra* 16a: '[Satan] comes down to earth and seduces, then ascends to heaven and awakens wrath; permission is granted him and he takes away the soul ... The Satan, the *Yetzer* (*ha-Ra*) and the Angel of Death are one'.
6. *Pirke de Rabbi Eliezer* (Warsaw: Bomberg, 1852), chap. 13, 32a.
7. Ibid., chap. 21, p.48a. See the English translation which is based on many manuscript variant readings: *Pirke de Rabbi Eliezer*, translated and annotated by Gerald Friedlander (London: n.p., 1916), pp.150–51.
8. *Genesis Rabbah* 17:8.
9. *Genesis Rabbah* 20:11.
10. For an extensive discussion of the relationship between sin and death, the effects of the sin of the first human couple, and for an analysis of the Talmudic text cited by Ravad and its

relationship to the Christian notion of original sin, see Ephraim Urbach, *The Sages*, trans. Israel Abrahams (Cambridge, Mass.: Harvard University Press, 1987), chap. 15, pp.420–31.

11. *Shabbat* 55b.
12. *Zohar* (Vilna: Romm, 1882), vol. 1, p.57b.
13. *Shabbat* 55a–b.
14. Samuel S. Cohon, 'Original Sin', *Hebrew Union College Annual* 21(1948): 306–11.
15. *Avot de Rabbi Natan*, Solomon Schechter (ed.) (2nd ed., New York: Feldheim, 1967), version B, chap. 42, pp.58b–59a.
16. Ibid., version B, p.59a. Compare *Genesis Rabbah* 20:6, where the biblical punishment of the pain of childbirth is extended to the discomfort of pregnancy and to the travails of bringing up children. According to *Genesis Rabbah* 17:8, Eve was punished with menstruation because she shed Adam's blood; her sin was the cause of his death.
17. Cohon, 'Original Sin', pp.275–330; Deborah Schechterman, 'Maimonides' View of Original Sin as Reflected in Jewish Thought in the Thirteenth and Fourteenth Centuries' [in Hebrew], *Da'at* 20 (1988): 65–135; Isaiah Tishbi, *The Doctrine of Evil and the Kelippah in Lurianic* Kabbalah [in Hebrew] (Jerusalem: Hebrew University of Jerusalem, 1963), pp.91–104; Dorith Cohen-Alorno, 'The Zohar's View of Magic as a Consequence of Original Sin' in Hebrew], *Da'at* 19 (1987): 31–65.
18. On polemics against the Christian doctrine of original sin in the Middle Ages, Joel E. Rembaum, 'Medieval Jewish Criticism of the Christian Doctrine of Original Sin', *AJS Review*, 1982–1983 (Cambridge, Mass.: Association for Jewish Studies, 1983), pp.353–82; Daniel Lasker, *Jewish Philosophical Polemics Against Christianity in the Middle Ages* (New York: Ktav, 1977), pp.18–19, 107–8.
19. Joseph Kimhi, *The Book of the Covenant* (*Sefer ha-Brit*), trans. Frank Talmage (Toronto: The Pontifical Institute of Medieval Studies, 1972), pp.30–32.
20. Rembaum, 'Medieval Jewish Criticism', pp.355–56.
21. For a clear contemporary expression of the Christian doctrine of original sin, see *Catechism of the Catholic Church* (Mahwah, N.J.: Paulist Press, 1994), secs. 389, 410–21, pp.98, 104–5.
22. *Avodah Zarah* 5b; *Baba Batra* 16a: 'If God has created the evil inclination, He also created the Torah as a spice [as a remedy] against it'.
23. Jeremy Cohen, 'Original Sin as the Evil Inclination', *Harvard Theological Review* vol. 73, nos. 3–4 (July/October 1980): 98.
24. See examples cited in Rembaum, 'Medieval Jewish Criticism'.
25. Thomas Aquinas's teachings on original sin somewhat replaced those of Augustine, but the teachings of Aquinas could not have been known by Ravad. On the development of the doctrine of original sin from Augustine to Aquinas, see Jeremy Cohen, 'Original Sin', pp.495–520. As Rembaum notes, 'Medieval Jewish Criticism' pp.378–79, many of the possible objections to the Christian doctrine of original sin that Aquinas notes but then tries to refute, were offered by Jewish polemicists. Yet Aquinas and other Jewish asa wellas Christian polemicists seemed unaware of Ravad's unique approach to this issue.

PART III
JEWISH THEOLOGIANS

CHAPTER FOURTEEN

Solomon Schechter

Let us begin at the end: 20 November 1915, the last day in the life of Solomon Schechter. In the morning, Schechter delivered his last lecture.[1] The topic was Jewish philanthropy. During his last year of life, Schechter was working on a study of *zedakah*, philanthropy in classical Jewish literature. Convinced by observation that philanthropy would be the religious act most characteristic of American Jewry, it was his hope that Jewish philanthropy would be conducted in an authentically Jewish manner. He began the task of decoding the classical Jewish religious sources to determine what characterizes a distinctively Jewish understanding of Jewish philanthropy.[2] But, he died, leaving the task unfinished.

After his lecture, Schechter went to attend to his administrative duties, but was taken ill. Despite his protests, he was confined to his bed. To relax, he started to re-read *The Antiquary* by one of his favourite authors, Sir Walter Scott. While he read, he had a fatal heart attack. Sabbath descended, but Solomon Schechter was gone. According to the Talmud he had studied and explicated, and the *Avot d'Rabbi Nathan* that he had edited, the righteous bid farewell to the world as the Sabbath falls upon the world.[3] Schechter was gone, but the deeds that characterized his extraordinary life, and the legacy that is uniquely his, remain even today.

Who was Solomon Schechter, this man of enormous scholarly breadth and depth, acute vision and insight, charm, wit, courage and conviction whom Rabbi Joseph Jacobs of London described as 'a blazing comet bursting upon us in the intellectual sky'?[4]

Why did this man, who had achieved international fame as a scholar at Cambridge University, the only Jewish scholar of his time formally recognized and awarded honorary degrees by both Cambridge and Oxford, leave the tranquility and esteem he enjoyed in England to come to the United States, a Jewish community then in turmoil, and largely devoid and unappreciative of Jewish learning, to head up a small, unknown institution of Jewish learning, The Jewish Theological Seminary of America, that was then on the verge of collapse?[5] Let's try to answer these questions by beginning now at the beginning.

Solomon Schechter was born in Foscani, Rumania in 1849, his father having migrated from Vollynia where he earned his living as a *shohet* (a ritual slaughterer), hence the surname 'Schechter'. Following Hasidic custom, his son was named Shneur Zalmen after the Hasidic *rebbe* his father followed, the founder of Lubavitch Hasidism, Shneur Zalmen of Liadi.[6]

The young Shneur Zalmen Schechter was an *illui*, a child prodigy. Bored with his studies in the *heder* (Jewish elementary school) in Foscani, the young red-headed Schechter would run away regularly from school, find a tall tree to climb, and there he would read Hebrew books.[7]

Growing up in an oppressive European society, Schechter was fascinated as a boy with stories he would read in Hebrew and in Yiddish with news of America, particularly with stories of the American President, Abraham Lincoln. Years later, Schechter would say that he considered the emancipation of the slaves in America to be the greatest social achievement of the nineteenth century. He became an expert on the American Civil War, and considered Lincoln one of the greatest figures in modern history. In 1909, on the 100th anniversary of Lincoln's birth, Schechter wrote his now classic essay on Abraham Lincoln, portraying Lincoln as a religious mystic. Throughout his life, Schechter was fond of quoting Lincoln's phrase, 'we cannot escape history'.[8]

In the Hebrew books Schechter read as a boy about Lincoln, there was no Hebrew term for 'rail-splitter', so Lincoln was described as *hoteiv etzeem*, a woodchopper. According to the Talmud, the Talmudic sage Hillel earned his living as a *hoteiv etzeem*. Consequently, Schechter identified Lincoln with Hillel.[9] From this, we see that already early in his life, Schechter's enormous admiration for the United States was firmly established. Unlike others in the Jewish east Europe of his day that considered America a barbarous wilderness, a place devoid of Torah, a *treifa medina* (impure land), Schechter considered it a wonderland, a place of opportunity, a challenge. Later in his life, he would take up the challenge offered by his adopted country.

During his teens, Schechter's father decided to send him to study at the great yeshivah in Lwow (Lemberg). He studied there until he had nothing more to learn, and there received the first of a number of rabbinic ordinations. In his late teens, Schechter was guided into an arranged marriage that – rare for his day – soon ended in divorce. Schechter was not to remarry for many years.[10]

From Lwow, Schechter went to study at the Jewish Theological Seminary of Vienna, where he first encountered modern Jewish scholarship and westernized Jewish scholars. After receiving a second ordination, he went at the age of 30 to Berlin to study at the liberal and prestigious Hochschule für die Wissenschaft des Judentums, where he received still another ordination.[11] But Schechter was unhappy there. He developed an antipathy towards everything German, which he expressed unabashedly the last year of his life when he urged America's entrance into the war against Germany in 1914 and 1915. Despite the financial support he and The Jewish Theological Seminary of America were receiving from largely pro-German, German-Jewish philanthropists, he often spoke out against the 'barbaric Hun' during his last months. He railed against Woodrow Wilson's hesitancy to enter the war, calling Wilson a *melamed*, a schoolteacher.[12] In 1914, recuperating from a serious operation, he wrote to the British Chief Rabbi, Joseph Hertz, that only a British victory could help his recovery. He agonized over the suffering of European Jewry during the war and over the apathy of American Jewry to their fate. Undoubtedly, his distress over the war cut short his life.[13]

In Berlin, Schechter met Claude Montefiore, a nephew of Sir Moses Montefiore, who took Schechter back to England to be his tutor, and who helped Schechter secure an academic appointment at Cambridge.[14] In England, Schechter's scholarly abilities blossomed. He met great scholars, like James Frazer who constantly consulted Schechter when Frazer, was writing his now classic work, *The Golden Bough*.[15] Schechter laboured hard to learn English, and read widely in British literature, especially Carlyle, Shakespeare, Byron, Dickens and Scott. He mastered a rich Victorian style of writing, peppered with citations from the entire range of British and Jewish literature. In 1887, he married Mathilde Roth. The wedding took place in the former home of Charles Dickens.[16]

During this time, Schechter published his critical editions with commentaries on two significant rabbinic works, *Midrash ha-Gadol* and *Avot d'Rabbi Natan*, his edition of the latter still being the standard one today.[17]

In 1896, two Scottish women brought him fragments of a parchment they had purchased during a visit to Egypt. One of these Hebrew parchments contained sections of the apocryphal book of Ben Sira, known until then only from Greek translations, the original Hebrew presumed to have been forever lost. Schechter realized the value of what had been discovered, and he travelled to Egypt to see what he could find. Gaining access to the Geniza, the literary storeroom of the Cairo synagogue, he literally fell into the greatest find in the history of modern Jewish scholarship, the Cairo Geniza, which scholars still today, all around the world, continue studying and deciphering.[18]

Schechter's publication of available parts of the reconstructed original Hebrew text of Ben Sira catapulted him into world renown, especially in non-Jewish circles. The publication of the original Hebrew text of a work, presumably written by a Palestinian Jew then thought to have been a contemporary compatriot of Jesus, engendered great excitement in Christian circles. (Today, however, scholars place Ben Sira about two centuries before Jesus.) Nevertheless, for Jewish scholars interested in shedding light on early rabbinic literature, linguistically and conceptually, the importance of Schechter's publication could not be underestimated. Comparing the newly discovered Hebrew text with extant Greek and Syriac translations, as well as with citations from Ben Sira in later Jewish literature, Schechter elucidated the nature and influence of this work.

Schechter brought back a mass of material from the Geniza to Cambridge where he began the arduous task of sorting and cataloguing the texts. This took vast amounts of time and required immense erudition. Among the works that emerged from these efforts was Schechter's study of the father of medieval Jewish philosophy, Saadya Gaon, as well as shorter studies of fragments of other works of Midrash, geonica and historical chronicles. Later in his life, in 1910, Schechter would publish studies on the Zadokite and Karaite sects based on the Geniza findings.[19]

Schechter's dream, never realized (nor realizable), was to complete his work on the documents from the Cairo Geniza. So why then, at the height of his scholarly attainment and powers, securely entrenched at Cambridge, with an eagerness to get on with his academic work, did Schechter – already in his mid-fifties – leave England for the United States to head up an undistinguished and almost moribund institution, a quickly dissolving Conservative Judaism, in the chaotic American Jewish community?

One possibility, expressed by Schechter in a letter to Cyrus Adler, had to do with his children. There was no Jewish community at Cambridge and Schechter missed being part of an active Jewish community.[20] He wrote of his desire to celebrate the Jewish holidays with other Jews and to raise his children in a Jewish environment. His two eldest daughters had flirted with Marxism. He wanted his son to be raised among Jews.[21] A second – and probably the major reason – why Schechter came to America was undoubtedly his love affair with the United States, mentioned above. Simply put, long before coming to America, Schechter observed that he saw America as the country holding forth the greatest promise for the future development of Judaism and Jewish scholarship.

Already in 1893, Schechter wrote, 'America must be a place of Torah, for the future of Judaism is across the seas ... Everything is at a standstill in Germany; England has too few Jews to exercise any real influence. What will happen to Jewish learning if America remains indifferent?'[22] And later, in 1913, despite the achievements of British, German and Austrian Jewish scholarship, despite the flourishing of the eastern European *yeshivot*, and despite the new influx of settlers in Palestine of which his twin brother was one, Schechter wrote, 'If there is a spot in the world where Jewish learning, which has so often migrated from land to land, should at last find a resting-place and develop freely in accordance with its own laws, it will be America'.[23]

The process of bringing Schechter to America had a number of steps. The first inquiry – to join the Seminary faculty – was made in 1890, but nothing came of it. In 1897, Sabato Morais, the Seminary's second president, died, and negotiations began to bring Schechter to America as Morais' successor. In 1899, Dr. Solomon Solis-Cohen of Philadelphia met with Schechter in Amsterdam and convinced him to come. Negotiations continued in 1900 in which Rabbi Stephen S. Wise played an active role. In 1901, the presidency of the Seminary's Board of Directors fell open due to the death of the former president, and a reorganization of the institution's governing body, desired by Schechter, was now under way. The reorganized board, led by Jacob Schiff, Louis Marshall and Cyrus Adler, raised an initial half-million dollar endowment. On 24 November 1901, Schechter accepted the appointment, and in April 1902, he arrived in America.[24]

It should also be mentioned that Schechter did visit the United States in 1895. There were two purposes for his trip. The first was to deliver an series of lectures by invitation in Philadelphia. These became his now classic book, [*Some*] *Aspects of Rabbinic Theology*. The second reason was to become acquainted with American Jewry which would help him decide whether to leave England for the United States.[25] In Philadelphia, Schechter met Henrietta Szold, later founder of Hadassah. At their first meeting, Schechter told Szold that he would be lecturing at Johns Hopkins University in Baltimore during his stay in America, and then invited himself to stay at the home of Henrietta Szold's parents in Baltimore, Henrietta Szold's father being the prominent Baltimore rabbi, Benjamin Szold.[26]

Having discussed why Schechter accepted the invitation to come to America, the question of why he was invited to direct The Jewish Theological Seminary still remains. In addressing this question, and in being aware of why it *is* a question, a number of facts need reviewing.

The invitation to Schechter came from the leaders of the reconstituted Seminary board. The first two presidents of the Seminary – Henry Pereira Mendes and Sabato Morais – were Sephardic Jews and the classes of the Seminary were held at the Spanish-Portuguese Synagogue, Shearith Israel.[27] Why did the new directors now want an east European Jew to lead the reorganized Seminary? The new directors were largely wealthy, well-established German Jews committed to *Reform* Judaism. Why were they involved with the *Conservative* Jewish Theological Seminary? And why did they *not* choose a German-Jewish scholar to direct it? Put another way, what was the agenda of the new directors for the newly reorganized Seminary, and how did Schechter fit into that agenda?

The turn of the century was a period in which massive waves of Jewish immigrants were coming to America from central and east Europe. The directors and funders of the Seminary, particularly

Louis Marshall and Jacob Schiff, were also leaders of American Jewry. They wanted to protect the social and financial status as Jews in America that they and their friends already had achieved. They perceived the east European Jews, with their quaint and to them, offensive manners, as a real threat to their own position as Jews in America. Therefore, they believed that the fastest possible process of the Americanization of the east European Jewish immigrants was desirable. They established and supported institutions to accomplish this goal. In Louis Marshall's words, there was an urgent need to 'civilize' the 'barbaric' east European Jews. Considering Orthodox Judaism to be merely a transplantation onto American soil of east European Judaism, they would not support Orthodox institutions, since they stifled the process of Americanization.[28] They also knew that German-American Reform Judaism would not appeal to east European Jews. Similarly, the Sephardic leadership of the Seminary in its earlier stage was foreign to the east European Jews. Only a traditional form of Judaism that also confronted the realities of Jewish life in America would be relevant to east European immigrants trying to become Americans while holding on to traditional Jewish observance. They therefore believed that the Conservative synagogue could serve as a vehicle for the Americanization of the newest American Jews.

A new kind of rabbi was required for this new kind of synagogue – a rabbi trained in the liberal arts as well as in the Talmud, a rabbi who could quote Shakespeare as easily as he could quote *Midrash*, a rabbi who was of east European background but who was a gifted English orator. In short, a role model for east European Jews coming to America was required. And to lead the institution to train such rabbis a particular kind of leader was required, a unique role-model was needed: an east European Jew who had 'made it' in the non-Jewish world, who was traditional in behaviour and orientation yet who knew how to live in a westernized country; who knew Jewish religious literature well but who was masterful in English and who could quote classics of English literature, who hailed from the east European ghetto but who had a passionate love of America. Without doubt, in the entire world of that time, Solomon Schechter was the person who best fitted the bill. Here was an east European Jew, with a big bushy beard, who observed Jewish law and was a leading scholar of Judaica. But, here was a Jew who had honorary degrees from Cambridge and Oxford, a Jew who had been accepted and acclaimed by the Christian scholarly world, and who wrote a masterful English. Here was the person they were looking for to further their agenda of Anglicizing, of Americanizing east European immigrants, who would develop and further a form of American Judaism conducive to making east European Jews into Americans, while retaining them as Jews.[29]

Yet Schechter's own agenda for American Jewry, his motivation for accepting the new position, was *not* identical to that of those who hired him. In fact, his agenda often clashed with theirs, but he held firm, courageously and persistently. In thirteen years, from 1902 when he came to America until his death in 1915, Schechter's implementation of his own agenda made an indelible imprint on American Jewish life. Let's now look at some of the features of Schechter's programme and the ideological foundations upon which it was based.

Schechter came to an America where Reform Judaism was entrenched. Here he saw an even more radical version of Reform Judaism than he had seen in Europe. Yet, despite the pervasiveness of Reform Judaism in the America to which he came, and despite the fact that his major financial backers were Reform Jews, Schechter, during his years in America, launched a relentless attack against Reform Judaism. In Schechter's view, *re*formed Judaism is *de*formed Judaism. Schechter's attack was ideological, not personal. He attacked an ideology, not individuals who espoused it. He was on good personal relations with leaders of American Reform, both lay and rabbinic, so much so that in 1913 Schechter was invited to deliver an address at the dedication of the new campus of the Reform Jewish rabbinical school, Hebrew Union College in Cincinnati. He titled his address, 'His Majesty's Opposition'.[30]

An examination of Schechter's opposition to Reform Judaism not only reveals what Schechter ideologically opposed, but it also elicits what he ideologically affirmed. Schechter perceived the American Reform Judaism of his day as a threat to Judaism proper, and to the future of American Judaism in particular. He believed that Isaac Mayer Wise and other leaders of American Reform had gone much too far in their attempts to reform and to modernize Judaism; so far, in fact, that they had turned American Judaism into a Christian sect and had made many American Jews into what

Schechter called 'amateur Christians'.[31] For example, to those American Reform Jews who defined themselves as 'Americans of the Mosaic persuasion', Schechter suggested that their rejection of Jewish observances such as *kashrut* (the Jewish dietary laws), would more correctly describe them as 'Jews of the ham and oyster persuasion'.[32]

In seeing what irked Schechter about American Reform in his day, we can determine some fundamental features of his own views on the nature of Judaism, on the features that characterize Conservative Judaism, and on what in his view is essential and what is tangential to Jewish religion. Reform Judaism had characterized Judaism as a form of 'ethical monotheism'. The first problem with this approach for Schechter is not what it states, but what it does *not* state: by depicting Judaism as 'ethical monotheism', this approach excludes Jewish peoplehood from being an essential aspect of Judaism.

Zacharias Frankel, the father of the Conservative Jewish ideology in Europe, had characterized Judaism as 'the religion of the Jews'.[33] Following this view, Schechter maintained that any definition of Judaism that is so universalistic as to exclude the notion of Jewish peoplehood as being *an* essential feature, if not *the* essential feature of Judaism, is not only incorrect and inauthentic, but is an apologetic attempt to make Judaism acceptable in a Christian environment by describing it in terms that make it sound like a variety of Christianity. Indeed, are not Christianity and Islam *also* forms of 'ethical monotheism'?

For Schechter, at the heart of Judaism, even at the heart of Jewish religious authority, is the Jewish people, *kelal yisrael* – the community of Israel. According to Schechter, the centre of Judaism, the source of Jewish vitality, is not an abstract universalistic slogan, but a living organism – the people of Israel. In Schechter's words, 'there is no other Jewish religion but that taught by the Torah and confirmed by the history and tradition, and sunk into the conscience of *kelal yisrael* (Catholic Israel)'.[34]

Flowing from this conviction that the Jewish people stands at the centre of Judaism is Schechter's view of the centrality of the Hebrew language for authentic Jewish existence. A people expresses itself through its language, and the language of the Jewish people is Hebrew. In affirming the centrality of the study of Hebrew as the primary language of Jewish prayer, Jewish literature and Jewish learning, Schechter was polemicizing against American-German Reform where the primary language of prayer and study was German, as well as against the view of those east European Jews who considered Yiddish to be the primary Jewish language. Against the Reform Jews who prayed and preached primarily in German, and against the Orthodox Jews who preached and studied primarily in Yiddish, Schechter advocated prayers primarily in Hebrew, a religious school curriculum where Hebrew is emphasized but where the language of instruction was English, and he strongly promoted the English sermon. In Schechter's words:

> the vital importance of Hebrew, the sacred tongue [is that] it is the great depository of all that is best in the soul-life of the congregation of Israel. Without it we will become a mere sect, without a past, and without a literature, and without a proper liturgy, and severed from the great tree which is life unto those that cling to it. Hellenistic Judaism is the only one known to history which dared to make this experiment of dispensing with the sacred language. The result was death ... Let us not deceive ourselves. There is no future in this country for a Judaism that resists either the English or the Hebrew language.[35]

Just as the Hebrew language is critical to Jewish peoplehood, and hence to Judaism, so for Schechter, is the land of Israel.

The American Judaism of Schechter's time was virulently anti-Zionist. In 1885, American Reform Judaism had adopted the Pittsburgh Platform which stated, 'We no longer consider ourselves a nation, but a religious community ... Therefore [we] expect no return to Palestine'.[36] Among the leading American anti-Zionists was Jacob Schiff, one of Schechter's major financial supporters.[37] In their view, since the notion of Jewish peoplehood is no longer pertinent, the attachment of Jews to the Jewish homeland is no longer valid. On the other side of the spectrum, Orthodoxy also maintained an anti-Zionist stance, claiming that only with the messianic advent could restoration of the Holy Land take place.

Despite fierce opposition from both the religious right and left, in 1906 Solomon Schechter became the first American Jewish religious leader to endorse Zionism. Schechter believed that attachment to Jewish peoplehood meant attachment to the land of Israel. Schechter believed that Zionism would provide a means for the eventual unification of a divided world Jewry, as well as a vehicle for returning the religiously disaffected back to Judaism.[38] One should note, however, that Schechter did not embrace the political Zionism of Theodore Herzl. While placing Jewish peoplehood at the centre of Jewish consciousness, Schechter nonetheless cautioned that a Zionism wedded to naked nationalism detached from Jewish religion and culture, is destined for 'spiritual disaster'. Zionism detached from the wellsprings of Jewish spirituality would lead, according to Schechter, to the assimilation both of Judaism and the Jew. While Jewish nationalists perceived political Zionism as a bulwark against the assimilation of the Jews, Schechter considered a Jewish nationalism uninformed by Jewish religion, tradition and spirituality as an invitation to the assimilation and disappearance of Judaism and the Jewish people. 'All this', Schechter wrote, 'is a consequence of preaching an aspect of nationalism more in harmony with Roman and similar modern models than with Jewish ideas and ideals'.[39] For Schechter, writing in 1906, Zionism 'had to re-create the Jewish consciousness before creating the Jewish state'.[40] In 1913, Schechter warned that if it became a form of unbridled secular nationalism, 'Zionism might become a danger to Judaism'.[41]

A second position of Reform Judaism that Schechter attacked was its wholesale dispensation with Jewish religious law, on the grounds that in modern, enlightened times, Jewish law was no longer binding nor necessary. Schechter evaluated this attitude as being historically naive and as a stance that would ultimately change Judaism into a form of Christianity. Some of the early reformers had maintained that the modern period of enlightenment and Jewish political emancipation was the realization of the messianic advent, that they were now living in a messianic age, when – according to certain early Jewish traditions – the law, Halakhah, would no longer be binding. Commenting on this, Schechter wrote, 'Not unlike the first Christians, they hoped for and believed in the speedy disappearance of the old world to be replaced by a new heaven and a new earth, in which rationalism would reign supreme. The Jews especially saw in the few crumbs of emancipation granted to them the redemption which was to include the whole humanity. The great day had already dawned upon humanity, with the messianic age looming in the not very far distance'.[42]

Jewish Reform had embraced the view of the Enlightenment that identified rationality with truth. Since, in this view, that which is rational is that which is true, for Judaism to be true, it had to be reduced to rationality, devoid of emotion or mysticism. This sentiment is expressed in the sixth plank of the Reform Pittsburgh Platform, which reads, 'We recognize in Judaism a progressive religion, ever striving to be in accord with the postulates of reason'.

Once held up as a standard of truth, reason became a criterion upon which to justify the process of reform. Those theological beliefs, laws, customs, rituals and practices that did not accord with reason would be discarded; those that did accord with reason would be retained. Schechter, however, considered a religion devoid of emotion and informed by rationality alone to be a sterile faith; indeed, not a religious faith at all. In Schechter's words, 'Rationalism ... could never properly value those qualities of obedience, submission, meekness and self-denial which constitute the holy life. The sentiments of grief and joy which make up the real life of the religionist, were largely unintelligible to the great majority of our rationalists inaugurating the Reform movement'.[43]

It is not surprising, therefore, that Schechter was one of the earliest modern Jewish scholars to write about Jewish mysticism with sympathy, appreciation and reverence. Modern Jewish thinkers and historians, most notably Heinrich Graetz, had tried to disparage Jewish mysticism, depicting Kabbalah, the Jewish mystical tradition, as a malevolent lunatic fringe in Judaism, and asserting that Judaism's essentially rationalistic nature leaves no room for Jewish mysticism. In opposition to this view, Schechter wrote, 'Mysticism is not an esoteric plant on the soil of Judaism, as some of our platitudinaries believe. There was always a certain tendency toward mysticism in Judaism of one kind or another'. Possibly with Heinrich Graetz in mind, Schechter continued, 'As every one knows who has occupied himself with the study of Jewish history, the greatest defects of many works in this field are due to the fact that their authors were largely ignorant of the Halachah and lacking in a real appreciation of Jewish mysticism. They have thus missed the central springs both of Jewish reason and of Jewish emotion'.[44]

In his multivolume work *Studies in Judaism*, Schechter wrote now classical studies of the Lurianic kabbalists on sixteenth-century Safed (a town in Galilee), on Nachmanides as a mystic, and on east European Hasidism as a form of Jewish mysticism. In his essay on Hasidism, Schechter was among the first authors writing in English to offer a positive view of Hasidism and of east European Jewish spiritual life.[45] In so doing, he was undoubtedly motivated by his correct perception of the attack against Kabbalah and Hasidism by German-Jewish scholars as *really* being a not-so-veiled expression of German-Jewish prejudice against east European Jewry.

Though Schechter opposed reform based upon convenience, rationality, notions of what constitutes a fleeting modernity, and belief that the messianic era had arrived, he was *not* opposed to either change or reform per se. His attitude was akin to that of Mark Twain who cautioned against confusing change with progress. Schechter advocated the reform of Judaism, but within certain perimeters. These are: first, that only the tangential and not the essentials of Judaism may be changed; second, that deliberate action and not the flights of momentary fashion dictate change; third, that the ultimate authority for change is the collective will of the Jewish people, and fourth, that change be dictated by internal and authentic Jewish categories of thought and not by the imposition or importation of foreign categories. Regarding this last criterion, Schechter wrote in a letter to Judge Mayer Sulzberger, dated 28 April 1905, 'I admit there *is* a good deal where reform would be desirable, but this reform can be done with the authority of the Bible and the Talmud which are elastic and wide enough for all reasonable purpose. This will be a [authentic] Jewish reform'.[46] And, a year later, he wrote, 'It is a tragedy to see sacred institutions as ancient as the mountains, to maintain which Israel for thousands of years shrank from no sacrifice, destroyed before our very eyes and exchanged for corresponding institutions borrowed from hostile religions'.[47] In 1902, reflecting on the source for reform, Schechter said, 'All I plead for is that the voice should come from Sinai, not Golgotha; that it should be the voice of Jacob, not of Esau ... Any attempt to place the center of gravity outside the Torah must end in disaster'.[48] With regard to change for the sake of contemporary fashion, Schechter admonished, 'There is something that is more important than modernity and that is eternity'.[49]

As was already discussed, Schechter held certain elements to be essential to Judaism: Jewish law, Jewish peoplehood, the Hebrew language and the mystical element in Judaism. Radical reform in such areas he considered to be spiritual suicide. In 1902 he observed, 'We must make an end to these constant amputations if we do not wish to see the body of Israel bleed to death before our very eyes'.[50] For Schechter, scholarly research can determine which beliefs, institutions and practices of Jewish life have been historically essential, such as *Shabbat* (Sabbath) and *kashrut*, and which have been tangential, such as polygamy. Ultimately, however, for Schechter, it is the people of Israel who define what Judaism is to be. According to Schechter, Jewish experience begins with God's revelation *to* Israel and continues with God's revelation *through* Israel. In Schechter's words:

> It is not the mere revealed Bible that is of first importance to the Jew, but the Bible as it repeats itself in history, in other words, as it is interpreted by tradition ... Since then the interpretation of Scripture or the secondary meaning is mainly a product of changing historical influences, it follows that the centre of authority is actually removed from the Bible and placed in some *living body*, which, by reason of its being in touch with the ideal aspirations and the religious needs of the age, is best able to determine the nature of the secondary meaning. This living body, however, is not represented by any section of the nation, or any corporate priesthood, or rabbihood, but by the collective conscience of Catholic Israel [*kelal yisrael*] as embodied in the universal synagogue ... It is 'God who has chosen the Torah, and Moses his servant, and Israel his people'. But indeed God's choice invariably coincides with the wishes of Israel; He 'performeth all things' upon which the councils of Israel, meeting under promise of the divine presence and communion, have previously agreed. As the Talmud somewhere expresses itself with regard to the Book of Esther, 'They have confirmed above what Israel has accepted below' ... Another consequence of this conception of tradition is that it is neither Scripture nor primitive Judaism, but general custom which forms the real rule of practice ... It was probably with a view to this communion that the later mystics introduced a short prayer to be said before the performance of any

religious ceremony, in which, among other things, the speaker professes his readiness to act 'in the name of all Israel'.[51]

The final issue that bears mention has to do with Schechter's critique and vision for Jewish life in America. In this regard, I should like to offer five 'snapshot' observations.

1. Schechter realized that which the history of Judaism had proven generation after generation, that both the survival and the revival of Judaism and the Jewish people were ultimately inextricably linked to Jewish learning and to the development of great centers of Jewish scholarship. Toward this end, Schechter laboured as president of The Jewish Theological Seminary to build a faculty of extraordinary scholars and a great library of Judaica. In accomplishing this goal, he made the Seminary in his time into the central institution for American Jewish scholarship, and for the training of American Jewish scholars and teachers for generations to come. In a letter to Dr Solis-Cohen, written 6 August 1899, Schechter states that 'a proper study of the Torah and real knowledge of our *past* will give us a *future*'.[52]

   What Schechter feared most was that American Jews would become Jewish ignoramuses. Already in his day he observed that, 'It is one of the great tragedies of modern Judaism that it knows itself so little'.[53] Once, commenting on the poor quality of knowledge of Judaism by Jews he encountered in America, Schechter lamented by paraphrasing Jesus' words on the cross. He said, 'Forgive them Father, for they know – nothing'.[54] Some fifty years later, Abraham Joshua Heschel echoed Schechter's view when he wrote, 'Judaism today is an unknown religion. The vital issues it raises, the sublime views it discloses, the noble goals it points to are forgotten. We have failed to learn how much Judaism has to say to the mind, to the soul'.[55]
2. Though scholarship was critical for Schechter, it was insufficient in itself. Schechter's ideal of the Jewish role model was not simply the scholar, but what he called 'the saint-scholar'. Spiritual, as well as intellectual cultivation, was necessary to sustain and to inspire the religious life.

In a number of popular essays and scholarly studies as well as in his private correspondence, Schechter continuously reiterated how crucial the 'saint-scholar' has been for Jewish life and thought. According to Schechter, the lives and works of the 'saint-scholars' of the past are the ultimate art form produced by the Jewish people. Contemplation of their lives, like works of art viewed in a museum, can inspire one to improve the spiritual quality of one's own life.[56] We may not be able to duplicate the spiritual and intellectual heights they achieved, but we may elevate the quality of our own individual spiritual existence by studying and reflecting upon what they accomplished.

With the great 'saint-scholars' as role models, the degeneracy of Jewish life into crass secular opportunism would, in Schechter's view, be stifled. For this reason, he especially encouraged rabbis to aspire to and emulate the model of the 'saint-scholar'.

To young rabbis, Schechter addressed these words: 'Let us not be *too* successful. For it is this consideration of ulterior motives which is responsible for the fact that latter day Judaism is almost entirely devoid of the element of saintliness, without which religion itself becomes profane and secularized'.[57] And elsewhere he despaired that the rabbinate had become 'reduced to a mere profession, a comfortable office, a smug berth in which men spend their lives along a certain routine. You may call such a routine practical and [such] men respectable, but the last thing you would call it is sacred'.[58]

3. Schechter recognized the need for and the importance of Jewish philanthropy. As was mentioned above, it was his hope that Jewish philanthropy in America would be guided by Jewish values. Nonetheless, he also recognized that making philanthropy and organizational efficiency into ends in themselves, rather than means to spiritual and religious ends, is an invitation to spiritual suicide, an entrée to the self-destruction of those very values that funding and institutional organization are there to support. Schechter deplored what he called 'the deification of the balance sheet, and the cold, stiff business-like spirit in which our institutions are conducted'. Already in 1901, Schechter repudiated the value system of the 'establishment, in

which by a peculiar history of its own, the man of business or the great organizer has of late years, gained the ascendancy over the man of thought and learning'. And elsewhere, Schechter stated that 'a religion cannot well convert itself suddenly into a large charity agency without doing serious injury to one of its important life-springs'.[59]

What concerned Schechter even more than the assimilation of the Jews was the assimilation of Judaism. He was more concerned about the '*galut ha-nephesh*', the alienation and assimilation of the Jewish soul, than he was about the alienation and assimilation of individual Jews.[60] The assimilation of Jews would lead to the diminution of the Jewish people, but in Schechter's view, the assimilation of Judaism, the exile of the Jewish soul from its spiritual roots, often encouraged by the secular nature of Jewish communal existence, would lead not simply to the diminution, but to the destruction of Judaism and hence of the Jewish people.

4. Schechter turned Conservative Judaism from a religious ideology into a religious movement. Until Schechter, both in Europe and America, Conservative Judaism was an idea without a constituency, a programme without a home. By catapulting the Seminary from obscurity into prominence, and by organizing the United Synagogue of America in 1913 as the congregational wing of Conservative Judaism, and finally by developing a programme for the training of Conservative rabbis and educators, Schechter laid the foundations for the emergence of Conservative Judaism as a dominant force in American Jewish life.
5. Finally, like Abraham Heschel, Solomon Schechter believed that Judaism is not only a way of living, but also a way of thinking. Without Jewish theology and spirituality, without an understanding of Jewish religious thought, there is no foundation upon which to base Jewish religious practice and Jewish organizational life. In Schechter's words, 'What value is life without thought, and least of all, what value has Jewish religious life without Jewish religious thought?' For Schechter, we not only have to *do* things, but we must also *think* things.[61] For Schechter, not anti-Semitism, but Jewish theological and cultural illiteracy, Jewish action detached from Jewish thought,

> and Jewish organizational life detached from Jewish spiritual life, are the greatest dangers to Jewish continuity and creativity. It is not coincidental, therefore, that Schechter's first lectures in America became his now classic work, *Aspects of Rabbinic Theology*.

For Schechter, an authentic Jewish theology must not only be derived from classical Jewish thinking, but must be permeated with the spiritual concerns and attitudes of the great minds and hearts of the Jewish past.[62] In his view, only a theology that is fully felt emotionally can be fully understood intellectually. For Schechter, existentialist commitment to specific beliefs and attitudes must precede theological speculation. The theologian must first be a person of intense faith before being a scholar who can formulate the features of religious belief. Theology needs to be experienced before it can be articulated. For Schechter, 'the health of a religion is to have a theology without being aware of it'.[63]

Unlike other Jewish theologians of the early twentieth century such as Kaufmann Kohler, Schechter's approach to Jewish theology was not influenced by trends in German Protestant theology of the time. In addition, he rejected the then common presupposition that to be valid, a theology had to be rationalistic and systematic. Precisely because rabbinic thought is not systematic by nature, a derivative rabbinic theology could not be systematically expressed. Indeed, he inveighs against confusing 'merciless logic for God-given truths'.[64] Overstating the case, Schechter claims that 'the Rabbis were a simple, naïve people, filled with a childlike scriptural faith neither wanting nor bearing much analysis and interpretation'.[65] However, recent scholarship has demonstrated that rabbinic thought is much more sophisticated than Schechter had imagined or depicted it to be.

For Schechter, there are 'aspects of rabbinic theology' that flow from the presupposition that we are citizens of the Kingdom of God, and there are duties (for example, the commandments) and attitudes (observing the commandments with devotion and joy) that articulate this presupposition. But, there are also dogmas and convictions that underlie both Jewish religious life and thought.[66]

Based upon the teachings of the Talmudic rabbis and the Jewish mystics, Schechter depicts the forging of an intimate, reciprocal relationship between God and the individual, God and the people of Israel, and God and the world, as being at the heart of Judaism.[67] Theology provides a road map as to how such a relationship can be established, as well as a guide to overcome factors, such as sin, that can stifle it. In addition, the mission of theology 'is just as much to teach the world that there *are* false gods as to bring it near to the true one'.[68] For Schechter, echoing the rabbis, 'if religion is anything, it is everything'.[69]

In his essay, 'The Dogmas of Judaism', Schechter writes:

> We are comparatively rich in productions of a theological nature … [Today] we seek the foundations of Judaism … in everything except religion … We usually urge that in Judaism religion means life; but we forget that a life without guiding principles and thoughts is a life not worth living. At least it was so considered by the greatest Jewish thinkers and hence their efforts to formulate the creed of Judaism, so that men should not only be able to do the right thing, but also to think the right thing.[70]

NOTES

1. On Schechter's last day, see Norman Bentwich, *Solomon Schechter: A Biography* (Philadelphia: Jewish Publication Society, 1938), p.230. Despite the personal relationship between Bentwich and Schechter that enhances Bentwich's biography of Schechter, a new, more expansive and perhaps more analytical biography is desirable.

   According to Mordecai Kaplan's diary, 1,500 people attended the funeral of Solomon Schechter. He died on 20 November 1915, a Friday afternoon, about 3:00 p.m., with Scott's *Antiquary* in one hand and a cigarette in the other. His daughter Amy was with him. See Mel Scult, 'The *Baale Boste* Reconsidered: The Life of Mathilde Roth Schechter (M.R.S.)', *Modern Judaism* 7:1 (February 1987): 17. It is perhaps ironic that Schechter's inaugural address as president of The Jewish Theological Seminary was also delivered on 20 November (1902).
2. Schechter's 'notes' for this lecture were posthumously published in Solomon Schechter, 'Notes of Lectures on Jewish Philanthropy', chap. in *Studies in Judaism: Third Series* (Philadelphia: Jewish Publication Society, 1924), pp.238–76.
3. See e.g., *Ketubot* 103b; *Avot d'Rabbi Natan*, Solomon Schechter (ed.), (2nd ed., New York: Feldheim, 1967), chap. 25, p.40b.
4. Cyrus Adler, 'Solomon Schechter: A Biographical Sketch', *American Jewish Yearbook* 17 (1916/1917): 30.
5. That Schechter had an honourary doctorate from Cambridge (1898) is well known. Louis Finkelstein once told me that he also had an honourary degree from Oxford. He also had one from Harvard; see Adler, 'Solomon Schechter', pp.25, 52.
6. According to Bentwich, *Solomon Schechter*, p.24, Schechter was born December 1849 or 1847. According to Adler, 'Solomon Schechter', p.25, he was born 7 December 1850; the Library of Congress gives the year of Schechter's birth as 1847 in its catalogue of his published work.
7. On Schechter's early life, see Bentwich, *Solomon Schechter*, pp.24–50.
8. Schechter, 'Abraham Lincoln', chap. in *Seminary Addresses and Other Papers* (New York:

Burning Bush Press, 1959), pp.145–69. On Schechter's prodigious knowledge of Civil War history and his infatuation with Lincoln, see, Adler, 'Solomon Schechter', p.57.

9. Bentwich, *Solomon Schechter*, p.164.
10. On this period in Schechter's life, see Bentwich, *Solomon Schechter*, pp.24–50.
11. It is important to identify some of Schechter's teachers. In Lwow, he studied as a teenager with the great Talmudist, Joseph Saul Nathanson. In Vienna, he studied with Adolph Jellinek, Isaac Hirsch Weiss and Meir Friedmann, who were innovative modern scholars in the study of rabbinics, especially Midrash. See Adler, 'Solomon Schechter', pp.26–7. For Schechter on Friedmann, see Schechter, *Seminary Addresses*, pp.135–45. He also knew scholars such as Moritz Steinschneider and Heinrich Graetz. See Schechter's essay on Steinschneider in *Seminary Addresses*, pp.119–25. In a letter dated 25 October 1899, Schechter states that he received an ordination in 1879 from the eminent scholar Isaac Hirsch Weiss in Vienna and a subsequent ordination from Pinkus Friedrich Frankl, Abraham Geiger's successor in Berlin. See Meir Ben-Horin, 'Solomon Schechter to Judge Mayer Sulzberger: Part I', *Jewish Social Studies* 25:4 (October 1963): 273.
12. Bentwich, *Solomon Schechter*, p.224.
13. Ibid., p.224. Almost prophetically, Schechter wrote during the Spanish-American War that 'The over-emphasis of the racial principle will be the destruction of our people'. See Adler, 'Solomon Schechter', p.49.
14. On Schechter and Claude Montefiore, see Bentwich, *Solomon Schechter*, pp.48–50, 77–79. Claude Goldsmid Montefiore, *Liber Freund*, Joshua B. Stein (ed.), (Lanham, Md.: University Press of America, 1988). On Schechter in England, see Bentwich, *Solomon Schechter*, pp.50–116.
15. On Schechter and Frazer, see Mathilde Schechter's diary description of their relationship, quoted in Scult, 'The *Baale Boster* Reconsidered', pp.6–7. See also a citation from Frazer's letter to Schechter, quoted in Adler, 'Solomon Schechter', p.54.
16. On Mathilde Roth Schechter, see Scult, 'The *Baale Boste* Reconsidered', pp.1–29. She was described by her friends in London as Schechter's 'tugboat'. When they met, Schechter was 37 years old and virtually unpublished. After this marriage, he began to publish. She served as his editor and secretary. On the marriage in Dickens's house, see Scult, 'The *Baale Boste* Reconsidered', p.3; Bentwich, *Solomon Schechter*, p.75.
17. For a valuable annotated bibliography of Schechter's work, Adolph S. Oko, *Solomon Schechter: A Bibliography* (Cambridge: Cambridge University Press, 1938).
18. On Schechter and the Geniza see Bentwich, *Solomon Schechter*, pp.136–64. For Mathilde Schechter's account, preserved in her diary, see Scult, 'The *Baale Boste* Reconsidered', pp.7–8. According to Mathilde, Schechter's first words, upon realizing that he was in possession of a fragment of the Hebrew original of Ben Sira, was, 'Wife, as long as the Bible lives, my name shall not die! This small torn scrap is a page of the Hebrew original of Ben Sira, which belongs to the Apocrypha of the Bible'. See also, Adler, 'Solomon Schechter', pp.40–5.
19. Oko, *Solomon Schechter*, pp.61–6.
20. Originally, in 1890, the idea was to bring Schechter to The Jewish Theological Seminary as an instructor. After Sabato Morais's death in 1897, when the presidency of the Seminary became vacant, the idea of bringing Schechter to head the Seminary gained momentum. In 1890, Schechter was virtually unknown, and struggling to make ends meet financially. However, by 1897, the discovery of the Hebrew version of Ben Sira and his role in researching the documents of the Cairo Geniza, put Schechter in a much more desirable position academically and economically.

    On the saga of Schechter's leaving England to come to New York to head The Jewish Theological Seminary, see Adler, 'Solomon Schechter', pp.37, 52, 55–58; Abraham Karp, 'Solomon Schechter Comes to America', chap. in Abraham Karp (ed.), *The Jewish Experience in America*, vol. 5 (New York: Ktav, 1969), pp.111–129. This period is discussed in Schechter's letters, particularly those to Judge Mayer Sulzberger of Philadelphia; see Meir Ben-Horin, 'Solomon Schechter', pp.249–87.

    Adler, 'Solomon Schechter', pp.54–55 noted that in England most of Schechter's students were non-Jews, and Schechter yearned to spread Jewish learning among Jews. Coming to the Seminary afforded him a unique opportunity in this regard, especially in view of Schechter's conviction that the future of Jewish learning was to be in America; see Schechter's letter to Sulzberger, 31 October 1895, quoted in Ben-Horin, 'Solomon

Schechter', pp.250, 268. On December 21, 1899 (p.275), Schechter wrote to Sulzberger saying, despite his material comfort in Cambridge, 'I would feel happier both for my sake and for the sake of my children if I lived among Jews ... It would lengthen my life ... to establish a school of Torah in America where the future of Judaism is'. Throughout these letters, Schechter expressed his frustration at the length and difficulty of the negotiations. In a letter dated 17 April 1901 (p.279), in exasperation, he stated, 'If they cannot see that I might do something for American [Judaism] ... then let them be d – d'.

21. The Schechters had three children: Ruth (1888), Frank (1890) and Amy. Ruth married Morris Alexander, the first Jew elected to the parliament of the Union of South Africa. Ruth, a staunch advocate of women's rights and an equally staunch opponent of apartheid, eventually divorced him and married a British non-Jewish classics professor. Schechter was apparently not enthused about her first marriage (and certainly not about her second). See Meir Ben-Horin, 'Solomon Schechter to Judge Mayer Sulzberger', *Jewish Social Studies* 30:4 (October 1968): 264. Her 'feminist' activities were not approved of by her father, or for that matter, by Henrietta Szold. See Scult, 'The *Baale Boster* Reconsidered', pp.15, 25; Irving Fineman, *Woman of Valor: The Life of Henrietta Szold* (New York: Simon and Schuster, 1961), p.255.

    Amy was a Marxist, and lived for a few years in the Soviet Union. Later, she worked as a union organizer in the textile mills of the American South. In 1929, during a textile strike in North Carolina, she was indicted on a contrived charge of murder, from which she was acquitted. Her lawyer was her brother, Frank. See Eli Ginzberg, 'The Seminary Family', in Arthur A. Chiel (ed.), *Perspectives on Jews and Judaism* (New York: The Rabbinical Assembly, 1978), p.121.

    Frank Schechter (1890–1937) was a prominent attorney and a leading expert in trademark law. He received the first Doctor of Jurisprudence degree from Columbia University in 1925. His work, *The Historical Foundations of the Law Relating to Trademarks*, is a classic in the field. He was a war hero during World War I. After the war, he gained an expertise in international law. Among his major clients was B.V.D. underwear. He wrote extensively on legal subjects and was active in Jewish communal affairs. His son, Daniel Schechter, moved to the Chicago area and was president of a leading Reform congregation. Daniel Schechter's son, Jon Schechter, was ordained a rabbi by The Jewish Theological Seminary. See Frank Schechter's obituary in the *New York Times*, 27 September 1937.

22. Quoted from a letter from Schechter to Alexander Kohut; see Bentwich, *Solomon Schechter*, p.167.

23. Schechter, *Seminary Addresses*, p.233.

24. On why Schechter was chosen and why he came, see Karp, 'Solomon Schechter Comes to America', pp.124–9.

25. Parts of Schechter's now classic volume, *[Some] Aspects of Rabbinic Theology* (New York: Macmillan, 1909) were first published in essay form, e.g., in the *Jewish Chronicle* during October, November, December 1894.

26. Schechter first met Henrietta Szold in February 1895 in Philadelphia when he delivered his lecture series that was to become *Aspects of Rabbinic Theology*. See Abraham E. Millgram and Emma G. Ehrlich, 'Nine Letters from Solomon Schechter to Henrietta Szold', *Conservative Judaism* 32:2 (Winter 1979); Joan Dash, *Summoned to Jerusalem: The Life of Henrietta Szold* (New York: Harper and Row, 1979), pp.43–47, 73–75. Szold attended classes at The Jewish Theological Seminary from 1903 to 1906. She had agreed, in advance of matriculation, not to apply for rabbinic ordination. This episode has some significance in terms of the later decision of the Seminary to ordain women. That she could have asked for ordination would imply that the ordination of women was deemed possible even then. Szold, both in a private capacity and in her capacity as 'secretary' of the Jewish Publication Society, helped many Seminary professors with their publications. For example, she prepared the index to Schechter's *Aspects of Rabbinic Theology*. However, much of her work was done for Professor Louis Ginzberg about whom she developed a romantic infatuation.

    The nature of the Szold-Ginzberg relationship is beyond the scope of this essay. According to one view, Ginzberg was oblivious to her interest in him, despite the constant company they kept for five years, during which she laboured without rest or reward on manuscripts of his writings, translating them and preparing them for publication. Szold was many years his senior, short, and very heavy. Another view contends that Ginzberg exploited her, utilizing her infatuation as a means of getting free 'slave labour' to advance his scholarly work and his career. A number of reported oral and written sources, including Mathilde Schechter's diary (Scult, 'The *Baale Boste* Reconsidered', p.14) maintain that Schechter was very angry with Ginzberg because of his treatment of Szold. Szold had come to New York after her father's death and Schechter possibly was a 'father figure' to her. Schechter clearly had great personal admiration for Szold. Indeed, Mrs Schechter's diary states that because of his bad treatment of Szold, Schechter prevented Ginzberg from being chosen his successor as president of the Seminary. I know from oral sources that this view was held by Alexander Marx, a professor and librarian of the Seminary. The Ginzberg-Szold relationship is discussed in great detail in Irving Fineman's biography of Szold, *Woman of Valor*. His reconstruction is based upon her diaries. In Joan Dash's biography of Szold, *Summoned to Jerusalem*, Dash notes (p.325, note 49) that after the appearance of Fineman's book, these diaries were sealed in the Central Zionist Archives. In the biography of his father, Eli Ginzberg discusses the relationship. See Eli Ginzberg, *Keeper of the Law: Louis Ginzberg* (Philadelphia: Jewish Publication Society, 1966), pp.105–30. For Ginzberg on Schechter, see Louis Ginzberg, 'Solomon Schechter', in *Students, Scholars and Saints* (Philadelphia: Jewish Publication Society, 1958), pp.241–52.

27. On the Seminary in the pre-Schechter era, including discussion of Mendes and Morais, see Moshe Davis, *The Emergence of Conservative Judaism* (Philadelphia: Jewish Publication Society, 1963).
28. Karp, 'Solomon Schechter Comes to America', pp.127–28. According to Mordecai M. Kaplan, Louis Marshall wanted 'to establish a training school for American rabbis who might stem the proliferation of gangsterism on the Jewish East Side'. According to Seminary donor Leonard Lewisohn, 'The Jewish Theological Seminary [is] ... the safest and surest means of ... Americanizing the foreign element'.
29. This description is drawn from an audiotape of an address by Louis Finkelstein. The date of the address, presumably to the Rabbinical Assembly, could not be determined.
30. Published in Schechter, *Seminary Addresses*, pp.239–44.
31. On Schechter's view of the similarity between Reform Judaism and Christianity, see e.g., Schechter, *Studies in Judaism–Third Series*, pp.62–63, 71–73. In a 28 April 1905 letter from Schechter to Mayer Sulzberger, Schechter characterizes the American Reform Judaism of Kaufmann Kohler, then president of Hebrew Union College, as 'simply [a] final conversion to Christianity'. See Meir Ben-Horin, 'Solomon Schechter to Judge Mayer Sulzberger: Part II', *Jewish Social Studies* 27:2 (April 1965): 85.
32. See Schechter's letter of 25 November 1902 to Dr Solis-Cohen, cited in Bernard Mandlebaum, *The Wisdom of Solomon Schechter* New York: Burning Bush Press, 1963), p.111.
33. On Frankel's teachings in this regard, see Ginzberg, 'Zechariah Frankel', in *Students, Scholars and Saints*, especially p.203.
34. Schechter, *Seminary Addresses*, pp.23, 62. See also Schechter, *Studies in Judaism: First Series* (Philadelphia: Jewish Publication Society, 1911), pp.xvii–xx; *Studies in Judaism: Second Series* (Philadelphia: Jewish Publication Society, 1908), p.116. The term 'Catholic Israel' was first used in this way by Isaac Leeser; see Davis, *The Emergence of Conservative Judaism*, p.132. Note Henrietta Szold's use of the term in her address, 'Catholic Israel', *American Hebrew* 65:1 (5 May 1899).
35. Schechter, *Seminary Addresses*, pp.88–89; see also, pp.110–11.
36. For the text of the 'Pittsburgh Platform,' see Davis, *The Emergence of Conservative Judaism*, pp.226–27.
37. For example, Jacob H. Schiff openly opposed Zionism and considered it incompatible with American citizenship. Schiff and Schechter engaged in a public debate on this issue in the pages of the *New York Times*. See Cyrus Adler, 'Jacob Henry Schiff: A Biographical Sketch', *American Jewish Yearbook* 23 (1921/1922): 55.
38. See Schechter, 'Zionism: A Statement', in *Seminary Addresses*, pp.91–105.
39. See Schechter's 'Preface', *Seminary Addresses*, pp.xxiv–xxv.
40. Ibid., p.100.
41. Quoted in Bentwich, *Solomon Schechter*, p.323. See also, Adler, 'Solomon Schechter', pp.65–6.
42. Schechter, *Studies in Judaism–Volume III*, p.71.
43. Schechter, *Studies in Judaism–Volume III*, p.72.
44. Schechter's endorsement of the importance of mysticism in Judaism is sprinkled throughout his work, see *Seminary Addresses*, p.59; *Studies in Judaism: First Series*, pp.xxiii–xxiv. In this

regard, Schechter's now classic essays on 'Nachmanides', 'Safed in the Sixteenth Century' and 'The Chassidim' are significant. However, one should note that Schechter nevertheless exhibited an ambivalence toward Jewish mysticism. In a letter to Sulzberger, Schechter 5 February 1896, wrote, 'The little time I can spare I must reserve for reading up mystics whom I both hate and love too much to neglect them'. See Ben-Horin, 'Solomon Schechter', p.255. In my view, Schechter's positive views on Jewish mysticism must be understood as part of his polemic against an arid Orthodox Jewish legalism on the one hand, and an over-rationalized, over-Anglicized, de-emotionalized arid Reform Judaism on the other hand. Schechter's ideal was the 'saint-scholar' who, more often than not, was a mystic. (Even his 'hero', Abraham Lincoln, he characterizes as a mystic.) This theme is found throughout his writings while still in England, such as his 1901 'Four Epistles to the Jews of England', and in American writings such as his 1905 essay, 'Saints and Saintliness' (both found in Schechter's *Studies in Judaism: Second Series*), as well as in his annual commencement addresses at the Seminary, found in *Seminary Addresses*. See also *Some Aspects of Rabbinic Theology*, p.78, where he writes, 'Indeed, no creed worthy of the name could or would ever dispense with that sprinkling of mystics representing the deeper elements of saintliness'.

45. Schechter's essay on Hasidism was originally written in German and subsequently translated into English. See Schechter, *Die Chassidim: Eine Studie über jüdische Mystik* (Berlin: Judischer Verlag, 1904). This was in turn based on a paper delivered in England in English in 1887.
46. Ben-Horin, 'Schechter to Sulzberger', p.85.
47. Schechter, *Seminary Addresses*, p.95.
48. Ibid., p.25.
49. Ibid., p.23.
50. Ibid., p.23.
51. Schechter, *Studies in Judaism: First Series*, pp.xviii–xx.
52. Mandelbaum, *The Wisdom of Solomon Schechter*, p.100.
53. Schechter, *Studies in Judaism: Second Series*, p.156.
54. This was told to me by Moshe Davis.
55. Abraham J. Heschel, *The Insecurity of Freedom* (New York: Farrar, Straus and Giroux, 1966), p.217. There are many close similarities between Schechter's and Heschel's thought, particularly on the goals of Jewish scholarship and the nature of Jewish spirituality. This issue, however, is beyond the scope of this essay.
56. See Schechter's 11 July 1904 letter to Solomon Solis-Cohen quoted in Bentwich, *Solomon Schechter*, p.238.
57. Schechter, *Seminary Addresses*, pp.42–43.
58. Ibid., pp.222–23.
59. Schechter, *Studies in Judaism: Second Series*, pp.196–97.
60. Ibid., pp.96–97.
61. Ibid., pp.200, 198.
62. Precisely because Schechter considered emotion and spirituality as critical aspects of theology, he urged utilizing liturgical texts in the formulation of Jewish theological discourse; see Schechter, *Aspects of Rabbinic Theology*, p.9.
63. See Schechter, *Aspects of Rabbinic Theology*, p.12.
64. Ibid., p.14.
65. Ibid., p.42.
66. See Schechter's essays, 'The Dogmas of Judaism' and 'The Doctrine of Divine Retribution in Rabbinic Literature' in Schechter, *Studies in Judaism: A Selection* (New York: Meridian Books, 1958).
67. See Schechter, *Aspects of Rabbinic Theology*, pp.33, 47.
68. Ibid., p.77.
69. Ibid., p.142.
70. Schechter, *Studies in Judaism: A Selection*, p.103.

CHAPTER FIFTEEN

Abraham Joshua Heschel

After Rabbi Uri of Strelisk died, the Rabbi of Kalev asked Rabbi Judah Zevi of Stretyn, what he had learned from his master. Rabbi Judah said, 'My master's teachings are like manna that enters the body but never leaves it'. But when the Rabbi of Kalev continued to press him, Rabbi Judah ripped open his shirt and cried, 'Look into my heart! There you will find what my master taught'.[1]

For Judaism, the master–disciple relationship is the holy of holies. What transpires within the sanctity and intimacy of its precincts determines whether the wisdom of the past will be perpetuated or whether it will suffer atrophy. The master who has received and who has acquired an embarrassment of riches from the past is obliged to convey that legacy to the future. Both for the master and for the tradition he embodies, the disciple represents continuity, life after death.

Like a necromancer, the master conjures up the spirits of the past and introduces them to the disciple so that the disciple may begin to develop the intimacy of relationship with them that the master already has attained. The disciple seeks to know what the master knows, though the disciple recognizes that he or she never will approximate either the knowledge or the wisdom of the master. In the process of transmission much is irretrievably and inevitably lost, some is unavoidably transformed. In imparting some of what he knows to another, the master is aware that both he and the disciple are but part of an extended conduit in the stream of tradition, and that a single rupture of that channel would relegate to certain oblivion the heritage they both cherish. Without the master, the disciple is a conclusion without a premise. Without the disciple, the master is a tree with roots, though barren of fruit. In their embrace, master and disciple become engaged in a sacred mission that transcends them both.

The bond of desire between master and disciple creates an alchemy between the one who influences and the one who is influenced. As it often happens, a disciple chooses a master long before the master even knows of the disciple. The disciple who has chosen must then await to be chosen in turn. Though the master may have many disciples, the disciple can have only one master. Though the disciple may have many teachers, only one may be chosen as a master.

For the disciple, the master is a text to be observed and examined in all aspects. As the disciple matures, even long after the master has departed from life, what the master had taught, and who the master was, become continuously revealed to the disciple. Acts performed, direction given, lessons taught, float in the disciple's psyche like recessive genes waiting to be activated during the unfolding of the disciple's own life and experience. What had been vague or incomprehensible to the disciple as a novice explodes like a time bomb in the disciple's consciousness as the disciple grows in knowledge and becomes enriched by experience.

The master knows that while the disciple is with him, the disciple must be nurtured and prepared for the time when the master will no longer be there. The interdependence of the master and disciple while the two are together must prepare for the inevitable independence of the disciple from the master. For the disciple, the death of the master is both an ending and a new beginning. At once, the disciple is paralyzed by profound grief at the death of the master, while manifesting an irrepressible and irrational anger at the master for what is then perceived as the ultimate act of abandonment. The disciple feels painfully alone, like a ship bereft of an anchor, a tree with severed roots.

With the passage of time, the pain increases, rather than being assuaged. The challenges confronting the disciple intensify. The decisions to be made become increasingly complex. The advice required becomes progressively intricate. At such times, the master's presence is needed more than ever before. The disciple needs the master to help adjust the rudder directing his or her course in life and learning. But the master is not there. The disciple yearns for the master's touch, gaze, word, but there is merely a chorus of silence emitting from a seemingly endless void. The disciple may become crippled by anxiety and uncertainty. However, once the disciple begins to recognize the wealth of wisdom the master had deposited in his or her mind and soul, once the disciple begins to hear again the master's voice in the words he has written and in memories recalled, the disciple begins to draw upon those precious links to the master's presence. Seeds planted by the master long before, now germinated by the disciple's own knowledge, experience and anxiety, suddenly begin to sprout. Unbeknown to the disciple, the master had bequeathed a trust aimed at providing for the disciple's needs long after the master's death.

The blending of the master's initial deposit with the disciple's subsequent self-development yields a principal capable of supporting the disciple through crisis after crisis. The master has provided the disciple with the means to confront situations and conditions that the master may have previsaged, as well as those that the master may not even have imagined. The bequest of the master combines with the knowledge, experience and resiliency of the disciple to confront the challenges that lie ahead. Hence, strengthened by what has been received from the master, the disciple feels as if both he or she and the master are responding in concert to the crisis at hand. And yet, despite and because of the disciple's joy at discovering that he or she had not been abandoned by the master, the disciple's love for the master deepens, and, the longing that can never be appeased becomes amplified beyond all previous expectation.

Longing now engenders duty; love precipitates obligation and responsibility. While the disciple recognizes that he or she cannot become a facsimile of the master, the disciple nonetheless knows that his or her own endeavour to create a life that is a work of art must incorporate what the master had bequeathed. Though the disciple is aware that, just as the master had transformed what he had received while also being faithful to the integrity of that inheritance, so must the disciple re-form and re-create what he or she had received from the master. But, most of all, the disciple is profoundly conscious of his or her role as a messenger with a message – a message delivered to the master from the past and passed on to the disciple to convey to the future.

Amnesia would squander the trust inherited from the master. Not to perpetuate the legacy once inherited by the master and now conveyed to the disciple, the bequest endowed in perpetuity for posterity, would deny the master part of his share in the World-to-Come, and would rob the disciple of part of his or her share in the here and now. As the master once was obliged to transmit the past to the future, as the master was duty-bound to imprint a vision of past masters upon the disciple, the disciple now becomes accountable to the future for the past. Paramount among the portraits of past masters which the disciple is obliged to portray is that of his or her own master.

Abraham Joshua Heschel is my master, my mentor. What precedes attempts to characterize some aspects of that relationship. What follows tries to provide a glimpse of some aspects of his spiritual portrait. Other sketches have been offered by others. Elsewhere, I have endeavoured to offer a more detailed portraiture.[2]

The richness and depth of Heschel's life and work means that any representation will be inadequate, incomplete. The subtlety and complexity of his personality compels one to see him in new and diverse ways, when viewed at different times and under the reflection of different lights and shadows. No one who has written about Heschel has managed completely to capture his spirit. None of his commentators have been able to surpass the astounding beauty or the profound perspicacity of his original text. Therefore, every attempt at a definitive portrait results in being a photographic snapshot at best. Every attempt at a complete commentary represents but a fragmentary exposition that palles in comparison to the primary text. Many books and monographs have been written attempting to examine *what* Heschel thought, taught and did. What follows suggests some insights into *why* Heschel thought, taught and did what he did.

What were some of the underlying motivations that helped shape Heschel's scholarly, theological and social contribution? Which features of his inner life provide an entrée to understand the coalescence of his scholarly researches, his theological expositions and his social action? What follows offers keys to unlock the pacemaker that drove Heschel's heart. While the keys might fit, they alone cannot fully disclose the nature and the meaning of the treasure trove that lies within.

Legend tells that when the Holy Temple in Jerusalem had been set ablaze by the enemy and its destruction was imminent, a group of priests climbed up to the roof and held the keys to the temple aloft. Thereupon, a hand reached down from heaven to reclaim the keys for safe keeping.[3] Centuries later, another conflagration began that ultimately would decimate the countless temples of stone, wood and flesh that constituted European Jewry. This time no angelic hand reached down to reclaim the keys to the Jewish spirit. They remained in the hands of the surviving remnant of a Jewish Atlantis consumed in a flood of fire.

Weeks before the volcano erupted in his native Poland, Abraham Heschel was able to leave Warsaw. Reflecting years later upon his escape, Heschel wrote, 'I am a brand plucked from the fire ... My destination was New York, it would have been Auschwitz or Treblinka'.[4] In the immediate aftermath of the destruction of the world he had known, Heschel fused anguish with memory and he wrote, 'We are either the last Jews or those who will hand over the entire past to generations to come. We will either forfeit or enrich the legacy of the ages ... We of this generation are still holding the key. Unless we remember, unless we unlock the realm of the spirit, the holiness of the ages will remain a secret of God'.[5]

No one could restore the lives that were lost. One could only strive to maintain and to transmit the surviving keys to the spiritual treasures of the Jewish soul. The alternative was to surrender a bounty of inherited insight, wisdom and experience to oblivion. To permit the bequest from the past to be irretrievably lost was, for Heschel, tantamount to a second Holocaust.[6] Despite what had happened, and precisely *because* of what had happened, Judaism could not be forgotten. For Heschel, the surviving remnant of the Jewish people could not afford to become messengers who forget the message they had been charged to convey.

In true Hasidic fashion, Heschel refused to be conquered by despair, even in the face of demonic horror, even despite staggering loss. Heschel taught that a person must believe in God, in spite of God.[7] One must wage war upon evil and injustice despite their holding sway in the world.[8] Each Jew must perpetuate Jewish learning though four-fifths of all Jewish scholars had been murdered. The Jewish people must preserve Jewish piety though the wellsprings of Jewish piety present in eastern Europe had been destroyed. The individual must search for truth and integrity though confronted with mendacity, and dare to love and to have the courage to embrace hope, despite the omnipresence of hate and adversity. The individual must strive for meaning beyond absurdity, and learn to be an optimist against his better judgment.[9]

The subject of Heschel's last book, the Hasidic master, Menachem Mendel of Kotzk, had taught that there are three ways to respond to sorrow. A person can scream. A person can be silent. Or, a person can transform sorrow into a song.[10] Following this teaching, Heschel marshaled his immense erudition, keen intellect and profound spiritual capacity to help ensure the continuity of the *niggun*, the melody of the Jewish spirit.

For Heschel, study plays a decisive role in the continuity of tradition. Study is an invitation to the past, an entrée to memory. Learning is a means of acquiring authenticity, self-enrichment and self-transformation. Through study, a link between a past otherwise destined to fade and an otherwise impoverished future is forged. In Heschel's words, one's 'total existence is, in a sense, a summation of past generations, a distillation of experiences and thoughts of his ancestors. The authentic individual is neither an end nor a beginning but a link between ages, both memory and expectation'.[11]

As philosophy begins with wonder, theology begins with faith. According to Heschel, faith is rooted in memory. A soul without memory is stunted. A person without memory is spiritually hollow. Heschel writes, 'The riches of a soul are stored up in its memory. This is the test of character – not whether a man follows daily fashion, but whether the past is alive in his present. When we want to understand ourselves, to find out what is precious in our lives, we should search our memory'.[12]

In the aftermath of the Holocaust, with the decimation of the great centre of Jewish learning in Europe, the preservation and transmission of Jewish memory became and remained one of Heschel's critical concerns. His apprehension that the Jewish people might become messengers who forget the messages, that amnesia might become an incurable illness for his people, haunted him, and served as a major force impelling his scholarship and his teaching.

Despite harsh criticism from his academic colleagues, Heschel tenaciously held to his conviction that Jewish scholarship could not afford to do 'business as usual'. The Holocaust had altered the script. Unlike those who wanted to perpetuate the agenda of the 'scientific study of Judaism' (*Jüdische Wissenschaft*), unlike those who perceived Jewish learning as a variety of humanistic research aimed at detached intellectual edification, unlike those who advocated academic voyeurism, who were more obsessed with footnotes and textual variants than with matters of the spirit, who were too preoccupied with the exotica of the Jewish past to be concerned with the demand for a Jewish future, Heschel contended that 'after the Holocaust, Jewish scholarship should be devoted to that which advances *Yiddishkeit* [Jewishness]'.[13]

In the Middle Ages, due to the scarcity of paper, people would often write new texts on top of earlier ones. Such writing is called 'palimpsest'. In Heschel's view, scholarship is ultimately a palimpsest.[14] Our individual lives are new compositions written upon the fabric of the memories of those who came before. The Ashkenazic Jewish tradition of naming children for deceased relatives expresses this view that no individual is a blank slate. Each person bears a name and a heritage from his or her forebears. Genealogy is a feature of biography. Indeed, Abraham Joshua Heschel's name was not his own. He inherited it from his ancestor, a Hasidic master, known as the Rabbi of Apt. According to Hasidic legend, Abraham Joshua Heschel of Apt believed in the transmigration of souls. He therefore taught that it is important to know who one once was, in order to understand who one presently is. The doctrine of transmigration of souls contains a profound religious truth. For one to know oneself, one must seek to understand one's past, one's heritage, the tradition from which one emerges.

Despite his fierce commitment to preserving and conveying the wisdom of the past, Heschel felt obliged to follow the advice of Rabbi Akiva to sing 'a new song every day', to compose new scores from old notes, to pave a new path down a well-trodden road.[15] Heschel knew that before one could become a pioneer, one first had to become an heir.[16]

Though deeply rooted in the past, Heschel insisted that he was 'not just a dwelling place for other people, an echo of the past'. Heschel endeavoured to make his life correlate with 'the supreme Hasidic imperative. Don't be old. Don't be stale'. 'I consider in my own intellectual existence', he wrote, 'that the greatest danger is to become obsolete ... I have one talent and that is the capacity to be tremendously surprised at life, at ideas ... Maybe this is my life. I always try to sing a *niggun*. I write another book and a Cossack gives me a beating. So I write another. The Cossack may be my greatest benefactor'.[17]

A goal of scholarship, for Heschel, is to make our ancestors our contemporaries, our companions, and to learn how to apply their insights to our situations. In one of his books, Heschel tells of a scholar who came to a certain Hasidic master. The master asked the scholar, 'What have you done all your life?' The scholar replied, 'I have gone through the entire Talmud three times'. To which the master said, 'Yes, but how much of the Talmud has gone through you?'[18] Elsewhere, Heschel rhetorically asks, 'What purpose was served in knowing the sacred text if one could not understand oneself?'[19]

Heschel was no armchair philosopher, no 'ivory tower' theologian, no clinically detached academician. For Heschel, life is too precarious, too precious, to become a game of trivial pursuit. Life is a work of art, and the challenge posed to each individual is whether to engage in a lifetime of labour to endeavour to produce a masterpiece, or whether to let sit dormant the possibilities for self-transcendence pregnant within each person.[20]

Heschel reminded us that human beings 'cannot live by sedatives alone'.[21] In *The Earth is the Lord's*, he approvingly quotes a leader of the nineteenth-century Lithuanian *Musar* movement who said, 'If I thought that I should always remain what I am, I would lay hands on myself. But, if I did not hope to be like the Gaon of Vilna, I would not be even what I am'.[22] Similarly, Heschel endorsed the motto of the Rabbi of Kotzk – *arbiten auf zich*, 'work on your self'.[23]

According to Heschel, no human being is found in a definitive edition. Authentic human existence entails a life long quest for self-understanding, for taking the ultimate risk of becoming whom one is able to become. This quest ends only with death. The human being is always in a process of development. Only God can say 'I am that I am'. God *is*, while human beings are always *becoming*. The challenge of self-understanding begins with the awareness that no one is self-made, that no individual is a *creatio ex nihilo*, a *Ding an sich* – a thing in oneself. As Mark Twain once observed, 'a self-made man is about as likely as a self-made egg'. Thus, for Heschel, the role of learning through which one encounters one's past, and the quest for self-understanding through which one forms one's future, are inextricably related. Learning offers us the raw materials from which we can construct the work of art that is each of our lives. But 'working with the self' – the process of self-understanding and of spiritual self-development – is also required, lest learning dissipate into an intellectual parlour game. For Heschel, each moment bears new possibilities. The present is a link between memory and expectation, between history and destiny, between who one is and who one may yet become.

Heschel's philosophy of religion and his philosophy of Judaism are expressions of his own quest for self-understanding, for self-transcendence. They are crucial strokes in the artistic masterpiece that was his own life. Heschel recognized that in the final analysis neither scholarship nor religious philosophy is an *apologia pro vita sua*, not a 'mirror reflecting other people's problems', but a window to the author's own soul.[24] His works may be read as a journal of a soul in search of self-understanding, as a 'self-help' manual in how to transform through concerted effort the materials bequeathed by tradition, the gifts God has bestowed, and the time fate has allotted, into a masterpiece of a life.

Just as an individual's life must be a constant exercise in self-understanding, so the life of a religious tradition must embrace a perpetual quest for self-understanding. Without persistent questing and questioning, a religious tradition is in danger of atrophy, of becoming stale. For Heschel the specific task of religious philosophy is 'religion's reflections upon its basic insights and basic attitudes, [the] ***radical self-understanding of religion in terms of its own spirit***' [emphasis in the original].[25]

Understanding Judaism on its own terms was a visceral part of Heschel's scholarly work, theological writings and his personal quest for self-understanding. Especially since Heschel was convinced that 'Judaism today is the least known religion',[26] he endeavoured to portray and to apply a uniquely and particularly *Jewish* way of thinking. His life long endeavour was to see how Judaism understands itself.[27]

Heschel warned against creating Judaism in our own image. Because Jews live in a largely non-Jewish world, they tend to think in non-Jewish categories, even about Judaism. Consequently, a primary goal in Heschel's scholarly, theological and personal agenda was to explicate a Jewish way of thinking. Beginning with his 1933 doctoral dissertation on the biblical prophets and continuing with his works on the Talmudic rabbis, the medieval Jewish philosophical and mystical thinkers, and the Hasidic masters, Heschel dealt with the problem of 'how to think in a Jewish way of thinking'.[28] In his writings on and participation in social issues, Heschel applied the categories and attitudes of Jewish thinking to the problems of his times. Both the paradox and the achievement of Abraham Heschel was his ability to apply the most particularly Jewish insights to the most universal issues, to demonstrate how ancient traditions most poignantly relate to the most contemporary problems.[29]

In locating, describing and defining the endemic categories of Jewish thinking, Heschel not only laid the intellectual and spiritual foundations for authentic Jewish self-understanding, but he also disclosed the dichotomy between Jewish thought and other forms of thinking. This led, amongst other things, to a relentless polemic against various forms of contemporary thinking that Heschel perceived as threats to ideas dear to Judaism, such as human dignity and sanctity.[30] His theological conclusions served as the premises upon which his preoccupation with social justice was based. In discussing the examples that follow, the relationship between Heschel's scholarly studies, theological expositions, polemical thrusts and social activities will be highlighted.

Heschel considered the category of the unique to be characteristic of theology in general and of Jewish theology in particular.[31] According to Heschel, theology is predicated upon unique events. Sinai is not a daily occurrence but a unique event. Each human being is unprecedented. No human being is a photocopy of another. In Heschel's words,

> No person can write his autobiography in advance. Generalization, by means of which theories evolve, fails in trying to understand man. For in dealing with a particular man, I do not come upon a generality but upon an individuality, a person. It is precisely the exclusive application of generalities to human situations that accounts for many of our failures ... My existence as an event is an original, not a copy. No two human beings are alike. A major mode of being human is uniqueness.[32]

The attempt of philosophy, of the natural and social sciences to fit all events and persons within prescribed rubrics poses, for Heschel, a threat to religious thinking, a danger that can lead to dehumanization. If Sinai was but a convocation, if the Exodus was but a result of the Hegelian master–slave dialectic, then the claims of Scripture pall into irrelevancies. If the human being is but an 'ingenious array of portable plumbing', then the claim that each human life is intrinsically sacred degenerates into a farce.[33] Though the physical sciences, social sciences and much of classical philosophy attempt to define the unique out of existence by subsuming individual persons and phenomena under artificially constructed universal laws, theories and rubrics, Heschel stressed the category of the unique as a way of apprehending fundamental religious claims and as a means of preserving the preciousness of being human.

To apply scientific thinking – predicated upon the establishment of generalizations and the subsuming of particular empirical situations under those general conceptual models – to religious thinking, is for Heschel a 'category mistake'.[34] Heschel cautioned theologians against thinking like scientists because of the moral as well as the intellectual implications of the application of scientific thinking to religious phenomena and to human beings. In Heschel's words, 'No other deficiency makes the soul more barren than the lack of the sense for the unique ... There is more discernment in sensing the ineffable uniqueness of an event than in trying to explain it away by stereotyped doubts'.[35]

At the foundation of Judaism is the claim that revelation occurred. To deny Sinai is to undermine Jewish thinking. Because revelation is unique, unprecedented, it is unacceptable to many moderns, to those who confuse their mental habits conditioned by scientific thinking with intellectual efficacy. Heschel writes:

> To most of us the idea of revelation is unacceptable, not because it cannot be proved or explained, but because it is *unprecedented* ... Trained in seeking to explain all that happens as a manifestation of a general law, every phenomenon as an example of a type, we find it hard to believe in the extraordinary, in the absolutely singular ... It is taken for granted in science that in the realm of space a process which happened once can happen all the time, but we have not the power to understand that in the realm of time certain events do not happen again and again. Now, revelation is an event that does not happen all the time but at a particular time, at a unique moment of time ... The category of the general is the key to the understanding of the world of space; the category of the individual is the key to the understanding of the world of time.[36]

The phenomenon of revelation is the central theological motif of Heschel's scholarly research and his theological exposition. From his 1933 dissertation on the prophets to the third volume of his Hebrew magnum opus, *Torah min-ha-Shamayim* (unfinished at the time of his death in 1972), the meaning of revelation and prophecy in biblical, rabbinic and medieval Jewish literature preoccupied Heschel.[37]

In probing the understanding of revelation in classical Jewish theological sources, Heschel encountered a paradox: the wholly-other God desires to enter into a relationship, a covenant, with human beings. The infinite God is profoundly concerned with finite human affairs. Human deeds somehow fulfil divine needs. However, as for the philosopher, Alfred North Whitehead, so for Heschel the theologian, paradox is not a calamity, but an opportunity. Indeed, Heschel maintains that 'To the Jewish tradition ... paradox is an essential way of understanding the world, history and nature ... tension, contradiction characterize all of reality'.[38]

Rather than *define*, classical Jewish thought *describes* various phenomena and relationships as the interaction of complementary polar opposites.[39] Definitions are limiting, restrictive. Paradox and polarity are dynamic, suggestive. Rather than questing after the elusive essence of things, rather than positing reductionist definitions of complex entities and phenomena, rather than reducing the profundities of existence to trite notionalism, Heschel advocated perceiving reality as the interplay between complementary polar opposites.[40] For example, religion embraces the polarity of the divine initiative and the human response, *God in Search of Man* and *Man's Quest for God*, divine revelation and human piety. The Jewish religious life develops within the polarities of faith and creed, word and deed, justice and love, truth and mercy, spontaneity (*kavanah*) and regularity (*keva*), theology (*agada*) and law (*halakhah*). The human being exists within the dichotomy of being 'dust and ashes' and a being created in the 'image of God'.

Heschel's investigations into the history and development of Judaism convinced him that Jewish thought is not monolithic, that there is no 'mainstream' of Judaism. Rather, there is a constant creative tension between the mystical and the rational. His *Torah min-ha-Shamayim* exhaustively probes the tension between the School of Rabbi Akiva and the School of Rabbi Yishmael. His

Yiddish magnum opus, *Kotzk: The Struggle for Integrity*, explores the tension in Hasidic thought between the Ba'al Shem Tov and Rabbi Mendel of Kotzk.

Revelation, for Heschel, consists of the giving ***and*** the receiving of the Torah. Prophecy is a 'revelation of God and a co-revelation of man'.[41] This polarity of God and human beings, of divine need and human deed relates to the most fundamental Jewish theological claim: the existence of a covenant between God and the people of Israel. For Heschel, the revelatory claim manifests itself in a covenantal relationship, in a partnership between the divine and the human. In Heschel's words:

> Life is a *partnership* of God and man ... God is a partner and a partisan in man's struggle for justice, peace, love, and beauty, and it is because of His being in need of man that He entered into a covenant with him for all time, a mutual bond embracing God and man, a relationship to which God, not alone man, is committed ... God's dream is not to be alone, to have mankind as a partner in the drama of continuous creation. By whatever we do, by every act we carry out, we either advance or obstruct the drama of redemption; we either reduce or enhance the power of evil.[42]

The performance of sacred deeds fulfils God's needs for human righteousness and piety. The sacred deed (***mitzvah***) is how human beings carry out their covenant, their partnership with God. As Heschel writes, 'The spirit of mitsvah is *togetherness*. We know, He is a partner to our act ... To fulfill a mitsvah is to be a partisan, to enter into fellowship with His will'.[43]

The divine–human partnership is, for Heschel, both intrinsic and essential to Judaism.

> There is only one way to define Jewish religion. It is the awareness of God's interest in man, the awareness of a covenant, of a responsibility that lies on Him as well as on us ... God is in need of man for the attainment of His ends, and religion, as Jewish tradition understands it, is a way of serving those ends ... Life is a partnership of God and man; God is not detached from or indifferent to our joys and griefs'.[44]

Elsewhere, Heschel writes, 'The Greek thinkers sought to understand man as a part of the universe: the prophets sought to understand man as a partner of God'.[45] And still elsewhere, Heschel elucidates further: 'His need is a self-imposed concern. God is now in need of man because He freely made him a partner in His enterprise, a partner in the work of creation.[46]

The idea of divine pathos, so central to classical Jewish thought according to Heschel, rests upon the paradox of the divine need for human collaboration, of the divine participation in the joys and grief of human existence. The God who is beyond all human apprehension and comprehension invites our participation in the inner life of the divine.[47] God, who transcends all human needs, somehow requires human actions to bring about redemption in the world. In this view, rooted in Scripture, amplified by the Talmudic rabbis and developed by the medieval Jewish mystics, 'man's relationship to God is not one of passive reliance upon His omnipotence but one of active assistance'.[48] This, for Heschel, is the paradox upon which Jewish theology and piety rest.

This paradox, this polarity, may serve as an example which demonstrates the nexus shared between Heschel's scholarly studies, his exposition of Jewish theological self-understanding, and his commitment to social action. These ideas, which Heschel described as critical to Judaism, are examined in his scholarly studies of the prophets, rabbinic theology, medieval Jewish mysticism and Hasidism. They are reformulated and expound in his philosophy of religion (*Man is Not Alone*) and in his philosophy of Judaism (*God in Search of Man*). They were translated into action in Heschel's massive efforts for social justice, such as his participation in the civil rights struggle and in the opposition to the war in Vietnam. May one example of this nexus suffice.

In rabbinic theology, the idea of divine pathos was expressed by the epithet for God called '*Shekhinah*'. The Shekhinah is the divine presence in the world. The disposition of Shekhinah in the world is effected by human deeds. Like the people of Israel, Shekhinah is in exile in the world awaiting messianic redemption. Through redemptive deeds, human beings can accelerate both the redemption of the world and the redemption of the divine presence in the world.[49]

It is not surprising that Heschel relates the idea of the exile of Shekhinah (*galut ha-shekhinah*) to his participation in social action.

In 1963, in his first significant public address on civil rights, Heschel uses the phrase the 'segregation of God'.[50] Since God (Shekhinah) is affected by the human condition, where human beings experience segregation or exile, so does the divine. By liberating human beings from segregation, the divine presence in their midst is also liberated. *Galut ha-shekhinah* is the 'segregation of God'. Acts of social justice help liberate the divine presence. Social action on behalf of God and in collaboration with God articulates the covenant, the partnership that we maintain with the divine. Similarly, in Heschel's response to the Vietnam war, theological claims rooted in erudite scholarship percolate to the surface: 'The encounter of man and God is an encounter within the world. We meet within a situation of shared suffering, of shared responsibility … God's presence unites us and God is present wherever man is afflicted.[51] Elsewhere Heschel writes, 'In light of God's mysterious dependence upon man the problem of anthropodicy and theodicy cannot be separated. The cardinal issue, why does the God of justice and compassion permit evil to persist? is bound up with the problem of how man should aid God so that His justice and compassion prevail'.[52]

For the last twenty-seven years of his life Heschel occupied a chair in Jewish ethics and mysticism at The Jewish Theological Seminary. Here, too, the polarity of theosophy and social action is evident. The polarities of Jewish thought are the polarities that characterize Heschel's biography and the contents of his bibliography.

According to Heschel, being the person one can become entails an encounter with the divine presence disguised in the self and in the world. 'God is of no importance unless He is of supreme importance', Heschel claims.[53] Being a messenger, a witness, a partner of God, is the premise and the promise of human, and certainly of Jewish existence. For Heschel, echoing the Hasidic master, Aaron of Karlin, 'The gravest sin for a Jew is to forget what he represents … We are God's stake in history … There is a war to wage against the vulgar, against the glorification of the absurd, a war that is incessant, universal. Loyal to the presence of the ultimate in the common, we may be able to make it clear that man is more than man, that in doing the finite he may perceive the infinite'.[54]

NOTES

1. Martin Buber, *Tales of the Hasidim: The Later Masters*, trans. Olga Marx (New York: Schocken, 1948), pp.148–49.
2. Byron L. Sherwin, *Abraham Joshua Heschel* (Atlanta: John Knox Press, 1979).
3. *Avot d'Rabbi Natan*, Solomon Schechter (ed.), (2nd ed., New York: Feldheim, 1967), p.12b.
4. Abraham J. Heschel, *Moral Grandeur and Spiritual Audacity* (New York: Farrar, Straus, and Giroux, 1996), p.235.
5. Heschel, *The Earth is the Lord's* (New York: Henry Schuman, 1950), p.107.
6. Heschel said this to me many times. He also said it to others. See for example, Richard L. Rubenstein, *Power Struggle* (New York: Scribner's, 1974), p.128, where Heschel is quoted as saying 'When I think of what our people have accumulated over the centuries that nobody will ever know about, it seems like a second holocaust. Hitler destroyed our people. Now we let their spirit die'. Towards the end of his life, Heschel was uncharacteristically pessimistic about the continuity of Jewish learning and spirituality in America. Writing in *Sh'ma* 10/185 (January 11, 1979):39, Arnold Jacob Wolf recalled, 'Weeks before Heschel died, he was in Lake Forest, Illinois. He called me over to talk to me for several hours ... he said he was in Germany in the great last days of years and the German-Jewish community almost succeeded. The renaissance of Jewish values almost made a coherent *Galut* [diaspora] possible and then Hitler came, and it was too late. He looked at me – I'll never forget this – and he said, "in America we have ten more years." (That was not his usual style.) He didn't say thirty or forty or sixty – he said *ten*. After that some factors will be irreversible'. See also Heschel, *Moral Grandeur and Spiritual Audacity*, p.23, from a 1965 address to the General Assembly of the Council of Jewish Federations and Welfare Funds: 'We may claim to be a success, but in the eyes of Jewish history we may be regarded as a failure'.

   Heschel was often criticized for not responding to the Holocaust. Yet, on numerous occasions, he spoke to me about it. In 1971 when viewing an exhibit on the Holocaust at the Spertus Museum in Chicago, he told me that he never understood this criticism since in every work, in all his work, he is dealing with it, often implicitly and sometimes explicitly. It was the Christian scholar, W .D. Davies who, I believe, was the first to write about the profound impact of the Holocaust on Heschel's theology and its relationship to his involvement in social action. Davies correctly observes that, 'The Holocaust does emerge in his writings, but his references to it, though devastating, are usually indirect ... The Holocaust did have a profound influence on his theology ... he expressed our social conscience. But I think that it was the holocaust that lent to his awareness its special urgency'. W. D. Davies, 'Conscience, Scholar, Witness', in *America* 128/9 (10 March 1973): 213.
7. Abraham J. Heschel, *Who is Man?* (Stanford: Stanford University Press, 1963), p. 80.
8. Heschel, *The Insecurity of Freedom* (New York: Farrar, Straus, Giroux, 1966), p.132.
9. See e.g., Abraham J. Heschel, *A Passion for Truth* (New York: Farrar, Straus and Giroux, 1973), pp 294–297; Abraham J. Heschel, 'In Search of Exaltation', in *Jewish Heritage* 13:3 (Fall 1971), p.29, where Heschel writes, 'I am an optimist against my better judgment'.
10. Heschel, *Passion for Truth*, p.283.
11. Heschel, *Who is Man?*, p.99.
12. Heschel, *Man is Not Alone* (Philadelphia: Jewish Publication Society, 1951), p.162.
13. Heschel, *The Circle of the Baal Shem Tov*, S. H. Dresner (ed.), (Chicago: University of Chicago Press, 1985), p.xxiv. See also the discussion there by Dresner on Heschel and *Jüdische Wissenschaft*, pp.xiv–xix. Note Heschel's statement in *Man is Not Alone*, p.231, 'Experts in religion are in danger of resembling the proverbial yeshivah-student who claimed to have understood and mastered all arts. Asked whether he could swim, he replied, "I do not know how to swim, but I understand swimming."'
14 Heschel often uses the analogy of palimpsest in his works.
15. Heschel, *Who is Man?*, p.118.
16. Ibid., Heschel, *Who is Man?*, p.99; *Man is Not Alone*, p.164; *Passion for Truth*, p.188.
17. Heschel, 'In Search of Exaltation', pp.29–30; also Heschel, *Passion for Truth*, pp.283–85.
18. Heschel, *The Earth is the Lord's*, p.83.
19. Heschel, *Passion for Truth*, p.107.
20. On Heschel's view of life as a work of art, *Who is Man?*, p.99; *Moral Grandeur and Spiritual Audacity*, p.412.
21. Heschel, 'In Search of Exaltation', p.30.

22. Heschel, *The Earth is the* Lord's, p.90.
23. Heschel, *Kotzk* [Yiddish] (Tel Aviv: Ha-Menorah, 1973), vol. 1, pp.131–6.
24. Heschel, *God in Search of Man* (Philadelphia: Jewish Publication Society, 1955), p.6. This approach is critical not only to understanding Heschel's theology, but his scholarship as well. In his scholarly writings, beginning with his very early studies of Abravanel and Maimonides, written in Germany in the 1930s, Heschel stresses the need for scholarship to examine the inner life of the subjects of scholarly research. This citation from *God in Search of Man* is found in earlier form in Heschel's first major work written in English, *The Quest for Certainty in Saadia's Philosophy* (New York: Feldheim, 1944), p.1, which originally appeared in *The Jewish Quarterly Review*, vols. 33 and 34, in 1943 and 1944.
25. *God in Search of Man*, p.8.
26. *The Earth is the Lord's*, p.107.
27. *Moral Grandeur and Spiritual Audacity*, p.156.
28. Like Solomon Schechter, Heschel stressed that Judaism is not only a way of doing, but a way of thinking as well. See e.g., Heschel, *The Insecurity of Freedom*, p.217, and Solomon Schechter, *Studies in Judaism: First Series* (Philadelphia: Jewish Publication Society, 1911), p.180; Heschel, *God in Search of Man*, p.23, no. 8.
29. Davies, 'Conscience, Scholar, Witness', p.215.
30. *Moral Grandeur and Spiritual Audacity*, pp.396–98, 404.
31. See e.g., Heschel, *Who is Man?*, pp.36–9.
32. Ibid., p.37.
33. Ibid., p.24; *God in Search of Man*, p.35.
34. For Heschel on science, *Man is Not Alone*, pp.30, 103; *God in Search of Man*, pp.43–44, 101–102. Heschel particularly inveighed against applying categories from the social sciences, especially psychology, to religious phenomena and experiences. *Man is Not Alone*, pp.221–22; *Insecurity of Freedom*, pp.226–29.
35. *God in Search of Man*, p.202.
36. Ibid, pp.201, 204.
37. Sherwin, *Abraham Joshua Heschel*, pp.30–33.
38. *The Insecurity of Freedom*, p.136.
39. *God in Search of Man*, pp.8, 102–4.
40. For Heschel on 'notionalism', 'The Jewish Notion of God and Christian Renewal', in *Renewal of Religious Thought*, vol. 1 of *Theology of Renewal*, L. K. Shook (ed.), (New York: Herder and Herder, 1968), pp.105–10. On polarity, *God in Search of Man*, pp.341–44.
41. Ibid., p.260.
42. *Who is Man?*, pp.75, 119.
43. *God in Search of Man*, p.287.
44. *Man is Not Alone*, p.241.
45. *Insecurity of Freedom*, p.152.
46. *Man is Not Alone*, p.243.
47. 'The Mystical Element in Judaism', in , *Moral Grandeur and Spiritual Audacity*, pp.164–84.
48. *Man is Not Alone*, p.243.
49. *Torah min-ha-Shamayim*, vol. 1 (London: Soncino, 1962), pp.65–90.
50. 'The Religious Basis of Equality of Opportunity – The Segregation of God', in Matthew Ahmann (ed.), *Race: Challenge to Religion* (Chicago: Henry Regnery, 1963), pp.55–73. This essay, delivered as an address at a 1963 conference in Chicago commemorating the 100th anniversary of the Emancipation Proclamation of President Lincoln is reprinted in *Insecurity of Freedom*, pp.85–101, with the title 'Religion and Race'; however, its original title included the phrase 'the segregation of God'. Heschel also uses this phrase, in his essay, 'Religion in a Free Society', in *Insecurity of Freedom*, p.8.
51. 'The Moral Outrage of Vietnam', in *Vietnam: Crisis of Conscience* (New York: Association Press, 1967), pp.52–3.
52. *Passion for Truth*, p.298.
53. *Man is Not Alone*, p.92.
54. *The Earth is the Lord's*, p.109. This seems to be a polemic against Hegel's claim that the Jews were incapable of perceiving the infinite.

CHAPTER SIXTEEN

Louis Jacobs

In generations yet to come, historians of British Jewry might very well conclude that 'Louis Jacobs' could not possibly represent the name of a single individual, but must refer to an entire school of rabbis and scholars. The scope of scholarly expertise, the breadth and depth of startling erudition, the massive corpus of published work, and the impact of rabbinic, religious, social, literary and academic activities identified with the name 'Louis Jacobs' could hardly but convince future chronicles that such legion attainments could not have been produced by a single individual during a single lifetime. Yet one of these chroniclers might find reports of a 2005 poll conducted by the *Jewish Chronicle* of London in which Louis Jacobs is designated as the greatest *individual* British Jew of all time, surpassing statesmen such as Benjamin Disraeli, philanthropists such as Moses Monterfiore, and all of those who have held the title of 'Chief Rabbi of the British Empire'.[1] For those of us fortunate enough to have counted Louis Jacobs among our friends and colleagues, he was indisputably a single and singular individual, the crown jewel of British Jewry, a person and a scholar who each of us would want to emulate.

For most of his long and distinguished career, Louis Jacobs served as a congregational rabbi in London, as an adjunct or visiting professor at various British and American academic institutions, and as a lecturer to a vast variety of academic and lay audiences. In almost forty books and hundreds of articles, Jacobs offers a dazzling display of range, depth, analysis, creativity and perspicacity. Yet, despite his legion intellectual and scholarly achievements, and his influence on many other rabbis, scholars and theologians, little has been written about Jacobs' academic and theological work. The purpose of what follows is to begin to redress this undeserved slight to one of contemporary Jewry's greatest theologians and most gifted and prolific scholars.

Though little has been written about Jacobs' scholarly oeuvre, much has been written about an ongoing episode in Jacobs' life that plagued him for decades, and that has stimulated much of his most significant theological and academic thought and writing – the so-called 'Jacobs Affair'. Though the arena of the Jacobs Affair has been Jewish communal life in Britain, at its core is a theological controversy centring on the nature and the products of the revelatory experience. In sum, the 'Jacobs Affair' was precipitated when Jacobs was denied a significant leadership position in the nominally Orthodox organizational structure of British Jewry because he did not accept the theological doctrine of Jewish fundamentalist inerrancy, that is, that every word of the Torah as we have it was revealed by God at Mount Sinai. Following universally accepted findings of modern scholarship, Jacobs arugued for a human element, both in the revelatory event and in the products of revelation such as the biblical text.

Jacobs' view, as stated in *We Have Reason to Believe* (1957), precipitated the 'Jacobs Affair' in the early 1960s that catapulted a Jewish theological controversy into a subject of international media attention.[2] As a result of the 'Jacobs Affair', an understanding of the nature of revelation and its implications (as will be discussed further below) has taken centre stage in Jacobs, many writings. However, Jacobs' theological position on revelation must be seen within the broader context of his endeavour to grapple with larger, more visceral issues: What can a modern Jew believe 'without subterfuge and with intellectual honesty?'[3] What can a modern Jew believe and how do those beliefs impact upon how he or she lives his or her life as a Jew? Jacobs' attempt to address these questions has led his investigations into virtually every nook and cranny of the vast corpus of Jewish thought. His many writings may be divided into four central areas of concern: theology, rabbinics, Jewish law and Jewish mysticism. As we shall see, Jacobs' writings in each of these areas relates to his life-long endeavour to forge and to defend 'traditionalism without fundamentalism'.[4] Always the teacher and preacher, Jacobs' writings also include many 'popular' works aimed at making Jewish thought accessible to the curious layperson as well as the seasoned scholar.

Jewish Theology

Consistent with the British proclivity to find a 'middle way' between alternative religious positions (as in the Anglican Church as a 'middle way' between Catholicism and other forms of Protestantism), Jacobs offers his view of 'supernaturalistic liberalism' or 'traditionalism without fundamentalism' as an alternative to a Jewish form of inerrant 'fundamentalism' characteristic of much of Orthodox Judaism, and to various forms of secular humanistic Judaism. He offers a version of 'conservative' or '*masorti*' ('traditional') Judaism as an alternative to Jewish Orthodoxy and to Jewish Reform.

'Supernaturalistic liberalism' represents a 'middle way' between 'liberal naturalism' and 'fundamentalist supernaturalism'.[5] 'Liberal naturalism' is essentially a form of secular humanism, in religious garb, that denies revelation, rejects a supernatural God, and sees sacred texts such as the Bible as being solely the product of human creativity. 'Fundamentalist supernaturalism' denies the presence of a human element in the revelatory event and in sacred texts that represent the record of such events. 'Supernaturalistic liberalism' considers revelation and its products to represent a coalescence of the divine and the human.

For Jacobs, the 'fundamentalist' posture that claims the Torah is the product of divine dictation devoid of a human element, a static body of divine truth handed down in tact throughout the generations, is a medieval dogmatic claim that can no longer be affirmed today. Both in his academic and theological writings, Jacobs demonstrates that not only modern critical scholarship but a large corpus of classical Jewish religious literature considers the Torah to contain both a divine as well as a human component, and that Judaism is a dynamic faith that has undergone continuous development and change, marked by creativity and flexibility.

Jacobs acknowledges that supernaturalism – belief in a transcendent yet personal God who enters into a relationship with human beings through revelation and various forms of mystical and religious experience – is considered by many modern Jews to be an untenable reactionary view bordering on the superstitious. However, for Jacobs, a secular or naturalistic Judaism (for example, following Mordecai Kaplan) is problematic for two reasons. First, it goes beyond 'the legitimate boundaries of traditional Jewish theology'.[6] In other words, though there are many options within Jewish theology, it nonetheless has boundaries. Ideas beyond these wide boundaries cannot be considered legitimate conceptual or historical options within Judaism. Second, for Jacobs, supernaturalism provides a foundation for individual and human meaning, rooted in belief in a personal God, that is unavailable in secularistic or naturalistic interpretations of Judaism. Jacobs' presentation of 'supernaturalistic liberalism' is found throughout his theological writings, both academic and 'popular'. These include *We Have Reason to Believe*; *Principles of the Jewish Faith*; *Beyond Reasonable Doubt*; *God, Torah, Israel*; and, *A Jewish Theology*.[7]

Jacobs' *A Jewish Theology* (1973) represents the first systematic presentation of the major themes of Jewish religious thought since Kaufmann Kohler's *Jewish Theology*, published more than fifty years before, in 1918.[8] Kohler's work is apologetic in nature, overwhelmingly rationalistic in orientation, and blatantly influenced by contemporary liberal Protestant theology. Jacobs' book, in contrast, offers a forthright and rounded portrait of Jewish theological concerns, including constant references to the Jewish mystical tradition. Unlike other thinkers who seek to apologize for Judaism or to defend it against intellectual or social challenges, Jacobs attempts to respond to a single question: what can Jews believe today? What kind of faith emerges '*within* traditional Judaism' when it encounters modernism? The theologian, he says, 'must try to present a coherent picture of what Jews can believe without subterfuge and with intellectual honesty'. For Jacobs, theologians must be 'committed to the truth they are seeking to explore', but they must also be practitioners of *Jüdische Wissenschaft*, the scientific study of Judaism.[9] For Jacobs, theology is both an art and a science. However, though science begins without presuppositions, theology begins with presuppositions developed within a faith tradition and affirmed in the life and thought of the theologian. Nonetheless, for Jacobs, 'a theology which seeks to overlook or to reject the findings of scholarship is bad theology'.[10]

Like Abraham Heschel, Jacobs rejects a monolithic view of Judaism as being unfaithful to the multifaceted complexity of Jewish religious thought. Jewish tradition, he maintains, has no 'mainstream', but many streams. It provides a variety of equally defensible traditional options for most theological, moral or personal problems.

The process of analysis, interpretation and selection of these options does not reduce tradition to the arbitrary selective will of the scholar, nor does it elevate modern tendencies into an absolute standard for judgment. But it does provide an opportunity for honest, careful confrontation with the tradition in order to elicit an authentic response to a contemporary problem.

In articulating his theology of Judaism, Jacobs harnesses the tools of analytic, linguistic philosophy to classical Jewish sources. Though many modern Jewish religious thinkers have allied themselves with the existentialist school, Jacobs demonstrates that analytic philosophy, in the 1960s and 1970s the dominant philosophical school of thought in Britain and America, need not be an enemy; it can be an ally of Jewish philosophical theology. His utilization of linguistic philosophy is most clearly evident in his 1968 work, *Faith*.[11]

By reason of its structure, *Faith* reads like a contemporary version of the medieval philosophical classic, Saadia's *Beliefs and Opinions*. Saadia moves from a discussion of how we know what we know, to a presentation of the content of Jewish belief. Similarly, Jacobs begins by discussing how we may come to believe what we believe. He then analyzes possible objections to that belief, that is, to theistic belief. Finally, he provides a brief description of the nature and content of Jewish belief. By his use of linguistic philosophical tools, Jacobs subtly demonstrates a methodological continuity between medieval Jewish philosophy and modern analytic philosophy. For both approaches, belief entails the affirmation of the truth value of propositions and the requirement for coherence among those propositions. Like Maimonides, Jacobs holds that since faith may mean assertion of the truth of a proposition, its clear, concise articulation is of great importance. Thus, his mastery of linguistic philosophy provides him with the impetus for clarity, so miserably lacking in many thinkers in the existentialist camp, and consequently, he offers a viable alternative to the often incoherent 'personal propaganda' that characterizes much that passes for contemporary Jewish thought.

Throughout his theological writings, Jacobs treats a wide range of issues of historical, conceptual and personal theological concern. These include God, theodicy, the after life, and Jewish peoplehood. However, because of the 'Jacobs Affair', revelation and its implications for Jewish thought, life, law and religious observance, have taken centre stage in Jacobs' oeuvre, particularly in his theological writings. Compared to his ongoing preoccupation with the problem of revelation and its implications, Jacobs' treatment of other theological issues is sometimes uneven.

Jacobs' position on revelation, as first stated in *We Have Reason to Believe*, rejects the fundamentalism posture. He asserts that the Bible is not revelation itself, not the verbatim word of God, but the *record* of revelation. As such, it contains a human as well as a divine element, and bears all the marks of human literary production. It can, therefore, be subjected to the critical methods of analysis which are used to clarify the meaning of other literary works. It is to the details of that position that we now turn our attention.

Jacobs deftly ties his discussion of revelation to an analysis of the theological underpinnings of Orthodox, Reform and Conservative Judaism. His own final position, which approximates the Conservative one, emerges from his polemical attacks on the theologies of revelation underlying Orthodoxy and Reform. His views on revelation provide theological conceptualization as well as a basis for practical implementation.[12]

Jacobs identifies the Orthodox position with a fundamentalist-inerrant understanding of revelation that considers the Torah and its commandments to be dictates of God that can neither be questioned nor altered by human initiative. They can only be obeyed. Humans worship God as a servant obeys his or her master, in passive obedience. According to this view, Jewish tradition in its entirety was given by God at Sinai; the rabbinic interpretations of Scripture were already revealed to Moses at Sinai. The Halakhah being totally of divine origin must be objectively and immutably true, for only that which is objectively true may be eternally valid and binding upon all generations. Being devoid of a subjective human element, the law proceeds according to an internal logic of its own, unaffected by social or intellectual factors or by historical development. Just as the prophet is a passive recipient of revelation rather than a partner is dialogue with God, so is the Halakhist a passive expositor of the law. He may elicit the inherent truth of the tradition revealed at Sinai, but he may not legislate. The tradition was given once and takes time to unfold. The prophet, the sage, the scholar, can only make the implicit become explicit. Human ingenuity and creativity only uncover; they do not innovate or create.

In addition, this position assumes that truth is regressive and static: the further we get from the source of truth – the revelation at Sinai when all truth was revealed – the less we know. This regressive notion of truth finds its classical expression in the Talmudic citation: 'If the early scholars were like angels, we are like men; if they are like men, then we are like asses'.[13] To hold to inerrant fundamentalism is to defend a single strand of Jewish thought and experience while overlooking other equally defensible ones within classical Judaism.

Though Jacobs finds the fundamentalist stance, which he identifies with Orthodoxy, to be wanting, so does he perceive the classical Reform view of revelation to be fallacious. Classical Reform Judaism's rejection of the binding quality of Jewish religious law (Halakhah) was based upon its assumption that revelation is 'progressive'; that is, as time goes on, as the human species 'evolves', God's truth is progressively revealed to human beings. Since Reform sees itself as the most recent expression of Judaism, it expresses, therefore, the highest truth now available.

For Jacobs, this notion of progressive revelation, which rejects the binding quality of Halakhah in the name of a higher, more recently revealed truth (often correlative with contemporary cultural trends), is specious. It is an improper attempt to apply a Darwinian theory of progressive evolution to revelation and to the history of Judaism. Though Judaism is continually changing and developing, it is not necessarily evolving from a lower to a higher form. In the wake of two world wars, the Holocaust, numerous other wars, social strife, ecological threats and economic uncertainties, the claim that humankind is making automatic progress in religious development, moral insight and quality of life, proves to be hopelessly naive. Jacobs writes:

> The doctrine of progressive revelation seems to imply that God has kept former generations in ignorance of the truth in its fullness until the spiritual supermen of the nineteenth and twentieth centuries came on the scene. It hints that in many ways we are spiritually superior to Amos, Isaiah, Akiba and Maimonides ... It comes perilously close to a belief in God who is constantly changing His mind.[14]

Having found both the fundamentalist and the 'progressive' views to be wanting, Jacobs proceeds to articulate his own position regarding revelation and the nature of Jewish law and tradition.

Revelation, Jacobs holds, is not revealed in 'propositional' terms, either all at once or progressively, but is an intense divine-human encounter embracing a divine initiative and a human response. 'Revelation is an event, not a series of propositions about God and His demands'.[15] There is a human partner in that event. Out of it, and in response to it, Jews have creatively developed the tradition known as 'Judaism'. For Jacobs, as for Zechariah Frankel, the 'father of Conservative Judaism', 'Judaism is the religion of the Jews'; that is, as a result of the revelatory experience and in continuous response to it, Jews continue to develop Jewish faith throughout the generations.

Accordingly, the Bible and subsequent Jewish tradition are neither dictates of God, nor are they a body of revelatory truths given to people intellectually and spiritually more primitive than we are, and subsequently made obsolete by the revelation of higher truth. On the contrary, 'the Bible is a *record* of how men were confronted by God'. Subsequent Jewish tradition is the record of how Jews in past generations confronted God, seeking to understand God's plan for humankind in general and God's will for the people of Israel in particular. As Jacobs writes:

> Revelation is a meeting or series of meetings with God Himself. Revelation is an event. It has been translated into words by human beings who experienced it and their words are found in the record we know as the Bible. From out of its pages we, too, can hear the voice of God speaking to us, but it is the voice of God speaking through the distortions of the fallible human record. Unless we ourselves are prophets how else could we hear God's voice? There is nothing in this view basically opposed to the Jewish idea, though it does involve, of course, a thorough reinterpretation of what revelation means.[16]

For Jacobs, the Bible is a record of a direct revelation from God. There is, however, a second indirect variety of revelation in which the people of Israel play an active and creative role. As in the Talmudic notion that Moses legislated certain laws on his own volition and God later ratified his decrees, so, in this view, the laws, traditions, ideas and observances accepted by the whole Community of Israel became binding *as* the word of God.[17] Thus, for Jacobs, revelation is neither 'regressive' nor 'progressive', but continuous. The Judaism of today can, at best, strive to be an authentic continuation of the past. The Judaism of today is neither the highest form of Jewish experience, nor is it the lowest. The challenge to contemporary Judaism is to try to be the best form of Jewish belief and practice for its day. But, there are no guarantees. The constant danger of atrophy on the one hand, and radical subjectivism on the other, may prevent the vibrant, creative development of a form of Judaism compatible with past traditions and current intellectual and spiritual needs.

In articulating this position in *Principles of the Jewish Faith*, Jacobs approximates the view of the founders of Conservative Judaism like Zechariah Frankel, Solomon Schechter and Louis Ginzberg, who held that the source of Jewish authority is ultimately not in the Bible but in the historical and religious experience of the people of Israel. In *A Jewish Theology*, Jacobs goes beyond this earlier view. Here, he expresses a 'theological approach' to the nature of Judaism – specifically, to Jewish law – saying that one must go beyond the 'historical' view of Frankel which perceives Judaism only in those terms. One must adapt an attitude which understands Judaism as a religion and not only as the historical product of the Jewish people. For one adopting this approach, the *mitzvot* are to be perceived as ways to God. Because they can succeed in bringing people to God, the *mitzvot*, though developed by the people of Israel, must be considered as binding *as* the will of God. Thus, for Jacobs, Halakhah remains binding, but individual laws, since they are not divine *dictates*, are continually open to change and analysis.[18]

Despite Jacobs' highly sophisticated theological efforts to articulate a non-fundamentalist position on the nature of revelation and Jewish law, and despite the many merits of that position, his stance creates many difficulties.[19] To equate the collective will of the Community of Israel with Judaism is problematic. Not only can such a notion be used to justify any idea or deed, no matter how intellectually preposterous or morally abhorrent, by invoking the motto *vox populi vox Dei*, but it suggests that any current generation of Jews, no matter how distant they may be from Jewish life or learning, may collectively decide the nature of Judaism. When Jews lived in the culturally unified *kehillot* (Jewish communities) of

Europe and were immersed in Jewish life and learning, such a position might be defensible, but at present, when most are ignorant of Jewish thought and practice, its viability may be doubted.[20] Furthermore, to claim that the collective voice of the people determined the tradition is to endanger the possibility for authentic minority dissent. Indeed, the views of minority dissenters, like Maimonides and Rabbi Mendel of Kotzk, cannot be eliminated from Judaism simply because they do not hold views in accordance with the collective will of the Community of Israel. To adapt this position is potentially to threaten Jacobs' own understanding of Judaism as a multifaceted rather than a monolithic faith.

To replace the absolutism of fundamentalism with the absolutism of the *Volkgeist* merely transfers authority from presumed divine dictates to the presumed collective will of the people, discarding an objective standard for a subjective, socially determined one. Furthermore, revelation remains monologic, rather than dialogic. For the fundamentalist, revelation is a monologue of God to Israel. In this approach of Jacobs, revelation is a monologue of Israel to God.

Jacobs' claim that because the *mitzvot*, developed by the people of Israel, bring people to God, they must, therefore, be considered as if they were commanded by God, is not adequately defended. It does not necessarily follow that because revelation is a monologue of Israel to God that it is also a monologue of God to Israel.

Jacobs' claim that 'the *whole* of the Torah is *minhag*, custom' is similarly problematic.[21] There are certainly adequate grounds in classical Judaism to defend the claim that *minhag* is Torah, that the customs and traditions developed by the people may become integrated into the Torah (in the generic, expansive use of the term, that is, into the Tradition).[22] However, it does not follow that Torah in its entirety, that all of Jewish tradition, is the product of the creative energies of the Jewish people. A non-fundamentalist alternative position to Jacobs might argue for a *dialogic* view of revelation in which Judaism is understood to consist of an objective, divine element and a subjective, human one. To posit both objective and subjective elements within Judaism would provide a non-fundamentalist stance which would prevent Judaism from becoming a socially determined or personally idiosyncratic affair.[23]

Though he *implies* that modernity ought to serve as the standard by which to measure the viability of various beliefs and observances, that is certainly not Jacobs' view, as he has written: 'It is only an attitude of cynical expediency that justifies the ruthless pruning of challenging ideas by labeling them 'outmoded'. The yardstick to be employed is not that nebulous concept 'modern thought' but Jewish tradition itself'.[24]

Jacobs is not unaware of the difficulties inherent within his position, yet, like so many others who hold similar views, he persists in trying to attain the elusive synthesis of tradition and change.

Rabbinics

Because of their highly technical nature, Jacobs' studies in rabbinics have not received much attention.[25] These studies rest upon assumptions set down in his theological works. Only once biblical, rabbinic and Halakhic literature are assumed to have been a product of human literary creativity and historical development rather than a product of divine dictation, does critical analysis become possible. As Jacobs writes, 'The fact that the rabbis were interested mainly in discussing the word of God and applying it to the life of their people need not blind us to the recognition of the literary form and style of their greatest monument, the Babylonian Talmud'.[26]

Like other modern critical scholars of rabbinic literature, Jacobs rejects a 'fundamentalist' posture that equates the Talmudic text with verbatim reports of discussions that took place in the ancient rabbinical academies. Like Louis Ginzberg and Louis Finkelstein, Jacobs' early work examines the influence of economic factors on the development of rabbinic texts.[27] Like Jacob Neusner and David Weiss Halivni, Jacobs engages in careful analysis of rabbinic texts to reveal a process of literary development. However, unlike Neusner and his students, Jacobs does not focus on a form-critical approach (an approach of modern scholarship that compares textual versions of the same tradition), and unlike Weiss-Halivni, he does not primarily utilize the approach of 'redaction criticism'.[28] Rather, Jacobs forges his own unique approach that combines methods of traditional Talmudic study with modern scholarly methodologies.[29] What emerges is a preoccupation with the logic and the form of 'Talmudic argument' and how they have shaped the development of the Talmudic text. By examining the process of rabbinic thought and reasoning, Jacobs attempts to elucidate the nature of rabbinic thought as well as the literary structure of the Talmudic text.

In his early work, Jacobs deals with forms of logical argument found in rabbinic literature. Both building upon and sharply critiquing the views of earlier scholars such as Adolf Schwartz who wrote about Talmudic logic, Jacobs establishes that not only deductive logic, but inductive logic as well, was utilized by the Talmudic rabbis. Jacobs further demonstrates how various rabbinic forms of logic bear a resemblance to the Indian form of inference known as *kimpunar* as well as to forms of inference discussed by John Stuart Mill. In his examination of the Talmudic form of argument known as *sebhara*, Jacobs demonstrates its similarity to the modern Anglo-American notion of 'common sense', and by implication to the 'reasonable man' criterion of Anglo-American jurisprudence.[30]

In *The Talmudic Argument*, Jacobs builds on his earlier work and provides a comprehensive portrait of his views regarding the nature of rabbinic reasoning and the development of the Talmudic text. As in some of his theological works, particularly *Faith*, Jacobs utilizes ideas and tools for linguistic analysis drawn from the school of analytic philosophy. For example, in this work Jacobs refers to the notion of the use of language as a 'game', bound by certain rules, manoeuvres and boundaries. By learning the rules of the game, one can participate in it. By becoming attuned to the logic and mental processes of the Talmudic rabbis, one can begin to anticipate the development of their arguments, and one can have the 'uncanny sense' of participating in their debates that took place so long ago. The goal, therefore, is not only to understand the 'game', but to 'play' it. Thereby, the student of the rabbinic text becomes an active participant in an ongoing discussion initiated by the Talmudic rabbis, and by implication in the rabbinic activity of legal decision-making. For Jacobs, precisely because the Babylonian Talmud is the most significant and influential work of Jewish religious literature, being able to penetrate and to participate in the workings of the rabbinic mind provides an entrée into the most representative and formative variety of Jewish thinking.[31]

In *The Talmudic Argument*, Jacobs delineates various key forms of the rhetoric of rabbinic logic and argumentation. These are compared to possible moves on a chessboard. Knowing these moves allows the student of the Talmudic text to anticipate how a discussion on a particular subject (particularly of law) might unfold. Without such knowledge, the Talmud can remain a 'closed book'.

In *The Talmudic Argument* and in his earlier works on rabbinic rhetoric, Jacobs examines the structure of the Talmudic *sugya*, a literary unit of discussion on a particular topic. From such an analysis, Jacobs concludes that the Talmudic text is not, as others had suggested, a haphazard collection of claims, counterclaims and cited texts, but a tightly argued, coherent and carefully crafted literary unit in which argument and counter-argument, question and answer, affirmation and refutation cumulatively lead step by coherent step toward a climax, often with dramatic effect. For Jacobs, the *sugya* of the Babylonian Talmud is 'a contrived literary product of great skill, in which older material has been reshaped by methods bearing a close resemblance to those of literary artists throughout the ages'.[32] Hence, the Talmudic *sugya* employs various forms of logical inference akin to that used in contemporary scientific investigation. Acting as literary artists, its editors molded it into a literary work somewhat akin to a historically based mystery story in which clues merge with inferential logic to produce a dramatic climax in which a resolution to the problem at hand eventually emerges.

In the Babylonian Talmud, there are over 300 instances in which a debate ends with the term *Teyku*. According to traditional Talmudic scholarship, these are cases of legal disputes which are to be left unresolved until the eschatological future. In *Teyku*, Jacobs thoroughly and painstakingly examines instances of the use of the term in the Talmud, and concludes that it refers to an insolvable issue. Once more comparing Talmudic argument to a 'game', Jacobs compares arguments ending in *Teyku* to a draw or a stalemate in a game like soccer or chess. In such debates, each side produces arguments of equal force and weight, thereby achieving a perfect balance in which neither view presented can prevail over the other.[33] Thus, for Jacobs, in Talmudic argument and in Jewish law, as in theology, there are matters that cannot be resolved through human reasoning. There are matters that transcend human comprehension and analysis, about which one reaches an impasse, and more cannot be said.

Despite the elegance and insight characteristic of Jacobs' analysis of rabbinic literature, certain implications of his approach remain problematic. One of these relates to Jewish legal decision making today. If the Talmud is the foundational textual resource for Jewish legal decision making, and if Talmudic discussions of legal matters reflect a contrived literary text based upon edited academic reflections in the early rabbinic academies, how can such texts serve as the basis for decision making about concrete legal matters related to actual persons obeying legal dictates in their everyday life?[34] This, and related questions, lead to a review of Jacobs' writings about Jewish religious law (Halakhah).

Jewish Law

In Jacobs' *Theology in the Responsa* (1975) and *A Tree of Life* (1984), his preoccupation with theology, rabbinics and Jewish law converge.[35] Responsa constitutes the largest genre of Jewish literature, stretching back from our own times to the geonic period. In *Theology in the Responsa*, Jacobs mines major collections of responsa over the centuries, and identifies those that address theological issues. By nature and definition, responsa are individual rabbinic legal decisions, examples of Jewish 'case law'. Yet Jacobs marshals considerable evidence to demonstrate that the most prominent adjudicators of post-Talmudic Jewish law were preoccupied with theological as well as legal questions. This work offers an implicit polemic against the often-stated view that Judaism is only a religion of practice and law, devoid of theological speculation. Further, in his analysis of how leading Halakhists dealt with theological issues in their responsa, Jacobs demonstrates that they did so with the same seriousness and rigour with which they dealt with purely legal issues.

In *A Tree of Life*, Jacobs is both the academic scholar and the theologian. Here, Jacobs adduces massive evidence to demonstrate that classical Jewish religious literature in general, and Jewish legal literature in particular, always recognized the vital role of the human element in revelation, in the literary records of revelation, and in the ongoing process of Halakhic decision making. Jacobs thereby demonstrates that a non-fundamentalist approach is not a deviation from traditional views, but is deeply rooted conceptually and historically in the tradition. Consequently, Jacobs concludes that the fundamentalist view that he opposes – more than the non-fundamentalist posture that he affirms both historically and theologically – is a deviation from well-established, well-documented views deeply embedded within classical Jewish sources, including Halakhic literature. In *A Tree of Life*, Jacobs marshals a significant body of evidence that demonstrates that Halakhic decision making did not and should not develop according to an 'objective', almost mathematical internal dynamic, as Soloveichik and others maintain, but that subjective, social, economic and even local climactic factors played a crucial role throughout Jewish legal history in the process of Jewish legal decision making.[36]

For Jacobs, modern critical scholarship has reaffirmed 'beyond reasonable doubt' that Jewish law is a developing organism rather than a static, frozen body of inerrant truth that dropped intact from heaven; that Jewish law has always embodied creativity, flexibility and change; that extra-halakhic considerations and subjective factors always played a critical role in the process of Halakhic decision making. In Jacobs' view, modern scholarship has merely made explicit that which the great halakhists of the past both knew and practised: that Halakhah is a dynamic, living organism, open to change and development, lest it become fossilized, static and frozen into atrophy. As Jacobs felicitously puts it, Jewish law should not be like kosher ice-cream – 'frozen under rabbinic supervision'.[37]

Jacobs' scholarly investigation of Talmudic literature and of Jewish law flow from the stance that precipitated the 'Jacobs Affair': his attempt to combine tradition and modernity, classical and modern scholarship, his rejection of the view that both sacred texts and their traditional interpretations are inerrant, static, and verbatim representations of divine revelation or of discussions actually held in the ancient rabbinical academies. As in his theological writings on revelation, so in his articulation of his approach to Jewish law, Jacobs formulates a 'middle way' between alternative views. For Jacobs, the Halakhists of the past and the modern scholars of more recent times embraced a middle way between legal atrophy and anarchy, legal rigidity and precipitous alterations of long-standing precedent based solely on a surrender to contemporary social trends.

Jacobs considers as theologically inauthentic and historically inaccurate any stance that denies the binding quality of Jewish law. Though an integral part of Halakhic tradition, justified change must not be confused with change for the sake of change, change as a sop to modernity, or a tacit rejection of the theological or jurisprudential presuppositions upon which Jewish law is based. Consequently, Jacobs finds as inauthentic the position of Reform Judaism, and of increasing numbers of Conservative Jewish thinkers, who claim that Jewish law is no longer authoritative and binding. For Jacobs, the findings of modern scholarship neither suggest, nor should they lead to, the undermining of the very foundations of Jewish law. The purpose of scholarship is to elucidate the history and development of Jewish law, and not to serve as the only determining factor in the process of contemporary Halakhic decision making. What Jacobs recommends is a symbiosis between the products of historical scholarship and Halakhic decision making where the former proves relevant to, but not primarily determinative of, the latter. Historical scholarship is capable of elucidating the history and development of law, but is not capable of contemporary Halakhic decision making.

Halakhic decisors are capable of making Halakhic decisions, but are limited in such capabilities if they are bereft of an awareness of the products of scholarly research into the nature, history and development of Jewish law and jurisprudence. A symbiosis of the historical scholar and the traditional legal decisor would, in Jacobs' view, lead to decisions that are more in tune with the historical dynamic of Halakhic decision making. For Jacobs, unless and until such a rapprochement occurs, Jewish law will either atrophy into fossilization or will dissipate into anarchy. Unfortunately, because so very few can equal Jacobs' vast knowledge of both domains, the symbiosis he envisions, and that he himself represents, is not very likely to obtain.

Jacobs' goal is the preservation of the dynamic though binding nature of Jewish law which he sees as essential to the continuity of Judaism as an authentic yet developing religious faith. Consequently, he rejects both those who would fossilize Jewish law as well as those who would dispense with its authority and would promiscuously alter certain long-standing traditions. For Jacobs, changes in Jewish law are justified when such changes are necessary to make practice correlatve with Jewish theological and ethical claims. When law and practice are not in step with Jewish ethical values, a change in the law, within the process for change endemic to halakhic tradition, becomes both necessary and justifiable. For Jacobs, 'where the Halakhah, as it presently [or has been traditionally] practiced, results in the kind of injustice that reasonable persons would see as detrimental to Judaism itself, a frank avowal is called for that there must be changes in the law'.[38] This is especially true with regard to ethical issues. Where 'no amount of legal tampering will succeed in removing an injustice ... a radical change in the law becomes imperative'.[39] This position flows from a theological stance that maintains that the act, the record and the interpretation of the message contained in revelation contain a human element, and are therefore fallible and not inerrant.

If Halakhah can be considered a form of 'practical theology', as the articulation of theological claims as they translate into prescribed action, then the relationship between theological discourse and Halakhic decision making is critical. In Jacobs' view, the process of Halakhic decision making in the past and in the present presumes certain theological and ethical postures. Consequently, to paraphrase Einstein, Halakhah without theology and ethics is lame; theology and ethics without Halakhah are mute. There both has been, and needs to be, a continuity, a flow, a consistency between theological and ethical claims and particular Halakhic decisions.

It is unfortunate that Jacobs has not applied his approach to specific contemporary social and ethical issues. Though he does call for change in areas of Jewish law such as *mamzerut* (relating to the legal status of a child born of an adulterous or incestuous union) and *agunah* (the 'chained wife', unable to secure a divorce when abandoned by her husband), and though he acknowledges that Halakhic injustices are to be found in the area of women's rights, Jacobs has neither produced responsa of his own, nor articulated specific Halakhic statements on issues of individual status, women's rights, business ethics, ecology, bio-ethics or social ethics.[40] It is also unfortunate that a scholar and pedagogue of Jacobs' extraordinary prowess did not engender a 'Jacobs school' of proteges and students capable of continuing and elucidating his scholarship and his teachings.

Jewish Mysticism

Jacobs' vast knowledge of the intricacies of Jewish mystical thought and practice is clearly evident throughout his theological and popular writings. Though ideas rooted in Jewish mysticism were largely ignored or marginalized in nineteenth-and early twentieth-century Jewish theological discourse, especially in western Europe and America, Jacobs unabashedly re-infuses Jewish mystical teachings into consideration of the 'principles of the Jewish faith'.

Jacobs' studies of Jewish mysticism were mostly written when the views of Gershom Scholem and his students dominated the field. Though aware of the approach of the 'Scholem school', Jacobs remained largely uninfluenced by it, developing instead his own approach to Jewish mysticism in general and to Hasidism in particular. For example, unlike Scholem, Jacobs does not see Sabbatean influences behind every Hasidic tree. While Scholem put undue stress on the intellectual history of Jewish mystical ideas to the neglect of Jewish mystical experience, Jacobs pays substantial attention to varieties of Jewish mystical experience as well as to types of Jewish mystical theology. Indeed, some of Jacobs' insights have been reinforced by recent scholarship. Neither a practising Kabbalist nor an apologist for Hasidism, Jacobs' works elucidate and analyze aspects of Jewish mysticism and Hasidism often overlooked by others. It is not surprising, therefore, that a collection of Jacobs' studies on Hasidism is subtitled, 'Unfamiliar Aspects of Hasidism'.[41]

One of Jacobs' studies is *Seeker of Unity*.[42] Here, he carefully examines the life and works of Rabbi Aaron of Starosselje. A little-known Hasidic master, Rabbi Aaron was an unconventional, but highly sophisticated, speculative mystic, and a disciple of Schneur Zalman of Liady, the founder of Lubavitch Hasidism. *Seeker of Unity* provides evidence, contrary to the views of popularizers of Hasidism like Martin Buber, that Hasidism did produce mystical theology of a highly complex and intricate nature. Besides portraying the 'cerebral' side of Hasidism, Jacobs also offers to the reader of *Seeker of Unity* what is arguably the clearest statement in English of the Zoharic doctrine of the *sefirot* (divine emanations, effusions) and the Lurianic concept of *zimzum* (divine contraction).

In this study of Rabbi Aaron, Jacobs shows how one specific Jewish mystic dealt with the theosophical problem that is at the root of Kabbalistic theological speculation: how does one account for the existence of anything other than God; how does one account for the emergence of a finite universe from an infinite God? Hence, Rabbi Aaron's system, as elucidated by Jacobs, deserves a chapter in the long history of philosophical cosmology as well as in the history of Jewish mysticism.

Toward the end of *Seeker of Unity*, Jacobs turns to a discussion of 'practical mysticism', of the knowledge gained during the mystical experience. This concern pervades *Tract on Ecstasy* and *Hasidic Prayer*.[43]

A significant, though unfortunate, characteristic of Jewish mystical literature is the virtual absence of 'diaries' in which the mystic describes the forms and stages of rapture that he has experienced.[44] An exception is *Kuntras ha-Hitpa'alut* of Dov Baer of Lubavitch. Jacobs' *Tract on Ecstasy* is a masterful translation of this rare gem of Kabbalistic literature. Generously introduced and annotated, this work invites both scholar and layperson into a fascinating but largely unexplored area. For those in search of a particularly and authentically Jewish guide to meditation, this work should be required reading. In this vein, reference should be made to Jacobs' *Jewish Mystical Testimonies*.[45] A major compilation of felicitously translated and clearly explained primary sources, it provides a pervasive survey of the varieties of Jewish mystical experiences to be found in the scant literature of Jewish mystical biography and autobiography.

Just as mystical diaries are a rarity in kabbalistic literature, so is the notion of *unio mystica* – the union of the mystic with the divine. Though it is an essential feature of other mystical traditions, Scholem claimed that it is virtually absent in Jewish mysticism. Jacobs, however, in his Kabbalistic studies, demonstrates its presence in both theoretical and practical Jewish mysticism.[46] Here, Jacobs shows that there is a strand of Judaism which held that the demarcation between the divine and the human is not absolute.

From biblical theology, through medieval Jewish philosophy and anti-Christian polemics, a concerted effort was made to distinguish the divine from the human, God and humans. However, as Jacobs shows, late Jewish mystical speculation endeavoured to blur that distinction. The human soul, rather than being considered a creation of God, was perceived to be 'a part of God'.[47] Hence, the goal of mystical experience, as presented by Rabbi Aaron and by Dov Baer, was reunification of the divine soul within the human being with the divine source from which it emerged. In this view, the aim of prayer at its highest level is 'annihilation of the self' in order to achieve a level of rapture in which *unio mystica* is attained. Both Rabbi Aaron and Dov Baer offer a road map as to how that ultimate mystical experience may be achieved.

In *Hasidic Prayer*, Jacobs implicitly rebuts a commonly asserted claim that Judaism is a 'this-wordly' religion. He demonstrates that for the greatest revivalist movement which Judaism has produced – Hasidism – the ultimate goal of religious existence, specifically of prayer, is to forsake the world; to abandon the self; to affirm our empirical observations as being saturated with illusion; to consider our world an illusion in the mind of God; to seek union with the ultimate Reality, with the Divine.

Before concluding a discussion of Jacobs' writings on Jewish mysticism, one should note his masterful translation of one of the great classics of Kabbalistic pietica, Moses Cordevero's *Palm Tree of Deborah*.[48] While much scholarly attention has been paid to the moralistic writings of the Jewish philosophers, little effort has been expended upon elucidating the nature of the ethical notions that emerge from the theosophical speculation of leading Kabbalists. The translation of this ethical treatise by classical Kabbala's greatest systematic thinker is a welcome contribution. It is noteworthy that Jacobs applies some of Cordevero's ideas in his own popular discussions of Jewish ethics.[49]

Popular Works

Jacobs' writings move across a spectrum ranging from the academic to the popular, and to points in between. Because of his penchant for clarity, his gift for explaining the most complex ideas in an accessible manner, and the weighty subjects he addresses in works addressed to the non-specialist, it is often difficult to draw a precise line of distinction between his scholarly and his popular writings.

Though many scholars find it nearly impossible to explain difficult texts and ideas in a comprehensible manner, and though many popular writers can do little else but vulgarize and distort the sublime and the complex, Jacobs' literary and pedagogic skills provide his readers with 'popularization' in the best sense of the term. For Jacobs, the popular need not be 'beneath the concern of the serious'. 'It is in many ways harder to write a popular book with clarity than a learned one'.[50]

Jacobs' first four books, published between 1955 and 1959, are written for the non-specialist: *Jewish Prayer*, *A Guide to Yom Kippur*, *We Have Reason to Believe*, and *A Guide to Rosh Hashanah*.[51] *We Have Reason to Believe* is a popular yet serious exposition of contemporary theological concerns. The other three treat various aspects of prayer, repentance and liturgy. In *Jewish Values* and *Jewish Personal and Social Ethics*, Jacobs discusses Jewish ethical values and problems.[52] In *Jewish Belief* and *The Book of Jewish Practice*, Jacobs offers lucid basic introductions to Jewish religious beliefs and practices for those with little or no prior study or practice of Judaism.[53] In *What Does Judaism Say About … ?*, and in *Ask the Rabbi*, Jacobs applies his vast erudition in responding to an enormous variety of questions asked of him during his long rabbinic career.[54] In these works, he treats issues ranging from change-of-sex operations to extrasensory perception, from hijacking to hypnotism, from nudity to reincarnation. Ever the preacher and always the teacher, a selection of Jacobs' homilies and sermons delivered over a period extending almost six decades may be found in his collection, *Jewish Preaching*.[55]

Precision and conciseness are the hallmark of the ability to compose articles on complex topics for inclusion in encyclopedias. These abilities are evident in Jacobs' many articles included in a variety of encyclopedias, such as the *Encyclopedia Judaica and Encyclopedia of Religion*. A large collection of Jacobs' short articles for encyclopedias on a stunning array of topics relating to Judaism is represented by his *Oxford Companion to Jewish Religion*.[56] Though most encyclopedic works are written by a variety of scholars, this volume is unusual in that it is the work of a single scholar.

In 1968, Jacobs published *Jewish Law*, the first volume in the 'Chain of Tradition' series.[57] Other volumes are: *Jewish Ethics, Philosophy and Mysticism*, *Jewish Thought Today*, *Hasidic Thought*, and *Jewish Biblical Exegesis*.[58] Of the latter volume, Jacobs has said, it 'is one of the best things I have ever written'.[59] Each volume is an anthology of classical Jewish texts, translated into English and crisply explained. Each volume serves as a lucid introduction to both well-known and recondite texts drawn from the entire spectrum of Jewish religious literature. In these works, Jacobs' skill, not only as an expositor of classical Jewish texts but also as a translator, is vividly evident. In this regard, Jacobs' other translations of Jewish texts, particularly from the mystical and Hasidic traditions, bear mention. These include Moses Cordevero's treatise on Jewish ethics, *The Palm Tree of Deborah*, Dov Baer of Lubavitch's *Tract on Ecstasy*, and Zevi Hirsch Eichenstein's *Turn Aside From Evil, and Do Good*.[60] In his groundbreaking anthology, *Jewish Mystical Testimonies*, Jacobs offers a wealth of translated and explicated texts on various types of the Jewish mystical experience, demonstrating that besides producing a complex mystical theology, the Jewish mystics also engaged in the attainment of paranormal mystical experiences.

Conclusion

In advocating flexibility within a theological and legal structure rather than either anarchy or inelasticity, intellectual honesty rather than the unreflective idolatry of ancestor worship,[61] development rather than progressive evolution, Jacobs offers a refreshing modicum of uncertainty in arenas too often dominated – both in the religious and secular worlds, on both the 'right' and the 'left' – by an unjustified dogmatic certainty. For Jacobs, theology, mysticism, law and religion itself are an ongoing quest, not limited to a single thinker or to a single generation. For Jacobs, the greatest danger to the dynamic nature and the very continuity of Judaism as a living yet authentic faith is to call a halt to this quest. It is not surprising, therefore, that Jacobs is fond of citing Judah Loew of Prague's observation that the quest for Torah is itself Torah. In this view, as Jacobs himself puts it, 'to seek is already to have found'.[62]

Louis Jacobs' penchant for clarity, his passion for cogency, and his always startling erudition make both his scholarly and his popular works an inestimable intellectual adventure for the scholar as well as for the layperson. His unrivalled ability to confront honestly and forcefully the theological problems of our times provides contemporary Jewry with a 'guide to the perplexed'.

NOTES

1. Paul Lewis, 'Rabbi Jacobs Voted Britain's Greatest Jew', *Guardian*, 30 December 2005. www.guardian.co.uk/religion/story/0,2763,1675264.00.
2. On the 'Jacobs Affair', Chaim Bermant, *Troubled Eden* (New York: Basic Books, 1970), chap. 19; Ignaz Maybaum, 'The Jacobs Affair', *Judaism* 13 (1964): 471–77; Alfred Sherman, 'The Jacobs Affair', *Commentary* 38 (October 1964): 60–64; Sefton Temkin, 'A crisis in Anglo-Jewry', *Conservative Judaism* 18 (Fall 1963): 18–35. For Jacobs' reflections, see his autobiography, Louis Jacobs, *Helping with Inquiries* (London: Vallentine Mitchell, 1989), pp.134–79, 211–22.
3. Louis Jacobs, *A Jewish Theology* (New York: Behrman House, 1973), p.14.
4. Louis Jacobs, *God, Torah, Israel: Traditionalism without Fundamentalism* (Cincinnati: Hebrew Union College Press, 1990).
5. Louis Jacobs, *Beyond Reasonable Doubt* (London: Littman Library of Jewish Civilization, 1999), p.50.
6. *God, Torah, Israel*, p.viii.
7. Louis Jacobs, *We Have Reason to Believe* (London: Vallentine Mitchell, 1957); *Principles of the Jewish Faith* (New York: Basic Books, 1964).
8. Kaufmann Kohler, *Jewish Theology: Systematically and Historically Considered* (1918; 2nd ed., New York: Ktav, 1968).
9. Citations in this paragraph are from *A Jewish Theology*, pp.14–15.
10. Jacobs has been criticized for too readily accepting the findings of modern scholarship; see Paul Morris, 'The Quest for a Jewish Theology and a Non-Fundamentalist Halakhah', in Dan Cohn-Sherbok (ed.), *A Traditional Quest: Essays in Honour of Louis Jacobs* (Sheffield: Sheffield Academic Press, 1991, pp.194–217, but such criticisms may be too harsh. For example, in *We Have Reason to Believe*, p.143, he writes: 'Scholarship can provide us with the

facts. It can inform us of what actually happened in the past. Our interpretation of the[se] facts will depend on large measure on our general attitude toward life'.

11. Louis Jacobs, *Faith* (New York: Basic Books, 1968).
12. For Jacobs' views on revelation and observance of Jewish law, *Principles of the Jewish Faith*, pp.289–301; *A Jewish Theology*, pp.199–230.
13. *Sabbath* 112b.
14. *A Jewish Theology*, p.202. Unfortunately, Jacobs limits his discussion of 'progressive revelation' to the articulation of that position embraced by classical Reform Judaism.
15. *A Jewish Theology*, p.203.
16. Ibid., p.214.
17. See the discussions and sources noted in Abraham J. Heschel, *Torah min ha-Shamayim*, vol. 2 (London: Soncino, 1965), pp.282–85.
18. *A Jewish Theology*, pp.226–30.
19. For an analysis of some of these difficulties, see e.g., Menahem Kellner, 'Louis Jacobs' Doctrine of Revelation', *Tradition* 14 (Fall 1974): 143–48.
20. Jacobs' position in this regard approximates Solomon Schechter's notion of 'Catholic Israel', which was formulated when the majority of Jews were observant. This concept was offered as an alternative to the innovations made by Reform rabbinic synods and to the Orthodox claim that the *Shulhan Arukh* legal code was the ultimate Halakhic authority. To assert this position at a time when the majority of Jews is not committed to Jewish religious life and practice is problematic for Schechter as well as for Jacobs. In *Principles of the Jewish Faith*, Jacobs himself notes the difficulties of this view. For example, at the time of Elijah, when most Jews worshipped the pagan god Baal and only the minority worshipped God, Baalism might have been said to represent the collective will of the community of Israel or Catholic Israel (p.297). To affirm this notion today, when the majority of Jews do not observe the Sabbath and the dietary laws, would imply that such observance is no longer part of Judaism as it does not express the collective will of the Jewish people. Jacobs might have considered attempts to reformulate Schechter's notion, such as that proposed by Robert Gordis, for whom Catholic Israel might be defined as referring, not to all Jews, but only to the majority or consensus of those Jews concerned with Jewish religious tradition and committed to its observance. See Robert Gordis in *Proceedings of the Rabbinical Assembly* (1942) and his *Judaism for the Modern Age*, (New York: Farrar, Straus, Cudahy, 1955), pp.166–86. For individuals such as Gordis and Jacobs who identify with Conservative Judaism, this redefinition is also problematic, for, if Catholic Israel is so defined, Orthodoxy might justifiably claim that it is Catholic Israel and that it should determine what Judaism is. One might suggest, however, that Catholic Israel might be usefully construed to denote not the collective will of the people of Israel or of committed Jews, but of the social factor in the development of Judaism; that is, not the sole factor, but one of a number of factors in determining Jewish belief and practice at a given time and place. See above, chap. 7.
21. *A Jewish Theology*, p.224.
22. See the statements of Jacob Mollin (Maharil) and Judah Loew of Prague (Maharal), 'The custom of our forefathers is Torah' (*minhag avoteinu torah hu*); Joseph Karo's *Shulhan Arukh* (Vilna: Romm, 1911), sec. *Yoreh Deah* 376:4 (Moses Isserles quoting Mollin in his gloss), and Judah Loew, *Netivot Olom* (New York: Judaica Press, 1969), sec. *Netiv ha-Torah*, chap. 7. On the role of custom in Jewish jurisprudence, see also chap. 7 above.
23. See chap. 7 above, and, Robert Gordis, *A Faith for Moderns* (New York: Bloch Publishing, 1960), pp.130–59. Jacobs defends the retention of institutions developed in Jewish history by the people which bring holiness to people's lives, such as the Sabbath and other holy days. But he finds their significance in socio-historical development. Similarly, Jacobs identifies certain 'interpretive beliefs' that do not change and that thereby ensure the continuity of Judaism; see Jacobs, *Principles of the Jewish Faith*, pp.271–72, 459–62, 'Faith', in Arthur Cohen and Paul Mendes-Flohr (eds), *Contemporary Jewish Religious Thought* (New York: Scribner's, 1987), pp.235–38. But here too, these significant theological essentials of Judaism are understood to be solely the product of Jewish historical and sociological development.
24. *Jewish Values* (London: Vallentine Mitchell, 1960), pp.9–10.
25. *Studies in Talmudic Logic and Methodology* (London: Vallentine Mitchell, 1961); 'Are There Fictitious Baraitot in the Babylonian Talmud?', *Hebrew Union College Annual* 42 (1971): 185–97; 'The Talmudic Sugya as a Literary Unit', *Journal of Jewish Studies* 34

(1973): 119–27; 'A Study of Four Parallel Sugyot', *Journal of Jewish Studies* 25 (1974): 389–411; 'How Much of the Babylonian Talmud is Pseudepigraphic', *Journal of Jewish Studies* 28 (1977): 46–60; *The Talmudic Argument* (London: Cambridge University Press, 1984).
26. *Studies in Talmudic Logic and Methodology*, p.69.
27. 'The Economic Situation of the Jews in Babylonia' [in Hebrew], *Melila* 5 (1955): 83–100; 'The Economic Conditions of the Jews in Babylonia in Talmudic Times Compared with Palestine', *Journal of Semitic Studies* (1957): 349–59.
28. For a discussion of these and related methodologies, Catherine Hezser, 'Classical Rabbinic Literature', in Martin Goodman (ed.), *The Oxford Handbook of Jewish Studies* (New York: Oxford University Press, 2002), pp.114–40.
29. *Helping with Inquiries*, p.80.
30. *Studies in Talmudic Logic and Methodologies.*
31. *The Talmudic Argument*, p.206.
32. *Studies in Talmudic Logic and Methodologies*, p.viii.
33. *Teyku: The Unsolved Problem in the Babylonian Talmud* (London: Cornwall Books, 1981), p.301.
34. Jacobs is not unaware of this problem; see *A Tree of Life* (New York: Oxford University Press, 1984), p.29.
35. *Theology in the Responsa* (London: Routledge and Kegan Paul, 1975. See also Jacobs' comment in his *Helping with Inquiries*, p.257.
36. *Tree of Life*, pp.14–15, 60–1.
37. *Helping with Inquiries*, p.70.
38. *Tree of Life*, p.236.
39. Ibid., p.236.
40. Jacobs deals with issues of *mamzerut* in *A Tree of Life*, pp.257–75, and mentions the problem of the *agunah* and women's rights in *A Jewish Theology*, pp.228–30. Jacobs' hesitancy to deal with such specific problems, some of which are addressed tersely in his popular works such as *What Does Judaism Say About ...?* (New York: Quardrangle Books, 1973), may be based upon his view that focusing upon specifics would deflect attention from the larger theological issues that underlie them. Jacobs also expresses his apprehension about ascribing views that to earlier traditions they could not possibly have held by applying 'artificial' contemporary categories upon a reading of classical texts. See *Judaism and Theology* (London: Vallentine Mitchell, 2005), p.82, where Jacobs writes: 'The task of the historian of Jewish ideas and rituals is to try to collate stray references in diverse sources, produced over lengthy periods of time, so as to produce some kind of systematic picture, being fully aware that in the very process he is imposing categories not really present in the sources'. See also pp.154–5, where Jacobs observes: 'Our topic [is it permissible to pray for the downfall of the wicked] provides as good an example as any of how precarious it is to speak of *the* Jewish attitude to complicated moral, ethical and religious problems, as if there were only one attitude, especially where powerful emotions are engaged and where both the cultural background and individual temperament have their influence on the opinions of even the most determinedly objective thinkers'.
41. *Their Heads in Heaven* (London: Vallentine Mitchell, 2005).
42. *Seeker of Unity* (New York: Basic Books, 1966).
43. *Tract on Ecstasy* (London: Vallentine Mitchell, 1963); *Hasidic Prayer* (New York: Schocken, 1973).
44. Gershom Scholem, *Major Trends in Jewish Mysticism* (New York: Schocken, 1941), p.121.
45. *Jewish Mystical Testimonies* (New York: Schocken, 1977).
46. Scholem, *Major Trends*, p.5.
47. *Judaism and Universalism* (London: Routledge and Kegan Paul, 1966), pp.87–115.
48. Moses Cordevero, *Palm Tree of Deborah*, trans. Louis Jacobs (London: Vallentine Mitchell, 1960).
49. *Jewish Values*, p.121.
50. *We Have Reason to Believe*, p.151.
51. *Jewish Prayer* (London: Jewish Chronicle, 1955); *A Guide to Yom Kippur* (London: Jewish Chronicle, 1957); *A Guide to Rosh Hashanah* (London: Jewish Chronicle, 1959).
52. *Jewish Personal and Social Ethics* (West Orange, NJ: Behrman House, 1990).
53. *Jewish Belief* (New York: Behrman House, 1984); *The Book of Jewish Practice* (New York: Behrman House, 1987).

54. *Ask the Rabbi* (London: Vallentine Mitchell, 1999).
55. *Jewish Preaching* (London: Vallentine Mitchell, 2004).
56. *The Jewish Religion: A Companion* (New York: Oxford University Press, 1995).
57. *Jewish Law* (New York: Behrman House, 1969).
58. Louis Jacobs, *Jewish Ethics, Philosophy and Mysticism* (New York: Behrman House, 1969); *Jewish Thought Today* (New York: Behrman House, 1970); *Jewish Biblical Exegesis* (New York: Behrman House, 1973); *Hasidic Thought* (New York: Behrman House, 1977).
59. *Helping with Inquiries*, p.260.
60. Zevi Hirsch Eichenstein, *Turn Aside From Evil and Do Good*, trans. Louis Jacobs (London: Littman Library of Jewish Civilization, 1995).
61. On this form of 'ancestor worship' as 'idolatry', see *A Tree of Life*, p.246.
62. 'Faith', p.238.

Jewish Theology in America

There is an old quip that compares the theological quest to a blind person entering a darkened room to look for a black cat that is not there. Throughout most of its history, American Jewry has adapted a similar attitude toward Jewish theology. Ignored at best, deemed irrelevant or divisive at worst, theological thinking has never been a priority item on the American Jewish communal agenda.

American Jewry has expressed its largesse in many ways, but the training and support of Jewish theologians has not been one of them. Until recently, even Jewish theological seminaries in the United States have been exceedingly lax in teaching Jewish theology or in training Jewish theologians. If the presence of trained theologians is a precondition for the production of theology, then their absence would seem to preclude the very existence of an American Jewish theology.[1] Yet American Jewish theology has developed in spite of, rather than because of, the interest or support of American Jewry.

According to the British Jewish theologian, Louis Jacobs, Jewish theology may be defined as 'an attempt to think through consistently the implications of the Jewish religion'.[2] Yet American Jewry has resisted such attempts for many reasons; one is because Americans tend to embrace practical action and pragmatism, often neglecting and indeed opposing doctrinal or ideological discourse. If Americans are basically activists, pragmatic and a-theological, then American Jews are too, but even more so. American Jews have tended to understand Judaism as a religion primarily concerned with doing things rather than thinking things, as a religion of action rather than doctrine, as an ethnic commitment rather than adherence to a transcendent faith.[3] Another reason why American Jewry has resisted attempts to develop an American Jewish theology is because American Jews tend to be secular. Indeed, they tend to be more secular than other Americans. Obviously, the more secular a community, the less likely it is to be concerned with theological thinking.

Though Americans tend to be activist and pragmatic, though they may be a-theological in the sense of not being very engaged in theological discourse, Americans nonetheless are a religious people. Almost from its inception, the United States has been described as a 'nation with the soul of a church'. In the landmark 1962 US Supreme Court case of Zorach v. Clausen, Justice William Douglas, in his majority opinion, wrote, 'We are a religious people whose institutions presuppose a Supreme Being'. Public opinion polls have regularly affirmed a high level of religious faith and commitment among Americans. The same studies have consistently found that the percentage of Jews who believe in God, who pray, and who affirm religious doctrines such as belief in an afterlife, is substantially lower than among other groups of Americans. Sociological studies confirm that American Jews, for the most part, are more secularized than other groups of Americans.

Observers of American Jewry have pointed out that the persecution of European Jews in generations past by religious (Christian) ideologies has embedded a fear of all religious doctrines among American Jews, including fear of their own religion. In this view, the secularity of American Jewry both reflects and articulates this fear of faith, this apprehension about the potentially oppressive nature of theological doctrines. In this view, American Jewry perceives secularism as a safe harbour against the dangers of the potentiality of religious coercion and oppression, even by one's fellow Jews. It sees religious belief as a threat to its own freedom and security.

Sociological studies and opinion polls consistently reveal that American Jews are more tenuous in their belief in God than other Americans. There is a higher proportion of agnostics or atheists among American Jews than among other groups of Americans. American Jews increasingly tend to pray less regularly than other Americans. Furthermore, faith in God does not play a major role in either Jewish identity or in Jewish communal activity. As sociologist Steven Cohen put it, 'American Jews are among the most religiously inactive, the most theologically skeptical, in short, the most secular [group in America]'.[4]

In 1967, sociologist Robert Bellah published his seminal essay on the American 'civil religion'. According to Bellah, besides various forms of denominational religious faith, Americans also embrace a common 'civil religion' with certain fundamental beliefs, values, holidays and rituals.[5] In 1986, Jonathan Woocher extended Bellah's insight to American Jewry by formulating and examining 'the civil religion of American Jews'. While Bellah found that belief in God plays a central role in American civil religion, Woocher found that it plays a 'thoroughly insignificant role in the civil religion of American Jews ... [The civil religion of American Jews] is a-theological – not atheistic – religion'.[6] Indeed, the God-idea is perceived as a cause for potential divisiveness among American Jews who embrace a substantial diversity of views on the subject, ranging from intransigent atheism to fervent religious faith.

Rejecting or ignoring traditional Jewish theological affirmations, the civil religion of American Jews had to posit an alternative basis for Jewish belief, identity, ethics and communal life. According to Woocher, the fundamental 'dogma' of the civil religion of American Jewry became 'Jewish survival'. The biological survival of the Jewish people became the ideological foundation for Jewish communal life in America. In this regard, the classical profession of Jewish religious faith of the *Shema* ('Hear O Israel, the Lord is our God, the Lord is One', Deut. 6:4) was replaced with the old Zionist slogan, 'We [the Jewish people] are one'. The people of Israel replaced the God of Israel as the foundation upon which Jewish existence was based. Particularly in the last decades of the twentieth century, the doctrine of Jewish survival became the prime directive and basic 'dogma' of Jewish communal life.[7]

The civil religion of American Jewry sought not only to supplement but to supplant Jewish religious thought. The civil religion introduced its own rituals, like the Jewish Federation fund-raising dinner, to articulate its various dogmas – foremost, Jewish survival. The dogma of Jewish survival evaluated various aspects of Jewish life as being worthwhile in terms of whether or not they were perceived as furthering the goal of Jewish biological survival. Classical Judaism, on the other hand, considers God and service to God to be ultimate, and the survival of the Jewish people as a means to that end.

The neglect of, opposition to, and marginalization of Jewish theological concerns precipitated the inception of alternative secular 'faiths' to Judaism. For many Jews, these were one or more of the 'isms' of the twentieth century (socialism, communism, humanism, rationalism), or one or more of the substitute 'Jewish' faiths, like Jewish nationalism. Louis Jacobs identifies three such substitute Jewish faiths: the worship of the Jewish people rather than the exclusive worship of God; making Jewish survival the ultimate goal of Jewish existence rather than the service of God; replacing the Torah with Jewish culture. These three approaches exclude the need for a Jewish theology.[8]

At the beginning of the twentieth century, no less a figure than Theodore Roosevelt proclaimed that no real American could be a hyphenated American. However, by the late 1960s and early 1970s, Americans began to proudly identify themselves as hyphenated Americans, through their ethnicity. The earlier 'melting pot' vision of America had been replaced by an understanding of the United States as a mosaic of diverse ethnic groups. The predominance of Jewish self-understanding primarily in ethnic terms served to further marginalize Jewish theological concerns.

The consolidation of Jewish communal power by Jewish Federations in the late 1960s and 1970s gave the civil religion of American Jews a position of centrality and authority in Jewish communal life. A prominent dogma of American civil religion, closely connected to Jewish survivalism, became the Holocaust-Israel, death-rebirth idea. This motif of death and resurrection, so reminiscent of Christian belief, demonstrated how the awareness of a certain understanding of the nexus between the Holocaust and the existence of the State of Israel had become a fundamental feature of American Jewish identity.[9]

Awareness of the Holocaust explains why Jewish biological survival had now become the prime directive for Jewish existence. Israel became the symbol of Jewish survival and the antidote to threats to Jewish survival. Jewish powerlessness was considered a condition that permitted anti-Semitism and the Holocaust to occur. Jewish power, the military power of Israel and the political power of American Jewry, was now considered to be the primary tool for helping to ensure Jewish survival. Consequently, political activity and fundraising on behalf of Israel became central 'sacred' activities according to the civil religion of American Jews.

Unlike other American ethnic groups that had deep emotional

ties with their countries of origin, American Jews viewed the countries from which they emigrated to America through unpleasant memories of oppression and anti-Semitism. American Jews adopted Israel as their homeland, rather than the native lands of their immigrant forebears. Israel became the foundation not only for the Jewish identity of American Jews, it also became a foundation, of their faith. Commitment to the dogmas of the civil religion of American Jews replaced classical Jewish theological beliefs for many American Jews, both secular and religious.

The Judaism of American Jewry was further recast so as to become consonant with the ideals and teachings of American political liberalism. As Steven Cohen has written:

> For many American Jews, politics – in particular pro-Israel and liberal activity – have come to constitute their principal working definition of Jewishness. In this sense modern Jewish political movements have served as functional alternatives to conventional religion ... Many American Jews were raised with the understanding that liberalism or political radicalism constituted the very essence of Judaism, that all the rest – the rituals, liturgy, communal organizations – were outdated, vestigial trappings for a religion with a great moral and political message embodied in liberalism.[10]

The publication of the *1990 National Jewish Population Study* sent a seismic tremor throughout the 'organized' Jewish community. This study showed that Jewish identity along ethnic lines, Jewish secularization, intermarriage, and the loss of Jews to Judaism through formal conversion to another religion, had severely diminished the number of American Jews professing Jewish religious faith of any variety. The strategy of Jewish survivalism clearly had failed in helping to ensure the survival of Jews as Jews, especially the survival of Jews as adherents to Judaism.

As the twenty-first century dawned, studies of American Jewry found that concern for and commitment to Israel was not as robust as it was assumed to be or as it actually had been in the 1970s. A decline of Jewish liberalism and social action as central determinants of Jewish self-identity was also found to be the case. Demographers began to predict that as the new century unfolds, the majority of

Americans of Jewish lineage would be practising a religion other than Judaism, or no religion at all. However, as Jews increasingly began to identify themselves in religious rather than ethnic categories, by spiritual rather than secular criteria, a hospitable environment for Jewish theological thinking began to develop. As the dogmas of the civil religion of American Jews began to lose their grip, and as Jews began to look to the intellectual and spiritual resources of their tradition as a source of wisdom, personal meaning and Jewish identity, the long-standing marginalization of Jewish theology promised to come to an end. Many Jews now began to ask: What is Judaism? What is Jewish faith? What does Judaism believe? What does Judaism teach about God, the meaning of life, life after death? These were precisely the kinds of questions with which theologians are concerned. Writing in 1994, Arthur Green observed that 'the Jewish people is ready for theology, needs it urgently ... Indeed thinking about our own Jewishness is precisely what we Jews need most to do ... We need to define our goals for the continuity of Jewish life. What do we mean by a Jewish future in America?'[11]

Despite the neglect and the marginalization of American Jewish theology for many years, and despite attempts to suppress Jewish theological thinking and writing when it challenged the secular assumptions, the Jewish communal agenda and the civil religion of American Jewish communal life, a long-standing tradition of American Jewish theology exists.

'Denominational' Jewish Theology

Five distinct trends in the history of American Jewish theology may be identified. The first is intra- and inter-'denominational' Jewish theology. Various studies of American Jewish theology focus exclusively upon certain individual Jewish thinkers but neglect theological discussion both within and across 'denominational' lines. American Jewish theology begins with the attempts of Reform Jewish theologians not only to define and to clarify the nature of Judaism, but to define and clarify the nature of American Judaism. The issues that preoccupied Reform Judaism in America as it developed were not only social and demographic, but were profoundly theological. They were not only matters of liturgy and ritual, but matters of theology. Indeed, changing theological perspectives in American Reform Judaism, as represented by its various 'platforms' (especially,

1885, 1937 and 1999), had a direct impact on the role of liturgy, ritual, ethics and observance within that movement.

As Conservative Judaism emerged in America in the early decades of the twentieth century, it became increasingly clear that the differences between Conservative and Reform Judaism were not simply sociological or demographic, but theological as well. As Orthodox Judaism experienced a resurgence in the post-World War II period, the three movements – Reform, Conservative and Orthodox – could be distinguished, not only on the basis of differences in religious practice, but also on the basis of visceral theological claims. While individual Jewish theologians produced works that were mostly read by an intellectual elite, and therefore have had a circumscribed impact, the theological discussions within and across 'denominational' lines undoubtedly have had a direct impact upon the extensive professional and lay constituencies of the movements that largely represent American Judaism.

Kaufmann Kohler, who played a central role in the development of Reform Judaism in the late nineteenth century and in the first decades of the twentieth century, may be considered the first significant American Jewish theologian. Kohler (1843–1926) was a German rabbi who arrived in the United States in 1869. After serving a number of congregations, he was appointed president of Hebrew Union College in 1903. At that time, Reform Judaism was the dominant form of American Judaism. For Kohler, Reform was not a movement within American Judaism; rather, it was Judaism in its most highly evolved and contemporary aspect.

In 1918, Kohler published *Jewish Theology*. A bold pioneering effort, this was the first systematic work on Jewish theology in the English language.[12] Kohler locates the essence of Judaism in the ethical monotheism of the biblical prophets, rather than in what he considered to be the legal particularism of the Talmudic and medieval rabbis. From this perspective, the mission of the people of Israel is to preserve and perpetuate the ethical message of the prophets until the time when it can become the unifying basis of a religion for all of humankind. Kohler's presentation of a socially and intellectually 'progressive', universalist, ethical (that is, non-legal), aggressively optimistic (that is, evil really does not exist) portrait of Judaism is paradigmatic of early twentieth-century American Reform Judaism. So is his rejection of Zionist aspirations. It is not surprising that the theological posture Kohler adapts in his lengthy *Jewish Theology* is an expansion of the views he succinctly set down in his proposed draft in the 1880s of the Pittsburgh Platform. In 1885, leaders of Reform Judaism largely adapted Kohler's draft as the defining statement of American Reform Judaism. To the seven 'planks' of the Pittsburgh Platform, basically drafted by Kohler, an eighth was added, affirming liberal political progressivism and calling for an active programme of social reform. The Pittsburgh Platform represents a precise statement of views on a wide variety of theological issues, including the nature of God, the nature of the Torah, the mission of the people of Israel, the afterlife, the Messianic Era, and the relationship of Judaism to other religions.[13]

The adaption in 1937 of the Columbus Platform by Reform Judaism represented not only a shift in policy, but a change in theology from the positions represented by the Pittsburgh Platform. As Kohler was the major force behind the Pittsburgh Platform, another significant Reform Jewish theologian, Samuel S. Cohon (1888–1959), was the primary author of the Columbus Platform. As Professor of Jewish Theology at Hebrew Union College for over three decades, Cohon played a decisive role in the shaping of Reform Jewish theology.

Cohon articulates his theology in a number of significant books and scores of articles. His never-completed *Jewish Theology* was published posthumously in 1971, as was a collection of his *Essays in Jewish Theology* (1986). In these works, Cohon's erudition and academic depth are clearly evident. However, because of his desire to inform and influence the layperson as well as the scholar, Cohon also wrote a number of more accessible books on Jewish belief and practice such as *Judaism: A Way of Life* (1948) and *What Jews Believe* (1971), first published in serial form in *The Jewish Layman* in 1930–31.

Unlike Kohler, Cohon does not begin his theology with general theological principles, but with the religious consciousness of the individual, specifically with the personal experience of the sacred. This encounter with the holy was, for Cohon, the basis of all religion. According to Cohon, Judaism shaped this primal religious experience into its own unique forms, symbols, values, beliefs and rituals. Unlike Kohler, Cohon had a positive view of Jewish particularism, Hebrew language, Jewish mysticism, religious observance, and Zionism.

Many of these views are embedded in the 1937 Columbus Platform.[14]

From its inception, Conservative Judaism resisted a clear and precise statement of its teachings. Indeed, it was not until 1988 when *Emet Ve-Emunah: Statement of Principles of Conservative Judaism* was published, that the Conservative movement issued a statement of its theological beliefs and principles.[15]

Though not a systematic theologian (like Kohler) or the author of a Jewish theology for the contemporary American Jew (like Cohon), Solomon Schechter (1849–1915), the 'father' of Conservative Judaism in America, did address Jewish theological issues throughout his many published works. Both implicitly and explicitly, Schechter polemicized against the views of Reform, particularly those represented in the Pittsburgh Platform. Schechter also formulated and articulated theological positions that would serve as the ideological foundation for Conservative Judaism, particularly in America.[16]

By 1999, when Reform Judaism in America adapted the second Pittsburgh Platform, most of the ideological and theological differences between Reform and Conservative Judaism that had existed in the days of Kohler and Schechter had been resolved, and were now passé. Because of this rapprochement, the 1999 Pittsburgh Platform was dubbed 'Conservative lite' by various observers. The process whereby Reform moved toward the Conservatives had already begun with the Columbus Platform. Meanwhile, the Conservative movement had been moving, in many ways, toward Reform.

Like early American Reform, early Conservative Judaism operated on the premise that it would eventually emerge as the dominant form of American Judaism. It was expected that Orthodoxy was too linked to European Jewry to survive in America beyond an immigrant generation. Reform, it was believed, would dissipate through the inevitable assimilation and secularization of its constituency. However, these beliefs proved incorrect. By the post-World War II period, three Jewish religious groups – Reform, Conservative and Orthodox – rather than one, characterized American Judaism. Like Christian denominations that distinguished themselves from others by theological stances, liturgy and religious practice, each of the three Jewish 'denominations' was obliged to do likewise. Though various theological issues divided the three movements, in none has their differences been more pronounced than in their views of divine revelation and religious authority.

Many Orthodox Jews maintain that there is no Jewish theology, that Judaism is essentially a system of religious law. However, underlying this claim is a theological presupposition that differentiates Orthodoxy from other contemporary forms of Judaism. That theological presupposition, called *Torah min ha-shamayim* ('Torah from Heaven') in classical Hebrew, asserts that the Torah has been directly revealed by God in its present form to the people of Israel, and that its contents are therefore inerrant. Revelation is viewed as a monologue of God to Israel. The role of the Jewish people is obedience to the word of God as found in the Torah and as interpreted by ongoing authoritative rabbinic tradition. This view of revelation and authority stands in sharp contrast to the views of non-Orthodox American Jewry.

For Schechter, there is both revelation to Israel and revelation through Israel. God's word and God's will become manifest through and within *Kelal Yisrael*, which Schechter translates (following Isaac Leeser) as 'Catholic Israel'. In this view, revelation is more of a dialogue with God than a monologue of God. Judaism is more of a creation of the interaction of the people of Israel with the revealed word of God than a system of divinely given dictates. For Schechter, the Jewish people is the final authority in determining the nature of Judaism. Historical research can determine which beliefs, practices and institutions have been and continue to be essential to Judaism.

Though oversimplified here, Schechter's view on revelation and authority represents early Conservative Judaism, contrasted not only with that of Orthodoxy but also with that of Reform. Throughout the history of Reform Judaism, first in Europe and then in America, the Kantian idea of individual autonomy served as the basis for religious and moral decision-making. In more recent Reform, individual autonomy and the authority of the tradition remain in a constant state of tension, as Eugene Borowitz has discussed in considerable detail.[17]

The classical Reform view of 'progressive revelation', influenced by Hegelian philosophy, claimed that as history unfolds, human beings automatically move to a higher perception of truth than previously.

The current generation, in this view, knows more than any previous generation, and consequently has the knowledge and hence the authority to reform the teachings of past traditions. Orthodoxy took the opposite view of revelation, identifying the revelation at Sinai as the apogee of revealed truth. From this perspective, the more chronologically proximate a religious authority is to Sinai, the greater his authority. Conservative Judaism embraced the idea of continuous revelation, where the revelation of the divine will continues through *Kelal Yisrael*, the community of Israel.

These approaches to revelation directly influenced each of the movements' philosophies of Jewish law. For Reform, the law (Halakhah) is no longer binding and authoritative. For Conservative Judaism, the law remains binding but is subject to change based upon certain historical and other meta-Halakhic considerations, such as the ethical principles of Judaism as well as certain socio-economic conditions. For Orthodoxy, not only is the law binding, but the last authoritative code of Jewish law, the ***Shulhan Arukh***, representing the quintessence of the Jewish legal tradition, is binding as well. Since the greater scholars dwelt in the past rather than in the present, change is discouraged. Halakhic alterations are viewed as 'deviationist'.[18]

The Reform notion of 'progressive revelation' is predicated on ideas rooted in the European Enlightenment: unbridled optimism (things are getting progressively better), individual autonomy, rationalism (since that which is rational is that which is true, and Judaism is true, Judaism can be defined and shaped only by that which is rational) and universalism. However, as the horrors of the twentieth century, particularly the Holocaust, became evident, Jewish theologians in America, including Reform theologians, began to back away from the founding assumptions that had animated liberal Judaism since the Enlightenment. The combination of the naive optimism characteristic of American culture coupled with the unrestrained optimistic tenor of Enlightenment thought was shattered by a confrontation with the effects of two world wars, the Depression, and the post-World War II threat of nuclear annihilation. American Jewish theologians confronted the grim realities of history by breaking with the presuppositions of Enlightenment thought that had been incorporated into earlier American Jewish theology.

The Existentialists

In the post-World War II era, American Jewish theologians began to formulate new approaches to understanding the nature of Jewish faith and to understanding the particular nature of American Judaism.[19] Until the 1950s, American Jewish theology was largely confined to intra- and inter-denominational thinking and writing. Few works of a Jewish theological nature had been produced by individual thinkers. However, the 1950s began with a salvo of works on Jewish theology. The authors, of these works, such as Will Herberg (1901–1977) and Abraham Joshua Heschel (1907–1972), were different in many ways. What they shared was an existentialist approach to thinking Judaism through.[20] It may be suggested that Jewish existentialist theology constitutes a second trend in the development of American Jewish theology. Though some American Jewish existentialist theologians were affiliated with one of the movements of American Judaism, their thought is not especially 'denominationally' oriented.

American Jewish existentialist theologians shifted the focus, agenda and presuppositions of American Jewish theology. Rather than initiating theological discourse by stating principles of religious belief, or by defining the 'essence' of Judaism, the existentialists began with questions about the meaning of human life and Jewish existence. This approach took a more positive view of past Jewish intellectual and theological tradition and of Jewish historical experience than had previously been the case in American Jewish theology. Earlier modern Jewish thought tended to subordinate classical Jewish literature, especially Talmudic and Kabbalistic literature, to modern European philosophy and to science. The Jewish existentialists, on the other hand, sought to articulate an 'authentic' Judaism, rooted in classical Jewish religious sources and ideas. For Abraham Heschel, for example, basic questions confronting Jewish religious thought are: What characterizes authentic Jewish thinking? What is *Jewish* about Jewish theology? Heschel maintained that Judaism is a way of thinking as well as a way of living, and that Jewish thinking is characterized by uniquely Jewish categories that are radically different from those of western philosophy. Furthermore, for Heschel and others, only an authentically Jewish way of thinking can serve as the basis for an authentically Jewish way of living. Thus, theological affirmations articulate themselves as a lifestyle. In this view, Judaism is a personal and existential commitment that is verified or refuted not by philosophical argument, but by one's lifestyle. The goal is to live out the beliefs that one affirms.

The Jewish existentialist theologians rejected the unbridled optimism, secularism, rationalism, acquiescence to science and technology, and other ideas drawn from Enlightenment thinking that had dominated earlier American Jewish life and thought. In their view, recent history, especially the two world wars, the Holocaust and the terrors of Stalinism, had adequately demonstrated the failures of the various secular 'isms' that had been pervasive in their times. No longer were rationalism or humanism considered to be viable foundations for Jewish life and thought. Historical events had demonstrated that neither human nature nor human history could provide a viable foundation for unbridled faith in the automatic improvement of the human condition, or for the belief in the innately beneficent nature of humankind.

In formulating their theological positions, the Jewish existentialists saw Jewish religious faith as holding the answer to the existential questions posed by the post-World War II period. Their approach focused not on theological principles or dogmas, but on the implications of a personal commitment to Judaism. Much of their thinking focused on the divine-human relationship. Their approach was less humanistic and more theocentric than that of their immediate predecessors.

Will Herberg identified religious faith as a matter of personal existential commitment, rather than as the intellectual affirmation of certain specific theological principles. For Herberg, there are two alternatives: faith in God or idolatry. For Herberg, only God is ultimate. Herberg defines idolatry as treating as ultimate that which is not ultimate. Consequently, for Herberg, committing to a secular ideology like communism (which he had done in his early life) is a form of idolatry.

For Jewish existentialists, ours is an unredeemed world where the human capacity for irrationality and evil is manifest in human experience. For Heschel, for example, the doctrine of human self-sufficiency is spurious. Human beings require the wisdom and insight rooted in divine revelation. For Heschel, revelation serves as the paradigm for the divine–human relationship, as the basis for religious authority, and as the bedrock of moral values and religious practice. It was not coincidental that revelation became the key issue in the theological works of Jewish existentialists such as Heschel.

A major theme of existentialist thought is the problem of how to overcome loneliness, absurdity and alienation. In a complex treatise combining Neo-Kantian, Jewish legal and philosophical as well as existentialist approaches, the leading Orthodox Jewish scholar and theologian, Joseph B. Soloveitchik (1903–1995) offers faith in God, commitment to traditional norms and social interaction within a religious community as paths to individual fulfillment and redemption.[21]

Mordecai M. Kaplan

Mordecai M. Kaplan represents a discrete trend in American Jewish theology in and of himself. He is not only unique in terms of his longevity (1881–1983), but also in terms of his thought and its impact upon American Judaism. Kaplan's thought in itself may be considered a third trend in American Jewish theology.[22]

Though Kaplan considered himself more of a sociologist than a theologian, his theology of Judaism is particularly American. Kaplan employed the endemically American philosophy of pragmatism in producing a philosophy and a programme for the reconstruction of American Judaism. Kaplan's life and thought had a profound impact upon American Jewish life, institutions, thought and thinkers (for example, Milton Steinberg, Richard Rubenstein, William Kaufman).[23]

Just as the leading American philosopher, John Dewey, sought 'reconstruction' in philosophy, Kaplan sought to reconstruct Judaism. Kaplan's goal was to provide a variety of reconstructed Judaism that would be relevant and challenging to modernized American Jews. Kaplan's ultimate hope was for a renaissance of Judaism in America. Eventually, Kaplan's work developed into, Reconstructionist Judaism a fourth movement in American Judaism. Unlike the other movements, it was the first native form of American Judaism.

In his writings, Kaplan critiques each of the other movements and finds them wanting and particularly problematic for the American milieu. He finds other contemporary approaches to Judaism reductionist. Classical Reform, in his view, affirms God, but neglects Torah and the peoplehood of Israel. Orthodoxy focuses on Torah and neglects God. Religious Judaism neglects Jewish culture and peoplehood. Jewish secular 'culturism' neglects Jewish religion and nationality. Jewish secular nationalism neglects religion and culture.

For Kaplan, what American Judaism needs is a more 'organic', comprehensive view of Judaism than was then being offered by Jewish nationalism, cultural, secularism, or the religious movements of American Judaism. For Kaplan, that need can best be fulfilled by understanding Judaism as an 'evolving religious civilization'. This means that Judaism is a total civilization, including religion, culture and nationality. It is evolving, hence, developing, and not static. It is religious: religion is not its totality but its core.

Kaplan radically reconstructs the three major issues of Jewish theological thinking – God, Torah and Israel – by severing them from their traditional theological meanings. For Kaplan, 'God' is no longer an abstract noun, but a functional noun. What is important for Kaplan is not so much the nature of God, but how God functions in our lives. The pragmatic application supersedes the theological concept. God, for Kaplan, is not a 'person', but a 'force' or a 'process' that operates in the universe and human life for goodness, meaning and salvation. Just as for Kaplan, God is not a supernatural being, so the Torah is not the product of a supernatural, divine revelation. God does not give us commandments. Rather, Judaism and Torah are expressions of the creative religious genius of the Jewish people. Jews observe certain practices, not because they have been dictated by God, but because they express the 'sancta' of the Jewish people. For Kaplan, the idea of Israel as a chosen people is also obsolete. Kaplan's reconstruction of Jewish theology led him to a reformulation of Jewish liturgical texts so that they might be correlative with the teachings of his reconstructed American Judaism.

It is not coincidental that many of the essays that comprise Richard Rubenstein's 1966 book, *After Auschwitz*, first appeared in the *Reconstructionist* magazine. Following Kaplan, Rubenstein had concluded that classical Jewish theological ideas had been rendered obsolete by the impact of modernity, secularism and historical events. But for Rubenstein, unlike Kaplan, the central modern event is the Holocaust. For Rubenstein, the Holocaust signifies the death of traditional theology, the rejection of traditional Judaism, and its replacement with a form of neo-paganism that he locates in secular Zionism and secular Israeli culture. For Rubenstein, now that 'God is dead', the Jewish community becomes of paramount importance.

Rubenstein's thought may be considered 'anti-theology'. However, the power of Rubenstein's writings and personality was largely responsible for placing thinking and writing about the Holocaust and the State of Israel at the heart of the Jewish theological agenda for the next two decades.

Post-Holocaust Theology

As a result of the perceived threat to the Jewish population in Israel during the 1967 Israel-Arab 'Six Day War', American Jewry experienced a deeper awareness of the Holocaust than it had until then. In addition, American Jews began to manifest a deeper commitment to Israel as a symbol of Jewish survival and rebirth than they had done previously. With an almost exclusive focus on the Holocaust and Israel in the 1970s and 1980s, American Jewish theology entered a fourth phase. For the first time, American Jewish theology and the civil religion of American Jewry came together, for example, in the teachings of Irving Greenberg.

As a German rabbi and naturalized Canadian citizen who later emigrated to Israel, Emil Fackenheim is beyond the scope of this essay. However, Fackenheim made a substantial contribution to Jewish theology and to Holocaust theology in particular.[24] Like the American Jewish theologian, Arthur Cohen, Fackenheim sees the Holocaust as a seismic, unprecedented event in Jewish and human history.[25] Unlike Richard Rubenstein, but like Cohen, Fackenheim reaffirms faith in the supernatural God. For Cohen, not only is God supernatural, but the people of Israel is also supernatural in its mission in the world, which includes bearing witness to the evil that infects humankind through the abuse of human freedom.

Like Cohen, the eminent Orthodox Jewish scholar and theologian, Eliezer Berkovits considers the Holocaust to be the result of a perversion of human freedom. However, Berkovits also utilizes the early notion of ***hester panim***, the hiding face of God, to address the Holocaust. God mysteriously and inexplicably and without any obvious cause such as human sin, hides from human beings. It is precisely this absence that makes human freedom, and hence human tragedy, possible. Further, Berkovits sees the Holocaust as proof of the endemic failure of western civilization and Christianity. Unlike Rubenstein and Fackenheim who utilize the unprecedented nature of the Holocaust to call for unprecedented Jewish responses, Berkovits deals with the theological issues posed by the Holocaust, particularly theodicy (the problem of evil), by employing traditional Jewish theological categories.[26]

Post-Modern Theology

A fifth phase in American Jewish theology began to emerge in the 1990s. According to Peter Haas, it is a 'post-modern' trend, represented for the first time exclusively by American-born and American-trained Jewish theologians.[27] Haas correctly indicates that with the emergence of this trend the legacy of the Enlightenment heritage has been completely discarded. The Holocaust and the State of Israel are dealt with, but neither is considered central to Jewish theological thinking. Neither rationalism, science, secularism, nor Jewish survival is considered to be a sine qua non for either human or Jewish meaning. The insights of Jewish mystical tradition are embraced. Classical Jewish sources are the raw materials out of which these theologians attempt to re-create an understanding of Judaism for the twenty-first century.

An issue that concerns 'post-modern' theologians is how a Jew goes about living out his or her commitment to the Jewish covenant with God. This concern leads them to formulations of views concerning issues such as revelation, philosophies of Jewish law, ethical behaviour, and the nature, interpretation and application of Jewish law. For 'post-modern' Jewish theologians, the task of theology is to provide a response and an alternative to the secularization of American Jewish life. Theological polemics with other faiths are not the issue here. Interreligious dialogue is presumed as being important and theologically enriching. The polemic here is against a de-spiritualized American Jewish community that suffers from spiritual anemia and yet which has begun to manifest a deep hunger for things Jewish and things spiritual. The goal is to produce a re-created yet authentic, traditional though non-Orthodox, American Jewish theology. For these thinkers – Eugene Borowitz, Arthur Green, Neil Gillman and Byron Sherwin, among others – the theological, mystical, spiritual, ethical and Halakhic elements of Judaism must be re-created and restated in a contemporary idiom, and then applied to the existential, social and communal problems confronting American Jews. For these theologians, Jewish theology is the key to providing American Judaism with a creative and meaningful future.[28]

In addition, a feature of this latest trend in American Jewish theology has been the beginning of the emergence of Jewish theological thinking and writing by women. Early works, like those of Judith Plaskow, have opened new agendas and have added new insights into the theological discussion of Judaism.[29] For example, they have stimulated new liturgies, a new sensitivity to the sexist use of religious language, the formulation of theologies of the human body as well as new approaches to pastoral theology and counseling.

Towards the Future

We must hope that American Jewish theologians of the present and the foreseeable future will be able to produce Jewish theology in a less hostile and more appreciative Jewish communal environment than their predecessors. Indeed, the future of American Judaism might depend upon precisely that. As the twenty-first century unfolds, new trends in American Jewish theology will inevitably develop. Just as the various past and present trends reviewed above were largely unpredicted in the periods that preceded them, so future trends must be currently uncertain. However, certain issues may be identified that are likely to preoccupy American Jewish theologians in the decades to come. Among these are the following.

The relationship between science and religion will be a growing concern of American theologians, including Jewish theologians. Of particular interest will be unfolding theories of cosmology and astrophysics as well as developments in genetics and biotechnology. The re-shaping of Jewish theological and social attitudes toward Christians and Christianity will continue in the twenty-first century. In addition, theological reconsideration of and dialogue with Islam, Buddhism and other religions will increase as America continues to become more religiously pluralistic. As theologies of feminism influenced Jewish theology in the late twentieth-century, theologies related to sexual preference are likely to develop in the first decades of the twenty-first century. The greatest challenge to American Jewish theologians in the near future may not be the 'isms' of the past, nor the secularism of the present, but the

American trend toward 'custom-made' individualized forms of religion in general and of Judaism in particular. What sociologists have called 'the sovereign self' will increasingly define the religious identity of many American Jews. Ideas and practices from other religions and ideologies will increasingly become elements of individual American Jews' religious identity. Whereas in recent decades, individual Jews wanted autonomously to decide which aspects of classical Jewish belief, ethics and ritual were meaningful for themselves, already emerging trends indicate that individual Jews now believe they can determine for themselves what Judaism is. This trend threatens to undermine both the continuity of Judaism as a historical theological tradition as well as the cohesion of the Jewish community.

Jewish theology historically has been open to change and innovation. It has been responsive throughout its history to contemporary social, cultural and philosophical trends. It has continuously reshaped its ideas in response to significant historical events. In all this, Jewish theology has nonetheless been characterized by a certain continuity and an inextricable link with the Jewish people. It has withstood the onslaught of religious disputation, historical trauma and ideological attacks from all sides, including those from within the Jewish community itself. How it will meet the challenges to continuity and community posed by individualized 'boutique' Judaisms, by the 'brave new world' of the unfolding 'biotech century', and by the dangers to America in a post-9/11 world, remains to be seen.

In 1947, after a visit to Hebrew Union College, Will Herberg commented, 'they take theology seriously, but their theology is not very serious'. The opposite may be said of the historical plight of American Jewish theologians: 'their theology is very serious, but their theology has not been taken very seriously by American Jewry'. It is to be hoped that, as the future unfolds, American Jewish theology will remain very serious, and will be taken very seriously.

NOTES

1. Arnold Eisen, 'Theology, Sociology, Ideology: Jewish Thought in America, 1925–1955', *Modern Judaism* 2:1 (February 1982): 91–104.
2. Louis Jacobs, *A Jewish Theology* (New York: Behrman House, 1973), p.1.
3. Norman Frimer, 'The A-Theological Judaism of the American Jewish Community', *Judaism* 11 (1962): 144–54.
4. Steven Cohen, *Content or Continuity?* (New York: American Jewish Committee, 1991), p.26.
5. Robert Bellah, 'Civil Religion in America', *Daedalus* (Winter 1967).

6. Jonathan S. Woocher, *Sacred Survival: The Civil Religion of American Jews* (Bloomington, IN: Indiana University Press, 1986), p.92.
7. Woocher, *Sacred Survival*, pp.72–76.
8. *A Jewish Theology*, pp.281–83.
9. Woocher, *Sacred Survival*, pp.132–36.
10. Steven Cohen, *American Modernity and Jewish Identity* (New York: Tavistock Publications, 1983), pp.32, 35.
11. Arthur Green, 'New Directions in Jewish Theology in America', in Elliot N. Dorff and Louis E. Newman (eds), *Contemporary Jewish Theology* (New York: Oxford University Press, 1999), p.487.
12. Kaufmann Kohler, *Jewish Theology: Systematically and Historically Considered*, (1918) (2nd. ed., New York: Ktav, 1968).
13. On Kohler's thought and his role in the 1885 Platform, see Michael A. Meyer, *Response to Modernity: A History of the Reform Movement in Judaism* (New York: Oxford University Press, 1988), pp.264–73. For the texts of the various Platforms, see pp.387–94.
14. On Cohon's thought and his influence on the 1937 Columbus Platform, see Meyer, pp.317–20. Cohon's major theological works are: Samuel S. Cohon, *Jewish Theology* (Assen, Netherlands: Royal Vangorcum, 1971); *Judaism: A Way of Life* (New York: Union of American Hebrew Congregations, 1948); *Essays in Jewish Theology* (Cincinnati: Hebrew Union College Press, 1986).
15. *Emet ve-Emunah* (New York: Jewish Theological Seminary, 1988).
16. Solomon Schechter, *Aspects of Rabbinic Theology* (New York: Macmillan, 1909).
17. Eugene Borowitz, *Renewing the Covenant: A Theology for Post-Modern Jews* (Philadelphia: Jewish Publication Society, 1991).
18. On these theologies of revelation and their application in Jewish law, Byron L. Sherwin, *In Partnership with God: Contemporary Jewish Law and Ethics* (Syracuse: Syracuse University Press, 1990), pp.16–46, and chap.7 above.
19. Robert G. Goldy, *The Emergence of Jewish Theology in America* (Bloomington, IN: University of Indiana Press, 1990).
20. Will Herberg, *Judaism and Modern Man* (New York: World Publishing Co., 1951); Abraham J. Heschel, *God in Search of Man* (Philadelphia: Jewish Publication Society, 1955).
21. Joseph B. Soloveichik, *Halakhic Man*, trans. Lawrence Kaplan (Philadelphia: Jewish Publication Society, 1983).
22. Mordecai M. Kaplan, *Judaism as a Civilization* (New York: Macmillan, 1934); *The Meaning of God in Modern Jewish Religion* (New York: Jewish Reconstructionist Foundation, 1947).
23. Milton Steinberg, 'The Theological Issues of the Hour', *Proceedings of the Rabbinical Assembly* 13 (1949): 356–408; Richard Rubenstein, *After Auschwitz* (Indianapolis: Bobbs-Merrill, 1966); William E. Kaufman, *The Evolving God in Jewish Process Theology* (Lewiston, NY: Edwin Mellen Press, 1997).
24. Emil Fackenheim, *God's Presence in History* (New York: NYU Press, 1970); *The Jewish Return into History* (New York: Schocken Books, 1978).
25. Arthur A. Cohen, *The Tremendum* (New York: Crossroad, 1983); *The Natural and the Supernatural Jew* (New York: McGraw Hill, 1964).
26. Eliezer Berkovits, *Faith After the Holocaust* (New York: Ktav, 1973).
27. Peter J. Haas, 'The Making of a New American Jewish Theology', *Central Conference of American Rabbis Journal* 39:3 (Fall 1992): 1–13.
28. Eugene Borowitz, *A New Jewish Theology in the Making* (Philadelphia: Westminster Press, 1968); Arthur Green, *Seek My Face, Speak My Name* (Northvale, N.J.: Jason Aronson, 1992); Neil Gillman, *Sacred Fragments* (Philadelphia: Jewish Publication Society, 1990); Byron L. Sherwin, *Toward a Jewish Theology* (Lewiston, N.Y.: Edwin Mellen Press, 1991).
29. Judith Plaskow, *Standing Again at Sinai* (San Francisco: Harper and Row, 1990).

Select Bibliography

The following books proved significant in the research and writing of this volume. These and other books and articles that have been utilized are cited with full references in the end-notes to each chapter.

Abravanel, Don Isaac. *Mashmiah Yeshuot*. Amsterdam: n.p., 1644.

Agadat Bereshit. Warsaw: Levensohn, 1876.

Albo, Joseph. *Sefer ha-Ikkarim – The Book of Principles*. 6 vols. Translated and edited by Isaac Husik. Philadelphia: Jewish Publication Society, 1946.

Arama, Isaac. *Akedat Yitzhak*. Pressburgh: n.p., 1849.

Ashkenazi, Eliezer. *Sefer Ma'aseh ha-Shem*. Venice: n.p., 1583.

Bamberger, Bernard. *The Search for Jewish Theology*. New York: Behrman House, 1978.

Ben Asher, Bahye. *Commentary on the Torah* [Hebrew]. 3 vols. Jerusalem: Mosad ha-Rav Kook, 1968.

——. *Kad ha-Kemah*. Lwow: n.p., 1897.

Ben Asher, Jacob. *Arba'ah Turim*. 4 vols. New York: Grossman, n.d.

Ben Bezalel, Hayyim. *Sefer ha-Hayyim*. Jerusalem: Weinfeld, 1968.

Ben David, Abraham. *Teshuvot u-Fesakim*. Jerusalem: Mosad ha-Rav Kook, 1964.

Ben Yehiel, Asher. *She'eilot u-Teshuvot ha-Rosh*. Jerusalem: n.p., 1965.

Bentwich, Norman. *Solomon Schechter: A Biography*. Philadelphia: Jewish Publication Society, 1938.

Berkovits, Eliezer. *God, Man and History*. New York: Jonathan David, 1959.

——. *Faith after the Holocaust*. New York: Ktav, 1973.

Bokser, Baruch M. *The Origins of the Seder*. Berkeley, CA: University of California Press, 1984.

Borowitz, Eugene. *A New Jewish Theology in the Making*. Philadelphia: Westminster Press, 1968.

——. *Renewing the Covenant: A Theology for Post-Modern Jews*. Philadelphia: Jewish Publication Society, 1991.

Buber, Martin. *Tales of the Hasidim*. Translated by Olga Marx. 2 vols. New York: Schocken, 1948.

Buber, Solomon (ed.). *Pesikta de-Rav Kahana*. Lyck: n.p., 1868.

——. *Midrash Tanhuma*. 2 vols. Vilna: n.p., 1885.

——. *Midrash Tehillim*. Vilna: Romm, 1891.

Cardozo, Benjamin. *The Nature of the Judicial Process*. New Haven, CT: Yale University Press, 1921.

Catechism of the Catholic Church. Mahwah, NJ: Paulist Press, 1994.

Chavel, Charles (ed.). *Kitve Rabbenu Moshe ben Nahman*. 2 vols. Jerusalem: Mosad ha-Rav Kook, 1963.

Cohen, Arthur A. *The Natural and the Supernatural Jew*. New York: McGraw Hill, 1964.

——. *The Tremendum*. New York: Crossroad, 1983.

Cohen, Arthur A., and, Paul Mendes-Flohr (eds). *Contemporary Jewish Religious Thought*. New York: Scribner's 1987.

Cohon, Samuel S. *Judaism: A Way of Life*. New York: Union of American Hebrew Congregations, 1948.

——. *Jewish Theology*. Assen: Royal Vangorcum, 1971.

——. *Essays in Jewish Theology*. Cincinnati: Hebrew Union College Press, 1986.

De Vidas, Elijah. *Reshit Hokhmah*. 3 vols. Jerusalem: Or ha-Musar, 1984.

Dorff, Eliot N., and, Louis E. Newman (eds). *Contemporary Jewish Theology*. New York: Oxford University Press, 1999.

Dresner, Samuel H. *Levi Yitzhak of Berditchev*. New York: Hartmore House, 1974.

Fackenheim, Emil. *Quest for Past and Future*. Boston: Beacon, 1968.

——. *God's Presence in History*. New York: NYU Press, 1970.

Faur, José. *Golden Doves with Silver Dots*. Bloomington, IN: Indiana University Press, 1986.

Finkelstein, Louis (ed.). *Sifrei – Devarim*. Berlin: Judischer Kulterband in Deutschland Abteilung Verlag, 1939.

Friedmann, Meir (ed.). *Pesikta Rabbati*. Vienna: Herausgebers, 1880.

——. *Seder Eliyahu Rabbah ve-Seder Eliyahu Zuta*. Vienna: Ahiyasaf, 1904.

Gerondi, Jonah. *Sha'arey Teshuvah*. Jerusalem: Eshkol, 1978.

Gilman, Neil. *Sacred Fragments*. Philadelphia: Jewish Publication Society, 1990.

Ginsburg, Elliot. *The Sabbath in Classical Kabbalah*. Albany, NY: SUNY Press, 1989.

Ginzberg, Louis. *Students, Scholars and Saints*. Philadelphia: Jewish Publication Society, 1958.

——. *The Legends of the Jews*. 7 vols. Philadelphia: Jewish Publication Society, 1968.

——. *On Jewish Law and Lore*. New York: Atheneum, 1970.

Gioia, Francesco (ed.). *Interreligious Dialogue: Official Teachings of the Catholic Church, 1963–1995*. Vatican: Pontifical Council for Interreligious Dialogue, 1997.

Goldy, Robert G. *The Emergence of Jewish Theology in America*. Bloomington, IN: University of Indiana Press, 1990.

Green, Arthur. *Tormented Master: A Life of Rabbi Nahman of Bratslav*. University, AL: University of Alabama Press, 1979.

——. *Seek My Face, Speak My Name*. Northvale, NJ: Jason Aronson, 1992.

Greenberg, Irving. *For the Sake of Heaven and Earth*. Philadelphia: Jewish Publication Society, 2004.

Halevi, Judah. *Kuzari*. Translated by Hartwig Hirschfield. New York: Schocken, 1964.

Halivni, David Weiss. *Midrash, Mishnah and Gemara*. Cambridge, MA: Harvard University Press, 1986.

Herberg, Will. *Judaism and Modern Man*. New York: World Publishing Co., 1951.

Heschel, Abraham J. *The Earth is the Lord's*. New York: Henry Schuman, 1950.

——. *God in Search of Man*. Philadelphia: Jewish Publication Society, 1955.

——. *The Insecurity of Freedom*. New York: Farrar, Straus and Giroux, 1966.

——. *Kotsk* [Yiddish]. 2 vols. Tel Aviv: Ha-Menorah, 1973.

——. *Man is Not Alone*. Philadelphia: Jewish Publication Society, 1951.

——. *Moral Grandeur and Spiritual Audacity*. New York: Farrar,

Straus and Giroux, 1996.
——. *A Passion for Truth*. New York: Farrar, Straus and Giroux, 1973.
——. *The Prophets*. Philadelphia: Jewish Publication Society, 1962.
——. *The Quest for Certainty in Saadia's Philosophy*. New York: Feldheim, 1944.
——. *The Sabbath*. New York: World, 1963.
——. *Torah min ha-Shamayim*. 2 vols. New York: Soncino, 1962–1965.
——. *Who is Man?* Stanford, CA: Stanford University Press, 1963.
Horovitz, Hayyim, and, Israel Rabin (eds). *Mekhilta de Rabbi Ishmael*. Jerusalem: Wahrmann, 1960.
Horowitz, Isaiah. *Shnei Luhot ha-Brit*. 3 vols. Jerusalem: Edison, 1960.
Hume, David. *Dialogues Concerning Natural Religion*. New York: Hafner, 1966.
Ibn Daud, David. *Emunah Ramah*. Frankfurt: n.p., 1852.
Ibn Gabbai, Meir. *Avodat ha-Kodesh*. Jerusalem: Levin-Epstein, 1954.
Ibn Pakudah, Bahya. *The Book of Direction to the Duties of the Heart*. Translated by Menahem M. Mansoor. London: Routledge and Kegan Paul, 1973.
Ibn Zimra, David. *Teshuvot ha-Radbaz*. 4 vols. Furth: n.p., 1781.
Idel, Moshe. *Absorbing Perfections*. New Haven, CT: Yale University Press, 2002.
——. *Kabbalah: New Perspectives*. New Haven, CT: Yale University Press, 1988.
——, *Studies in Ecstatic Kabbalah*. Albany, NY: SUNY Press, 1988.
Isserles, Moses. *Responsa* [Hebrew]. Jerusalem: n.p., 1970.
Jacob Joseph of Polnoyye. *Toledot Ya'akov Yosef*. 2 vols. Jerusalem: Sifrei Musar va-Hasidut, 1967.
Jacobs, Louis. *We Have Reason to Believe*. London: Vallentine Mitchell, 1957.
——. *Jewish Values*. London: Vallentine Mitchell, 1960.
——. *Studies in Talmudic Logic and Methodology*. London: Vallentine Mitchell, 1961.
——. *Principles of the Jewish Faith*. New York: Basic Books, 1964.
——. *Seeker of Unity*. New York: Basic Books, 1966.
——. *Faith*. New York: Basic Books, 1968.

——. *Hasidic Prayer*. New York: Schocken, 1972.
——. *A Jewish Theology*. New York: Behrman House, 1973.
——. *Theology in the Responsa*. London: Routledge and Kegal Paul, 1975.
——. *A Tree of Life*. New York: Oxford University Press, 1984.
——. *Helping with Inquiries*. London: Vallentine Mitchell, 1989.
——. *Beyond Reasonable Doubt*. London: Littman Library of Jewish Civilization, 1999.
Jellinek, Adolph (ed.). *Beit ha-Midrash*. 6 vols. 2nd ed. Jerusalem: Wahrmann, 1967.
John Paul II. *Crossing the Threshold of Hope*. New York: Knopf, 1994.
Joseph, Morris. *Judaism as Creed and Life*. New York: Bloch, 1903.
Kadushin, Max. *The Rabbinic Mind*. New York: Jewish Theological Seminary, 1952.
Kaplan, Moredecai M. *Judaism as a Civilization*. New York: Macmillan, 1934.
——. *The Meaning of God in Modern Jewish Religion*. New York: Jewish Reconstructionist Foundation, 1947.
——. *Greater Judaism in the Making*. New York: Reconstructionist Press, 1960.
Karo, Joseph. *Shulhan Arukh*. 4 vols. Reprint: Vilna: Romm, 1911.
Katz, Dov. *Tenuat ha-Musar*. 4 vols. Tel Aviv: Menorah, 1973.
Kaufman, William. *Contemporary Jewish Philosophies*. New York: Reconstructionist Press, 1976.
——. *The Evolving God in Jewish Process Theology*. Lewiston, NY: Edwin Mellen Press, 1997.
Kellner, Menahem. *Dogma in Medieval Jewish Thought*. New York: Oxford University Press, 1986.
Klausner, Joseph. *The Messianic Idea in Israel*. Translated by William F. Stinespring. New York: Macmillan, 1955.
Kochan, Lionel. *The Jew and His History*. Chico, CA: Scholars Press, 1985.
Kohler, Kaufmann. *Jewish Theology: Systematically and Historically Considered*. 2nd ed. New York: Ktav, 1968.
Langer, Jiri. *Nine Gates to the Chassidic Mysteries*. London: Clarke, 1961.
Lasker, Daniel. *Jewish Philosophical Polemics Against Christianity in the Middle Ages*. New York: Ktav, 1977.

Liebes, Yehudah. *Studies in the Zohar*. Albany, NY: SUNY Press, 1993.

Liebman, Charles S., and, Eliezer Don-Yehiya. *Civil Religion in Israel*. Berkeley, CA: University of California Press, 1983.

Loew, Judah. *Ner Mitzvah*. Bnai Brak, Israel: Yahadut, 1962.

——. *Be'er ha-Golah*. New York: Judaica Press, 1969.

——. *Hiddushei Aggadot*. 4 vols. New York: Judaica, 1969.

——. *Netivot Olom*. 2 vols. New York: Judaica Press, 1969.

——. *Nezah Yisrael*. New York: Judaica Press, 1969.

——. *Tiferet Yisrael*. New York: Judaica Press, 1969.

——. *Gur Aryeih*. 5 vols. Jerusalem: Yahadut, 1972.

Luria, Solomon. *Responsa* [Hebrew]. Lublin: n.p., 1774.

——. *Yam shel Shlomo*. Stettin: Shrenzel, 1861.

Luzzatto, Moses Hayyim. *Mesillat Yesharim—The Path of the Upright*. Translated by Mordecai M. Kaplan. Philadelphia: Jewish Publication Society, 1936.

Maimonides, Moses. *Teshuvot ha-Rambam*. Tel Aviv: Mekitzei Nirdamim, 1934.

——. *Guide of the Perplexed*. Translated by Shlomo Pines. Chicago: University of Chicago Press, 1963.

——. *Mishneh Torah* [with commentaries]. 6 vols. New York: Friedman, 1963.

——. *Sefer ha-Mitzvot*. Jerusalem: Levin-Epstein, 1965.

Mandelbaum, Bernard (ed.). *Pesikta de-Rav Kahana*. 2 vols. New York: The Jewish Theological Seminary, 1962.

Margaliot, Reuven (ed.). *Sefer ha-Bahir*. Jerusalem: Mosad ha-Rav Kook, 1951.

——. *Sefer Hasidim*. Jerusalem: Mosad ha-Rav Kook, 1960.

Meyer, Michael. *The Origins of the Modern Jew*. Detroit: Wayne State Press, 1967.

Midrash Rabbah [with commentaries]. 2 vols. Vilna: Romm, 1921.

Mikraot Gedolot [Hebrew Scripture with commentaries]. 5 vols. New York, Tanach, 1959.

Mishnah [with commentaries]. Jerusalem: Horeb, 1952.

Mordecai of Chernobyl. *Likkutei Torah*. New York: Noble Printing Co., 1954.

Moore, George Foot. *Judaism in the First Centuries of the Christian Era*. 2 vols. Cambridge, MA: Harvard University Press, 1927.

Moses Hayyim Ephraim of Sudlykow. *Degel Mahane-Ephraim*.

Jerusalem: Hadar, 1963.

Novak, David. *Jewish–Christian Dialogue: A Jewish Justification*. New York: Oxford University Press, 1989.

Orhot Zaddikim. Translated by Seymour J. Cohen. New York: Feldheim, 1960.

Ortega y Gasset, José. *Revolt of the Masses*. New York: W.W. Norton, 1957.

Palestinian Talmud [with commentaries]. Krotoschin: n.p., 1886.

Philipson, David. *The Reform Movement in Judaism*. New York: Macmillan, 1907.

Pirke de Rabbi Eliezer. Warsaw: n.p., 1852.

Plaskow, Judith. *Standing Again at Sinai*. San Francisco: Harper and Row, 1990.

Ringrenn, Helmer. *Israelite Religion*. Philadelphia: Fortress Press, 1966.

Rosenzweig, Franz. *The Star of Redemption*. Translated by William H. Hallo. New York: Holt, Rinehart and Winston, 1970.

——. *On Jewish Learning*. New York: Schocken, 1955.

Rubenstein, Richard. *After Auschwitz*. Indianapolis, IN: Bobbs-Merrill, 1966.

Saadya Gaon. *The Book of Beliefs and Opinions*. Translated by Samuel Rosenblatt. New Haven, CT: Yale University Press, 1948.

Samuel of Uceda. *Midrash Shmuel*. Jerusalem: Brody-Katz, n.d..

Sarna, Nahumm. *Understanding Genesis*. New York: Schocken, 1966.

Schechter, Solomon (ed.). *Studies in Judaism: Second Series*. Philadelphia: Jewish Publication Society, 1908.

——. *Aspects of Rabbinic Theology*. New York: Macmillan, 1909.

——. *Studies in Judaism: First Series*. Philadelphia: Jewish Publication Society, 1911.

——. *Studies in Judaism: Third Series*. Philadelphia: Jewish Publication Society, 1924.

——. *Studies in Judaism*. New York: Meridian, 1958.

——. *Seminary Addresses and Other Papers*. New York: Burning Bush Press, 1959.

——. *Avot d'Rabbi Natan*. 2nd ed., New York: Feldheim, 1967.

Scholem, Gershom. *On the Kabbalah and Its Symbolism*. Translated by Ralph Mannheim. New York: Schocken, 1965.

——. *The Messianic Idea in Judaism*. New York: Schocken, 1971.

——. *On the Mystical Shape of the Godhead*. New York: Schocken, 1991.

Sefer ha-Hinukh. Jerusalem: Eshkol, 1946.

Sefer Raziel. Amsterdam, n.p., 1701.

Sherwin, Byron L. *Abraham Joshua Heschel*. Atlanta: John Knox Press, 1979.

——. *Mystical Theology and Social Dissent. The Life and Works of Judah Loew of Prague*. Oxford: Oxford University Press, 1982.

——. *In Partnership with God: Contemporary Jewish Law and Ethics*. Syracuse, NY: Syracuse University Press, 1990.

——. *Toward a Jewish Theology*. Lewiston, NY: Edwin Mellen Press, 1991.

Sherwin, Byron, and, Harold Kasimow (eds). *John Paul II and Interreligious Dialogue*. Maryknoll, NY: Orbis Books, 1999.

Shneur Zalman of Liady. *Lekutei Amarim* [Tanya]. Brooklyn: Otzar ha-Hasidim, 1965.

Soloveichik, Joseph B. *Halakhic Man*. Translated by Lawrence Kaplan. Philadelphia: Jewish Publication Society, 1983.

——. *The Halakhic Mind*. New York: Macmillan, 1986.

Talmud [with commentaries]. Vilna: Romm, 1895. Reprint. 20 vols. New York: Otzar ha-Sefarim, 1958.

Tchernowitz, Chaim. *Toledot ha-Poskim*. 4 vols. New York: n.p., 1947.

Tishbi, Isaiah. *The Wisdom of the Zohar*. Translated by David Goldstein. London: Oxford University Press, 1989.

Urbach, Ephraim. *The Sages*. Translated by Israel Abrahams. Cambridge, MA: Harvard University Press, 1987.

Vital, Hayyim. *Sefer Pri Etz Hayyim*. Koretz: n.p., 1784.

——. *Shaar ha-Gilgulim*. Jerusalem: Eshel, 1963.

Werblowsky, R. J. Zwi. *Joseph Karo*. Philadelphia: Jewish Publication Society, 1977.

Wolfson, Harry. *Philo*. 2 vols. Cambridge, MA: Harvard University Press, 1947.

Woocher, Jonathan S. *Sacred Survival: The Civil Religion of American Jews*. Bloomington, IN: Indiana University Press, 1986.

Yalkut Shimoni. 2 vols. New York: Pardes. 1944.

Yerushalmi, Yosef Hayyim. *Zakhor: Jewish History and Jewish Memory*. Seattle, WA: University of Washington Press, 1982.

Zadok ha-Kohein of Lublin. *Zidkat ha-Zaddik*. New York: n.p., 1947.

Zohar. 3 vols. Vilna: Romm, 1882.

Index

Rabbinic Thought in the Talmud
Louis Jacobs

Ever since the publication of his pioneering work Studies in Talmudic Logic and Methodology, over forty years ago, the author's views on the form, structure and history of the Babylonian Talmud have awakened much interest. This book provides four detailed understandings of the nature and scope of the Babylonian Talmud, outlining the state-of-the-art studies of the subject as well as some problems still awaiting solution, such as who were the actual editors of the Bavli and how they went about their work. This is followed by seven comprehensive examinations of the Talmudic method as seen from the complete unit of the Talmud, the Sugya. Here the author advances his original view, now widely accepted by scholars, that the Talmudic Sugya is not simply a plain account of the various arguments but a carefully constructed literary work, a contrived statement in which one point leads to another in a dynamic way. A further essay seeks to show that that *kal va-homer*, found throughout the Talmud and Midrashic literature, finds anticipation as a mode of reasoning in scriptural passages. Another essay seeks to convey the economic background of the Babylonian Talmud, while a further essay subjects to criticism Montefiore and Loewe's Rabbinic Anthology. The concluding section of the book deals with Rabbinics, the works of post-Talmudic scholars who sought to bring the Talmudic discussions to life in the Jewish community. This book is highly technical in parts, of interest chiefly to Talmudic scholars, but the author's gift of clarity in presentation will enable non-experts to grasp the nature and methodology of the Talmud and Rabbinics.

2005, 216 pages
ISBN 978 0 85303 564 0 (cloth) £39.50 / $62.95
ISBN 978 0 85303 568 8 (paper) £17.95 / $28.95

Studies in Talmudic Logic and Methodology

Louis Jacobs

In the traditional Talmudic Methodologies the subjects of Talmudic logic and methodology are generally treated together. With a few notable exceptions, there has been little attempt at a systematic presentation of such matters as the structure of the Talmudic arguments, the division of the *sugya* into its component parts, the methods of Talmudic reasoning, and the literary style and character of the Amoraic debates.

This book notes some of the problems in this field and suggests some tentative solutions. The first part sheds light on Talmudic logic, in particular suggesting the ancients were aware of the process of Induction. The second part examines the literary analysis of the Amoraic literature, and argues that the *Gemara* in its present form is a 'contrived' literary product of great skill in which the older material used has been reshaped by methods similar to literary artists throughout the ages.

Although the book is presented for the considerations of students of the Talmud it may be of interest to the layman who has a desire of gaining a closer acquaintance with the full flavour of Talmudic reasoning.

February 2007, 208 pages
ISBN 978 0 85303 737 8 (paper) £17.95 / $27.95

Judaism in Contemporary Context
Enduring Issues and Chronic Crises
Jacob Neusner

The essays collected here form a contribution to a half-century of Jewish public life. From the 1950s to the present day Jacob Neusner has served as one of the public intellectuals of the English-speaking community of Judaism. The essays claim a hearing for two reasons. First, the issues persist for a new generation to confront. Second, there is the story of a generation now passing that remains to be told. The essays concern both Judaism the religion viewed in its own terms, and also Judaism the amalgam of religious and ethnic components viewed in the political setting of the Jewish People, with special reference to the English-speaking component of that People. These enduring issues are captured by the words 'Holocaust' and 'State of Israel'.

The impact of the Holocaust has defined the condition and consciousness of world Jewry from the Second World War onward. For not a few it takes the place of Judaism. So too, the State of Israel and Zionism define paramount parts of that amalgam, and for many these two substitute for Judaism. The Holocaust, Zionism and the State of Israel represent claims upon the consciousness and conscience of the diaspora that none would contemplate dismissing.

Neusner has spent the last fifty years engaging with the perennial issues that Judaism confronts, which remain as relevant in the twenty-first century as ever.

February 2007, 208 pages
ISBN 978 0 85303 665 4 (cloth) £45.00 / $75.00
ISBN 978 0 85303 737 8 (paper) £19.95 / $29.50

Divine Pathos and the Human Being
The Theology of Abraham Joshua Heschel
Michael A. Chester

Abraham Joshua Heschel, a Jewish refugee from Nazism, became a significant theologian and social activist in the USA, though relatively unknown in the UK. The first part of the book contains a brief biography which puts his work into context, personally, culturally and historically. His style is examined and he is located as a theologian, with an examination of his 'depth theology'. Part Two is an examination of 'divine pathos', its influence on Christian theologians, its major critics, the theological anthropology that relies on it and interfaith dialogue made possible by it.

2005, 240 pages
ISBN 978 0 85303 569 5 (cloth) £37.50 / $65.00
ISBN 978 0 85303 570 1 (paper) £18.95 / $29.95

Judaism and Homosexuality

Chaim Rapoport

In the light of modern changes in attitude regarding homosexuality and recent controversy surrounding government legislation, Rabbi Chaim Rapoport explores the Jewish stance on homosexuality.

Rabbi Rapoport combines an unswerving commitment to Jewish Law with a deep understanding of the philosophical and moral issues involved. He advocates the adoption of a fair and balanced perspective and attitude.

This work will undoubtedly facilitate greater appreciation of the issues that lie at the heart of a great deal of debate, not to mention prejudice and discrimination. The book combines clearly written prose for instant and easy access with exhaustive endnotes for all those who wish to explore the issues further.

Judaism and Homosexuality is in effect the first comprehensive work on Jewish attitudes to homosexuality, and will be a 'must have' for the desks of all professionals who find themselves in positions of guidance within the Jewish community.

2004, 230 pages
ISBN 978 0 85303 501 5 (cloth) £40.00 / $64.95
ISBN 978 0 85303 452 0 (paper) £16.95 / $26.95

Orthodox Judaism since 1913
An Ideology Forsaken

Miri J. Freud-Kandel

Foreword by Chimen Abramsky

In 1991, just as Jonathan Sacks was acceding to the post of Chief Rabbi, the United Synagogue, the largest synagogal institution in British Jewry, commissioned a report entitled *A Time for Change*. This report identified the significant difficulties in which many of the Orthodox institutions of British Jewry found themselves: the United Synagogue itself, the Chief Rabbinate, and the *Bet Din* – its religious court. It suggested that the root cause of the problems was a shift away from '*minhag Anglia*, a celebration of the twofold blessing of being Jewish and British'.

This work examines the thought and influence of the three Chief Rabbis whose terms in office have begun and ended during the twentieth century. It follows the theological shifts that have occurred amongst the religious leadership of Orthodox Judaism in Britain and assesses the influence of factors such as immigration and the so-called 'Jacobs Affair' in effecting these changes.

The Jewish community in Britain provides a model of a religious minority group's attempt to secure its survival in the midst of a host society that espouses alternative values derived either from secularism or an alternative religious system. Through an in-depth analysis of the theology of Chief Rabbi Joseph Herman Hertz, this work identifies a paradigm that was established for Jews in Britain of a strong and confident Orthodoxy that champions interaction in the host society. The Chief Rabbinates of Israel Brodie and Immanuel Jakobovits were each influenced in different ways by the burgeoning influence of alternative models for Orthodox Judaism. This work considers how this facilitated the displacement of the community's fervour for unity with religious polarisation; and analyses how its religious leadership adopted a theology which seemed to call on Anglo-Jewry to forsake its ideology of meaningful interaction to secure its religious identity.

September 2006, 236 pages
ISBN 978 0 85303 713 2 (cloth) £45.00 / $75.00
ISBN 978 0 85303 714 9 (paper) £19.95 / $35.00